Elements, Government, and Licensing

Elements, Government, and Licensing

Developments in phonology

Edited by Florian Breit, Yuko Yoshida, and Connor Youngberg

First published in 2023 by
UCL Press
University College London
Gower Street
London WC1E 6BT

Available to download free: www.uclpress.co.uk

Collection © Editors, 2023
Text © Contributors, 2023
Images © Contributors and copyright holders named in captions, 2023

The authors have asserted their rights under the Copyright, Designs and Patents Act 1988 to be identified as the authors of this work.

A CIP catalogue record for this book is available from The British Library.

Any third-party material in this book is not covered by the book's Creative Commons licence. Details of the copyright ownership and permitted use of third-party material is given in the image (or extract) credit lines. If you would like to reuse any third-party material not covered by the book's Creative Commons licence, you will need to obtain permission directly from the copyright owner.

This book is published under a Creative Commons Attribution-Non-Commercial 4.0 International licence (CC BY-NC 4.0), https://creativecommons.org/licenses/by-nc/4.0/. This licence allows you to share and adapt the work for non-commercial use providing attribution is made to the author and publisher (but not in any way that suggests that they endorse you or your use of the work) and any changes are indicated. Attribution should include the following information:

Breit, F., Yoshida, Y., and Youngberg, C. (eds) 2023. *Elements, Government, and Licensing: Developments in phonology*. London: UCL Press. https://doi.org/10.14324/111.9781800085282

Further details about Creative Commons licences are available at https://creativecommons.org/licenses/

ISBN: 978-1-80008-530-5 (Hbk)
ISBN: 978-1-80008-529-9 (Pbk)
ISBN: 978-1-80008-528-2 (PDF)
ISBN: 978-1-80008-531-2 (epub)
DOI: https://doi.org/10.14324/111.9781800085282

The idea for this book was conceived a few years ago, at a meeting on the occasion of Monik Charette's retirement from the School of Oriental and African Studies. Not only has Monik been a steadfast member of London's phonological community over many decades, she was also a driving force in making it a *community*, to the extent that most who have pursued graduate studies or research in phonology at SOAS and UCL, or indeed other nearby establishments, might well have had the impression she might have been a member of any of the institutions at which they had just met her.

Those who know Monik would undoubtedly agree that she is valued not only as a highly influential phonologist but also as an extremely charming and charitable person. Indeed, over time she has brought many students and scholars from all over the world to the field of phonology, particularly to research on phonological empty categories and licensing. Monik's work has had a profound impact both on Government Phonology itself and those conducting research in the framework and its many descendants, as exemplified by many contributions in the present book.

We (and we include all contributors to the book in this 'we') are indebted to Monik for helping us forge connections, both within the wider phonological community and between the myriad respective intellectual interests and ideas harboured by of each of us. The work presented here is dedicated to her:

Momo, as our dear friend, mentor, and colleague, we cannot thank you enough – but let us at least express our profound gratitude by means of the phonology contained herein.

Contents

List of figures   x
List of tables   xi
List of symbols and abbreviations   xii
Notes on contributors   xiv

1 Principles and parameters in phonology: an introduction and overview   1
Connor Youngberg, Yuko Yoshida, and Florian Breit

Part 1: Melody and segmental representation

2 Melody and segmental representation: a brief introduction   13
Florian Breit

3 On hedgehogs and gold in Bavarian: *l*-vocalisation in Upper Austrian German   19
Sabrina Bendjaballah

4 Sets of (sets of) elements   33
Florian Breit

5 Production bias and substance-free representation of laryngeal distinctions   49
Eugeniusz Cyran

6 The no-crossing constraint: a neglected licensing constraint   60
John R. Rennison

Part 2: Prosody and constituent structure

7 Prosody and constituent structure: a brief introduction   73
Yuko Yoshida

8 Prevocalic Tenseness in English, binarity and the typology of long vowel distributions   77
Katalin Balogné Bérces and Shanti Ulfsbjorninn

9 Vowel length and prominence in Cairene Arabic   89
Radwa Fathi

10	#sC in stereo: a dichotic-listening study of initial clusters in Cypriot Greek *John Harris and Faith Chiu*	98
11	The segholate verbs of English *Jean Lowenstamm*	112
12	From me to [juː]: on government licensing and light diphthongs *Markus A. Pöchtrager*	124
13	Licensor tier and culminativity *Yuko Yoshida*	139

Part 3: Emptiness, schwa, and epenthesis

14	Emptiness, schwa, and epenthesis: a brief introduction *Connor Youngberg*	155
15	Turbid government *Edoardo Cavirani*	161
16	Word-final onsets: a Brazilian Portuguese case study *Thaïs Cristófaro Silva*	174
17	A note on the svarabhakti vowels in Connemara Irish *Michael J. Kenstowicz*	185
18	Domino effects and licensing chains in government licensing: sequential NC clusters in Bantu *Nancy C. Kula*	197
19	CəCj in French *Tobias Scheer*	209
20	The prince and the nymph: interconsonantal plosive–zero alternation in English *Péter Szigetvári*	219

Part 4: Prosodic structure and recursion

21	Prosodic structure and recursion: a brief introduction *Connor Youngberg and Florian Breit*	235

22	Nasal vowels in French: a precedence-free approach *Phillip Backley and Kuniya Nasukawa*	238
23	Recursive syllable structure in RCVP *Harry van der Hulst*	255

Subject Index   274
Language Index   277

List of figures

10.1 Cypriot Greek dichotic listening: participants' preference for fused percepts (%Fused) classified by the major class of pairs of input consonants. — 107

10.2 Cypriot Greek dichotic listening: participants' preference for the sonority sequencing (Rise versus Fall) of fused input consonant pairs consisting of the two major-class combinations most susceptible to fusion, Stop|Liquid and Nonsibiliant Fricative|Liquid. — 109

17.1 Duration (in ms) of first (left plot) and second (right plot) vowels of the svarabhakti (CVCC) and organic (CVCVC) stems. — 190

17.2 Duration (in ms) of the medial nonrhotic sonorant consonant in svarabhakti (CVCC) and organic (CVCVC) stems. — 190

17.3 First (y axis) and second (x axis) formant values (in Hz) for the second (reduced) vowel in svarabhakti (CVCC) and organic (CVCVC) stems. — 191

17.4 F0 plots of time-normalised organic (CVCVC), svarabhakti (CVRC) and monosyllabic stems. — 192

17.5 Second formant values (in Hz) of the medial sonorant consonant in svarabhakti (CVCC) and organic (CVCVC) stems. — 194

17.6 Second formant values (in Hz) of the initial vowel in citation (left side) and inflected palatised form (right side) of svarabhakti (CVCC) and organic (CVCVC) stems. — 194

List of tables

4.1	Licensing constraints reframed as a complement in Σ.	44
10.1	Word-initial consonant clusters in Cypriot Greek.	102
10.2	Consonant pairs used in the dichotic listening study.	106
10.3	Possible responses to dichotically presented nonword stimuli.	107
12.1	Systematic comparison of permitted glide plus vowel sequences and structural conditions for (a) French, (b) Japanese, and (c) English. '—' indicates systematic gaps that exist independently of light diphthongs.	133
20.1	The results of the survey.	226

List of symbols and abbreviations

ATR	Advanced Tongue Root
BP	Brazilian Portuguese
C	Consonant
COND	conditional
CPP	Cracow-Poznań Polish
CV	Consonant-Vowel sequence
CVCV	Alternative name for Strict CV Theory
D	Voiced obstruent; Determiner
ECP	Empty Category Principle
eN	empty-cum-floater Nucleus
EN	Empty Nucleus
EP	European Portuguese
ET	Element Theory
F0	Fundamental frequency
FeN	Final empty-cum-floater Nucleus
FEN	Final Empty Nucleus
FNV	French nasal vowel
FOD	Final obstruent devoicing
GB	Government and Binding
GL	Government Licensing
GP	Government Phonology
Gvt	Government
H	High tone; the noise/fortis element |H|
HVD	High Vowel Devoicing
INF	infinitive
IO-gvt	Interonset Government
IWV	Irregular weak verbs
L	Low tone; the nasal/lenis element |L|
Lar	Laryngeal
LarLic	Laryngeal licensing
LC	Licensing Constraint
LH	Low-High contour tone
LIP	Licensing Inheritance Principle
LPD	Longman Pronunciation Dictionary
LSP	Language specific phonetics

M	The mean
MEN	Medial Empty Nucleus
ML	Meinhof's Law
MR	Melodic Representation
MW	Merriam-Webster dictionary
N	Nucleus
NCC	No-Crossing Constraint
NHG	New High German
O	Onset
OCP	Obligatory Contour Principle
OT	Optimality Theory
P	Phrase
$\mathcal{P}$	Prominence
PE	Phonological Expression
PfP	Precedence-Free Phonology
PG	Proper Government
PT	Prevocalic Tenseness
R	Sonorant
RCVP	Radical CV Phonology
RP	Received Pronunciation
RT	Sonorant-Obstruent sequence
SD	Standard Deviation
SG	Scottish Gaelic
SGP	Standard Government Phonology
SOHC	Single Optional Headedness Condition
SPE	The Sound Pattern of English (Chomsky and Halle 1968)
SSB	Standard Southern British English
T	Obstruent; Tense
TP	Tense Phrase
TR	Obstruent-Sonorant sequence
TT	Turbidity Theory
UHP	Ultimate Head Parameter
UP	Universal Phonetics
V	Vowel
VH	Vowel Harmony
vP	little-v Phrase
voi	voice
VZA	Vowel-Zero Alternation
WP	Warsaw Polish

Notes on contributors

Phillip Backley (PhD University College London 1998) is Professor of English Linguistics at Tohoku Gakuin University. His research interests are mainly concerned with theoretical phonology (Element Theory, sound change, melody-prosody relations) and with aspects of the history of English.

Sabrina Bendjaballah (PhD Université Paris Diderot 1999) is Senior Research Scientist at the French National Centre for Scientific Research (CNRS). She has published on the phonology and the morphology of Berber, German, Modern South Arabian, and Somali.

Katalin Balogné Bérces (PhD Eötvös Loránd University 2006) is Associate Professor in English and Theoretical Linguistics at the Institute of English and American Studies, Pázmány Péter Catholic University, and the Department of English Language and Literature, Catholic University in Ružomberok. Her field of research is the phonology of English, especially its syllable structure and consonantal processes. Besides a number of organisations, she is a member of the Government Phonology Round Table and a regular organiser of its meetings.

Florian Breit (PhD University College London 2019) is Research Officer in Linguistics at Bangor University and Honorary Research Fellow in Linguistics at University College London. His research is concerned with the building blocks of melodic representation and how they may or may not interact with other levels of linguistic representation, particularly mutation at the morphosyntax-phonology interface and the voice-nasality connection.

Edoardo Cavirani (PhD Leiden University and Pisa University 2015) is currently an FWO Marie Skłodowska-Curie Actions – Seal of Excellence postdoc researcher and Italian Linguistics lecturer at the KU Leuven. His research interests include theoretical phonology, the interfaces of phonology with phonetics and morphosyntax, and microvariation.

Faith Chiu (PhD University College London 2018) is Lecturer in Phonetics at the University of Glasgow. She studies speech perception and auditory processing in adverse listening conditions. She is interested in incorporating techniques from cognitive psychology, psychoacoustics and neuroscience to support experimental work in phonetics and phonology.

Thaïs Cristófaro Silva (PhD School of Oriental and African Studies 1992) is Researcher at the Brazilian National Council for Scientific and Technological Development (CNPq) and Professor of Linguistics at the Federal University of Minas Gerais. She was formerly the president of the Linguistic Association of Brazil. Her research focuses mainly on the study of sound variation and change using Exemplar Model and Laboratory Phonology approaches.

Eugeniusz Cyran (PhD Catholic University of Lublin 1995) is full Professor at the Institute of Linguistics, John Paul II Catholic University of Lublin. His research is mainly concerned with the representational aspects of phonological theory, syllable and melody related phenomena in Celtic and Slavic languages, and the phonetics-phonology interface in voicing phenomena.

Radwa Fathi (PhD Université Paris Diderot 2013) is Associate Researcher at the Linguistics Laboratory, Nantes Université and Lecturer in Arabic at the Institut National des Langues et Civilisations Orientales. She is interested in the phonology and morphosyntax of Semitic languages, especially the realisation of Gender and Number at the interface with phonology.

John Harris (PhD University of Edinburgh 1983) is Emeritus Professor of Linguistics at University College London. His main areas of research include phonological theory, experimental phonology, the phonetics-phonology interface, accents of English, sound change, and phonological disorder.

Michael J. Kenstowicz (PhD University of Illinois 1971) is Professor of Linguistics at the Massachusetts Institute of Technology. He is the (co)-author more than 100 research articles and two widely used phonology textbooks. His research interests have included tone and accent, cyclic phonology, and more recently the phonetic basis of phonological contrasts. He has been an editor of the phonology sections of *Natural Language and Linguistic Theory* and the *Journal of East Asian Linguistics* for many years.

Nancy C. Kula (PhD University of Leiden 2002) is Professor of Linguistics at the University of Essex. Her research empirically focuses on Bantu languages where she works on phonology, prosody, phonology-syntax interface and morphosyntax. She is particularly interested in morphophonology and its interaction with segmental representations.

Jean Lowenstamm (PhD University of Massachusetts Amherst 1979) is Professor Emeritus in the Linguistics Department at the Université Paris Diderot. His research covers phonology, morphology, morphosyntax, and Afroasiatic languages.

Kuniya Nasukawa (PhD University College London 2000) is Professor of English Linguistics at Tohoku Gakuin University. His research interests include prosody-melody interaction, precedence-free phonology, and evolinguistics. He has written many articles covering a wide range of topics in phonological theory.

Markus A. Pöchtrager (PhD University of Vienna 2006) is Lecturer at the University of Vienna. His research focuses on phonology, phonological metatheory, phonology-morphology interaction, linguistics as a cognitive science, Finno-Ugric and Scandinavian languages, Turkic, and Caucasian languages. He is particularly interested in the structural reinterpretation of various properties usually considered melodic.

John R. Rennison (PhD University of Salzburg 1979) is Emeritus Professor at the University of Vienna and was born a native speaker of Yorkshire English. He first investigated the 'exotic' Bavarian dialects of German, then moved on to West Africa and to Koromfe, the language he has worked on for more than 40 years. His theoretical interests have always been the structure of phonological representations and the relationship between lexical and systematic-phonetic forms.

Tobias Scheer (PhD Université Paris Diderot 1996) is Directeur de Recherche at the CNRS in Nice. He is a phonologist with specific interests in the interfaces (with morpho-syntax and phonetics) and related aspects of cognitive science, more recently also regarding EEG-based experimental work. He mainly works on the synchrony and diachrony of Slavic languages and French and is a representative of Government Phonology (Strict CV).

Péter Szigetvári (PhD Eötvös Loránd University 2000) is Associate Professor and Head of the Department of English Linguistics at Eötvös Loránd University. He gives courses on the phonology of English, phonology in general, linguistics, and typography. He is currently working on a simplified description of the phonology of (British) English.

Shanti Ulfsbjorninn (PhD School of Oriental and African Studies 2015) is moving to Assistant Professor at Memorial University of Newfoundland.

Before this, they were first a Marie Curie Post-Doctoral Research Fellow at the University of Lyon. Their work has mostly focused on the interplay of syllabic and metrical structure and contributions toward a modular, autosegmental framework of morpho-phonology. Recently, they have been exploring the use of technology to carry out linguistic fieldwork on endangered and lesser studied languages. They are also a co-editor of *Radical: A Journal of Phonology*.

Harry van der Hulst (PhD Leiden University 1984) is Professor of Linguistics at the University of Connecticut. He specialises in the phonology of spoken and signed languages, has published 4 books, over 170 articles, edited over 32 books and 6 journal theme issues. He is Editor-in-Chief of *The Linguistic Review* and co-editor of the series 'Studies in generative grammar' with Mouton de Gruyter.

Yuko Yoshida (PhD School of Oriental and African Studies 1995) is Professor at the Faculty of Global Communications at Doshisha University. Her research pursues the nature of prosodic features in languages, especially pitch accent of Japanese varieties, in relation to syllabic structure, melodic content and morphosyntactic organisation, at the same time providing acoustic phonetic evidence. Most of her work centres round parameter settings between the varieties, mainly those spoken in the Kansai region, contributing to developments of the theory of Government Phonology.

Connor Youngberg (PhD School of Oriental and African Studies 2017) is an Associate Fellow in the Department of Language & Linguistics at the University of Essex. His research focuses on linguistic variation, vowel inventories and vocalic interaction in Japanese, with additional work on accent at the morpho-syntax interface and moraic nasals. Connor also has research interests in intergenerational attrition of dialects in Japanese and English and has contributed to projects within the domains of prosodic variation and Japanese language acquisition.

1
Principles and parameters in phonology: an introduction and overview

Connor Youngberg, Yuko Yoshida, and Florian Breit

This book is the culmination of state-of-the-art research in phonology from 2019 to 2022, with an eye on both theoretical proposals and careful investigation of individual languages.[1]

The work presented broadly covers segmental structure, prosodic structure, phonotactics and vowel-zero alternations, including traditional descriptive and analytical work, laboratory and experimental results, and generative and representational phonology. Much of this work is inspired by topics and representational issues discussed in Charette (1991) and other seminal work in the canon of Government Phonology (Kaye et al. (KLV) 1990), Element Theory (Kaye et al. 1985), Strict CV (Lowenstamm 1996) and Dependency Phonology (Anderson and Jones 1974; Anderson and Ewen 1987), as well as Optimality Theory (Prince and Smolensky 2004). Naturally, given the breadth of this work we cannot give an exhaustive overview of all the theoretical approaches and frameworks involved here. For this we refer the reader to Dresher and van der Hulst (2022) as a general broad overview, as well as chapters from Ritter (2022) and Staun (2022) for those readers unfamiliar with Government Phonology and Dependency Phonology. Not all of the work presented here is theoretical, however, and some contributions provide new work oriented towards fresh data and experimental results.

The contributions provide theoretical advances, new empirical evidence and analyses challenging previous generalisations, and we believe that the insights offered here will be equally exciting for phonologists working on related issues inside and outside frameworks with a focus on representational phonology, for example, researchers working in Optimality Theory or classical rule-based phonology.

The principles and parameters approach: Government Phonology

Government Phonology (GP) is a theory that can be broadly construed as a framework which explores the unification of forces from Principles and Parameters theory (Chomsky 1981; Chomsky and Lasnik 1993) with phonological structure, representation, and generation. The framework has its origins in early work on syllabicity from Kaye and Lowenstamm (1984) and Lowenstamm and Kaye (1986). These concepts were developed further in the programme of Government Phonology through the 1980s and 1990s, with early seminal works including Kaye et al. (1985, 1990), Charette (1991), and Harris (1994). More recent work continues to further the development of GP, such as the proposal that all syllables are composed exclusively of consonant-vowel pairs in CV phonology (Lowenstamm 1996; Scheer 2004) and the incorporation of structure in addition to elements or features into subsegmental representations (Jensen 1994; Rennison and Neubarth 2003; Pöchtrager 2006).

The main premise of this programme is the idea that phonology and syntax may not be as radically different mentally as they were often proposed to be in contemporary work (cf. Halle and Bromberger 1989). Instead, Government Phonology proposes that many of the fundamental mechanisms and principles may be shared across the two, such as the presence of empty categories, government and licensing relations, and the regulation of the surface-complexity of constituent and segmental structure through parameterisation and principles operating in conjunction with government and licensing relations. A further notable differentiating factor is the central role given to mental representations (see, for example, Harris 2007).

The nature of segmental melody was similarly re-evaluated, here leading to a more radical departure from the notion that phonology is really about deriving 'phonetic' representations from more abstract 'phonological' representations (for an overview and current work on debates surrounding the nature of phonological primitives, see also Breit et al. 2023), with no significant level of phonetic substance being acknowledged at any level of phonological representation (Harris and Lindsey 1995). Instead of the common equipollent articulatory features popularised with *The Sound Pattern of English* (Chomsky and Halle 1968), melody is represented by combination of more abstract, privative features known as elements, similar but not identical to the privative features found in Dependency Phonology (Anderson and Jones 1974; Anderson and Ewen 1987) and Particle Phonology (Schane 1984). Element Theory can now be considered its own representational framework which is used both within and outside of Government Phonology (Backley 2011).

A broad overview of frameworks in this tradition can be found in Scheer and Cyran (2018a,b), Scheer and Kula (2018), and Ritter (2022).

'Standard GP': a brief overview

As already mentioned briefly, major research themes in Government Phonology (GP) include the proposal that government and licensing relations regulate both syntax and phonology, the recognition of empty categories/constituents in phonology, and the parameterisation and restriction of structural representation and generation both at the syllable and segmental level. Standard versions of GP recognise the constituent categories *onset*, *nucleus*, and *rhyme* (where the rhyme is, strictly, a projection of the nucleus) – codas are notably not recognised as constituents in their own right. All of these are limited to binary branching, and segments are associated to a skeletal tier below these constituents. What is often most striking to non-GP phonologists are the syllable structures evidenced in this theory, such as those given below for the Southern British English words *splay* and *sent*. These include multiple empty constituents including a word-initial 'coda' in *splay* and a final onset preceding an empty nucleus rather than a complex coda in *sent*. Empty constituents are not distributed freely. They are highly restricted by conditions on government (on which more is found in the short introductions to the various parts of this book, for example, Chapters 7 and 14). Governing and Licensing relations regulate interconstituent and intersegmental relations, as well as the highly restricted – and potentially silent – empty nuclei. These relations are not shown in the below diagrams, but relevant concepts are discussed in the later chapters of this book and in the aforementioned references. Empty constituents and positions silenced through government or parameterisation are conventionally shown underlined in representations, as in the examples below and throughout this book.

(1) Example GP structure for *splay*

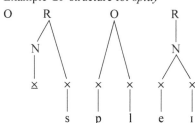

(2) Example GP structure for *sent*

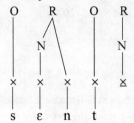

What is apparent is that while the initial *spl* of *splay* may be a complex onset or an appendix plus onset structure in other frameworks, word initial s+C sequences and others with falling sonority are treated as an empty syllable with only a rhymal complement or 'coda' (Kaye 1992; Goad 2012). Word-final clusters with a final falling sonority cluster such as the *nt* of *sent* are treated as a rhymal complement ('coda') followed by an onset (Kaye et al. 1990; Kaye 1990). This is supported by a wealth of evidence which implies that word-final consonants are in fact onsets of a syllable containing an empty nucleus (see, for example, Harris and Gussmann 1998, 2002).

Some Standard GP analyses eschew the use of branching constituents and treat most or all consonant clusters as onsets surrounding an empty nucleus. Examples include work on Polish (Gussmann and Kaye 1993; Cyran 2010), Japanese (Yoshida 1995), and Bemba (Kula 2002, 2008). Such a state of affairs might be viewed as the consequence of a parameter regulating constituent-branching traditionally, but has latterly given rise to a rich body of work within the Strict CV or CVCV approach (Lowenstamm 1996, 1999; Scheer 2004, 2012), which rejects constituent-branching and conflates the constituent and skeletal tiers. Under this view, all words are composed of strictly repeating Consonant-Vowel (CV) pairs and all consonant clusters enclose an empty V position, as shown in (3) for the English word *trap*.

(3) CVCV representation of *trap*

There are also several studies exploring the use of GP or CV structures combined with Optimality Theory (OT) (Polgárdi 1998, 2015; Rowicka 1999; Cavirani 2015), while others employ a VC skeleton or a 'loose' rather than a 'strict' CV skeleton (Dienes and Szigetvári 1999; Polgárdi 2008).

Segmental representations in GP utilise *elements*, which are a set of privative features encoding relatively broad phonological characteristics or acoustic categories (Kaye et al. 1985; Harris and Lindsey 1995; Charette and Göksel 1996; Backley 2011), though Element Theory can well be considered a separate framework of melodic representation which is now often used in work not subscribing to GP's approach to prosodic structure. Most versions of Element Theory employ six elements: |A|, |I|, |U|, |H|, |L|, and |ʔ|, which are used in both consonant and vowel representations. In vowels, |A|, |I|, and |U| broadly correlate with low, front, and round vowels, respectively, while |H|, |L|, and |ʔ| correlate to devoicing/breathiness, nasality, and creakiness. In consonants, |A|, |I|, and |U| broadly correlate to the place categories coronal/pharyngeal, palatal/coronal, and velar/labial, while |H|, |L|, and |ʔ| broadly correlate to aspiration/frication, nasality/voicing, and occlusion/obstruency. What all of the elements have in common is that they may occur and be interpreted both independently (as a sole property of some vowel or consonant) as well as in combination with other elements to form more complex segmental representations. For more details on Element Theory see Chapter 2.

Recent developments and current questions

In recent years, increased attention has been given to topics such as the accuracy of GP's syllabification approach, how to deal with accent and stress in a framework which does not formally recognise feet and other metrical constituents, and how to best capture the varying character of segments in terms of their phonological behaviour and phonetic realisation. There are central debates as to whether syllabic and segmental structure can be further reduced or even unified, and there has been increasing recognition of the fact that while GP has been very successful in modelling representational aspects of phonology, the specifics of phonological computation and phonological processes as well as the analysis of tone and lexical stress currently leave much to be desired. The framework makes strong predictions and places heavy restrictions upon what may be expected to exist or how certain data ought to be understood, and more recent examinations of data new and old heavily challenge some of our theoretical assumptions.

A large body of recent work examines how CV templates and segmental structure may be utilised at the morphosyntax–phonology interface, seeking to better understand what a morpheme is and how phonological representation can feed into that understanding. This includes but is not limited to work from Lowenstamm (2008), Bendjaballah and Haiden (2008), Bendjaballah (2012), Scheer (2012), Lampitelli (2014), Fathi and Lowenstamm (2016), Barillot et al. (2018), and Breit (2019).

Another major avenue of current investigation concerns the question of whether syllabic and segmental structure can (and should) be further reduced and unified. This typically means reducing the number of elements representing melody and accounting for the properties thus not independently encoded through (potentially more restrictive) structural means instead. The principal ongoing development in this direction is GP 2.0 (Živanović and Pöchtrager 2010; Pöchtrager 2020), which proposes that the set of elements be further reduced while more complex, embedded representations account for, for example, the effects of lowness instead, thereby linking them explicitly with length phenomena. Other proposals examining segmental structure in a similar vein include Precedence-Free Phonology (Nasukawa 2014; see also Chapter 22) and Onset Prominence (Schwartz 2012), which posit a richer and more fine-grained structural resolution of melodic representation, as well as Radical CV (van der Hulst 2020; see also Chapter 23), which is more closely tied to Dependency Phonology and reduces melodic representation to just two elements (C and V), encoding various complex melodic properties through the same rich, embedded structure and dependency relations that also obtain at segmental and syllabic levels.

Outline of the present work

Our book is divided into four Parts, reflecting major active research themes both in the GP programme and research on phonology as a broader field. Each begins with a brief introduction outlining the GP view of the broad themes treated and introducing the chapters contained therein. By adopting this 'distributed introduction' approach we hope to make the work presented here more accessible to readers who are less familiar with the framework. Part 1 focuses on melodic and segmental representations. Part 2 examines the role of prosodic and constituent structure in relation to processes and distributions. Part 3 is devoted to the role of vowel-zero alternations, syncope, and epenthesis in various languages, and how the role of schwa can be understood. Finally, Part 4 considers the role of recursive structures in phonology.

While each chapter addresses key issues and questions relevant specifically to the framework and research programme we have outlined above, not all of these are framed within Government Phonology terms. Some take a theory neutral approach, focusing on empirical and experimental data which challenges commonly held phonological assumptions and generalisations taken to be true by many theoreticians, such as what a cluster in English is or what generalisations we can make about svarabakhti in Irish. Many of the chapters represent exciting new endeavours to develop and push theory further, including new work on the interaction of GP and OT computation and proposals for further suprasegmental parameterisation seeking to better explain prosodic phenomena. We believe that the work presented here offers interesting ideas, findings, and data, not only for those fluent with the GP literature but also those who are new to the framework or simply curious about current issues, developments, and thought from various quarters of phonology. We hope that both the theoretical developments and the careful studies of French, Bavarian, Irish, Cypriot Greek, Japanese, and other language varieties contained herein will encourage further debate, discussion, and cross-theoretical interaction in works yet to come.

Note

1. This book and also this chapter are an equal-contribution editorship/authorship; there is no significance to the author order for either.

References

Anderson, J. M., and Ewen, C. J. (1987). *Principles of Dependency Phonology*. Cambridge: Cambridge University Press. https://doi.org/10.1017/CBO9780511753442.

Anderson, J. M., and Jones, C. (1974). 'Three theses concerning phonological representations'. *Journal of Linguistics* 10(1), 1–26. https://doi.org/10.1017/S0022226700003972.

Backley, P. (2011). *An Introduction to Element Theory*. Edinburgh: Edinburgh University Press.

Barillot, X., Bendjaballah, S., and Lampitelli, N. (2018). 'Verbal classes in Somali: Allomorphy has no classificatory function'. *Journal of Linguistics* 54(1), 3–43. https://doi.org/10.1017/S002222671700024X.

Bendjaballah, S. (2012). *La grammaire des gabarits*. Habilitation thesis, Université de Paris Diderot.

Bendjaballah, S., and Haiden, M. (2008). 'A typology of emptiness in templates'. In *The Sounds of Silence: Empty elements in syntax and phonology*, edited by J. Hartmann, V. Hegedüs, and H. van Riemsdjik, 21–57. Amsterdam: Elsevier.

Breit, F. (2019). *Welsh Mutation and Strict Modularity*. Doctoral dissertation, UCL.

Breit, F., Botma, B., van t' Veer, M., and van Oostendorp, M. (eds). (2023). *Primitives of Phonological Structure*. Oxford: Oxford University Press. https://doi.org/10.1093/oso/9780198791126.001.0001.

Cavirani, E. (2015) *Modeling Phonologization*. Utrecht: LOT Publishing.

Charette, M. (1991). *Conditions on Phonological Government*. Cambridge: Cambridge University Press.

Charette, M., and Göksel, A. (1996). 'Switching and vowel harmony in Turkic languages'. In *A Festschrift for Edmund Gussmann From his Friends and Colleagues*, edited by K. Henryk and S. Bogdan, 29–57. Lublin: Wydawnictwo KUL.

Chomsky, N. (1981). *Lectures on Government and Binding: The Pisa Lectures*. Dordrecht: Foris Publications.

Chomsky, N., and Halle, M. (1968). *The Sound Pattern of English*. New York: Harper & Row.

Chomsky, N., and Lasnik, H. (1993). 'Principles and Parameters Theory'. In *Syntax: An international handbook of contemporary research*, edited by J. Jacobs, A. von Stechow, W. Sternfeld, and T. Vennemann. Berlin: De Gruyter.

Cyran, E. (2010). *Complexity Scales and Licensing in Phonology*. Berlin: De Gruyter.

Dienes, P., and Szigetvári, P. (1999). 'Repartitioning the skeleton: VC phonology'. Unpublished manuscript, Eötvös Loránd University, Budapest.

Dresher, B. E., and van der Hulst, H. (2022). *The Oxford History of Phonology*. Oxford: Oxford University Press.

Fathi, R., and Lowenstamm, J. (2016). 'The gender assignment pattern of French nouns'. *Morphology* 26, 477–509. https://doi.org/10.1007/s11525-016-9287-2.

Goad, H. (2012). 'sC clusters are (almost always) coda-initial'. *The Linguistic Review* 29, 335–73.
Gussmann, E., and Kaye, J. D. (1993). 'Polish notes from a Dubrovnik café: I. The yers'. *SOAS Working Papers in Linguistics and Phonetics* 3, 427–62.
Halle, M., and Bromberger, S. (1989). 'Why phonology is different'. *Linguistic Inquiry* 20(1), 51–70.
Harris, J. (1994). *English Sound Structure*. Oxford: Blackwell.
Harris, J. (2007). 'Representation'. In *The Cambridge Handbook of Phonology*, edited by P. de Lacy, 119–138. Cambridge: Cambridge University Press. https://doi.org/10.1017/CBO9780511486371.007.
Harris, J., and Gussmann, E. (1998). 'Final codas: why the West was wrong'. In *Structure and Interpretation: Studies in Phonology*, edited by E. Cyran, 139–162. Lublin: Folium.
Harris, J., and Gussmann, E. (2002). 'Word-final onsets'. *UCL Working Papers in Linguistics*, 14, 1–42.
Harris, J., and Lindsey, G. (1995). 'The elements of phonological representation'. In *Frontiers of Phonology: Atoms, structures, derivations*, edited by J. Durand and F. Katamba, 34–79. London: Longman.
Jensen, S. (1994). 'Is ʔ an Element? Towards a non-segmental phonology'. *SOAS Working Papers in Linguistics and Phonetics* 4, 7–78.
Kaye, J. (1990). '"Coda" Licensing'. *Phonology* 7(1), 301–30. https://doi.org/10.1017/S0952675700001214.
Kaye, J. (1992). 'Do you believe in magic? The story of s+C sequences'. *SOAS Working Papers in Linguistics and Phonetics* 2, 293–313.
Kaye, J., and Lowenstamm, J. (1984). 'De la syllabicité'. In *Forme sonore du langage: Structure des représentations en phonologie*, edited by F. Dell, D. Hirst, and J. -R. Vergnaud, 123–59. Paris: Hermann.
Kaye, J., Lowenstamm, J., and Vergnaud, J.-R. (1985). 'The internal structure of phonological representations: A theory of Charm and Government'. *Phonology Yearbook* 2, 305–28.
Kaye, J., Lowenstamm, J., and Vergnaud, J.-R. (1990). 'Constituent structure and government in phonology'. *Phonology* 7(2), 193–231.
Kula, N. C. (2002). *The Phonology of Verbal Derivation in Bemba*. Utrecht: LOT Publications.
Kula, N. C. (2008). 'Derived environment effects: A representational approach'. *Lingua* 118(9), 1328–43. https://doi.org/10.1016/j.lingua.2007.09.011.
Lampitelli, N. (2014). 'The Romance plural isogloss and linguistic change: A comparative study of Romance nouns'. *Lingua* 140, 158–79. https://doi.org/10.1016/j.lingua.2013.12.011.
Lowenstamm, J. (1996). 'CV as the only syllable type'. In *Current Trends in Phonology: Models and methods*, edited by J. Durand and B. Laks, 419–42. Salford: European Studies Research Institute.
Lowenstamm, J. (1999). 'The beginning of the word'. In *Phonologica 1996*, edited by J. Rennison and K. Kühnhammer, 153–66. The Hague: Holland Academic Graphics.
Lowenstamm, J. (2008). 'On little n, √, and types of nouns'. In *The Sounds of Silence: Empty elements in syntax and phonology*, edited by J. Hartmann, V. Hegedűs, and H. van Riemsdjik, 105–44. Amsterdam: Elsevier.
Lowenstamm, J., and Kaye, J. D. (1986). 'Compensatory lengthening in Tiberian Hebrew'. In *Studies in Compensatory Lengthening*, edited by L. Wetzels and E. Sezer, 97–132. Berlin: De Gruyter. https://doi.org/10.1515/9783110821666-006.
Nasukawa, K. (2014). 'Features and recursive structure'. *Nordlyd* 41(1), 1–19.
Prince, A., and Smolensky, P. (2004). *Optimality Theory: Constraint interaction in generative grammar*. Cambridge: Blackwell.
Polgárdi, K. (1998). *Vowel Harmony: An account in terms of Government and Optimality*. Utrecht: LOT.
Polgárdi, K. (2008). 'The representation of lax vowels in Dutch: A Loose CV approach'. *Lingua* 118(9), 1375–92. http://doi.org/10.1016/j.lingua.2007.09.008.
Polgárdi, K. (2015). 'Syncope, syllabic consonant formation, and the distribution of stressed vowels in English'. *Journal of Linguistics* 51(2), 383–423. https://doi.org/10.1017/S0022226714000486.
Pöchtrager, M. A. (2006) *The Structure of Length*. Doctoral dissertation, University of Vienna.
Pöchtrager, M. A. (2020). 'Tense? (Re)lax! A new formalisation for a controversial contrast'. *Acta Linguistica Academica* 67(1), 53–71. https://doi.org/10.1556/2062.2020.00005.
Rennison, J. R., and Neubarth, F. (2003). 'An x-bar theory of Government Phonology'. In *Living on the Edge: 28 Papers in honour of Jonathan Kaye*, edited by S. Ploch, 95–130. Berlin: De Gruyter. https://doi.org/10.1515/9783110890563.95.
Ritter, N. (2022). 'Government Phonology in historical perspective'. In *The Oxford History of Phonology*, edited by B. E. Dresher and H. van der Hulst, 509–29. Oxford: Oxford University Press. https://doi.org/10.1093/oso/9780198796800.003.0024.

Rowicka, G. (1999). *On Ghost Vowels: A strict CV Approach*. The Hague: LOT.

Schane, S. A. (1984). 'The fundamentals of Particle Phonology'. *Phonology Yearbook* 1, 129–55.

Scheer, T. (2004). *A Lateral Theory of Phonology, Volume 1. What is CVCV and why should it be?* Berlin: De Gruyter.

Scheer, T. (2012). *A Lateral Theory of Phonology, Volume 2. Direct Interface and one-channel translation*. Berlin: De Gruyter.

Scheer, T., and Cyran, E. (2018a). 'Syllable structure in Government Phonology'. In *The Routledge Handbook of Phonological Theory*, edited by S. J. Hannahs and A. Bosch 262–92. London: Routledge.

Scheer, T. and Cyran, E. (2018b) 'Interfaces in Government Phonology'. In *The Routledge Handbook of Phonological Theory*, edited by S. J. Hannahs and A. Bosch, 293–324. London: Routledge.

Scheer, T. and Kula, N. (2018) 'Government Phonology: Element Theory, conceptual issues and introduction'. In *The Routledge Handbook of Phonological Theory*, edited by S. J. Hannahs and A. Bosch, 226–61. London: Routledge.

Schwartz, G. (2012). 'Glides and initial vowels within the onset prominence representational environment'. *Poznań Studies in Contemporary Linguistics* 48(4), 661–85. https://doi.org/10.1515/psicl-2012-0029.

Staun, J. (2022). 'Dependency Phonology'. In *The Oxford History of Phonology*, edited by B. E. Dresher and H. van der Hulst, 485–508. Oxford: Oxford University Press. https://doi.org/10.1093/oso/9780198796800.003.0023.

van der Hulst, H. (2020). *Principles of Radical CV Phonology: A theory of segmental and syllabic structure*. Edinburgh: Edinburgh University Press.

Yoshida, Y. (1995). *On Pitch Accent Phenomena in Standard Japanese*. Doctoral dissertation, School of Oriental and African Studies, University of London. https://doi.org/10.25501/SOAS.00033572.

Živanović, S., and Pöchtrager, M. A. (2010). 'GP 2, and Putonghua too'. *Acta Linguistica Hungarica* 57(4), 357–80.

Part 1
Melody and segmental representation

2
Melody and segmental representation: a brief introduction
Florian Breit

Introduction

Element Theory (ET) has undergone many revisions since its first inception with Dependency Phonology (Anderson and Jones 1974; Anderson and Ewen 1987) and Particle Phonology (Schane 1975, 1984) and subsequent adoption in early Government Phonology (Kaye et al. (KLV) 1985). For instance, the set of elements assumed has undergone much change. While mainstream ET has for some time now settled on a set of six features (|H, L, ʔ, A, I, U|), early versions included, among others, the neutral element |@|, a noise element |h|, and a nasal element |N|. Yet in some current versions there is a drive to further reduce this set, typically by adopting structural conventions to encode relevant distinctions, such as the disposal of |A, H, ʔ| in GP 2.0 (for example, cf. Pöchtrager and Kaye 2013). Variation also concerns other matters such as the role of headedness and dependency, the role of substance (see also van 't Veer et al. 2023), and representational organisation. For a more in-depth overview of variation within ET see Backley (2012).

Consonant-vowel unity

Although some elements, especially |ʔ|, have not been linked to a consistent role within nuclei, ET assumes *consonant-vowel unity* (cf. Backley and Nasukawa 2010). That is, segmental melody is represented by the same set of elements regardless of the segment's dominating category (that is, *onset* or *nucleus*). This carries the theoretically interesting implication that, although we might be able to link specific elements to typical phonetic exponents dependent on such categories, ET proper makes no use (or, has no knowledge) of a distinction between such entities as vowels and consonants.

Privativity

Many theories of phonological primitives have a notion of multivalency. For example the feature theory of Chomsky and Halle's (1968) SPE employs equipollent binary features such as [+high] and [−high], while other feature theories may have unary but explicitly matched (and thus in a sense equipollent) pairs of features, such as [compact] and [diffuse] in Jakobson et al. (1952). In contrast, ET assumes that all melodic primitives (viz. the elements) are strictly monovalent and privative. This means that in ET, the primitives have no 'negative' or 'unmarked' counterparts at any theoretically relevant level. Only the presence of an element within a melodic representation is recognised, and the absence of an element is neither referenceable nor interpretable.

Binary distinctive features have been a mainstay of work conducted in the tradition of linear phonology, such as Jakobson et al. (1952), Jakobson and Halle (1956), and especially Chomsky and Halle (1968). Such features have traditionally been employed not only to encode those categorial distinctions pertaining to the phonetic identity of phonological segments, but also to encode aspects such as stress, syllabicity, boundary information, and so on. As such, no explicit distinction was made between prosodic and melodic (that is, segmental) information. Later work however showed the need to formally distinguish these two levels of phonological representation, leading to the development of nonlinear models of phonology such as Autosegmental Phonology (Goldsmith 1972), which non-monotonically link melodic and prosodic information on different tiers of phonological representation, and this is the view taken by both Government Phonology and ET (cf. Harris 2007).

Interpretability

Another important property distinguishing ET from most other theories of melodic representation concerns the interpretive requirements of melodic material. Whereas it is standardly assumed that the melodic output of phonology is interpretable only as a fully specified matrix of features in, for example, SPE-type theories, elements are understood as inherently interpretable units, fully sufficient to receive phonetic interpretation in their own right (Lindsey and Harris 1990; Harris and Lindsey 1995). This means that any element, say |I|, is interpretable both as the sole melodic specification of a segment as well as in combination with other elements (for example, in the compound expressions |I, A| and |I, H, ʔ|). An important consequence of this view is that an element-theoretic representation is interpretable at all times – there is no sense in ET in which for instance the underlying representation of some form can be said to lack the necessary melodic specification to be phonetically interpretable, as would be the case with most SPE-type underlying representations that are heavily underspecified lexically and rely on phonological processing and feature-filling rules to reach a state of interpretability.

The set of elements

Current mainstream ET assumes a set of six primitives: |A, I, U| and |H, L, ʔ| (cf. Backley 2011, 2012; Kaye 2000). The former three are commonly known as *resonance elements* (also *place* or *colour*) and principally correlate with vocalic quality and place of articulation. The latter are often termed the *manner elements* because they principally correlate with manner of articulation (though that term is too strict to cover the range of their phonetic correlates). A brief summary of the six elements, their mnemonic names and principal characteristics is given in (1).

(1) | **Element** | **Name** | **Characteristics** |
|---|---|---|
| |A| | *mAss* | Lowness, uvular and pharyngeal place |
| |I| | *dIp* | Frontness, palatal and coronal place |
| |U| | *rUmp* | Roundness, velar place |
| |H| | *high* | High tone, aspiration, frication |
| |L| | *low* | Low tone, voicing, nasality |
| |ʔ| | *edge* | Noncontinuancy ('stopness') |

Segmental composition

As mentioned, the elements may appear in melodic representations by themselves as well as in combination with one another. However, in addition to this, ET also recognises an empty representation (a necessary consequence of adopting the Empty Category Principle in GP) and recognises that elements in compound representations may enter into a head-dependent (or head-operator) relationship.

Empty representations receive a language-dependent default interpretation when not licensed to be silent (that is, to remain uninterpreted) by Proper Government. For nuclei this is typically a neutral central vowel such as /ə/ or /ɨ/. As is often the case, the situation has been less well investigated with consonants to date, but, for example, in German empty initial onsets are interpreted as a glottal stop.

The head-dependent relationship that elements may enter into is much more restricted in ET than, for example, in classical Dependency Phonology. ET standardly allows only a single element within a melodic representation to assume head status (though Backley 2017 argues for multiple headedness), while the others remain as dependents. At the same time, melodic representations do not have to be headed in ET, so that |I|, |$\underline{I}$|, |I, A|, |$\underline{I}$, A|, and |I, $\underline{A}$| (heads underlined) are all distinct melodic representations.

Closely connected to this highly restrictive conception of a dependency relation (vis-à-vis segment-internal structural asymmetry) is that ET assumes that melodic representations permit isomerism (though always achiral) and operations thereon are idempotent, in the sense that (unlike, for example, in Schane's Particle Phonology) an element is either present or absent from a representation without any notion of multiplicity and that two melodic representations are distinct if, and only if, either they are composed of different elements or the head of the representation is different (Breit 2013, 4–5). Consequently, compounding an element |I| into a representation such as |A, I| results in identical output, that is |A, I|, and while |A, I|, |$\underline{A}$, I|, and |A, $\underline{I}$| are all distinct by virtue of the different head, there is no difference between notations such as |$\underline{A}$, I| and |I, $\underline{A}$| since they contain the same elements and have the same head (that is, order is irrelevant).

Themes addressed in Part 1

The chapters in Part 1 address a variety of current research themes in ET and its application. Bendjaballah (Chapter 3) contributes to our understanding of the internal make-up and behaviour of liquids, which have long presented puzzles for segmental phonologists, regardless of the assumed framework. In ET, it is often assumed that such liquids feature a combination of either |A, I| or |A, U| while |U| and |I| themselves function antagonistically to one another (see, for example, Backley 2011). Conversely, Bendjaballah demonstrates through an analysis of Bavarian *l*-localisation that the process can simultaneously show affinities suggesting that both |U| and |I| play an active role, with surface effects dependent on sequential licensing issues rather than segment-internal antagonistic relations. In doing so, she is able to present a unified analysis of post-vocalic and post-consonantal environments in which /l/ lenites in these varieties and to make strong arguments suggesting that the behaviour seen is indeed in the grasp of phonological explanation, rather than having to be relegated to lexical encoding and diachrony.

Turning his attention to final-obstruent devoicing in Polish, Cyran (Chapter 5) explores the separation of explanation across linguistic levels for certain marginal phenomena such as voicing-retention in the context of arguments for a more substance-free/relativistic approach to laryngeal categories (see, for example, Cyran 2014). Cyran argues that there are good reasons to believe that a separation of concerns is not only feasible but also desirable, showing that apparently conflicting phenomenology may be reconciled if we correctly consider their origin and distribution across the interface between segmental phonology and language-specific phonetics.

Breit (Chapter 4) is more concerned with the theoretic characterisation of ET itself, revisiting an earlier formalism (Breit 2013) and arguing explicitly for a derivational characterisation that draws out possible cognitive homology across linguistic modules. Extending previous work, he also seeks to formally integrate and characterise Licensing Constraints (LCs; for example, Charette and Göksel 1996), which opens up the possibility for further investigation of their role in the generation and distribution of various segmental systems.

The issue of LCs and the encoding of restrictions commonly attributed to them is also taken up by Rennison (Chapter 6), who argues that we ought to give consideration to different explanatory hypotheses in light of LCs' potential arbitrariness. Instead of arbitrary LCs, Rennison argues that we should revisit geometric constraint mechanisms by showing that these are able to encode a more conservative and simultaneously revealing set of restrictions in the context of Turkish Vowel Harmony, one of the original sources of evidence for the modern theory of LCs.

References

Anderson, J. M., and Ewen, C. J. (1987). *Principles of Dependency Phonology*. Cambridge: Cambridge University Press. https://doi.org/10.1017/CBO9780511753442.
Anderson, J. M., and Jones, C. (1974). 'Three theses concerning phonological representations'. *Journal of Linguistics* 10(1), 1–26. https://doi.org/10.1017/S0022226700003972.
Backley, P. (2011). *An Introduction to Element Theory*. Edinburgh: Edinburgh University Press.
Backley, P. (2012). 'Variation in Element Theory'. *Linguistic Variation* 12(1), 57–102. https://doi.org/10.1075/lv.12.1.03bac.
Backley, P. (2017). 'Headedness in Element Theory: The case for multiple heads'. *Glossa* 2(1), 1–17. https://doi.org/10.5334/gigl.463.
Backley, P., and Nasukawa, K. (2010). 'Consonant-vowel unity in Element Theory'. *Phonological Studies* 13, 21–8.

Breit, F. (2013). *Formal Aspects of Element Theory*. MRes dissertation, UCL.

Charette, M., and Göksel, A. (1996) 'Switching and vowel harmony in Turkic languages'. In *A Festschrift for Edmund Gussmann From his Friends and Colleagues*, edited by K. Henryk and S. Bogdan, 29–57. Lublin: Wydawnictwo KUL.

Chomsky, N., and Halle, M. (1968). *The Sound Pattern of English*. New York: Harper & Row.

Cyran, E. (2014). *Between Phonology and Phonetics: Polish voicing*. Berlin: De Gruyter.

Goldsmith, J. (1972). *Autosegmental Phonology*. Doctoral dissertation, Massachusetts Institute of Technology (MIT).

Harris, J. (2007). 'Representation'. In *The Cambridge Handbook of Phonology*, edited by P. de Lacy, 119–38. Cambridge: Cambridge University Press. https://doi.org/10.1017/CBO9780511486371.007.

Harris, J., and Lindsey, G. (1995). 'The elements of phonological representation'. In *Frontiers of Phonology: Atoms, structures, derivations*, edited by J. Durand and F. Katamba, 34–79. London: Longman.

Jakobson, R., and Halle, M. (1956). *Fundamentals of Language*. The Hague: Mouton & Co.

Jakobson, R., Fant, C. G. M., and Halle, M. (1952). *Preliminaries to Speech Analysis: The distinctive features and their correlates*. Boston, MA: MIT Press.

Kaye, J. (2000). 'A users' guide to Government Phonology'. Unpublished manuscript. https://www2.ung.si/~jezik/jkaye/Documents/guide.pdf.

Kaye, J., Lowenstamm, J., and Vergnaud, J.-R. (1985). 'The internal structure of phonological representations: A theory of Charm and Government'. *Phonology Yearbook* 2, 305–28.

Lindsey, G., and Harris, J. (1990). 'Phonetic interpretation in generative grammar'. *UCL Working Papers in Linguistics* 2, 355–69.

Pöchtrager, M. A., and Kaye, J. (2013). 'GP2.0'. *SOAS Working Papers in Linguistics* 16, 51–64.

Schane, S. A. (1975). 'Some diachronic deletion processes and their synchronic consequences in French'. In *Diachronic Studies in Romance Linguistics*, edited by M. Saltarelli and D. Wanner, 183–94. Berlin: De Gruyter.

Schane, S. A. (1984). 'The fundamentals of Particle Phonology'. *Phonology Yearbook* 1, 129–55.

van 't Veer, M., Botma, B., Breit, F., and van Oostendorp, M. (2023). 'The structure and content of phonological primitives'. In *Primitives of Phonological Structure*, edited by F. Breit, B. Botma, M. van 't Veer, and M. van Oostendorp, 1–36. Oxford: Oxford University Press. https://doi.org/10.1093/oso/9780198791126.003.0001.

3
On hedgehogs and gold in Bavarian: *l*-vocalisation in Upper Austrian German

Sabrina Bendjaballah

Introduction

Liquids are known for their peculiar behaviour crosslinguistically and the question of their internal structure has been much debated in the literature.[1,2] In this context, *l*-vocalisation in Bavarian has been discussed in different frameworks (for example, Kranzmayer 1956; Rennison 1978; Wiesinger 1990; Kühnhammer 2004; Djabbari et al. 2010; Kaye and Pöchtrager 2015; Noelliste 2017). This phenomenon refers to the fact that post-vocalic *l* in Standard German does not correspond to post-vocalic *l* in various Bavarian languages, for example, Upper Austrian German [goɪd] 'gold' versus Standard German *Gold*.

This phenomenon however does not exclusively obtain in post-vocalic context: it is also observed in post-consonantal context, for example, Upper Austrian German [yːgɪ] 'hedgehog' versus Standard German *Igel*. This fact has largely been ignored in the literature. My aim in this chapter is twofold. First, I propose an analysis of the phenomenon in post-consonantal context. More specifically, applying an Element Theory analysis (Kaye et al. (KLV) 1985, 1990; Charette 1991; Backley 2011) to data from a particular Bavarian language (Weyer Bavarian, Oberösterreich, Austria), I show that the processes in post-consonantal and in post-vocalic context can be unified. Second, I examine the implications of the analysis on the status of *l*-vocalisation as a synchronically active phonological process in Bavarian. The analysis will attempt to disentangle the intricacies of the behaviour of |I| and |U|, which have been beautifully handled in Turkic languages by Charette and Göksel (1996).

The three sections that follow present the data, the analysis, and then evaluate the implications of the analysis and conclude the chapter, respectively.

Data

Introduction

l-lenition[3] regularly takes place in coda position and results in [w] crosslinguistically. The process is reported both synchronically and diachronically. The probably most widely discussed languages are English dialects, for example, *milk* realised in London English as [mɪwk]. However this type of *l*-lenition is attested in many genetically unrelated languages; see, for example, Omani Mehri (Semitic, Modern South Arabian): [jəlúːbəd] versus [jəwbéːd] /jəlbéːd/, √lbd 'hit' IPF.3ms versus SBJ.3ms (Bendjaballah and Tifrit 2018). *l* > [j] is less common, but it is also attested in various languages; see, for example, Standard Taqbaylit Berber [ali] versus Ouadhia Taqbaylit Berber [aji] 'climb' (Bedar and Quellec 2020).

l thus presents an affinity both with |I| and |U|. The question arises as to whether these elements combine in the internal structure of *l*, or whether *l* has either |U| (for example, Omani Mehri), or |I| (for example, Ouadhia Berber). Backley (2011, 178) supposes that |U| and |I| 'do not easily combine' and proposes that laterals are composed either of |A| and |U|, or of |A| and |I|.[4]

It has long been noticed that the surface realisations of coda *l* in Bavarian involve both |I| and |U|, as seen respectively in /gold/ [goɪd] 'gold', and /ɛlf/ [œːf] 'eleven' (for recent analyses in an Element Theory framework, cf. Djabbari et al. 2010; Bendjaballah 2012). However, the existence of the phenomenon as a synchronically active phonological process has been challenged in Kaye and Pöchtrager (2015), who argue that the surface realisations reflect the underlying representations: there is no /l/ in examples such as [goɪd] 'gold' and [œːf] 'eleven', and therefore no *l*-lenition.

Vowels

In the literature, the discussion of *l*-lenition in Bavarian focuses on the interaction of coda /l/ with its preceding nucleus. Two subsets must be distinguished depending on the identity of this nucleus. The first column in (1) exemplifies the phenomenon after a back vowel. The second column gives a related form where /l/, being in an onset position, surfaces as such, thus establishing its presence at the underlying level in the examples of the first column:

(1)   **coda /l/**   **onset /l/**
    /u/   [ʃuːɪ]   'school'   [ʃulɐbuɐ]   'schoolboy'
    /o/   [ʁoɪn]   'roll'.INF   [ʁoːlɐd]   'roll'.COND
    /ɔ/   [fɔɪn]   'fall'.INF   [fɔːlɐd]   'fall'.COND

(2), below, exemplifies the phenomenon after a front vowel. As in (1), the second column provides related forms where /l/ surfaces. The underlying identity of the vowels in the forms in the first column of (2) is a matter of debate: Is it identical to the surface (y, œ, ø), or does it have the identity that can be seen in the corresponding Standard German forms (i, e, ɛ)? The stem-vowel is identical in the forms with and without [l]. This casts doubt on the assumption of /i, e, ɛ/. However, additional data support an analysis in terms of rounding triggered by /l/. For this reason, I assume rounding of /i, e, ɛ/ to [y, œ, ø] for the time being, and will come back to this issue below.

(2)   **coda /l/**   **onset /l/**   **Standard German**

	coda /l/		onset /l/		Standard German
[y] /i/	[ʒbyːn]	'play'.INF	[ʒbyːlɐd]	'play'.COND	*spielen*
[œ] /e/	[mœː]	'flour'	[mœːlɪ(g)]	'tasting like flour'	*Mehl*
[ø] /ɛ/	[ʃøːn]	'peel'.INF	[ʃøːlɐd]	'peel'.COND	*schälen*

The following distributional generalisation can be established:

(3)   If the vowel preceding coda /l/ contains
     a. |U|, but not |I| /l/ surfaces as [ɪ]
     b. |I|, but not |U| /l/ does not surface, and the preceding vowel is rounded.[5]

Diphthongs

l-lenition after diphthongs is less often discussed, if at all. As illustrated in (4a), the off-glide preceding /l/ is neither [ɪ] nor [ʊ], but [ɥ]. (4b) illustrates the fact that [aɥ] never surfaces if the consonant following the off-glide is not /l/. Following Kaye and Lowenstamm (1984), and many others, I assume that the internal structure of glides consists of |U| [w], |I| [j] and a combination thereof |U.I| [ɥ]. An off-glide preceding /l/ is always realised as |U.I| [ɥ].

(4)

		infinitive	conditional		Standard German
	a.	dɐfaɥn	dɐfaɥlɐd	'rot'	*verfaulen*
		daɥn	daɥlɐd	'divide'	*teilen*
		faɥn	faɥlɐd	'file, grate'	*feilen*
	b.	ʁaɪ̯m	ʁaɪbɐd	'rub'	*reiben*
		saʊffa	saʊffɐd	'booze'	*saufen*
		saʊŋ	saʊgɐd	'suck'	*saugen*

Consonants

The question of the interaction of /l/ with a preceding consonant is remarkably absent, or at best marginal, in the literature on *l*-vocalisation in Bavarian.[6]

The realisation of /l/ after a consonant depends on the identity of the consonant, exactly as was the case post-vocalically. The distributional facts are summarised in (5) and illustrated in (6) and (7). As shown in the second column of (6), if a vowel-initial suffix is added, /l/ surfaces as such. I take this to establish its existence in the underlying representation of the lexical items under consideration.

(5) If the consonant preceding /l/ is
    a. a labial or a velar (≠ ɣ)   /l/ surfaces as [ɪ]
    b. a dental-alveolar (≠ n, d) /l/ surfaces as [l̩]

(6)
		infinitive	**conditional**	
a.	labial__	[auf dy:βɪn]	[auf dyβlɐd]	'fix, make stick'
		[ɔː daɥfɪn]	[ɔː daɥflɐd]	'throw a fit'
		[ãʊ̯ hymmɪn]	[ãʊ̯ hymlɐd]	'praise to the skies'
b.	velar__	[kuːgɪn]	[kuːglɐd]	'roll'

		noun	**adjective**	
		[buːgɪ]	[buːglɐd]	'back', 'bumpy'

(7)   dental-alveolar__   [fuxdl̩n]   'gesticulate'.INF
                                  [muʃʃl̩]   'mussel'
                                  [ʃnitsl̩]   'escalope'

/n, d, ɣ/ must be excluded in (5) because they trigger additional phenomena: n+l is realised as [ndl]; the acoustic realisation of {ɣ, d}+l requires a detailed phonetic analysis. In this chapter, I will transcribe the resulting segment as L and leave the question of its exact realisation for further research.[7]

Finally, the realisation of /l/ after palatals cannot be tested, since Upper Austrian German does not have underlying palatal obstruents: [ç] is the realisation of an underlying velar. /l/ preceded by [ç] behaves as expected: it surfaces as [ɪ], for example, [syççɪ] 'sickle'. The only context after palatal is thus after an off-glide, cf. (4).

The affinity between labials and velars has often been noted in Element Theory, and it has been ascribed to the presence of |U| in both classes of consonants. (See for example, Backley 2011, 81ff.: 'this [...] supports the idea that velars and labials are phonologically related [...] this relation is based on the presence of a shared |U| element'.) Assuming in addition that the only consonant with |I| in Upper Austrian German is [ɾ], we conclude that

(8) If the consonant preceding /l/
    a. contains |U| but not |I| /l/ surfaces as [ɪ]
    b. contains neither |U| nor |I| /l/ surfaces as [l̩]

Note that (8) is not sensitive to the morphological status of /l/: it applies exactly in the same way in cases where /l/ has affixal status, as illustrated in (9). Diminutive -*l* is realised as [ɪ] after labials and velars, and as [l̩] after dental-alveolars.

(9)
	base	*l*-diminutive	
labial__	[koːpf]	[køppfɪ]	'head'
velar__	[duɐx]	[dyɐççɪ]	'cloth'
dental-alveolar__	[hẽːn]	[hẽːndl̩]	'hen'

Action at a distance

/l/ also interacts with a segment located at a distance. The facts are exemplified in (10). The forms in the first column are /l/-final nouns; the forms in the second column are diminutives, that are built by suffixation of *-erl*. As noted above, I transcribe the surface realisation of /l/ as [L] while the exact phonetic character remains to be determined.

(10)
	stem-vowel		*l*-final noun	*erl*-diminutive	
a.	y ~ i	labial__	[dy̱ːβɪ]	[di̱ːβɐL]	'dowel, bump'
		velar__	[y̱ːgɪ]	[i̱ːgɐL]	'hedgehog'
b.	ø ~ e	labial__	[ʒdø̱mbbɪ]	[ʒdɛ̱mbbɐL]	'stamp'
		velar__	[dø̱ːgɪ]	[de̱ːgɐL]	'container'
c.[8]	o	labial__	[kno̱ːfɪ]	[kno̱ːfɐL]	'garlic'
		velar__	[fo̱ːgɪ]	[fo̱ːgɐL]	'bird'
	u	labial__	[ʒdu̱ːmmɪ]	[ʒdu̱ːmmɐL]	'short cylinder'
		velar__	[ku̱ːgɪ]	[ku̱ːgɐL]	'ball'

The internal structures of the vowels are summed up in (11): the vowel in the *l*-final noun systematically contains an additional |U|. (If the vowel contains |U|, this addition is not reflected on the surface, and no alternation is observed.)

(11)
VC-*l* (*noun*)		VC-*ɐL* (*diminutive*)	
y	|U.I|	i	|I|
ø, œ	|A.U.I|	e, ɛ	|A.I|
o	|A.U|		
u	|U|		

I propose to interpret these facts as follows:

(12) a. *ɐL*-diminutives make it possible to recover the underlying quality of the stem-vowel.
    b. Final /l/ triggers rounding (+|U|) of the stem-vowel.

In order to establish (12), we must first exclude the outside interference of an independent, morphologically conditioned, phenomenon: Umlaut. Umlaut in Upper Austrian German obeys (13):

(13) $|U| \rightarrow |I|$

As seen above, Upper Austrian German has two diminutive suffixes: -*l* and -*ɐL*. -*l* is not productive and is used in a closed class of lexicalised items; -*ɐL* is more productive. Diminutive -*l* always triggers Umlaut:

(14)
			base	*l*-diminutive	
a.	/u/ → i / _ l_{DIM}		[vuɐʃt]	[viɐʃtl̩]	'sausage'
			[haʊs]	[haɪsl̩]	'house'
	/o/ → e / _ l_{DIM}		[ʁoːs]	[ʁessl̩]	'horse'
b.	i — i		[kind]	[kindl̩]	'child'
	e — e		[hẽːn]	[hẽːndl̩]	'hen'

Now note in (10) that *l*-final nouns always build their diminutives via suffixation of -*ɐL* to the nominal base <u>without final /l/</u>. The fact that final /l/ is systematically absent in the diminutive suggests that it functions as a (class marker) suffix: *l* has affixal status in *l*-final nouns. The question thus arises as to whether it triggers Umlaut. Such is not the case in (15). Diminutive -*l* triggers Umlaut while class marker -*l* does not.

(15)

stem-vowel	*l*-final noun +|U|	Umlaut |U| → |I|
/i/	[y]	[i]
/u/	[u]	
/e, ɛ/	[ø, œ]	[e]
/o/	[o]	

Diminutive -ɐL triggers Umlaut for some roots, only (16a versus 16b).[9]

(16)
		base	ɐL-diminutive	
a.	/u/ → i / _ ɐL$_{DIM}$	[dʁumm]	[dʁimmɐL]	'large lump'
	/o/ → e / _ ɐL$_{DIM}$	[koɐb]	[keɐβɐL]	'basket'
b.	u — u	[hund]	[hundɐL]	'dog'
	o — o	[boːt]	[boːtɐL]	'boat'
c.	i — i	[fiːç]	[fiːçɐL]	'animal'
	e — e	[veːg]	[veːgaL]	'path'

The question is whether [i], [e] in the diminutives in (10a,b) result from Umlaut. If yes, the underlying identity of the corresponding stem-vowels is /u/, /o/ respectively. This leads to the pattern in (17): the underlying vowel of a word like *dy̰ːβɪ* 'dowel' is /u/, and final /l/ adds |I| to this vowel. [i] in the corresponding diminutive (*diːβɐL*) results from Umlaut. By contrast, in a word like *kṵːgɪ* 'ball', final /l/ does not add |I|, and the corresponding diminutive does not undergo Umlaut.

(17)

	l-final N				ɐL-diminutive		
/u/	y	(+|I|)	i	(+Uml)	[dyːβɪ]	[diːβɐL]	alternating
/o/	ø	(+|I|)	e	(+Uml)	[døːgɪ]	[deːgɐL]	
/u/		u			[kṵːgɪ]	[kṵːgɐL]	non-alternating
/o/		o			[fo̰ːgɪ]	[fo̰ːgɐL]	

We are faced with a choice between the following options: either we maintain a unified behaviour of final /l/ (/l/ always has the same effect on a given vowel quality), or we maintain a unified behaviour of roots (certain roots always alternate, others never alternate, and this feature has to be specified in the lexical entry of the root). I adopt the first option: the effect of /l/ is a regular, predictable, phonological process, and the diminutive makes it possible to recover the underlying identity of the stem-vowel. Under the second option, underlying /u, o/ in words like *dy̰ːβɪ*, *do̰ːgɪ* would never be recoverable from any form in the language.

I conclude that [i], [e] in the diminutives in (10a,b) do not result from Umlaut, but are the underlying stem-vowels. Diminutives make it possible to filter out the effect of final /l/ on the stem-vowel and reveal the underlying vowel quality. The non-diminutive forms reveal the effect of /l/ on this underlying vowel: rounding.[10]

Conclusions

/l/ has both a local effect, and a distance effect:

(18) **Local effect:**
   a. After a segment (C/V) that contains |U| but not |I|, /l/ surfaces as [ɪ]
   b. After a segment (C/V) that contains |I| but not |U|, /l/ does not surface, and triggers rounding.

(19) **Distance effect:**
   In V(:)Cl#, if C contains |U|, /l/ surfaces as [ɪ], and triggers rounding of V.

Analysis

The representations to follow will be cast in the CV-framework of Government Phonology (Lowenstamm 1996). (20) provides a summary of the empirical generalisations the analysis has to account for.

(20) **Generalisations:**
   a. *l*-lenition takes place ⇒
      – /l/ is not licensed by its nucleus.
      – the immediately preceding segment contains either |I|, or |U|.
   b. If this segment contains |U| but not |I|, /l/ surfaces as [ɪ], and triggers rounding to its left, up to V_1 in a V_1Cl sequence.
   c. If this segment contains |I| but not |U|, /l/ does not surface, and triggers rounding of the immediately preceding segment.

(20a) pertains to the conditions under which *l*-lenition takes place. If /l/ is followed by its nucleus, it is licensed, no matter what the internal structure of the preceding segment is (21a). If /l/ is not licensed by a nucleus with vocalic content, lenition is triggered (in the spirit of Harris 1994).[11] The presence of |I| and |U| in the preceding segment conditions the realisation of /l/. I take this to indicate that /l/ contains at least |I| and |U| (cf. Djabbari et al. 2010 for a similar assumption), and that *l*-lenition involves dissimilation: if /l/ shares part of its internal structure with the preceding segment, *l*-lenition obtains. If /l/ does not share part of its internal structure with the preceding segment, it is realised as [ɫ] (21b).

(21) a.   b.

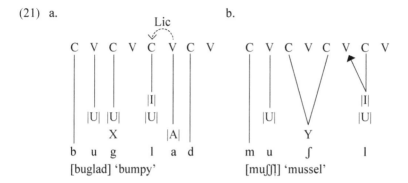

(X and Y represent any other element in the internal structure of C.)

Let us now consider (20b–c). *l*-lenition is a partial (20b) or total (20c) disassociation of the internal structure of /l/. Which part is disassociated depends on the identity of the segment immediately preceding /l/:[12]

(22) a. If the preceding segment contains |I|, |I| is disassociated and disappears altogether. Otherwise, |I| remains associated.
b. |U| is always disassociated and spreads to the left.

The configurations after vowel and consonant are represented in (23) and (24) respectively. (23/24a) show that if the preceding segment contains |U|, only |I| remains associated. I assume |U| to disassociate from C and spread to the left, even though |U|-spreading is not visible since the preceding segment contains |U|. (23/24b) illustrate the situation after a segment containing |I|, namely |I| is disassociated, and |U| spreads to the left. |U|-spreading is visible on the surface.

(23)

(|I| disassociation)
|U| disassociation
|U|-spreading

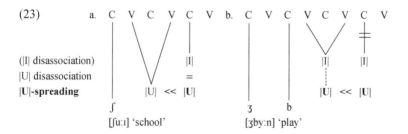

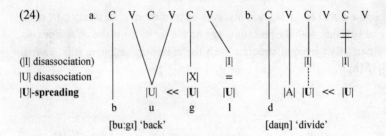

Finally, the configurations where |U| spreads at a distance are represented in (25). Note that for this process to take place, the intervening segment must contain |U|. This supports an analysis in terms of spreading rather than harmony.

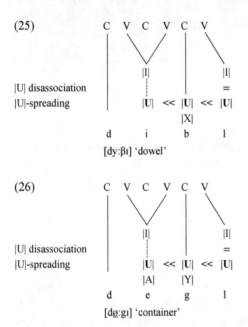

According to this analysis:

- |I| must be disassociated if preceded by |I|. I take this to result from an OCP/dissimilation effect. (For a different instantiation of liquid dissimilation in Bavarian, see Hall 2009.)
- |U| behaves uniformly: it must always disassociate, and spread as far as it can to the left. Note the peculiarity of |A|, that resists rounding in the first part of the diphthong in (24b).[13]

Dissimilation does not apply between labials/velars and preceding |U|-vowels, as can be seen, for example, in [buːgɪ] 'back'. Neither does it apply between *j* and preceding |I|-vowels, for example, [ʃijssn̩]¹⁴ 'shoot'. Getting back to Backley's observation that |I| and |U| do not easily combine, I propose that the dissimilation of *l* should be ascribed to this 'difficulty in combining': Upper Austrian German shows that in a language where |I| and |U| combine within a segment, this segment is unstable, and its internal structure is subject to disassociation. Note that in Upper Austrian German, *l*-lenition does not imply loss of elemental content altogether. Rather, the information on the internal structure of /l/ is recoverable from the context.

Conclusion: a phonological process?

We are now in a position to evaluate the status of *l*-lenition in Upper Austrian German: is it a synchronically active phonological process?

The problem

Recall that the absence of vowel-alternation in pairs like [mœː] 'flour', [mœːlig] 'tasting like flour' casts doubt on the assumption of underlying /l/ in this type of forms: do we need to posit underlying /eːl/ in [mœː], or is /œː/ the underlying vowel? Kaye and Pöchtrager (2015) argue in favour of this second option. They state that both rounding of the preceding vowel and 'the case of intrusive l' are not phonological: '*schnell* [ʃnœː] 'fast' / *schneller* [ʃnœlɐ] 'faster' are different lexical entries [...] and thus not derived from each other'. I do not question the fact that *schnell* and *schneller* are two lexical entries – all forms are lexical entries, even if they are productively derived from another form. However, this does not mean that we must get rid of phonology entirely, and that the underlying representations are identical with the surface realisations of the lexical entries under consideration.

The argument

The behaviour of /l/ after a consonant reveals two salient facts that suggest that the issue should be revisited, and that a phonological analysis should not be discarded. First, the realisations of /l/ obey the same generalisations post-consonantally and post-vocalically. Second, /l/ triggers a stem-vowel alternation at a distance, whose pattern is identical with the one observed locally in (post-vocalic) coda position. The fact that the processes after vowel, after consonant, and at a distance obey the same regularity supports the analysis of *l*-lenition as a phonologically active phenomenon. A lexicalist view seems to miss this parallelism.

In addition, the process applies irrespectively of the morphological status of /l/: diminutive -*l* and class marker -*l* behave on a par with respect to the realisation of /l/ and rounding (crucially, not with respect to Umlaut). I take this fact to indicate that *l*-lenition is a phonological process.

Finally, Kaye and Pöchtrager (2015) note that 'Crucially no kind of suffixation would help to recover the correct UR, acquisition is only possible if child knows the standard'. *ɐL*-diminutives systematically reveal the underlying identity of the stem-vowel. The child does not need to know Standard German to decide on the identity of the stem-vowel: s/he knows that [dø:gɪ] 'container' alternates with [de̝:gɐL] 'small container', and that [dy:βɪ] 'dowel, bump' alternates with [di̝:βɐL] 'small dowel, bump'. One can hypothesise that s/he will learn this rule quite early since diminutives are particularly widespread in baby talk.

Notes

1. This chapter is dedicated to Monik Charette whose inspired work on vowel harmony, elements, and licensing has shaped phonological thinking in and beyond the Government Phonology framework. I thank Connor Youngberg for inviting me to contribute to this book, and for valuable comments on this chapter.
2. Abbreviations: INF = infinitive, COND = conditional, DIM = diminutive, IPF = imperfective, SBJ = subjunctive, N = noun, ADJ = adjective.
3. In this chapter I use '*l*-lenition' instead of '*l*-vocalisation': as will become apparent, /l/ does not always surface as a vowel in the data under discussion.
4. See Kaye et al. (1985, 308) and subsequent work for the marked character of the combination of |I| and |U|.
5. Upper Austrian German does have [a], for example, [ba:m] 'tree'. Interestingly the only [al] sequences I could find appear in loanwords, for example, [a:l] 'eel'. Upper Austrian German [l] thus seems to be incompatible with preceding |A|. I get back to this observation in Note 8.
6. Djabbari et al. (2010) note that 'there also exists a vocalic variant of syllabic /l/ which occurs after labial consonants.' However, they do not go into more detail concerning the distribution and the phonological effects of this 'vocalic variant.'
7. See, for example, Kranzmayer (1956, 124), Hall (2009), and Noelliste (2017, 167) for the realisation of this segment in different Bavarian languages.
8. ɔ ~ a alternations are also observed in (i). However, they cannot straightforwardly be analysed as /a/ being rounded to [ɔ] in the context of /l/, because they also obtain in the absence of /l/ (ii).

		noun	diminutive	
(i)	*l*-final	[gɔ:βɪ]	[ga:βɐL]	'fork'
		[ɔpfɪ]	[apfɐL]	'apple'
(ii)	not *l*-final	[hɔ:z]	[ha:zɐL]	'rabbit'
		[bɔ:x]	[baxxɐL]	'stream'

These alternations involve additional complications related to the status of |A| in Upper Austrian German. Standard German [a] and [al] regularly correspond to Upper Austrian German [ɔ] and [ɔɪ], for example, [dax] versus [dɔx] 'roof', [bal] versus [bɔɪ] 'ball'. However, Upper Austrian German does have [a], for example, [ba:m] 'tree'. It thus seems to be the case that Upper Austrian German [l] is incompatible with preceding |A|. In addition, |A| resists the process of rounding at a distance triggered by /l/: daʊ̃n, *dɔʊ̃n 'divide'.INF, kã͂m / kãmpɪ,*kɔ̃mpɪ 'comb' / 'comb'.DIM. Clearly, more research on the status of |A| in Upper Austrian German is needed. For various cross-linguistic generalisations on |A|, cf. Pöchtrager (2006).

9. In addition, both suffixes sometimes trigger stem-vowel shortening. This alternation is outside the scope of this chapter. For details and an analysis in terms of Lowenstamm (2008), cf. Bendjaballah (2008).
10. If rounding is a phonologically active rule, it should not be restricted to *l*-final nouns: it should apply irrespectively of the morphological status of /l/, and we expect it to take place in (lexicalised) *l*-diminutives, too. Given the context during which this chapter was written, I could not conduct fieldwork and test this prediction. For a recent discussion of 'vowel dissimilation' in Bavarian, see, for example, Noelliste (2017, 146ff.).
11. On licensing conditions, see among many others Harris (1990), Charette (1991), Cyran (2010).
12. See Charette and Göksel (1996) for the analysis of various harmony processes in Turkic languages where |I| and |U| are involved in an asymmetrical fashion.
13. See also Note 8.
14. Some native speakers perceive [j] as a lower back vowel in this form, and would transcribe it as [ɐ]. This is probably related to the peculiar status of |A| in Upper Austrian German, and its resistance to rounding, cf. Note 8.

References

Backley, P. (2011). *An Introduction to Element Theory*. Edinburgh: Edinburgh University Press.
Bedar, A., and Quellec, L. (2020). 'l-alternations in Taqbaylit'. In *Phonological and Phonetic Explorations*, edited by J. Szpyra-Kozłowska, 11–27. Lublin: Wydawnictwo KUL.
Bendjaballah, S. (2008). 'Some remarks on Upper Austrian German diminutive formation'. *Workshop on Templates*, 27–28 May 2008, Université Paris 8.
Bendjaballah, S. (2012). *La grammaire des gabarits*. Habilitation dissertation, Université Paris Diderot.
Bendjaballah, S., and Tifrit, A. (2018). '*l*-vocalisation in Mehri'. *OCP* 15, 12–14 January 2018, UCL, London.
Charette, M. (1991). *Conditions on Phonological Government*. Cambridge: Cambridge University Press.
Charette, M., and Göksel, A. (1996). 'Licensing constraints and vowel harmony in Turkic languages'. *SOAS Working Papers in Linguistics and Phonetics* 6, 1–25.
Cyran, E. (2010). *Complexity Scales and Licensing in Phonology*. Berlin: De Gruyter.
Djabbari, D., Fischer, B., Hildenbrandt, T., Neubarth, F., and Rennison J. (2010). '"Liquid vocalisation" in German. "Herr Wirt, vier Bier will ich: viere und schnell!"'. Unpublished manuscript, University of Vienna.
Hall, T. A. (2009). 'Liquid dissimilation in Bavarian German'. *Journal of Germanic Linguistics* 21(1), 1–36.
Harris, J. (1990). 'Segmental complexity and phonological government'. *Phonology Yearbook* 7, 255–300.
Harris, J. (1994). *English Sound Structure*. Oxford: Blackwell.
Kaye, J., and Lowenstamm, J. (1984). 'De la syllabicité'. In *Forme Sonore du Langage*, edited by F. Dell, D. Hirst and J.-R. Vergnaud, 123–59. Paris: Hermann.
Kaye, J., Lowenstamm, J., and Vergnaud, J.-R. (1985). 'The internal structure of phonological representations: A theory of Charm and Government'. *Phonology Yearbook*, 2, 305–28.
Kaye, J., Lowenstamm, J., and Vergnaud, J.-R. (1990). 'Constituent structure and government in phonology'. *Phonology* 7(2), 193–231.
Kaye, J., and Pöchtrager, M. A. (2015). 'All that glitters is not gold: The problem of phonological self-deception'. *Government Phonology Round Table*, 1–3 May 2015, Vienna.
Kranzmayer, E. (1956). *Historische Lautgeographie des gesamtbairischen Dialektraumes*. Graz: Böhlau.
Kühnhammer, K. (2004). *Isochrony in German*. Master's dissertation, University of Vienna.
Lowenstamm, J. (1996). 'CV as the only syllable type'. In *Current Trends in Phonology Models and Methods*, edited by J. Durand and B. Laks, 419–42. Salford: European Studies Research Institute.
Lowenstamm, J. (2008). 'On little *n*, √, and types of nouns'. In *The Sounds of Silence: Empty elements in syntax and phonology*, edited by J. Hartmann, V. Hegedus, and H. van Riemsdjik, 105–44. Amsterdam: Elsevier.
Noelliste, E. (2017). *The Phonology of Sonorants in Bavarian German*. Doctoral dissertation, Indiana University.

Pöchtrager, M. A. (2006). *The Structure of Length*. Doctoral dissertation, University of Vienna.

Rennison, J. (1978). *Bidialektale Phonologie: Die Kompetenz eines Salzburger Sprechers*. Doctoral dissertation, University of Salzburg.

Wiesinger, P. (1990). 'The Central and Southern Bavarian Dialects in Bavaria and Austria'. In *The Dialects of Modern German*, edited by C. V. J. Russ, 438–519. London: Routledge.

4
Sets of (sets of) elements
Florian Breit

Introduction

In this chapter, I propose a revised formalisation of Element Theory (ET; Backley 2011; Charette and Göksel 1998; Cyran 1995; Harris and Lindsey 1995; Kaye et al. (KLV) 1985; Lindsey and Harris 1990), building on the model in Breit (2013).[1] I propose revisions both to the structure building process and the architecture of an 'element-theoretic grammar', that is, a grammar of melodic representations (MRs).[2] This aligns the model more closely with a shift away from templatic structure and (asymmetric) pair-merge in minimalist syntax (cf. also Ulfsbjorninn 2021), forming a base-point to discuss cross-modular homology – an aspect that has long been a driving force behind developments in Government Phonology (Chapter 1 of this book; Kaye 1990; Kaye 2012; Pöchtrager 2006; Pöchtrager and Kaye 2013; cf. also Bromberger and Halle 1989). The architectural reframing also allows for a unified account of Licensing Constraints (LCs; Charette and Göksel 1996, 1998; Kaye 2001), 'parameterised' elements (Cyran 1996) and (tentatively) elemental antagonism (Backley 2011, 2017). The chapter explores central aspects of the revised model, its correspondence with Standard ET and some variants, and discusses important questions and insights framed by formalisation.

Element-theoretic assumptions

There are many variants of ET, both historically and in current theory development. While this certainly makes an extended exposition of specific assumptions desirable, due to limited space I can but give an extremely terse summary of my assumptions here. I take these to describe what I term

'Standard ET', a (perhaps conservative-leaning) version I take to be representative of the mainstream ET baseline over the last decade or so. Breit (2013, 3–16) provides a more detailed technical exposition and Backley (2011) gives a comprehensive introduction to the theory (though I do not subscribe to multiple headedness and remain sceptical of admitting phonetic substance). Backley (2012) gives an overview of commonalities and differences across various version of ET. See also the overview in Chapter 2.

Stenographically, I assume: (i) consonant-vowel harmony, that is, the same primitives are active in consonantal and vocalic representation (cf. Backley and Nasukawa 2010); (ii) the set of primitives (called *elements*) consists of |H, L, ʔ, A, I, U|; (iii) elements are strictly privative and monovalent; (iv) elements are interpretable both independently and combined with other elements (Independent Interpretability Principle); (v) the empty representation | | is well-formed and interpretable; (vi) MRs have exactly one head or none (Single Optional Headedness Condition, SOHC); (vii) MRs are achiral, that is, they are distinguished solely by the elements occupying head and complement position.

Preliminary considerations

It is relatively obvious that the set of all possible MRs defined by Standard ET is finite, given that the terminal vocabulary is finite, repetition is not allowed (|A, A| = |A|, or *|A, A|; *pace* Schane 1984), and MRs do not permit infinite embedding (recursion; *pace* Backley and Nasukawa, Chapter 22; Backley and Nasukawa 2020; Ulfsbjorninn 2021).

The point is that MRs are rather simple compared to, for example, syntactic representations. This makes it relatively trivial, and tempting perhaps, to formally define the set of all possible MRs by equally simple means. The model I propose may thus at first seem unreasonably complex, but the reasoning is easily made apparent by briefly entertaining two (overly) simple approaches.

The least complex but formally satisfactory definition of the set of possible MRs (that is, the formal language $L(ET)$ defined by ET) can be given by simply enumerating all its members. Assuming the elements |H, L, ʔ, A, I, U| and short Kuratowski pair definition[3] to represent head and complement (cf. Breit 2013, 21ff.), we might give $L(ET)$ as shown in (1) (including only |A| and |I| for brevity):

(1) $L(ET) = \{\emptyset, \{A\}, \{A, \{A\}\}, \{I\}, \{I, \{I\}\}, \{A, I\}, \{A, \{A, I\}\},$
     $\{I, \{A, I\}\}, \ldots\}.$

The enumeration approach is obviously facile, being neither helpful nor insightful in any significant way. Apart from assigning some unique and templatically consistent set of representation to each MR defined by ET, we have learned nothing about the underlying cognitive system we are attempting to model (see also the criticism of templatism in Ulfsbjorninn 2021).

Despite the relative brevity ($|L(ET)| = 256$) of an enumerated definition of $L(ET)$, we could of course define a simple formal grammar $G_{ET} = \langle V_T, V_N, S, R \rangle$ instead, with terminal vocabulary $V_T = \{A, I, U, H, L, ?\}$, non-terminal vocabulary V_N (consisting solely of the start symbol S), and a set of rewrite rules R, given cursorily by

(2) $R = \begin{cases} S \\ S \rightarrow \text{any } X \in \wp(V_T) \\ \text{any } X \in \wp(V_T) \rightarrow \text{any } \{Y, X\} \text{ such that } Y \in X \end{cases}$.

Applying these rules to derive sets which do not contain non-terminal S from the set $V_T \cup V_N$ in the usual way, G_{ET} generates the language $L(G_{ET})$ illustrated in (3) – which is of course identical to (1).

(3) $L(G_{ET}) = \{\emptyset, \{A\}, \{A, \{A\}\}, \{I\}, \{I, \{I\}\}, \{A, I\}, \{A, \{A, I\}\},$
$\{I, \{A, I\}\}, \ldots\}$.

This is conceptually more pleasing than enumeration because it makes the structure building process explicit: the first step always involves rewriting the start symbol with any set in $\wp(V_T)$, followed by an optional step of rewriting this set as one consisting of itself and any of its members (essentially internal merge). We can take G_{ET} as a model making claims as to the psychological reality of an intensional system, thus potentially furnishing actual insight about MRs. The model also allows us to engage in model comparison, asking, for example, how $L(G_{ET})$ would be affected if we modified V_T or N in one way or another, thus being theoretically helpful.

The way in which the second model falls short is in its content, that is, in the mechanism from which we have constructed G_{ET}, which is not rich enough in detail and speciation to model the actually postulated underlying mental system. Consider for a moment the fact that $|L|$ and $|H|$ cannot combine in many languages. To encode this fact we would have to replace the very general rule $S \rightarrow \text{any } X \in \wp(V_T)$, breaking it down in such a way that a specific language might show an absence of whatever rule allows the pairing $\{L, H\}$. We then consider that in yet many other languages, $|U|$ and $|I|$ cannot combine, that in certain languages such combinations are possible when one is the head, etc. etc. Eventually we must arrive at a system which breaks down the general patterns of these rewrite rules in such a way that we do not capture a large proportion of the insights that are to be made about MRs but rather end up with something resembling the enumeration of possibilities rather than modelling the mental processes by which they are built. For instance, as discussed further in the section 'The constraint set C', the set of possible restrictions upon MRs itself is very much a system governed by rather few general yet well-constrained mechanisms.

The revised model

Given the discussion above, a conceptually more satisfactory and insightful model of ET must strive toward explanatory adequacy, that is, the aim must be to closely model the hypothesised mental mechanisms of ET and their integration within the cognitive architecture of the phonological component.

Conceding that ET is but one part of a more complex phonological theory (whether it be Standard GP, Strict CV, or some other theory), often quite tightly integrated with other aspects of that theory, I propose that we can nonetheless fruitfully model it as a specific subcomponent of phonology. To stretch the computational metaphor, it seems apt to characterise ET as a relatively discrete submodule of phonology implementing processes to build and carry out computations over MRs, exposing a part of this functionality to its parent module (providing a 'public API' of sorts) while keeping certain parts of its workings private. That is, ET provides phonology with a system to (a) derive MRs from a symbolic vocabulary V, (b) relate and map MRs, and (c) exclude MRs of certain types.

By way of an overview before diving into more detail, what I propose is that a grammar G modelling ET is a triplet $\langle V, R, C \rangle$ consisting of: (i) a universally fixed vocabulary of atomic symbols V (the set of elements), (ii) a set of relations R, also universally fixed, by which MRs can be derived from other MRs following specific principles, and (iii) a language-specific constraint set C, which delineates the set of well-formed MRs in $L(G)$ by means of licensing constraints. Given such a grammar, we define Σ as the set of all MRs derivable from V by means of R (respecting the principles of application), and a language L as a subset of Σ such that L contains all the MRs derivable from V except those in C (that is, $L(G) = \Sigma - C_G$ and $L(G) = \Sigma \leftrightarrow C_G = \emptyset$; note also that $L(G)$ with $C_G = \emptyset$ essentially $\equiv L(G_{ET}) \equiv L(\text{ET})$ above).

Note again that I assume that G characterises not just an output $L(G)$, but models a subcomponent which other phonological processes can interact with (via the set of relations R). I also assume the absence of non-terminal symbols, that all relations map like-to-like (MR $\mapsto$ MR) and that the only language-specific part of the grammar are the constraints on MR composition encoded in C, which suggests that $L(G)$ for any given language is (potentially much) greater than the set of MRs actually employed in its phonological representations.

The vocabulary

A major variable factor across versions of ET are the elements assumed. Apart from the labels we may attach to these atoms, the only significant way in which the set of vocabulary items affects the grammar is the generative capacity GC of G, since $|GC(G)| \propto |\Sigma| \propto |V|$. Independent of the specific elements assumed we state,

(4) Given a grammar $G = \langle V, R, C \rangle$, let V be a finite set of atomic symbols.

However, for each specific version of ET it is generally held that V is universal, that is, identical across human phonologies and not subject to language-specific variation. The generalised version in (4) is thus of interest if comparing versions of ET which assume differently sized sets of elements only. For all Gs implementing Standard ET, V is defined by

(5) $V \doteq \{A, I, U, H, L, ?\}$.

A possible exception to the universality assumption is Cyran (1997, 2010). He proposes that some elements (specifically, the noise element |h|) may be parametrically present or absent in some languages. While this can be implemented by varying V parametrically (as, for example, in Breit 2013), I propose that it is best to keep the assumption that the set of elements is a universally fixed part of the underlying cognitive machinery. As shown in this chapter's section 'The constraint set C', 'parametric elements' are already accounted for as part of the language-specific constraint mechanism.

Melodic representations

The primary objects that an element-theoretic subcomponent deals with are MRs, more than individual elements. As foreshadowed, I here espouse an explicitly derivational view. MRs are sets constructed from members of V according to a specific set of principles (or axioms). As Ulfsbjorninn (2021) rightly criticises, many recent approaches to ET take an essentially templatic approach where segmental representations are but a schematic structure with slots that can be populated as needed. Not only does this miss potentially important insights (such as the hypothesis that an element in the head position of an MR may imply its phonetic interpretation as a complement; cf. Breit 2017; Ulfsbjorninn 2021), it also prevents us from making observations about the proposed underlying cognitive processes. For instance, while Breit (2013, 21) explicitly links the proposed structures to those produced by the syntactic adjunction operation (pair-)$merge(\alpha,\beta) = \{\alpha,\{\alpha,\beta\}\}$ (Chomsky 1995), the derivational process is not further elucidated.

I propose to revise Breit's (2013) account in two important ways. First, I follow Ulfsbjorninn (2021) in assuming only set-merge as the underlying structure building operation (in line with other work proposing to eliminate pair-merge from syntax, cf., for example, Oseki, 2015). Second, I propose that relations in ET uniformly map MRs to MRs. The latter modification gives us the Independent Interpretability Principle for free, since bare elements are never exposed.

Concretely, I propose that MRs are built by the (set-)*merge* operation, defined in (6).

(6) $merge(\alpha,\beta) \doteq \{\alpha,\beta\}$.

Set-merge is one of the simplest possible cognitive operations, being not much more than ad-hoc categorisation. Of course, in syntax *merge* may apply recursively (potentially ad infinitum), whereas MRs are severely limited structurally. Per the SOHC, an MR in Standard ET consists minimally of a subset of V, and maximally of a subset of V plus one element in head position. If we want to capture this property of standard ET (rather than propose a new infinitely embeddable variant as in the Bare Element Geometry of Ulfsbjorninn 2021), an interesting question arises: If both syntactic and melodic representations are built by the same operation, how is it that syntax ends up with strictly binary branching trees (for example, $\{W,\{X,Y\}\}$) while MRs may be 'imbalanced' (for example, $\{X,Y,Z\}$ or $\{W,\{X,Y,Z\}\}$)?

It has been suggested that the binarity of *merge* in syntax is a domain-specific restriction, perhaps driven by computational requirements (for a brief discussion see, for example, Chomsky 2005, 11ff.), though n-ary merge might not be an insensible choice for ET. After all, ad-hoc categorisation is generally constrained more by factors such as subitisability and working memory than some need for symmetry. Even so, I propose to maintain the assumption that melodic structure building is based on binary (set-)*merge*. We need not allow an arbitrary number of objects to combine (for example, $merge(\alpha_1,\ldots,\alpha_n) = \{\alpha_1,\ldots,\alpha_n\}$) to explain 'imbalanced' MRs.

There is an alternate candidate for the apparent imbalance in MRs, namely the *numeration*. The numeration v is a subset of items drawn from V at the start of a derivation, containing the items to be combined during the derivation. Since at least for ET, V consists only of atoms, we can say that v is a possible numeration precisely if $v \in \wp(V)$, which gives us the corollary that all numerations in ET are MRs, including among others the empty set $\emptyset$ and a finite number of sets of cardinality n such that $n \leq |V|$ (maximally V itself).

What I propose is that the numeration itself is essentially employed as first merge in the building of melodic structure. This fits well with a general oddity of first merge, namely that it is the only step in a syntactic derivation which applies external merge to more than one external item. A possible explanation for syntactic first merge not admitting the full numeration could be that this would not allow for other necessary conditions to be obtainable, for example, subcategorisation, feature checking, interface requirements, etc., upon second merge. Since an MR consists only of atoms, without feature-checking requirements or similar, the restriction does not arise.

(7)   (a) Given a grammar $G = \langle V, R, C \rangle$, let any $v \in \wp(V)$ be called a *numeration*.
       (b) Every derivation in G must begin with a numeration.
       (c) Every numeration in G is a *melodic representation (MR)* in G.

From (7), we get all the possible unheaded MRs, including the empty representation | |. Given that any subset of V is an MR, we should be able to apply *merge* to that MR. If we apply merge to a non-empty numeration and merge with some $x \in v$ (that is, we apply *internal merge*), we get an overall asymmetric, potentially 'imbalanced' structure. For example, let $v = \{H, ?, U\}$. If we stop the derivation here, we have the unheaded MR |H, ?, U|. If we now apply second merge (axiomatically always internal merge) on some $x \in v$, say H, we have $merge(H, \{H, ?, U\}) = \{H, \{H, ?, U\}\}$, where H is what we conventionally call the head in a singly headed MR such as |H̲, ?, U| (a more formal characterisation of *head* and *complement* follows). Note that, if $v = \emptyset$, internal merge is not possible. Example (8) illustrates some correspondences between MRs in set- and conventional ET-notation.

(8) | | = ∅,
       |A, I| = {A, I},
       |A, I̲| = {I, {A, I}},
       |A̲, L, ?| = {A, {A, L, ?}}.

Much like Breit (2013) and Ulfsbjorninn (2021), this suggests that the basic mechanism of structure building underlying melody (vis-à-vis phonology) and syntax may show deep homology. The most striking and fundamental difference is that melodic structure building (at least under standard assumptions) is limited to second merge:

(9) Given a numeration v in G, $merge(\alpha, \beta)$ may be applied iff $\alpha \in \beta$ and $\beta \in v$.

In other words, the set of all possible MRs Σ is exhausted by numeration followed by at most one application of internal merge.

Before moving on, let us briefly consider whether weakening restriction (9) may be desirable. Explanatorily, the answer ought to be *yes*, (9) is stipulative, and one would hope that we could explain the restriction as arising from some third factor, for example, requirements at the interface to phonetic interpretation. Extensionally, under the most restrictive variant of standard ET, we cannot forgo it however, adding further to the impression of severely constrained structure building in this subcomponent. However, there is also a relatively well-established view in ET that some melodic expressions are 'unfused', argued to represent contour segments such as [t͡ʃ] and light diphthongs. Breit (2017) suggests that these could be modelled by representations where a higher primitive is not a member of first merge. In the terms of this model, that 'unfused' melody is external merge. Allowing one cycle of external merge (and excluding internal after external merge) would give us additional specifier-like structures such as $\{H, \{I, \{I, ?\}\}\}$ (= unfused |I, ?|⌢|H|) and $\{I, \{A\}\}$ (= unfused |A|⌢|I|).

Head and complement

The head-dependency relation is one of the most important aspects of ET representations, which matters not only for (prosodic) well-formedness and phonological processes, but also at phonetic interpretation. Let us first turn our attention to the head relation $head \subseteq (\Sigma \times \wp(V))$. As shown in the section above, the derived sets are all either of the form $\emptyset$, $\{\alpha, \ldots\}$ or $\{\alpha, \{\alpha, \ldots\}\}$. The former two are headless, the latter has a head α. *head* should thus map representations of the first two types to $\emptyset$, and the latter to $\{\alpha\}$ (recall that $\alpha \notin \Sigma$). This is actually (and perhaps surprisingly) very close to the effect of the labelling relation proposed in Chomsky (2008), which states that for a syntactic object $\kappa = \{\alpha, \beta\}$, α is the label of κ if α is a lexical item and β is an XP. The definition in (10) adapts this to ET:

(10) (a) A member α of an MR X is called the *head* of X iff α is a vocabulary item and at least one member of X contains α.
(b) $head(X) \doteq \{\alpha \in V: (\alpha, \beta \in X) \land (\alpha \in \beta)\}$.

Example (11) illustrates the relation (10b) for a selection of MRs:

(11) $head(\emptyset) = \emptyset$, $||\rightarrow||$
     $head(\{A, H, ?\}) = \emptyset$, $|A, H, ?| \rightarrow ||$
     $head(\{A, \{A, H, ?\}\}) = \{A\}$, $|\underline{A}, H, ?| \rightarrow |A|$
     $head(\{A, \{A\}\}) = \{A\}$. $|\underline{A}| \rightarrow |A|$

A perhaps more contentious question is what the right characterisation of the set of dependents should be. Kaye (2000, 2001), following Kaye et al. (1985), calls these the *operators* (the term *dependents* is also used) and means all the elements in a representation that are *not* the head. Breit (2013, 2017) and Ulfsbjorninn (2021) argue for a view of a (structural) *complement* which explicitly includes the embedded copy of the head. I will side with the latter view. Suffice it to say once we have a relation $cmpl \subseteq (\Sigma \times \wp(V))$ mapping to the complement of a representation, we can define the relation to the set of operators simply as $ops(X) \doteq cmpl(X) - head(X)$. The complement and its relation $cmpl$ are defined (preliminarily[4]) as the set of vocabulary items (embedded) in the symmetric difference of X and its head, as in (12).

(12) (a) A member α in a (potentially flattened) MR X is called a *complement* of X iff α is not a head of X.
(b) $cmpl(X) \doteq \{\alpha \in V: (\alpha \in (X \ominus head(X))) \lor (\alpha \in \beta \land \beta \in (X \ominus head(X)))\}$.

Example (13) illustrates the relation (12b) for a selection of MRs:

(13) $cmpl(\emptyset) = \emptyset$, $||\rightarrow||$
     $cmpl(\{A, H, ?\}) = \{A, H, ?\}$, $|A, H, ?| \rightarrow |A, H, ?|$
     $cmpl(\{A, \{A, H, ?\}\}) = \{A, H, ?\}$, $|\underline{A}, H, ?| \rightarrow |A, H, ?|$
     $cmpl(\{A, \{A\}\}) = \{A\}$. $|\underline{A}| \rightarrow |A|$

A relatively interesting consequence of taking this more explicitly cyclic derivational approach based on symmetric merge is that *head* and *cmpl* now both range over $\wp(V)$, not Σ as in Breit (2013). As such these relations, important for specifying the conditions under which phonological processes take place, essentially implement syntactic *demerge*, argued by Fukui and Takano (1998) to play an important role in top-down linearisation.

Composition and decomposition

Another important set of relations implements the composition and decomposition of primitives on existing representations. Following the arguments in Breit (2013, 28–31), I suggest these come in a complement- and a head-oriented flavour each, for example, *compc*, *comph*, *decompc*, *decomph* (all in $\langle \Sigma, \wp(V) \rangle \times \Sigma$). Due to limited space, and because I have nothing much to add over Breit (2013), I will not further define or discuss the composition/decomposition operations here, though note that this proposed split fits rather well with the head and complement relations' *demerge*-like character.

The constraint set C

I have argued that all the components of G discussed thus far (assuming of course a single version of ET) are universal. However, were this the case for the entire grammar, it would imply the claim that the range of generated/generable MRs is identical across all languages. Were this so, the fact that the attested inventories of MRs employed frequently differs from language to language would have to be explained merely as a consequence of diachronic happenchance. That is to say, the reason that for instance English makes use of |A, U| but not *|I, U|, while Finnish employs |I, U| but not *|A, U| is simply a consequence of the way in which their phonetic surface forms and lexical items have been shaped over time, in each case simply implementing the optimal encoding according to some shared algorithm given as its input the experienced phonetic surface forms of a sizeable proportion of the respective languages' lexicon. Consequently, an English speaker would be free at any time to posit a new underlying representation containing |I, U| if that were the optimal representation for what they needed to represent, as would a Finnish speaker with |A, U|.

Albeit perhaps counter to the intuitions or inclinations of many working in the 'maximally restrictive' tradition of GP, I propose that we should actually adopt an only slightly more constrained version of this hypothesis. What the above formulation is failing to account for is that some languages provide hard evidence (that is, evidence within their respective phonological system) that certain configurations of elements are not permitted, or *actively* ruled out, by their phonology. In ET, specific MRs are ruled out through *Licensing Constraints* (LCs; Charette and Göksel 1996, 1998; Kaye 1993, 2001; Ploch 1999). While there is still much work to be done on LCs, especially in consonants, it has become clear by now that these are highly systematic. Example (14) attempts to give an exhaustive list of the types of LCs employed in ET, where $\alpha, \beta \in V, \alpha \neq \beta$, and *operator* means $\alpha \in cmpl(X) - head(X)$:

(14) (a) All MRs must be headed.
(b) α may not license operators.
(c) α must license operators.
(d) α must be licensed.
(e) α may not be licensed.
(f) α may not be head.
(g) α must be head.
(h) α may not license β.
(i) α and β may not combine.

Using such LCs, the English–Finnish situation above is usually accounted for by assuming that in English |I| and |U| may not combine (14i), while in Finnish |U| may not be licensed (14e).

What I propose is that the constraint set C is essentially a set of predicates, limited to a very specific form, which taken together delineate a subset K of Σ, functioning as a filter on what G can generate with R over V (note that C does not properly partition Σ since potentially $K \in \{\emptyset, \Sigma\}$). Importantly, LCs do not interfere directly with the structure building process (for example, blocking a certain numeration). They instead place a limit on the eventual output condition of a derivational chain, meaning that intermediate steps in a derivation may violate some LC, but the final derived object may not. Based on this we can define the specific set of MRs $L(G)$ generated by G as follows:

(15) A grammar $G = \langle V, R, C \rangle$ generates an MR $S \in \Sigma$ if there is a sequence of MRs $S_i, \ldots, S_n$ such that $S_i \in \wp(V)$, S_i is derivable from S_{i-1} by a relation in R for each $2 \leq i \leq n$, and $S_n \notin K$.

LCs can be systematised as predicates, each of which selects a subset of Σ, so that K is the infinitary union of those sets (since we have construed $L(G)$ as $C_\Sigma K$). Table 4.1 shows the LCs with proposed predicate forms. Stated in this way it becomes immediately apparent that there is a very restrictive definition of what is a well-formed constraint predicate, promising further reduction and generalisability of LCs.

Though I am optimistic that LCs can be successfully generalised even further going forward, for now it at least seems clear that we need at most three general forms:

First, (a–c) are about head-complement (non)-identity. Their range can be captured with two variables P, A with domains $\{=, \neq\}$ and $\{A: A \subseteq V \land |A| \leq 1\}$, so that we can generate their predicates with a function $conident(P, A) \mapsto A = head(S) \land A \, P \, cmpl(S)$. LC (a') does not form part of the established

Table 4.1 Licensing constraints reframed as a complement in Σ.

	Condition	As $C_\Sigma - \{S \in \Sigma:...\}$
(a)	All MRs must be headed	$\{\} = head(S) \land \{\} \neq cmpl(S)$
(a')	(no empty representation)	$\{\} = head(S) \land \{\} = cmpl(S)$
(b)	α may not license operators	$\{\alpha\} = head(S) \land \{\alpha\} \neq cmpl(S)$
(c)	α must license operators†	$\{\alpha\} = head(S) \land \{\alpha\} \neq cmpl(S)$
(d)	α must be licensed	$\{\} = head(S) \land \{\} \subseteq cmpl(S)$
(e)	α may not be licensed	$\{\} \neq head(S) \land \{\} \subseteq cmpl(S)$
(f)	α may not be head	$\{\alpha\} = head(S) \land \{\alpha\} \subseteq cmpl(S)$
(g)	α must be head	$\{\alpha\} \neq head(S) \land \{\alpha\} \subseteq cmpl(S)$
(h)	α may not license β	$\{\alpha\} \neq head(S) \land \{\beta\} \subseteq cmpl(S)$
(h')	(only α may license β)	$\{\alpha\} \neq head(S) \land \{\beta\} \subseteq cmpl(S)$
(i)	α and β may not combine	$\{\alpha\} \subseteq cmpl(S) \land \{\beta\} \subseteq cmpl(S)$

† in conjunction with (g).

LC canon, but is implied by this generalisation, and actually reflected in a known property, namely that in some languages (non-p-licensed) empty skeletal positions are not permitted.

Second, (d-h) are about head-complement distribution. Looking over these constraints, we notice that they imply (h') – again not part of the established canon – and that LCs (d-g) are special cases of (h,h'), with the first set ∅ in (d,e), and both sets being identical in (f,g). Three variables P, A, B are required to capture the range of distributional constraints. P, A have the same domain as with conident, and B has the domain $\{B: B \subseteq V \land |B| = 1\}$ (that is, the domain of A without ∅). Thus $condist(P, A, B) \mapsto A \ P \ head(S) \land B \subseteq cmpl(S)$ captures the range of these LCs.

Third, (i) implements co-occurrence constraints and is set apart principally by not enforcing any condition on the head. Assuming two variables A, B again with the domains already given we can generate their predicates by $conco(A, B) \mapsto A \subseteq cmpl(S) \land B \subseteq cmpl(S)$.

As mentioned in the section 'The vocabulary', this constraint mechanism readily captures parameterisation of individual elements (Cyran 1996, 2010). Given an element $x \in V$, x is totally excluded from $L(G)$ if $\{condist(=, \emptyset, \{x\}), condist(\neq, \emptyset, \{x\})\} \subseteq C_G$, that is, if x simultaneously must be licensed (d) and may not be licensed (e). In fact, if we assume that the domain of the variable A of $conco$ permits the empty set (as suggested above), excluding an element x may be even more trivial via $conco(\emptyset, \{x\})$. Since ∅ is a subset of any set by definition, $\emptyset \subseteq cmpl(S)$ is always true and $conco(\emptyset, \{x\})$ equivalent to $\{x\} \subseteq cmpl(S)$.

Elemental antagonism (Backley 2011, 2017) attempts to capture certain postulated combinatory restrictions of pairs of elements that share substantive traits. For instance, the antagonist hypothesis argues that because |L| and |H| both correlate with frequency modulation, their combination is marked and if they combine the compound must be asymmetric (that is, |L̲, H| or |L, H̲| but not *|L, H| or *|L̲, H̲|). A principal motivation is to restrain multiple headedness to $\frac{|V|}{2}$ (or three heads assuming $|V| = 6$; Backley 2017, 11). While the model I have discussed above assumes single headedness (the SOHC), if it is modified to allow 'complex' (aka multiple) heads, it seems reasonable in turn to also obviate the cardinality restriction on variables in the constraint predicates, that is, allowing sets with cardinality greater than 1 for A, B in *conident*, *condist*, and *conco*. This would allow constraints such as $conident(=, \{x,y\})$ to rule out the double-headed expression |x̲, y̲|, in conjunction with $condist(=, \emptyset, \{x,y\})$ to rule out the headless antagonistic pair |x, y|. However, even though this seems feasible when considering just two elements in isolation, as soon as we consider $|V| > 2$ it becomes clear that there is no straightforward means to generally rule out a symmetric antagonistic pair in compounds with further elements (for example, capturing |x, y, z̲|, |x, y, w̲|, ... without explicit enumeration of |z, w, ...|). This makes clear that while the antagonistic relation proposed by Backley seems to fit well into the broad category of LCs, the multiheaded version of ET cannot be sufficiently captured purely by weakening the model's cardinality restrictions. Instead, the nature, and possibly number, of constraint mechanisms required appears to also be more complex.

Conclusion

In this chapter I have proposed several revisions to the formal model of ET proposed in Breit (2013), making the model both more comprehensive and simpler in several respects.

As pointed out by Ulfsbjorninn (2021) and argued in this chapter, templatism doesn't appear to align well with the research agenda of Government Phonology and ET, which among other things have always sought to explore cognitive homology between (morpho-)syntax and phonology and to reduce where possible that which is supposed to be 'special' about phonology vis-à-vis related cognitive faculties. It has been proposed that the structure building process underlying both syntax and melodic phonology may be essentially the same, namely simple symmetric set-merge. While there is much work in the GP/ET sphere that similarly explores more homologous structure building (for example, Pöchtrager and Kaye 2013 for GP 2.0; Nasukawa 2014 for Precedence-free Phonology; Cavirani and van Oostendorp 2020 for vowel-internal recursion; Ulfsbjorninn 2021 for Bare Element Geometry; see also

Chapters 21–23) these all depart quite radically from the most well-established mainstream of ET in several ways. What is novel in the specific context given here, is that it has been shown that, even within the highly restrictive, non-recursive, single-headed standard implementation of ET, there is potentially much to be gained not only in elucidating the actual underlying mechanisms of melodic structure building (versus focusing on just the resultant representations) but in learning what may give rise to observed and/or hypothesised differences of the processes involved. For example, it has been suggested here that the fairly different structures derived by melody versus syntax may result from factors not directly attributable to the underlying cognitive process itself, but for instance: to a lack of feature-checking and subcategorisation in melody (in turn the result of ET's monovalent atomic primitives) which permits the entire numeration to feature as an input to merge; to a more strictly fixed sequence of derivational cycles (possibly linked to the specific processing needs of phonology, which must yield very rapid and robust output to facilitate fast lexical access); and to the different interface-requirements faced by the two modules. It certainly seems worthwhile to explore these factors much further as they clearly have the potential to arrive at better explanations regarding melody-specific assumptions.

The other main revision proposed concerns the integration of licensing constraints within the model of melody. What I have proposed is that LCs operate as an output filter on the structures generable by the ET grammar, rather than operating either during derivation of those structures or at the level of syllabic/prosodic phonology. It has been proposed that all LCs in ET can essentially be reduced to three types, constraining head-complement identity, head-complement distribution, and co-occurrence respectively. It may be possible that further work on LCs can lead to even better generalisations over the set of possible LCs. Integrating LCs at this stage of the grammar offers several interesting questions to pursue further, for instance to what degree there is evidence that melodic representations not employed by a given language (in the absence of positive evidence for a learner to posit an LC) are available to speakers of that language (for example, in representing the melody of loans). Another interesting aspect concerns generative capacity: it has often been seen as an argument for ET that it predicts much smaller segment inventories and fewer languages, closer to what is attested than say SPE-style feature theories (cf. Breit 2013, and references therein), though it has been pointed out that this may not be the true metric we might want to apply concerning melody (Reiss 2012). ET with integrated LCs offers a different mechanism by which segment inventories are generated and it is quite likely that many different constraint sets give rise to the same final inventory, so that further investigation on possible constraint sets in ET offers novel measures on the predicted sizes and distributions of various melodic systems rather than just two flat measures of possible segments and possible inventories as in previous work on the generative capacity of ET.

Extending the application of the LC mechanism to elemental antagonism in multiheaded ET revealed that while, on the one hand, the implementation of the antagonism hypothesis itself may not necessitate changes and additions to the structural assumptions about ET beyond allowing multiple heads (contra to what Backley 2017 seems to suggest), on the other it seems clear that either the specific consequences of antagonism (especially with respect to the unheaded occurrence of both elements in an antagonistic pair) or the species of LCs required in multiheaded ET must be revisited, potentially pointing to another aspect in which that version of ET is less parsimonious than single-headed ET.

Notes

1. I thank Andrew Nevins, Connor Youngberg, Kuniya Nasukawa, Markus Pöchtrager, Shanti Ulfsbjorninn, Sixto Rodriguez, Tobias Scheer, and especially John Harris and Monik Charette, for encouragement and useful discussions on some of these ideas.
2. MRs are also commonly referred to as phonological expressions (PEs) or (sub-)segmental representations. I use the term MR here to avoid ambiguity (*expression* versus *representation*; *phonology* versus *melody*; 'SR' could refer to 'surface representation').
3. Kuratowski (1921) proposes $\langle x,y \rangle \doteq \{\{x\}, \{x,y\}\}$, often adapted to 'short Kuratowski' $\{x, \{x,y\}\}$ (for example, pair-merge in Chomsky 1995).
4. The simple definition in (12) hinges on the limited, single merge cycle, which does not allow structures of the form $\{\gamma, \{\alpha, \beta, \ldots\}\}$ (where $\gamma \notin \{\alpha, \beta\}$). If we want to incorporate such structures (for instance to cover Bare Element Geometry, or unfused melodic expressions, the definition of the *cmpl* relation needs to be revised. Note also the clumsy disjunction to extract embedded members if $head(X) \neq \emptyset$, a consequence of the mixed member types in short Kuratowski pair notation $\{\alpha, \{\alpha, \beta\}\}$ (infinitary union resolves this more elegantly with $\{\{\alpha\}, \{\alpha, \beta\}\}$).

References

Backley, P. (2011). *An Introduction to Element Theory*. Edinburgh: Edinburgh University Press.
Backley, P. (2012). 'Variation in Element Theory'. *Linguistic Variation* 12(1), 57–102. https://doi.org/10.1075/lv.12.1.03bac.
Backley, P. (2017). 'Headedness in Element Theory: The case for multiple heads'. *Glossa* 2(1), 1–17. https://doi.org/10.5334/gigl.463.
Backley, P., and Nasukawa, K. (2010). 'Consonant-vowel unity in Element Theory'. *Phonological Studies* 13, 21–8.
Backley, P., and Nasukawa, K. (2020). 'Recursion in melodic-prosodic structure'. In *Morpheme-internal Recursion in Phonology*, edited by K. Nasukawa, 11–35. Berlin: De Gruyter. https://doi.org/10.1515/9781501512582-002.
Breit, F. (2013). *Formal Aspects of Element Theory*. MRes dissertation, UCL.
Breit, F. (2017). 'Melodic heads, saliency, and strength in voicing and nasality'. *Glossa* 2(1), 85. https://doi.org/10.5334/gjgl.462.
Bromberger, S., and Halle, M. (1989). 'Why phonology is different'. *Linguistic Inquiry*, 20(1), 51–70.

Cavirani, E. and van Oostendorp, M. (2020). 'A theory of the theory of vowels'. In *Morpheme-internal Recursion in Phonology*, edited by K. Nasukawa, 37–56. Berlin: De Gruyter. https://doi.org/10.1515/9781501512582-003.

Charette, M., and Göksel, A. (1996) 'Switching and vowel harmony in Turkic languages'. In *A Festschrift for Edmund Gussmann From his Friends and Colleagues*, edited by K. Henryk and S. Bogdan, 29–57. Lublin: Wydawnictwo KUL.

Charette, M., and Göksel, A. (1998). 'Licensing constraints and vowel harmony in Turkic languages'. In *Structure and Interpretation: Studies in phonology*, edited by E. Cyran, 65–89. Lublin: Folium.

Chomsky, N. (1995). *The Minimalist Program*. Boston, MA: MIT Press.

Chomsky, N. (2005). 'Three factors in language design'. *Linguistic Inquiry* 36(1), 1–22. https://doi.org/10.1162/0024389052993655.

Chomsky, N. (2008). 'On phases'. In *Foundational Issues in Linguistic Theory: Essays in honor of Jean-Roger Vergnaud*, edited by R. Freidin, C. P. Otero, and L. Zubizarreta, 132–66. Boston, MA: MIT Press. https://doi.org/10.7551/mitpress/9780262062787.003.0007.

Cyran, E. (1995). *Vocalic Elements in Phonology: A study in Munster Irish*. Doctoral dissertation, Catholic University of Lublin.

Cyran, E. (1996). 'The parametric occurrence of elements in phonological systems'. In *A Festschrift for Edmund Gussmann From his Friends and Colleagues*, edited by K. Henryk and S. Bogdan, 75–98. Lublin: Wydawnictwo KUL.

Cyran, E. (1997). *Resonance Elements in Phonology: A study in Munster Irish*. Lublin: Folium.

Cyran, E. (2010). *Complexity Scales and Licensing in Phonology*. Berlin: De Gruyter.

Fukui, N., and Takano, Y. (1998). 'Symmetry in syntax: Merge and demerge'. *Journal of East Asian Linguistics* 7, 27–86.

Harris, J., and Lindsey, G. (1995). 'The elements of phonological representation'. In *Frontiers of Phonology: Atoms, structures, derivations*, edited by J. Durand and F. Katamba, 34–79. London: Longman.

Kaye, J. (1990). 'What ever happened to dialect B?' In *Grammar in Progress: GLOW essays for Henk van Riemsdijk*, edited by J. Mascaró and M. Nespor, 259–63. Berlin: De Gruyter.

Kaye, J. (1993). *Current Issues in Phonology* (Lecture series). School of Oriental and African Studies, University of London.

Kaye, J. (2000). 'A users' guide to Government Phonology'. Unpublished manuscript. https://www2.ung.si/~jezik/jkaye/Documents/guide.pdf.

Kaye, J. (2001). 'Working with licensing constraints'. In *Constraints and Preferences*, edited by K. Dziubalska-Kolaczyk, 251–68. Berlin: De Gruyter. https://doi.org/10.1515/9783110881066.251.

Kaye, J. (2012). 'Canadian raising, eh?'. In *Sound Structure and Sense: Studies in memory of Edmund Gussmann*, edited by E. Cyran, H. Kardela, and B. Szymanek, 321–52. Lublin: Wydawnictwo KUL.

Kaye, J., Lowenstamm, J., and Vergnaud, J.-R. (1985). 'The internal structure of phonological representations: A theory of Charm and Government'. *Phonology Yearbook* 2, 305–28.

Kuratowski, C. (1921). 'Sur la notion de l'ordre dans la Théorie des Ensembles'. *Fundamenta Mathematicæ* 2(1), 161–71.

Lindsey, G., and Harris, J. (1990). 'Phonetic interpretation in generative grammar'. *UCL Working Papers in Linguistics* 2, 355–69.

Nasukawa, K. (2014). 'Features and recursive structure'. *Nordlyd* 41(1), 1–19.

Oseki, Y. (2015). 'Eliminating pair-merge'. In *Proceedings of the 32nd West Coast Conference on Formal Linguistics*, edited by U. Steindl, 303–12. Somerville, MA: Cascadilla.

Ploch, S. (1999). *Nasals on my Mind: The phonetic and the cognitive approach to the phonology of nasality*. Doctoral dissertation, SOAS, University of London.

Pöchtrager, M. A. (2006). *The Structure of Length*. Doctoral dissertation, University of Vienna.

Pöchtrager, M. A., and Kaye, J. (2013). 'GP2.0'. *SOAS Working Papers in Linguistics* 16, 51–64.

Reiss, C. (2012). 'Towards a bottom-up approach to phonological typology'. In *Towards a Biolinguistic Understanding of Grammar: Essays on interfaces*, edited by A. M. Di Sciullo, 169–91. Amsterdam: John Benjamins.

Schane, S. A. (1984). 'The fundamentals of Particle Phonology'. *Phonology Yearbook* 1, 129–55.

Ulfsbjorninn, S. (2021). 'Labiovelars and the labial-velar hypothesis: Phonological headedness in Bare Element Geometry'. *Glossa* 6(1), 111. https://doi.org/10.16995/glossa.5718.

5
Production bias and substance-free representation of laryngeal distinctions
Eugeniusz Cyran

Introduction

A rather marginal yet intriguing phenomenon of voicing retention occurs in Polish in the phonological context for final obstruent devoicing (FOD). It has a number of sources: phonetic, pragmatic, and possibly also phonological. It may be argued that it is similar in nature to the problem of incomplete neutralisation. One well-known example of voicing retention, which is clearly motivated by pragmatics, arises to disambiguate the message, avoid homophony, or even rudeness, as in *dób* [dup] 'day and night, gen.pl.' and *kod* [kɔt] 'code', which are homophonous with *dup* [dup] 'arse, gen.pl.' and *kot* [kɔt] 'cat'. Polish speakers consciously avoid the homophony by pronouncing the former two as [dub] and [kɔd] (Gussmann 2007). Whatever explanation is given to account for such variation occurring in monitored speech, modularity suggests that pragmatics, or even phonetics should have no access to phonology. However, the question remains as to how it is possible to bypass regular phonology when voicing is retained. It will be argued that such phenomena provide us with a number of analytically relevant tips as to how sound systems work.

Theoretical context

It is generally assumed that the linguistic utterances we produce are externalisations of phonological forms, or result from phonological derivation. Given a system in which the phonology has a process of devoicing, voicing retention suggests that the 'rule' of devoicing is blocked, or that, for some reason, what is pronounced is based directly on the underlying form, which amounts to the same thing. Thus, for phonology, if this is where the phenomenon is rooted, the question is two-fold: (i) how retention can be formally captured, and (ii) what is the nature of the interaction between phonology on the one hand, and the extra-linguistic aspects listed above.

Phonology is responsible for the nature and distribution of the laryngeal categories in the phonological representation. In this chapter, the representation of the laryngeal distinction is assumed to be strictly privative. In a language with two series of obstruents only one is marked, while sonorant consonants and vowels are never marked laryngeally. These tenets are widely accepted within, for example, Element Theory (Backley 2011; Harris and Lindsey 1995) and more generally within Laryngeal Realism (Beckman et al. 2013; Harris 1994; Honeybone 2002; Iverson and Salmons 1995), according to which, Polish, which is a 'voice' system, marks the voiced series of obstruents, for example, /p°/ versus /b^{Lar}/.

The second aspect of phonological conditioning, which underlies the distribution of the laryngeal prime in phonological representation, is the mechanism of licensing (Charette 1990). In Polish, as in other Slavic languages, the laryngeal licensing (LarLic) is discharged by vowels. The licensing goes from the melodically filled nucleus to the preceding obstruent, with or without an intervening sonorant (Cyran 2014). If the nucleus is empty, the laryngeal licensing fails. Schematically, we may therefore refer to the following two types of strings: licensing $C^{Lar}(R)V$ and unlicensing $C^{o}(R)\emptyset$.

To answer the question *where* the phenomena of voicing retention belong a particular view of *sound system* is assumed in this chapter. It comprises the phonological module with its representation and computation on the one hand, and language specific phonetics (LSP), which is the totality of phonetic knowledge concerning a given language, and universal phonetics (UP) on the other. The two domains of the sound system are mediated by largely arbitrary, that is, lexicalised spell-out relations (Scheer 2014).

(1) **Sound System**
 Phonology ⟵ spell-out ⟶ LSP+UP

A distinction should be made between *sound systems* and *sound patterns*. The latter is understood as the totality of phonetic, surface, effects and knowledge that speakers are consciously aware of, and linguists collect as data. In other words, a sound pattern is synonymous with LSP, and merely constitutes a fragment of a given sound system.

Below, we consider each of the above aspects of the laryngeal sound system beginning with a possible phonological analysis of voicing retention.

Hypothesis I: a phonological approach in which delaryngealisation is blocked

Under this hypothesis devoicing is due to delaryngealisation. Voicing retention, on the other hand, is a case of the phonetic interpretation of the underlying representation, rather than the post-phonological form. Given that the distribution of the laryngeal distinctions in Polish is regulated by licensing, one way of capturing register switches, or hyper-correction, is to refer to strengthening of the licensing properties of nuclei.

An ad hoc phonological analysis to this effect is offered in Cyran (2014). It builds on the observation that languages seem to employ slightly different licensing properties of different types of nuclei depending on the register. One example comes from Malayalam in which the final empty nucleus is allowed to license more types of consonants in formal than in colloquial speech, producing variation of the type [paal ~ paalə] 'milk', [wayar ~ wayarə] 'stomach'. Malayalam resembles Polish voicing retention in that the final empty nucleus can license more in formal speech than in colloquial/unguarded speech. When voicing is retained in *kod* and *dób*, it appears that Polish modifies the target of licensing rather than the trigger: there is no observable change in the licensor. However, phonologically, we could claim that the modification is in fact in the trigger: it is given more licensing power in monitored speech, than it generally has. The analysis of voice retention in *kod* [kɔt ~ kɔd] 'code' is illustrated below in (2).

(2) **Unguarded speech** [kɔt]   **Monitored speech** [kɔd]

```
a.  C  V  C  V                  b.  C  V  C  V
    |  |  |         LarLic          |  |  |
    k  ɔ  d      strengthening      k  ɔ  d
       ǂ                                  |
       Lar                                Lar
```

Generally, the idea is that there is a critical point at which a given type of licensor can barely license the preceding structure. This is where variation connected with register switches occurs in Malayalam and possibly Polish. There are a few theoretical consequences of the above proposal. The biggest one is that grammar-external considerations influence the computation of the phonological module. This is at odds with the modular architecture of grammar.

Hypothesis II: there is no phonological delaryngealisation ever

An alternative assumption to the one in which retention is a case of delaryngealisation blocking could be that the actual computational phenomenon of phonological delaryngealisation simply does not exist. As a consequence the existence of laryngeal licensing becomes superfluous.

The idea that there is no delaryngealisation is explicitly proposed by van der Hulst (2015). It is claimed that the property called |fortis| is present in voiceless obstruents in both aspiration and voicing languages. The difference between such systems follows from language specific implementation enhancement rules. In some adverse contexts, for example, word-finally, such rules do not operate leaving a phonological distinction which is deprived of phonetic enhancement, but no |fortis|-loss occurs. The remaining prime is claimed to be responsible for the small distinctions between the lexically voiced and lexically voiceless obstruents which are known as incomplete neutralisation (for example, Slowiaczek and Dinnsen 1985).

Thus, the attraction of the no-delaryngealisation hypothesis is obvious. It is a viable phonological response to the growing evidence for the incompleteness of neutralisation. As a consequence of this proposal, the explanation for FOD, and indeed voice retention phenomena, rests completely outside phonology. The obvious candidates that are left are the spell-out and the phonetics (LSP+UP).

Apart from the fact that laryngeal licensing becomes redundant, virtually all computation to do with |Lar| vanishes, possibly, including |Lar|-spreading. Thus, what is left in the phonology is merely the lexicalised distinction which is responsible for the voiced/voiceless contrast, or, in fact, the lexical distinction which will determine which phonological objects undergo which battery of phonetic enhancement rules in relevant contexts. Without the enhancement rules, the distinction between the lexical representations may only produce very similar objects in a particular context.

Let us consider where exactly the implementation rules reside in our tripartite model of the sound system. Is it in the spell-out, or in LSP?

The nature of spell-out

Within Element Theory and Government Phonology (Charette 1990; Harris 1994; Harris and Lindsey 1995; Kaye et al. (KLV) 1990), phonetic interpretation of phonological representations seems to be construed mainly as interpretation of segments based on prior phonological processing due to the prosodic context, rather than interpretation of segments in context.[1] Thus, given that [p] and [b] in Polish are /U,h,ʔ/ and /U,h,ʔ,L/, respectively, FOD is a case of phonological lenition under weak licensing (for example, Harris 1990, 1994), whereby a segment /C^{Lar}/ is turned into /C°/. The following empty nucleus itself is not taken into account in the interpretation. The prosodic context is assumed to have modified the internal representation of a given segment before it is phonetically interpreted. This view is echoed in recent proposals (for example, Scheer 2014) in which spell-out (↔) is understood as lexicalised lists of segment types, for example, /X/ ↔ [b] versus /Y/ ↔ [p], rather than strings of the type /XØ/ ↔ [p] versus /XV/ ↔ [b].

On the other hand, in van der Hulst (2015) the context is crucial for the interpretation because it triggers particular enhancement rules, or not. The question is, if it is the phonological or the phonetic context that must be taken into account. The answer should probably be as follows: phonetic, because the enhancement rules are in the phonetics, or at least outside phonology. Thus, under the non-delaryngealisation assumption, there is almost no phonological computation in FOD. The phonological object makes it through the phonological processing unscathed, and is phonetically interpreted depending on the phonetic context. It may, therefore, be claimed that if there is any computation it occurs in the phonetic domain. There is no phonological allophony, but only a phonetic one. Consequently, what begins to loom large is the question of the nature of the computation at the level of phonetics, that is in LSP.[2]

Both hypotheses discussed above seem to rely on the same premise: that there is no delaryngealisation. However, they differ markedly with respect to the phenomenon of voice retention in Polish. The phonological analysis of retention in the section of this chapter 'Hypothesis I: A phonological approach …' assumes the absence of delaryngealisation only in the case of the interaction between phonology and pragmatics. In this approach, FOD, when it does occur, is a result of phonological computation. In the 'no-delaryngealisation-ever' approach, FOD is a result of the absence of phonological and indeed phonetic computation. FOD follows from the absence of enhancement rules in a given context.

Since in van der Hulst (2015) it is the voiceless series that carries the property |fortis| and the voiced series is only voiced due to the enhancement rules, it may be assumed that in the case of Polish voicing retention in *kod* the rules of voice enhancement are simply generalised to all positions. The problem of modularity does not arise, because LSP may be viewed as the domain of grammar-external knowledge. That is, one that is not a result of phonological acquisition, but rather the basis for phonological acquisition. This is where the knowledge of language specific phonetics, that is, the knowledge of major allophones, alternations, and other observable sound patterns interact with the knowledge of spelling, pragmatics, etc.

To sum up, the 'no-delaryngealisation-ever' hypothesis leads to a number of positive outcomes. It allows us to automatically place phenomena such as voice retention in the domain in which it guarantees that modularity is not undermined. It also offers a surprisingly simple explanation of incomplete neutralisation. This assumption, however, also has some grave consequences for phonology. One of them is that almost no phonological computation is left to describe or explain the sound patterns related to voicing phenomena. Another interesting outcome of such a strong component of enhancement rules within LSP is that it seems no longer linguistically relevant which obstruent should be marked in a two-way system. The only thing that is important is that one of them is. The rest is due to the relevant enhancement rules.

Below, we consider an assumption which combines some elements of both approaches discussed above.

Hypothesis III: Polish has phonological delaryngealisation, voice retention is an LSP phenomenon, it does matter which series of obstruents is marked, enhancement has something to do with articulatory planning, less so with computation

There is evidence that FOD is at least partly phonological in Polish – as delaryngealisation due to the absence of laryngeal licensing – and that voicing retention, just as incomplete neutralisation, is entirely restricted to LSP. There is also evidence that it matters which series of obstruents is marked. The evidence comes from sandhi phenomena.

Depending on whether word-boundary is visible to the application of enhancement rules, the 'no-delaryngealisation-ever' assumption predicts two sandhi patterns, of which one possibly corresponds with Macedonian (Korytowska 2012), and the other with the Warsaw Polish (WP) dialect. What is not predicted is the existence of Pattern 3, which is found in Cracow-Poznań Polish (CPP). All the patterns involve FOD in final position, unless retention occurs (Pattern 4).

(3) **'no-delaryngealisation-ever', boundary visibility and retention**

	# boundary visibility		voicing retention
No	Yes		as lexical identity
Pattern 1	Pattern 2	Pattern 3	Pattern 4
Macedonian	WP	CPP	Mac., WP, CPP
/D/# → [T]	/D/# → [T]	/D/# → [T]	/D/# → [D]
/D/#/V/ → [D]	/D/#/V/ → [T]	/D/#/V/ → [D]	/D/#/V/ → [D]
/T/#/V/ → [T]	/T/#/V/ → [T]	/T/#/V/ → [D]	/T/#/V/ → [T]

Pattern 1 indicates that enhancement rules do not apply word-finally, hence FOD takes place. The lexical identity is maintained across a word boundary, which means that the enhancement rules do see the following vowel and apply, ignoring the intervening boundary. This alone suggests surface (LSP) conditioning of the enhancement rules. The other pattern which is consistent with the 'no-delaryngealisation-ever' hypothesis is Pattern 2. This time, however, one has to assume that the word boundary is visible and blocks the enhancement rules, suggesting that either the enhancement rules must operate on deeper representation, or that the underlying distinction between /D/ and /T/ is no longer present, for example, due to delaryngealisation. The problem concerning the level of application of the enhancement rules is further complicated by Pattern 3. It partly corresponds to Pattern 1, in that FOD occurs word-finally, and /D/ is enhanced before a vowel-initial word, suggesting boundary invisibility. However, it would not be correct to say that the word boundary is ignored because the lexical /T/ is enhanced, as if it was a /D/. Enhancement, as the name suggests, should amplify the lexical distinction, not neutralise it. Therefore, one should conclude that in Pattern 3 the boundary is visible and it provides a phonological context for the loss of the laryngeal distinction. On the other hand, enhancement operates at the phonetic level and is blind to the boundaries. Finally, Pattern 4 is found in all the example languages as a case of voicing retention which ignores both boundaries and enhancement contexts.

As argued in Cyran (2014), the distinction between Patterns 2 and 3 can be understood within a strictly privative account only if it is assumed that (i) word-final obstruents are delaryngealised in both dialects; (ii) the laryngeal representation of the obstruents in CPP is the opposite of WP, that is, WP has $/D^{Lar}/ = [d]$ versus $/T^{o}/ = [t]$ and CPP has $/D^{o}/ = [d]$ versus $/T^{Lar}/ = [t]$, and (iii) there is no difference between word-internal C^oV and the sandhi $C^o\#V$ contexts with respect to enhancement of $/C^o/$. Whether it is phonetically interpreted as voiced or voiceless is strictly related to the regular spell-out relations established for the unmarked obstruent in the respective systems during acquisition.

Production bias and acquisitional amnesia

First of all, the laryngeal relativism described above rejects the realist view that /C°/ has a universal phonetic interpretation as voiceless unaspirated. Likewise, |Lar| corresponds to neither voicing nor aspiration. Its choice does not *a priori* determine the surface phonetic categories, that is, whether it is a voicing system [b-p], or an aspiration one [p-pʰ]. The deterministic approach to laryngeal marking will be viewed here as an instance of production bias. We assume that the choice of the phonetic categories, for example, [b-p], is an LSP choice, based on the [b-p-pʰ] distinction provided by UP (4a).

The acquisition of the laryngeal system proceeds from LSP, where languages divide into 'voicing' and 'aspiration' systems (4c).

(4) **Acquisition of the laryngeal system**

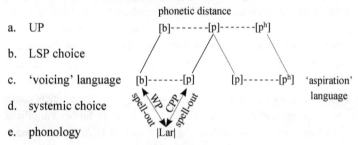

a. UP
b. LSP choice
c. 'voicing' language
d. systemic choice
e. phonology

By the time the acquisitional decision is made concerning the way the relevant two-way distinction is to be represented in the phonology (4d), the LSP knowledge already comprises a number of aspects which constitute the basis of this systemic choice. The decision is an automatic act of establishing the spell-out relations between the surface phonetic object representing a totality of acoustic, perceptual, and articulatory aspects and the symbolic privative representation of the laryngeal distinction.

LSP involves knowing the main distinctive phonetic categories/major allophones, for example, [b, p], that they are fully distinctive as targets of spell-out in the context __(R)V, and that they are related to particular modified forms in other contexts than __(R)V. These sound patterns constitute the basis for the systemic choice/acquisition of the phonological representation and computation that generalise the patterns in the mind.

(5) **LSP patterns**
   a. /B/ → [b] / __(R)V
      /B/ → [b] / __C^{+voi} and __#(R)V in CPP
      /B/ → [p] / __#, __C^{-voi} and __#(R)V in WP
   b. /P/ → [p] / __(R)V
      /P/ → [p] / __#, __C^{-voi} and __#(R)V in WP
      /P/ → [b] / __C^{+voi} and __#(R)V in CPP

LSP has two important properties: (i) it constitutes the basis of phonological acquisition, and (ii) this knowledge does not disappear after phonological acquisition is complete, and, together with UP, plays a role in phonetic implementation.

The representational choice has to reflect the patterns in (5), but it need not be a direct translation of phonetic patterns into phonological rules, or a direct translation of acoustic properties into phonological features. Importantly, it is not a phonetic decision. The choice of the marked series will have no bearing on the phonetic categories in (4c), because they are already given: the input to acquisition will later constitute the output of production. What matters in the representational decision is the phonological behaviour of the marked segments, for example, that they require licensing. It follows that the property |Lar| can indeed be fully symbolic and need not contain substance and the interpretation of the neutral obstruent is system specific. Thus, in principle, there is nothing wrong with the fact that /C°/ is phonetically interpreted as [p] in one system and [b] in another.

As for phonetic interpretation, we may assume that the target of, say, /b/ at spell-out is the [b] which is found in the __(R)V context. It may be somewhat idealised as a gross acoustic pattern (Harris and Lindsey 1995). However, spell-out does not consider the phonetic context. The context will have an effect on the final phonetic interpretation of the target. Thus, spell-out, or translation, may be viewed as slightly different from phonetic interpretation. The former is automatic and arbitrary, while phonetic interpretation involves contextual influence. If so, then enhancement rules may be viewed as an effect of articulatory planning, rather than computation of any sort.

Finally, the knowledge of LSP is not forgotten. It is the basis for the phonological acquisition and remains as the speakers' conscious competence. This fact can be used in explaining the phenomenon of voicing retention, as well as, it is hoped, incomplete neutralisation.

Voice retention, an LSP take

It should be recalled that what FOD, voicing retention, and incomplete neutralisation have in common is the word-final context, in which the LSP knowledge, for example, that illustrated in (5), involves not only the awareness that obstruents must be voiceless, but also the fact that they have two lexical sources: a voiceless obstruent, or a voiced one. This is because at this level of linguistic knowledge speakers know the alternations and they are able to identify the major allophones. This is also where other grammar-external aspects interact, such as experience, pragmatics, knowledge of spelling, word familiarity, etc. It is in LSP that speakers can consciously manipulate phonetic forms on the basis of the LSP patterns and various relations, and this is where voice retention should belong.

Incomplete neutralisation

Since the early 80s, experimental studies have been showing that the neutralisation of the voicing contrast in languages like Polish is incomplete, and that it requires a phonological account (for example, Slowiaczek and Dinnsen 1985). In the light of our discussion of the laryngeal system, the idea that incomplete neutralisation should be expressed in the phonology is based on two misconceptions: production bias and acquisitional amnesia. This view wrongly assumes that phonetic forms (sound patterns) are generated by the phonological system and implementation rules, with no reference to the crucial aspect of sound systems, that is, LSP. The domain in which conscious awareness of the patterns prevails. It is in LSP that the variants are controlled by such aspects as word familiarity, frequency, tempo of speech, degree of speech monitoring by speakers, spelling, pragmatics, and more importantly, also the familiarity with the sounds patterns, such as alternations.

Conclusion

This chapter addressed the question of the structure of the sound system in relation to familiar though marginal laryngeal phenomena in Polish. The analysis of voicing retention in Polish, which is a case of suspension of a regular phenomenon of final obstruent devoicing, allowed us to clarify the role of phonology, spell-out conventions, and language specific phonetics in sound systems. The acquisition-centred perspective affords a view in which phonological categories may be deprived of substance, and phonological computation is rather small. It is restricted to licensing or unlicensing of the category |Lar| in the phonology.

A simple view of LSP is advocated, in which no computation is assumed. What might appear to be contextual phonetic implementation rules, or enhancement rules, are claimed to be the result of articulatory planning, which is part of LSP, and universal phonetics. It is suggested that laryngeal phenomena such as voicing retention or incomplete neutralisation are best viewed as LSP phenomena.

Notes

1. One exception is the interpretation of empty positions which are vocalised if not p-licensed (Kaye et al. 1990).
2. Alternatively, the spell-out is not list-like, but process-like, which also has its consequences.

References

Backley, P. (2011). *An Introduction to Element Theory*. Edinburgh: Edinburgh University Press.
Beckman, J., Jessen, M., and Ringen, C. (2013). 'Empirical evidence for laryngeal features: Aspirating vs. true voice languages'. *Journal of Linguistics* 49(2), 259–84.
Charette, M. (1990). 'Licence to govern'. *Phonology* 7(1), 233–53. https://doi.org/10.1017/S0952675700001196.
Cyran, E. (2014). *Between Phonology and Phonetics. Polish voicing*. Berlin: De Gruyter.
Gussmann, E. (2007). *The Phonology of Polish*. Oxford: Oxford University Press.
Harris, J. (1990). 'Segmental complexity and phonological government'. *Phonology* 7(1), 255–300. https://doi.org/10.1017/S0952675700001202.
Harris, J. (1994). *English Sound Structure*. Oxford: Blackwell.
Harris, J., and Lindsey, G. (1995). 'The elements of phonological representation'. In *Frontiers of Phonology: Atoms, structures, derivations*, edited by J. Durand and F. Katamba, 34–79. New York: Longman.
Honeybone, P. (2002). 'Germanic obstruent lenition: Some implications of theoretical and historical phonology'. Doctoral dissertation, University of Newcastle upon Tyne.
Iverson, G., and Salmons, J. (1995). 'Aspiration and laryngeal representation in Germanic'. *Phonology* 12(3), 369–96.
Kaye, J., Lowenstamm, J., and Vergnaud, J.-R. (1990). 'Constituent structure and government in phonology'. *Phonology* 7(1), 193–231.
Korytowska, A. (2012). *Sandhi w standardzie języka macedońskiego* [Sandhi in standard Macedonian]. Wydawnictwo Naukowe Uniwersytetu Mikołaja Kopernika.
Scheer, T. (2014). 'Spell-out, post-phonological'. In *Crossing Phonetics-Phonology Lines*, edited by E. Cyran and J. Szpyra-Kozłowska, 255–75. Cambridge: Cambridge Scholars Publishing.
Slowiaczek, L., and Dinnsen, D. A. (1985). 'On the neutralizing status of Polish word-final devoicing'. *Journal of Phonetics* 13, 325–41.
van der Hulst, H. (2015). 'The laryngeal class in RcvP and voice phenomena in Dutch'. In *Above and Beyond the Segments: Experimental linguistics and phonetics*, edited by J. Caspers, Y. Chen, W. Heeren, J. Pacilly, N. O. Schiller, and E. van Zanten, 323–49. Amsterdam: John Benjamins.

6
The no-crossing constraint: a neglected licensing constraint
John R. Rennison

Background

In Rennison (1996), I proposed an analysis of the ATR harmony of Mòoré based on the relative ordering of the elements |A| and |ATR| on their shared or 'fused' tier, working in conjunction with the No-Crossing Constraint (NCC), which for reference is stated in (1).

(1) The 'No-Crossing Constraint' (NCC)
Association lines do not cross. (Goldsmith 1976, 48)[1]

This is the only proposal I know of that accounts for the fact that in Mòoré only high ATR vowels (that is, /i/ and /u/) trigger harmony, but mid ATR vowels do not (and there is no lexical low ATR vowel). In other words: the stem vowels {i, u} trigger ATR harmony, but {ɪ, e, ɛ, a, ɔ, o, ʊ} do not. This is exemplified in (2) with the stem vowels /i/ and /e/. Suffix vowels are /ɪ, ʊ, a/ (that is, never mid, never ATR, never nasal). When ATR-harmonised they become /i, u, ʌ/ respectively.

(2) ATR harmony in Mòoré. Only high vowels trigger harmony. ✗ marks an NCC violation.

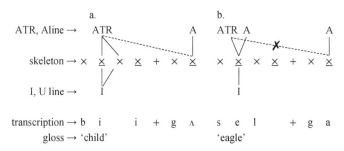

This unusual restriction means that even though the word is the domain of ATR harmony, there are plenty of disharmonic words in the language – namely those with /e/ or /o/ in their stem.

In this chapter, I will augment this extraordinary case with a new analysis of Turkish vowel harmony (VH) in which the elements |A| and |U| share a tier. In this way I will demonstrate that (a) tier fusions beyond |I/U| are not uncommon, and therefore (b) many LCs are in fact epiphenomena of more basic aspects of the theory of GP.

How can one justify a fusion of tiers? Or, conversely, how can one justify the non-fusion of tiers? The theory allows (or once allowed) elements to reside on lines/tiers, and the precise configuration of the elements and lines remained a matter for empirical investigation. In Kaye et al. (KLV) (1985, 307) the fusion of the |I| and |U| tiers is dealt with very briefly and with little justification. It is assumed that no skeletal point can be associated to two different elements on the fused tier (for example, to both |I| and |U|). In fact, the allocation of elements to tiers deserved far more attention (for some early ideas on this, see Rennison 1990.). As a first hypothesis, let us assume that *any* constellation of tiers is possible. For the purposes of this chapter, I will restrict myself to the four elements |I|, |U|, |A|, and |ATR| within vowel systems. Note that these elements are by no means equal in status. In particular, the element |ATR| demands that at least one other element be present in the vowel. Also, for our present typological purposes we will largely ignore the elements |H|, |L|, and |R|.

The minimum number of elements in a vowel system is probably zero, if Circassian [a] is a geminate schwa, as Job (1981) suggests. I am unaware of a language in which every logically possible combination of {I, U, A, ATR} is fully active/contrastive (giving a vowel system like /œ, y, ʏ, e, ɛ, i, ɪ, o, ɔ, u, ʊ, ʌ, a, ɘ, ə/), and its existence would be surprising, since additional elements bring additional markedness and additional phonological strength.

In this chapter I will ignore headedness because we still do not know enough about it, and also because it does not seem to play any role in the vowel systems and processes under consideration here. The case of Mòoré outlined above shows clearly that |ATR| is a normal element (and subject to the NCC); therefore, it cannot have anything to do with headedness, and switching is not an option.

Turkish vowel harmony

In Rennison (1987) I gave my first account of Turkish VH within the framework of Government Phonology (GP). Since then we have learned more about VH systems and the research programme of GP has advanced and matured. Other analyses of Turkish VH have been proposed, notably Charette and Göksel (1994, 1996). In the latter study they claim that 'licensing constraints not only determine the vocalic inventory but also explain how vowel harmony operates' (Charette and Göksel 1996, 86). However, I share Pöchtrager's (2010) mistrust of licensing constraints in GP.[2] These are extremely problematic because they are completely unrestricted and therefore devoid of any explanatory power. Indeed, even the notion of headedness in the melodic structure of sounds (to which both licensing constraints and Pöchtrager refer) is not well understood (though see Rennison and Neubarth 2003). On the other hand, Charette and Göksel (1994, 1996) and Pöchtrager (2010) nowhere show any tiers of elements, and it is not clear whether they even have any – even though they make ample use of the autosegmental device of spreading.

My earlier analysis

Apart from the use of |L| (labial) as the name of what we now call the |U| element, the diagrams of eight words, that is, one per stem vowel, each in four inflectional forms, are still presentable today. In (3) I give the melodic content of the Turkish vowels in terms of elements, and in (4) my earlier representations (more neatly formatted, with |U| in place of |L|).

(3) The melodies of Turkish vowels, without consideration of tiers or headedness (for the final version, see (7) below)

vowel	i	ü	e	ö	a	o	u	ɨ
elements	|I|	|IU|	|IA|	|IUA|	|A|	|UA|	|U|	| |

(4) Turkish harmonised noun forms (numbered (19) in Rennison 1987, 351–53). The lexical shape of the genitive suffix is /in/ and of the plural suffix /lar/. To save space, transcriptions are shown instead of x's on the skeleton.

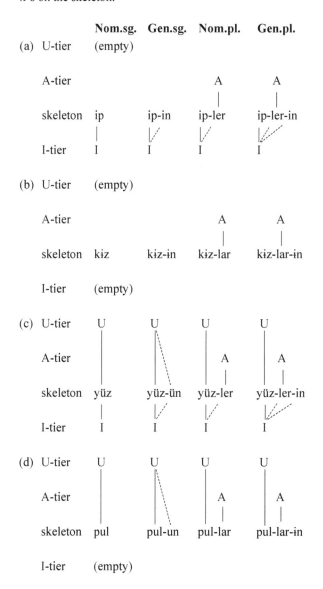

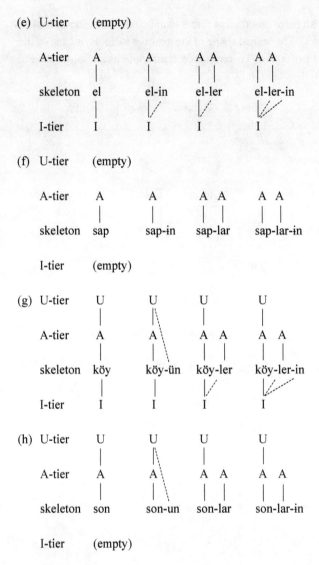

Under this analysis, all VH in Turkish involves the left-to-right spreading of an element from the (last) stem vowel to the suffix vowels. The |I| element spreads without restriction, and the |A| element does not spread at all. The |U| element spreads only to vowel positions that are not associated to an |A| element and cannot skip over a vowel that is associated to an |A|. Thus in the fourth column of (4) none of the final morphemes has a |U| element because the penultimate morpheme (ler/lar) always contains an |A| element.

A tier-sharing analysis

Tier sharing and multiple associations

If every phonological element were located on its own independent tier, the question of double[3] associations of a skeletal point to the elements of a particular tier would not arise.[4] However, from the beginnings of Government Phonology it has been generally assumed that the elements |I| and |U| share a tier in many languages. The existence of multiple associations from a tier to a skeletal point raises a further issue relating to the NCC. Is it possible to have only single associations in the lexicon, but to produce double associations in the phonology? This hypothetical case is illustrated in (5).

(5) Phonological double associations with only single lexical associations: four logical possibilities. NB: B and C, and the x's to which they are associated are not necessarily strictly adjacent.

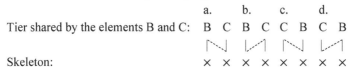

Old High German I-umlaut

It can easily be seen that this scenario must have been responsible for the creation of the majority of front rounded vowels in German: an |I| element near the end of a word was allowed to associate to the neighbouring lexically specified vowel to its left. This is shown in (6).

(6) Old High German I-umlaut.

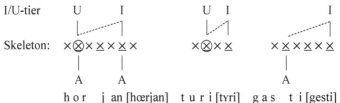

h o r   j an [hœrjan]   t u r i [tyri]   g a s   t i [gesti]

Examples: <horjan>, New High German *hören* 'to hear'; <turi>, NHG *Tür(e)* 'door'; <gasti>, NHG [gɛstə] 'guests'.

The resulting vowels, indicated by circles in (6), now have double associations to elements on the I/U-tier within the phonology, although in the lexicon there are only single associations (namely to |U|, but not to |I|).

Let us now investigate the double associations of Turkish vowels.

A new analysis of Turkish vowel harmony

My new proposal for Turkish VH involves the notion that failures of spreading are caused not only by the NCC but also by the ordering of tier-sharing elements within a segment. In other words, if we take the NCC seriously, then the reason why |U| spreads to the right sometimes, but not always, can only be that |U| shares a tier with some element whose association lines or whose ordering relative to |U| block that spreading. In Turkish, the only candidate element is |A|.

More formally: In Turkish the elements |U| and |A| may be associated to a single vowel position in the lexicon only in the order |A| – |U|, but the order |U| – |A| is banned both in the lexicon and in derivations.[5,6] This prohibits the spreading of |U| to a position already associated with |A|. The vowels of Turkish therefore have the representations in (7); but the two vowels in (8) are illicit.

(7) The vowels of Turkish when U and A share a tier and are ordered A – U.

(8) Two vowels that are disallowed in Turkish because they violate the element ordering |A| – |U| within segments.

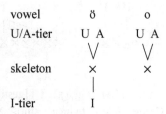

Now consider the representations in (9), in which the elements |U| and |A| share the same tier. Here only the words that have both |U| and |A| are considered; the other words have effectively the same representations as in (4) – but with a fused |U| and |A| tier.

(9) The relevant nouns of (4) on a tier-sharing analysis; all other nouns retain the representation in (4), except that the |U| and |A| tiers are conflated. The lexical shape of the genitive suffix remains /in/ and of the plural suffix /lar/.
✗ = NCC violation, !✗ = element ordering violation

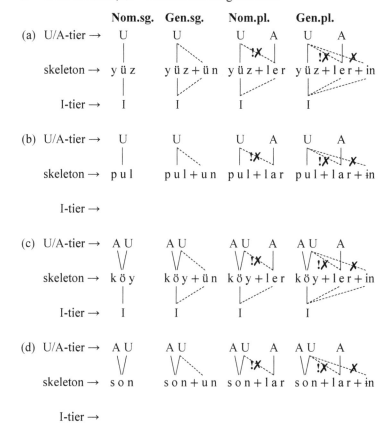

Each of the !✗ association failures would result in a segment having associations to the U/A-tier in the illicit order |U| – |A|. However, in (9d) the first vowel is associated to both |U| and |A| in the order |A| – |U| and therefore perfectly okay.

So finally we arrive at the two new simplified rules of Turkish vowel harmony:

1. I spreads to the right.[7]
2. U spreads to the right.

Everything else is taken care of by the element/tier configuration, and there is no need for segment-level licensing constraints.

Conclusion

I have proposed here a unified theory in which two old friends, the no-crossing constraint and the autosegmental tiers, are used to define possible segment inventories and phonological processes (and the constraints on them). This is accomplished at the cost of an additional theoretical device: that of *element ordering*, whereby elements which share the same tier and are connected to the same skeletal point must occur in a specific linear order. A project for future research will therefore be to examine element ordering more closely.

Notes

1. This original formulation of the NCC was the second part of the Well-Formedness Condition (of which the first part is not relevant here). For the purposes of GP, since tiers are arranged cylindrically around the skeleton, we should perhaps add 'in the same plane'.
2. Tier sharing, element ordering, and the option of double attachments from tiers to segments determine the vowel inventory of a language. Thus for example Nyangumarda (Western Australia) has the elements |I, U, A| on a single tier and allows only single attachments from tier to segment. Therefore the language has precisely three vowels: /i, u, a/.
3. I know of no case where more than two elements which share a tier can be associated to a single skeletal point. Languages like Nyangumarta quite definitely have three elements |I, U, A| on a single tier, but I have found no such language (so far) that seems to allow more than single associations of these elements to a single vowel. I suspect that this may be some kind of restriction on overall complexity.
4. This assumes that the autosegmental tiers of elements are arranged cylindrically around the skeleton, thus in principle allowing the elements of each tier to associate with the skeleton without interference of any kind from elements on any other tier.
5. It would be nice if the ordering of elements were derived from some higher principle.
6. The only rule in a phonological derivation is 'License!'. There is no rule ordering. But I am avoiding the word 'license' here in order to be perfectly clear about there being no segmental licensing constraints.
7. Whether the direction of spreading needs to be stated is another question that I am not equipped to answer.

References

Charette, M., and Göksel, A. (1996) 'Switching and vowel harmony in Turkic languages'. In *A Festschrift for Edmund Gussmann From his Friends and Colleagues*, edited by K. Henryk and S. Bogdan, 29–57. Lublin: Wydawnictwo KUL.
Charette, M., and Göksel, A. (1998). 'Licensing constraints and vowel harmony in Turkic languages'. In *Structure and Interpretation: Studies in phonology*, edited by E. Cyran, 65–89. Lublin: Folium.
Goldsmith, J. A. (1976). *Autosegmental Phonology*. Doctoral dissertation, Massachusetts Institute of Technology (MIT).
Job, D. M. (1981). 'Circassian vowels: one, two, three'. In *Phonologica 1980*. Akten der vierten internationalen Phonologie-Tagung, Wien, 29. Juni-2. Juli 1980, Innsbrucker Beiträge zur Sprachwissenschaft 36, edited by W. U. Dressler, O. E. Pfeiffer, and J. R. Rennison, 231–36. Innsbruck: Institut für Sprachwissenschaft der Universität Innsbruck.
Kaye, J., Lowenstamm, J., and Vergnaud, J.-R. (1985). 'The internal structure of phonological elements: A theory of Charm and Government'. *Phonology Yearbook* 2, 305–28.
Pöchtrager, M. A. (2010). 'Does Turkish diss harmony?'. *Acta Linguistica Hungarica* 57(4), 458–73.

Rennison, J. R. (1987). 'Vowel harmony and tridirectional vowel features'. *Folia Linguistica* XXI, 337–54.

Rennison, J. R. (1990). 'On the elements of phonological representations: The evidence from vowel systems and vowel processes'. *Folia Linguistica* XXIV, 175–244.

Rennison, J. R. (1996). 'Mòoré vowels revisited'. Government Phonology Workshop (2 Nov. 1996), *8th International Phonology Meeting*, Vienna. https://www.univie.ac.at/linguistics/gp/rennison.pdf.

Rennison, J. R., and Neubarth, F. (2003). 'An x-bar theory of Government Phonology'. In *Living on the Edge. 28 Papers in honour of Jonathan Kaye*, edited by S. Ploch, 95–130. Berlin: De Gruyter.

Part 2
Prosody and constituent structure

7
Prosody and constituent structure: a brief introduction
Yuko Yoshida

Introduction

Prosodic and constituent structure in Government Phonology (GP) has undergone complexification since the initial syllable proposal of Kahn (1976) and divided into approaches where words are composed of syllables and moras (Hayes 1983) and constituents which link to a skeletal tier in GP (Kaye and Lowenstamm 1984; Kaye et al. (KLV) 1990). 'Deforestation' in phonology has been a goal since the proposal of Strict CV by Lowenstamm (1996), with a lateral alternative replacing the arboreal syllable structures of the standard theories (Scheer 2004). The questions posed are what prosodic constituency looks like, as well as where and how prosodic phonology operates.

Elements that constitute segments (see Part 1), constituents, and prosodic properties pivot around the timing slots, or the timing skeleton, in Standard Government Phonology (SGP) (Kaye et al. 1985; 1990; Charette 1991). The SGP representations enabled GPists to explicate numerous phonological phenomena including syllabic processes with arboreal structures that indicate autosegmental behaviour of the constituents. Before those works, McCarthy (1979) proposed an intervening tier between segments and syllable structure in the analysis of Semitic languages differently from SGP. SGP allowed the use of branching rhymal constituents, though Lowenstamm (1996) later boiled down syllable structure to only CV constituents, corresponding to ON in SGP. Presence of the rhyme meant a banned operation in SGP of 'resyllabification': the word final consonant (R) is syllabified as the initial onset of the suffixal element in the SGP canon.

Constituents and government

SGP recognises branching onsets, branching nuclei, and branching rhymes in a strictly binary fashion – no complex onsets of the shape *CCC are permitted, and 'codas' are defined as rhymal complements consisting of a single segment. Central to the discussion of many of the chapters that follow is the concept of Government Licensing (GL) (Charette 1990, 1991), which provides support from nuclei to their preceding onset to form either a coda-onset cluster (direct GL) or a branching onset (indirect GL). Charette (1990, 1991) provides an account for the asymmetric behaviour between the consonants associated to the onset and 'coda', understood in SGP to be the rhymal complement. Traditionally, 'coda' consonants have been understood to be weak because they are subject to both the Constituent Government (CG) of the preceding nucleus, which licenses its complement, and the Transconstituent Government (TG) of the following onset, as exemplified in (1).

(1)

However, the analysis of clusters and codas has evolved since this period and different proposals for the analysis of weak segments such as codas have been made, especially in lateral theories such as Strict CV which do away with the skeletal slot as well as projection, and therefore also cannot model coda consonants as rhymal adjuncts in the way that standard GP does.

Issues addressed in Part 2

The chapters in Part 2 focus on the behaviour and representational analysis of different segmental combinations and their constituent structure. Pöchtrager (Chapter 12) revisits the issue of representing light diphthongs (traditionally represented as two unfused melodies attached to a single skeletal point), shedding light on the properties observed both in light and heavy diphthongs, evincing typological issues from English, French, and Japanese. This chapter crucially parallels the pattern of diphthongs to the asymmetry of (final) empty nuclei (for example, lampØ, *laprØ) elucidating the difference between empty nuclei, complex nuclei, and simplex, realised nuclei.

Harris and Chiu (Chapter 10) provide experimental results from Cypriot Greek listeners, which revisits the necessity of a one-size fits all approach to syllabifying consonant clusters as complex onsets. An intriguing result of a dichotic-listening experiment with Cypriot Greek speakers furnishes support for the unique behaviour of sibilants in #sC clusters, reinforcing the possibility that these clusters are not branching onsets.

Multiple contributions within this section consider vowel length in relation to stress assignment and morphological operations. Fathi (Chapter 9) presents a re-examination of Cairene Arabic focusing on accent and aspects of the vowel length in English and Cairene Arabic. Crucially, a re-examination of the facts as they have been presented in the phonological literature provides not only a promising understanding of the vocalic phonology of Cairene Arabic, but also a fresh account of accent assignment in Cairene Arabic as linked to prominence. Fathi questions the alternating length of vowels in Cairene Arabic and claims that the vowels are underlyingly long. Unlike McCarthy (2005), the vowels do not undergo shortening, and length is one of the bundled properties of stress, along with pitch-induced prominence and an increase in duration. In another fundamental re-analysis, Lowenstamm (Chapter 11) presents a templatic analysis of English irregular weak verbs, proposing that they are similar to Arabic segholates, focusing on verbs involving vowel length alternations, as in *keep/kept*. The templatic treatment also accounts for the activity of voicing of the stem-final consonant and the past morpheme in 'regular' verb forms, providing a full story for the behaviour of vowel length, clusters, and voicing for verbs that would normally be considered suppletive forms.

Two proposals consider the utility of applying a strict CVCV template to English vowels and stress. Quantity effects in Strict CV are often dealt with by Incorporation (Ulfsbjorninn 2014; Faust and Ulfsbjorninn 2018), where a metrically significant empty V-slot is 'identified' by the adjacent filled V-slot projected. Balogne Bérces and Ulfsbjorninn (Chapter 8) connect the Current Southern British English process of Prevocalic Tenseness (PT), that is, monophthongisation, locating the language in the typology of 'long-vowels' distribution. The analysis of PT offers the use of universal fixed parameter hierarchies. This is a model of cross-linguistic variation based on Charette's formal typological distribution (Charette 1990, 1991, 1992). A revisitation of Charette's Licensor Projection (1990) leads Yoshida (Chapter 13) to propose a new tier where prosodic heads meet, where only the licensor Vs, for example, the head member of a 'long vowel', are projected. Analysis on Japanese licensor Vs and licensed Vs involved in geminates, 'long vowels', 'moraic' /N/ and devoiced high-vowels, is now reflected on English stress-assignment focusing on underlyingly long vowels.

References

Charette, M. (1990). 'License to govern'. *Phonology* 7, 233–53.
Charette, M. (1991). *Conditions on Phonological Government*. Cambridge: Cambridge University Press.
Charette, M. (1992). 'Polish and Mongolian meet Government Licensing'. *SOAS Working Papers in Linguistics and Phonetics* 2, 275–91.
Faust, N., and Ulfsbjorninn, S. (2018). 'Arabic stress in Strict CV, with no moras, no syllables, no feet and no extrametricality'. *The Linguistic Review* 35(4), 561–600.
Hayes, B. (1983). 'Compensatory lengthening in moraic phonology'. *Linguistic Inquiry* 20(2), 253–306.
Kahn, D. (1976). *Syllable-Based Generalizations in English Phonology*. Doctoral dissertation, Massachusetts Institute of Technology (MIT).
Kaye, J. D., and Charette, M. (1981). 'Tone sensitive rules in Dida'. *Studies in African Linguistics* 12(Suppl. 8), 82–5.
Kaye, J., and Lowenstamm, J. (1984). 'De la syllabicité'. In *La forme sonore du langage*, edited by F. Dell, J.-R. Vergnaud, and D. Hirst, 123–59. Paris: Hermann.
Kaye, J., Lowenstamm, J., and Vergnaud, J.-R. (1985). 'The internal structure of phonological representations: A theory of Charm and Government'. *Phonology Yearbook* 2, 305–28.
Kaye, J., Lowenstamm, J., and Vergnaud, J.-R. (1990). 'Constituent structure and government in phonology'. *Phonology* 7(2), 193–231.
Lowenstamm, J. (1996). 'CV as the only syllable type'. In *Current Trends in Phonology: Models and methods*, edited by J. Durand and B. Laks, 419–41. Salford: European Studies Research Institute.
McCarthy, J. (1979). *Formal Problems in Semitic Phonology and Morphology*. Doctoral dissertation, Massachusetts Institute of Technology (MIT).
McCarthy, J. (2005). 'The length of stem-final vowels in Colloquial Arabic'. In *Perspectives on Arabic Linguistics XVII–XVIII: Papers from the 17th and 18th Annual Symposia on Arabic Linguistics*, M. T. Alhawary and E. Benmamoun, 1–26. Amsterdam: John Benjamins.
Scheer, T. (2004). *A Lateral Theory of Phonology, Volume 1: What is CVCV and why should it be?* Studies in Generative Grammar 68. Berlin: De Gruyter.
Ulfsbjorninn, S. (2014). *A Field Theory of Stress*. Doctoral dissertation, SOAS, University of London.

8
Prevocalic Tenseness in English, binarity and the typology of long vowel distributions

Katalin Balogné Bérces and Shanti Ulfsbjorninn

Introduction

This chapter aims to provide a better understanding of binarity, long vowels, diphthongs, and hiatuses in the framework of Strict CV Phonology (Lowenstamm 1996; Scheer 2004). It offers an explanation for Prevocalic Tenseness (PT) in Standard Southern British English (SSBE) by embedding the SSBE facts into a working typology of positional restrictions on long vowel distributions. Our analysis draws on insight coming from two directions: on the one hand, we resort to a novel mechanism for formalising typological variation and implicational relationships: (Phonological) Parameter Hierarchies (Ulfsbjorninn 2014, 2017; Benz and Ulfsbjorninn 2018; cf. Vaxman 2018); on the other hand, we utilise a Strict CV interpretation of quantity: Incorporation (Ulfsbjorninn 2014; Faust and Torres-Tamarit 2017; Faust and Ulfsbjorninn 2018). This model provides an analysis where English vowel length (not tenseness) is contingent on English's binary phonological quantity. This resolves a long-standing paradox created by moraic theory: if English allows trimoraic syllables CVVC (in words like *shoulder*), why doesn't it allow CVVV(CV)?

The problem stems from the fact that, *a priori*, Strict CV cannot distinguish diphthongs from hiatuses or VC sequences due to its recasting of constituency into flat dependency (Scheer 2013). However, the PT-cum-monophthongisation, that is, vocalic spreading, data (see below, section 'VV in current SSBE') demands an interpretation of this contrast, since monophthongisation affects *V+schwa* sequences but not V:+*schwa* ones. Apparently only binary vocalic spreading is possible; however, as we show in the section 'Long vowel typology and the parameter hierarchy', below, this does not follow from the distributional restrictions on V:s. In English, a vowel may spread to any V position that is (a) licensed by a filled vowel, (b) in absolute word-final position, or (c) before a Final Empty Nucleus (FEN) (but not before a Medial Empty Nucleus). Accordingly, there would be nothing improper about having ternary monophthongisation.

To restrict monophthongisation in these forms, we first propose that (in English) Incorporation is obligatorily binary, even if 'superheavy' syllables are attested. Despite appearances, but without contradiction of any attested phonological behaviour, there are only *two* degrees of quantity in English: Heavy (VC, VV) > Light (V). Secondly, we propose the restriction that vowels can only spread into incorporated positions (cf. Arabic; Faust and Ulfsbjorninn 2018). Since incorporation is binary, this will make vowel lengthening binary, thereby cementing the state where English only has long tense prevocalic vowels. This interacts with an unrelated process whereby high vowels become tense when they spread into empty onsets forming glides (VCs), thus robbing English of its only other prevocalic lax vowels.

Background

VV in current SSBE

We deal with current SSBE (referred to as General British/GB in, for example, Cruttenden 2014; see 'Accent'[1] in Szigetvári and Lindsey 2013– for a sociolinguistic definition and a brief historical background, including its relation to classic RP).

Wells-era RP (for example, Wells 2008) exhibited an exceptionless static distribution affecting lexical vowel hiatuses, standardly called Prevocalic Tenseness (PT).

(1) Prevocalic Tenseness: in English the first member of a hiatus, if stressed, is always tense.

Accordingly, the first member of a hiatus was either a closing diphthong (as in *cr*a*yon*, *hi*a*tus*[2], *vo*y*age*, *No*a*m*, *flo*w*er*) or /iː, uː/ (phonetically of diphthongal quality: [ɪj] and [uw, ʉw], respectively; for example, *Le*o, *rui*n) (see Balogné Bérces and Szentgyörgyi 2006, 43).

However, in current SSBE, PT also applies to unstressed vowels. 'HAPPY-tensing' ([ɪ] → [i]; Wells, 1982, 257–8) is not only restricted to word/stem-final unstressed position but it has extended to pretonic prevocalic (for example, *re*a*ct*, *radi*a*tion*) and non-pretonic prevocalic (mostly, pre-schwa) positions (for example, *glori*o*us*), as well as to unstressed /ʊ/ (for example, *thank y<u>ou</u>; t<u>ui</u>tion, sit<u>ua</u>tion; infl<u>ue</u>nce*) (see Wells 2008). We summarise these developments in (2).

(2) a. **Pretonic tenseness** $\frac{KIT}{FOOT} \rightarrow \frac{FLEECE}{GOOSE}$ / __ V́

  b. **Pre-schwa tenseness** $\frac{KIT}{FOOT} \rightarrow \frac{FLEECE}{GOOSE}$ / __ ə

(1) and (2) combined, the result is a system where all prevocalic vowels, stressed and unstressed, are tense. Consequently, only tense vowels precede schwa. Moreover, in this variety, there are no prevocalic schwas, for example, *m<u>e</u>ow* */*mə.áu/, for independent reasons (see section 'Pretonic PT', below). Throughout the chapter, ungrammatical examples are shown marked by an asterisk (*).

Yet another process affects VV sequences in current SSBE. The centring diphthongs of classic RP (that is, tautosyllabic V+ə strings) variably undergo monophthongisation: descriptions do not agree on the extent of this change.[3] We identify SSBE as the variety in which all three relevant lexical sets have completed it (and which is, therefore, closest to the one modelled by Szigetvári and Lindsey 2013–). The processes in question are illustrated in (3)–(5).

(3) SQUARE eə or ɛə → [ɛː]   e.g., *stairs, p<u>a</u>rent, Hung<u>a</u>rian*

(4) NEAR   ɪə   → [ɪː][4]   e.g., *Lear/leer, h<u>e</u>ro, sinc<u>e</u>re*

(5) CURE   ʊə   → [oː]   e.g., *poor, sure, t<u>ou</u>rist, sec<u>u</u>rity*

Note that all the original centring diphthongs contain a lax vowel as the first term (due to the historical process 'Pre-schwa Laxing'; Wells 1982) – consequently, the monophthongisation eliminates lax vowel + schwa sequences. Also, as remarked by all major sources including Wells (1982, 288) and Cruttenden (2014, 84), the monophthongisation affects V+schwa sequences but not Vː+schwa ones, which leads to the crucial difference between diphthongs and hiatuses in (6).

(6) (a) [lɪə] → [lɪː]   *Lear/leer* vs. [liːə] *Leah*
    (b) [ʃʊə] → [ʃoː]   *sure*   vs. [sʉːə] *sewer*

In sum, it appears that in current SSBE, PT has gained such a general scope that it now also applies in all VV sequences irrespective of stress relations between (or of the (un)reduced nature of) the vowels involved. There are also reasons to assume that the monophthonging process in (3)–(5) is underway in order to enforce it by getting rid of the ill-formed lax vowel + schwa sequences, while retaining the lexical set contrast between diphthong and hiatus of RP.

This is hard to understand in English, however, because we could have expected smoothing to completely remove vowel-schwa sequences. Instead, smoothing in *sewer*-words is not even incipient.[5] This is also theoretically puzzling since a flat Strict CV (Scheer 2013) does not make an *a priori* distinction between diphthongs and hiatuses. One might imagine that the impediment would be a ban on super-heavy syllables; however, *prima facie* English does allow trimoraic syllables: *shoulder*, *mound*, *oinking* (verb), and a simple ban solely on ternary long vowels would appear circular or stipulative. Furthermore, from the Strict CV perspective, a ban on V:: cannot be constructed from English-specific settings of the typology of long vowel distributions.

Phonological parameter hierarchies and long vowel typology

Based on the formal typology that is original to Charette (1990, 1992), it is argued in Ulfsbjorninn (2014, 2017) and Benz and Ulfsbjorninn (2018) that the phonological parameter settings responsible for cross-linguistic structural differences are organised into universal implicational hierarchies.

We assume a CVCV skeleton, whose slots may be associated with melody (constituted by phonological expressions – see the segment symbols used as shorthand notation in our representations) either lexically or via spreading, or remain empty. Both spreading and emptiness are constrained by parametric requirements. Of immediate relevance to the present discussion are those parameters, referred to in the theory as 'licensing' (Scheer 2004), that are responsible for the well-formedness of long vowels.

There is a well-established cross-linguistic observation that if a language allows V:s then it universally allows V:s preceding a *filled* V (as in hypothetical [baːra]; see (7)) – we therefore conclude that the most fundamental licensor type for V spreading is a filled V that immediately follows the long vowel (Yoshida 1993; Kaye 1995; Scheer 2004).

(7)   **The site of a V:'s spreading is licensed by the following V**

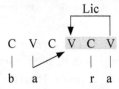

However, we note that cross-linguistically long vowels are also found in other environments, which we will assume require further parametric specification on Licensing. These include a V: before a Medial Empty Nucleus (MEN) producing forms like [ba:mØpi] (8a) and a V: before a Final Empty Nucleus (FEN), leading to forms like [ba:mØ] (8b); and whether a FEN can be the target of spreading as in [bama:] (9).

(8) **V: licensing by EN**
   a. *Medial Empty Nucleus* (MEN)
   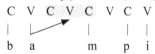
   b. *Final Empty Nucleus* (FEN)

(9) **FEN is part of the V:**

We will show that these environments are actually implicationally related to each other. To capture this formally, we propose that there is a fixed hierarchy among these V: licensing parameters.

Long vowel typology and the parameter hierarchy

The chart in (10) below summarises the positional restrictions on long vowels that we identify in the language types specified in the first column. The other three columns provide the environments (that is, licensing by MEN (8a), by FEN (8b), and FENinV: (9), respectively) in which language data are either attested (indicated with '✓') or not ('✗').

(10) **Positional restrictions on V**:

Lang \ Env	V:C.CV/# ba:mpi/Ø	V:C# ba:m	V:# bama:
Licensor type	MEN	FEN	FENinV:
Type 1			
Chugach, Italian	✗	✗	✗
Type 2			
Turkish	✗	✗	✓[6]
Hausa	✗	✗	✓
Type 3			
Icelandic	✗[7]	✓	✓
Type 4			
Cairene Arabic	✗	✓	✗
Type 5			
Palestinian Arabic	✓[8]	✓	✗
Type 6			
Hungarian[9], Pulaar	✓	✓	✓

On the basis of this typology, we establish a parameter hierarchy diagrammed in (11), where the stacked parameters are shown together with an example language.[10] Height in the hierarchy is graphically represented: higher-stacked parameters are positioned above lower-stacked ones to symbolise the dominance relation, from which the implications follow (lower implies higher). The highest parameter is *Filled* (see 7), located at the top of the hierarchy. Whenever the setting is 'yes' for a given parameter, the subordinate parameter begs to be set. Note that *Empty* implies *Filled*, and *Medial* implies *Final*.[11]

(11) **Parameter hierarchy for long vowels** (English settings <u>underlined</u>)

```
                        Filled ────── no (no V:) Spanish
                           │
no ──── FENinV: ┄┄┄┄ yes ┄┄┄┄ Final Empty ────── no (ba:ma only) Italian
         │                           │
        yes                         yes ┄┄┄┄┄┄ Medial Empty ──── no
      (maba:)                                        │        (maba:m)
     Hungarian                                      yes        Cairene
                                                 (ba:mpa)
                                                Hungarian
```

An additional function of the diagram in (11) is to indicate V: settings for English (in double underline). Given these parameter settings, a vowel in English may spread to any V position that is (a) licensed by a filled vowel; (b) in absolute word-final position; or (c) before a FEN but not before a MEN. A significant consequence of this for spreading is that, theoretically, (b) and (c) may combine in the way shown in (12): a FEN is capable of licensing spreading from V_1 to V_2 and receive docking melody at the same time. This creates the (false) grammaticality of ternary monophthongs.

(12) **Ternary monophthong ([lɪːː])**

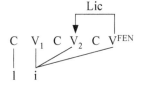

One way out of this problem is to simply stipulate that vocalic spreading is binary in English. However, an alternative solution that uses an independently justified (though apparently unrelated) mechanism is possible.

Why is long vowel spreading binary? Quantity

Quantity and stress in Strict CV

In Strict CV, stress is regulated by parameters on the projection of V-slots, filled or empty (Larsen 1998; Yoshida 1999; Harris and Gussmann 2002; Scheer and Szigetvári 2005; Charette 2008; Ulfsbjorninn 2014; Faust and Ulfsbjorninn 2018).

In English, all light nouns tend to have antepenultimate stress (for example, c[á]libre 'calibre'), and word-final singleton consonants (onsets) are 'extrametrical' (Charette 1984; Burzio 1994; Harris 1994; Balogné Bérces and Szentgyörgyi 2006), for example, p[ɛ́]lica<n> 'pelican'. But the language is quantity-sensitive, therefore heavy penultimate syllables tend to attract stress: mar[íː]na 'marina', cor[əu]na 'corona', pol[ɛ́n]ta 'polenta'. Final long vowels are always stressed, for example, jambor[íː] 'jamboree'.

Quantity effects in Strict CV are handled by the mechanism of Incorporation (Ulfsbjorninn 2014; Faust and Ulfsbjorninn 2018), where a metrically significant empty V-slot is 'identified' by the heightened projection of an adjacent filled V-slot. The V-slots of the incorporation environment/ domain are shown grey-shaded beneath.

(13) **Incorporation in Strict CV**
   a. Project a V to L3 if it precedes an empty V
   b. *polénta*

English does have (C)**VVC**.CV syllables; however, there is no phonological behaviour that identifies these as *super*-heavy. Although segmentally 'syllables' may be large, in terms of quantity, there is only heavy and light. Pulaar and Kashmiri, in contrast, do show that CVVCs are heavier than heavy syllables (CVV > CVC) since the former outcompete the latter in stress assignment. This shows that, formally, even empty V-slots that are not strictly local to a filled V can be incorporated. However, English incorporation is strictly local, resultantly quantity is strictly binary.

(14) **Incorporation (binary)**
   Incorporation is strictly local.

(15) **CVVC and incorporation:** [ʃɔuldə] *shoulder*

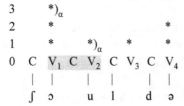

Given this metrical condition on quantity, we propose the following condition on vowel length in English (identical to that of Arabic, see Faust and Ulfsbjorninn 2018).

(16) Long vowel spreading only targets incorporated positions.

Effectively, vowel length is piggy-backing on quantity. This explains why smoothing targets 'diphthong' schwa (17a) but not hiatus schwa (17b).

(17) a. **[lɪː]** *Lear/leer*   b. **[liːə]** *Leah*

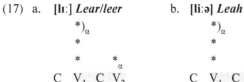

Pretonic PT

To complete the picture, we now turn to the cases of what we call *meow*-words (introduced in (2a) above) (18a). Here we observe that in SSBE these lax vowels have tensed and glided into the onset of the oncoming hiatus (18b). For some speakers, this is further accompanied by (near) loss of the vocalic position ('High vowel gliding' – 18c).

(18) **Pretonic PT**
 a. *mɪ.áu / *mɛ.áu / *mə.áu
 b. [miʲáw]   *meow*
    [tʉʷíʃən]   *tuition*
 c. [mjáw]   *meow*
    [twíʃən]   *tuition*

For reasons that are not clear, it seems that gliding is always accompanied by the tensing of the vowel. This may be perhaps related to the fact that effectively no language contrasts tense/lax consonantal glides (though as consonantal high vowel analogues such a contrast is conceivable).

(19) **Pretonic tenseness:** [miʲáw] 'meow'

Whatever the explanation, this tensing removes the only other source of pre-vocalic lax vowels in the phonological system (without entering into a discussion of triphthongs, which would take us too far afield).

Conclusion

PT is nearing completion as a process in SSBE. Some of this has been achieved through smoothing of pre-schwa diphthongs. However, no such smoothing is even incipient in hiatus+schwa sequences. Lax vowels are eliminated before schwa but the language forbids the creation of CVVV sequences thus preserving tense vowel+schwa hiatus sequences. Blocking CVVV sequences does not follow from typological or even language-specific bans on this syllable type. We claim, however, that vowel length in English is inextricably tied to quantity, and quantity in English is binary. Although English has CVVC syllables, these are just ordinarily heavy and there are no CVVVs. Moreover, Pretonic PT comes as a product of gliding into a stressed syllable.

(20)	**Contexts**		**Process**
Pretonic lax (e.g., *tuition*, *create*)	>	Tensing
Pre-schwa lax (e.g., *bear*, *beer*, *sure*)	>	Deletion of schwa
Pre-schwa tense (e.g., *Leah*)		

Distribution   Lax and tense before vowels   No lax before vowels

Notes

1. http://cube.elte.hu/accent.html.
2. It is irrelevant to the present discussion in what sense the first vowel of *hiatus* is stressed – it *is* an unreduced vowel.
3. Of the three lexical sets, Wells (1982, vol. 1, especially 3.2.7) only discusses [ɔː] as an RP pronunciation variant of CURE (referring to the change by various names incl. CURE-FORCE/THOUGHT Merger, Second FORCE Merger, CURE Lowering), the other two are centring diphthongs in his analysis. More recently and in contrast, Cruttenden (2014) considers the SQUARE vowel to have completed the monophthongisation, and already transcribes it as /ɛː/, noting that '[o]lder speakers of GB may have a diphthong [ɛə]' (Cruttenden 2014, 118); the other two are treated in his system as centring diphthongs (2014, 84–5), and the monophthongal pronunciations are only mentioned as marginal variants (2014, 154, 156). CURE monophthonging is considered highly variable in Cruttenden (2014, 156), and the variation in lexical incidence observed with CURE is also mentioned by Wells (1982, vol. 2, 4.1.5). In Szigetvári and Lindsey (2013–), all three are long monophthongs, transcribed as shown in (3)–(5), with the note in the 'Accent' section that in CURE, '[w]hen preceded by a palatal consonant, many speakers have [øː], for example, *Europe*, *security*, *during*, *mature*'.
4. [ɪjə] when heavily accentuated. Classified as a 'broad London' pronunciation in Cruttenden (2014, 154).
5. In some cases, such as *theatre* [θiːətə or θiɛtə or θɪːtə] there *is* variation in the lexical set of the item; however, smoothing only occurs in cases where this token has changed into the NEAR-set (diphthong, never directly from a hiatus source) *th*[iː(ː)]*tre*. In a later change, some speakers with NEAR smoothing have begun to lax the Leah set.
6. Only in monosyllables.
7. However, the language does allow mysterious light rising diphthongs (Árnason 2011).
8. These are only permitted in derived words, however.
9. Length in this environment can be extremely restricted. However, we are only looking at *positional* environments, not melodic ones. The presence of even one V: in this syllable structure configuration would be enough to set the parameter to <yes>.

10. These are used in syntax (Baker 2001; Biberauer et al. 2013; Sheehan 2014; *pace* Boeckx and Leivada 2013).
11. Interestingly, the implicational statement 'Empty implies Filled' opens the door for third factor explanations. First, Emptiness is more marked than Filledness considering that phonology is a module devoted to externalisation (Chomsky et al. 2002; Chomsky 2005) and therefore phonological objects that will receive no phonetic interpretation need extra licensing and extra stipulations in the grammar (not less). Cyran (2003) discusses complexity scales and markedness in a closely related way. However, Medial implies Final does not seem to follow so easily from general principles, which begs the question: how did it become this way? Crucially these questions can only be asked with such clarity due to the formalism employed in the analysis of the typology (specifically Strict CV principles). In an instance of McCarthy's famous edict: 'if the representations are right, the rules will follow' (1988, 84).

References

Árnason, K. (2011). *The Phonology of Icelandic and Faroese*. Oxford: Oxford University Press.
Baker, M. C. (2001). *The Atoms of Language: The mind's hidden rules of grammar*. New York: Basic Books.
Balogné Bérces, K., and Szentgyörgyi, Sz. (2006). *The Pronunciation of English*. Budapest: Bölcsész Konzorcium.
Balogné Bérces, K., and Ulfsbjorninn, S. (2018a). 'Prevocalic Tenseness in English, binarity and the typology of long vowel distributions'. Conference presentation, *The 26th Manchester Phonology Meeting (mfm26)*, 24–26 May 2018, Manchester.
Balogné Bérces, K., and Ulfsbjorninn, S. (2018b). 'English Prevocalic Tenseness and the typology of vowel length in Strict CV'. Conference presentation, *Réseau Français de Phonologie (RFP) 2018*, 27–29 June 2018, Paris.
Benz, J., and Ulfsbjorninn, S. (2018). 'Improving the formalism of phonological parameter hierarchies'. Conference talk, *Phonological Theory Agora (PTA) Workshop, Generative Linguistics in the Old World (GLOW) 41*, 10–14 April 2018, Budapest.
Biberauer, T., Roberts, I., and Sheehan, M. (2013). 'No-choice parameters and the limits of syntactic variation'. In *Proceedings of the 31st West Coast Conference on Formal Linguistics (WCCFL 31)*, edited by R. E. Santana-LaBarge, 46–55. Somerville, MA: Cascadilla Press.
Boeckx, C., and Leivada, E. (2013). 'Entangled parametric hierarchies: Problems for an overspecified Universal Grammar'. *PLoS ONE* 8(9), e72357.
Burzio, L. (1994). *Principles of English Stress*. Cambridge: Cambridge University Press.
Charette, M. (1984). 'The appendix in parametric phonology'. *Studies in African Linguistics* Supplement 9, 49–53.
Charette, M. (1990). 'License to govern'. *Phonology* 7, 233–53.
Charette, M. (1992). 'Polish and Mongolian meet Government Licensing'. *SOAS Working Papers in Linguistics and Phonetics* 2, 275–91.
Charette, M. (2008). 'The vital role of the trochaic foot in explaining Turkish word endings'. *Lingua* 118, 46–65.
Chomsky, N. (2005). 'Some simple Evo-Devo theses'. Unpublished manuscript, MIT.
Chomsky, N., Hauser, M. D., and Fitch, W. T. (2002). 'The faculty of language: What is it, who has it, and how did it evolve?'. *Science* 298, 1569–79.
Cruttenden, A. (2014). *Gimson's Pronunciation of English*. 8th edition. London: Routledge.
Cyran, E. (2003). *Complexity Scales and Licensing in Phonology*. 1st edition. Lublin: Wydawnictwo KUL.
Faust, N., and Torres-Tamarit, F. (2017). 'Stress and final /n/ deletion in Catalan: Combining Strict CV and OT'. *Glossa* 2(1), 63.
Faust, N., and Ulfsbjorninn, S. (2018). 'Arabic stress in Strict CV, with no moras, no syllables, no feet and no extrametricality'. *The Linguistic Review* 35(4), 561–600.
Harris, J. (1994). *English Sound Structure*. Oxford: Blackwell.
Harris, J., and Gussmann, E. (2002). 'Word-final onsets'. *UCL Working Papers in Linguistics* 14, 1–14.
Kaye, J. (1995). 'Derivations and interfaces'. In *Frontiers of Phonology: Atoms, structures, derivations*, edited by J. Durand and F. Katamba, 289–332. London: Longman.

Larsen, B. U. (1998). 'Vowel length, Raddoppiamento Sintattico and the selection of the definite article in Italian'. In *Langues et Grammaire II–III: Phonologie*, edited by P. Sauzet, 87–102. Paris: Université Paris 8.

Lowenstamm, J. (1996). 'CV as the only syllable type'. In *Current Trends in Phonology: Models and methods*, edited by J. Durand and B. Laks, 419–41. Salford: European Studies Research Institute.

McCarthy, J. J. (1988). 'Feature geometry and dependency: A review'. *Phonetica* 45, 84–108.

Scheer, T. (2004). *A Lateral Theory of Phonology. Vol 1: What is CVCV, and why should it be?* Berlin: De Gruyter.

Scheer, T. (2013). 'Why phonology is flat: The role of concatenation and linearity'. *Language Sciences* 39, 54–74.

Scheer, T., and Szigetvári, P. (2005). 'Unified representations for stress and the syllable'. *Phonology* 22(1), 37–75.

Sheehan, M. (2014). 'Towards a parameter hierarchy for alignment'. In *Proceedings of WCCFL 31*, edited by R. E. Santana-LaBarge, 399–408. Somerville, MA: Cascadilla Press.

Szigetvári, P., and Lindsey, G. (2013–). *CUBE: Current British English searchable transcriptions.* http://cube.elte.hu (accessed 6 February 2023).

Ulfsbjorninn, S. (2014). *A Field Theory of Stress: The role of empty nuclei in stress systems*. Doctoral dissertation, SOAS, University of London.

Ulfsbjorninn, S. (2017). 'Markedness and formalising phonological representations'. In *Beyond Markedness in Formal Phonology*, edited by B. D. Samuels, 153–90. Amsterdam: John Benjamins.

Vaxman, A. (2018). 'Contribution of parameter dependencies to descriptive adequacy of accent theory'. Conference talk, *Réseau Français de Phonologie (RFP) 16*, 27–29 June 2018, Paris.

Wells, J. C. (1982). *Accents of English*. Cambridge: Cambridge University Press.

Wells, J. C. (2008). *Longman Pronunciation Dictionary*. 3rd edition. London: Pearson Longman.

Yoshida, S. (1993). 'Licensing of empty nuclei: The case of Palestinian vowel harmony'. *The Linguistic Review* 10, 127–59.

Yoshida, Y. (1999). *On Pitch Accent Phenomena in Standard Japanese*. The Hague: Holland Academic Graphics.

9
Vowel length and prominence in Cairene Arabic
Radwa Fathi

Introduction

Cairene Arabic implements the characteristic alternating pattern documented in (1). The usual view (implicit in the representations below) is that the final vowels in the words at the left in (1) are short whereas the same vowels are long in the various environments on the right.

(1)
i. ʕáša   'dinner'   vs. ʕašá:k (ʕaša+k)   'your (masc.sg.) dinner'
ii. kálti   'you (fem.sg.) ate' vs. makaltí:š (ma+kalti+ š)   'you (fem.sg.) didn't eat'
iii. rámu   'they threw'   vs. ramú:ha (ramu+ha)   'they threw it (fem.)'

Some process is evidently at work in (1). Repeated application of that process is illustrated in (2).

(2)
i.   kátabu   'they wrote'   (katab-u)
ii. katabú:ha   'they wrote it (fem.)'   (katab-u+ha)
iii. katabuhá:li   'they wrote it (fem.) to me'   (katab-u+ha+l+i)
iv. makatabuhalí:š   'they did not write it (fem.) to me' (ma+katab-u+ha+l+i+š)

One question raised by the data in (1) and (2) is the directionality of the process: are the alternating vowels underlyingly short and lengthened in a specific context? Or are they underlyingly long and shortened under definable conditions?

Watson (2002) argues that vowels behaving as shown above are underlyingly short and lengthen (cyclically) before a suffix on account of a rule of Pre-Suffix Vowel Lengthening, for example, /kátabu+ha/ → [katabú:ha], /katab-u+ha+li/ → [katabuhá:li], etc. Pre-Suffix Vowel Lengthening in turn feeds a rule of Unstressed Vowel Shortening which forces all vowels lengthened on a previous cycle to resume their original brevity; thus [katab*u*há:li], not *[katab*u*:há:li], [makatabuhalí:š], not *[makatab*u*:ha:lí:š], etc.[1]

McCarthy (2005) rejects Pre-suffix Vowel Lengthening, arguing that the final vowels targeted by the process illustrated in (1) and (2) are underlyingly long, then shortened in the appropriate environment.

I accept McCarthy's view that the alternating vowels are underlyingly long, though I will argue that they do not undergo shortening. My claim, in other words, is that the alternations in (1) and (2) are not length alternations at all. In the next section, I review McCarthy's arguments. In the next two sections, I re-evaluate the evidence, and develop the idea that 'length' has very little to do with the alternations in (1) and (2). Pitch-induced prominence, I claim, is key to their understanding. In the section that follows this, I discuss an empirical consequence of my proposal.[2]

McCarthy's proposal

McCarthy's argumentation proceeds in two steps. In a first step, he shows based on theory internal considerations how the underlying length of pre-suffixal vowels follows as a theorem from OT. The second step consists of matching this result with evidence. I briefly review two of the empirical arguments adduced by McCarthy in the course of that second step.

Argument 1

Syncope deletes unstressed high vowels in environment VC_CV, as in for example, *húwwa m_dárris* 'he (is a) teacher' (< /húwwa + mudárris/) or *šír_b il?áhwa* 'he drank the coffee' (< /šírib + il-?áhwa/). Word-final unstressed high vowels, however, never delete in that very same context; thus, *kátabu gawá:b* 'they wrote (a) letter', and never **kátab_gawá:b* and *tiktíbi gawá:b* 'you (fem.sg.) write (a) letter', and never *tiktíb_gawá:b*. According to McCarthy, the fact that the vowels of the last two examples resist syncope is a direct reflection of their underlying length (McCarthy, 2005, 18).

Argument 2

Here, I quote from McCarthy (2005, 20) *verbatim*:

(3) A [third] point in support of an analysis with underlying stem-final long vowels is the existence in Cairene of a derived contrast between

tense and lax short high vowels (Mitchell 1956: 10–11, 112). Long i: and u: are pronounced as the tense vowels [i:] and [u:], while their short counterparts i and u are pronounced as the lax vowels [ɪ] and [ʊ].[3] But when a surface short vowel is derived from an underlying long vowel, it is pronounced as tense.[4] For instance, šilí:h 'take (fem.) it (masc.) away!' is pronounced as [šilí:h] and not *[šɪlí:h]. That is because the vowel of the first syllable is underlyingly long and has been shortened in an unstressed syllable, as shown by forms like ši:l 'take away (masc.)'. The same goes for [síbha] 'leave it (fem.)!', where /i:/ has been shortened in a closed syllable.

According to Mitchell, final short i and u are also pronounced as tense: [ší:li] and not [ší:lɪ] for 'take away (fem.)' […], this observation suggests that final vowels are tense because they are underlyingly long.

McCarthy's arguments are quite insightful. The fact that stem final high vowels defy syncope and retain their height and tenseness is fully consistent with the conjecture that they are underlyingly long and fully inconsistent with the alternative. But, as McCarthy notes, his two arguments involve a paradox: those vowels behave just like long vowels, as he points out, but they are *not* long. I intend to reappraise McCarthy's interpretation, but before I do this, a point of fact demands attention.

McCarthy's second argument above mentions two statements from Mitchell (1956):

(4) The qualities of *ii* and *i* in *ší:li* 'take away (fem.)!', *šilí:h* 'take (fem.) it (masc.) away!', *siib* 'leave!' and *síbha* 'leave it (fem.)!' are substantially the same, and the *i* of, for example, *síbha* is not pronounced as *i* in, for example, *bint* 'girl' (Mitchell 1956, 112).

ii is regularly shortened in certain contexts, for example, *šilhum* 'remove them!', but the sound of the vowel remains as for *ii* (Mitchell 1956, 10–11).

Mitchell is quite right about *ii* and *i* being the same in *ší:li*, in *šilí:h*, and in *siib*. On the other hand, he is entirely incorrect about the quality of the first vowel in *šílhum* or *síbha*: that vowel is definitely not the same as the first vowel in šilí:h or the last vowel in *ší:li*; rather, it *is* the same as the vowel in [bent] (or [bɪnt]).[5] Indeed, a rule exceptionlessly shortens and lowers long high vowels in non-final closed syllables: /ši:l+hum/ → [šelhum] (or [šɪlhum]), /si:b+ha/ → [sébha] (or [sɪbha]).

That correction will prove important in the next section. We can now return to the evidence considered by McCarthy and re-evaluate it.

Re-evaluating the evidence

How can we detect brevity? The data discussed so far provides two unambiguous indications of how true brevity is reflected in the pronunciation of underlying high vowels. First, if the vowel is underlyingly short, it redundantly lowers to the mid-range as in, for example, /zimi:l/ → [zemí:l] (or [zɪmí:l]) 'colleague', /zibu:n/ → [zebú:n] (or [zɪbú:n]) 'client', etc. Second, when the vowel is underlyingly long and ends up in a non-final closed syllable, it shortens. This is one of the most solidly established generalisations in the phonology of the Semitic languages. Shortening redundantly entails lowering to the mid-range, as could be seen with the example of, for example, [sébha] (< /si:b+ha/). In neither case does height survive. Evidently, a Cairene Arabic vowel cannot maintain its underlying height whether *it was short to begin with* or *if it underwent shortening*. I submit that (5) holds.

(5) Height is licensed by length

In light of this, what can we make of the first vowel of, for example, *sibí:(h)* 'leave (fem.sg.) him!' or the last vowel of, for example, *sí:bi* 'leave (fem. sg.)!' which have retained their height and their tenseness even though they supposedly lost all length? One approach is to simply label that phenomenon 'opaque', a mere observation which leaves the problem intact. An alternative is to question whether those vowels really lost their length and consider the possibility that they behave as long vowels because they *are* long vowels. I will explore the hypothesis in (6).

(6) a. Height is licensed by length (5).
     b. The vowels underscored in *sibí:(h)* and *sí:bi* have retained their height.
     c. Therefore, they are long.

In the rest of this chapter, I explore the consequences of a strong version of (6c):

(7) The grammar of Cairene Arabic includes no rule of unstressed vowel shortening.

At first sight, and in view of the facts of (1) and (2), arguing for (7) looks like an uphill battle. However, in order to evaluate the plausibility of (7), we have to compare the weight of the various pieces of evidence available to us. With /zimi:l/ → [zemí:l], we have incontrovertible indication that its first vowel is short. Not only does it lower, it syncopates at the first opportunity: *ya z_mí:li* 'O my colleague!' (< /ya + zimi:l+i/). With /si:b+ha/ → [sébha], we are dealing with one of the sturdiest phenomena of Semitic phonology, the shortening of a long vowel in a non-final closed syllable. This is all hard phonological evidence.

When it comes to the putative brevity of the first vowel in *sibí:(h)* and the last vowel in *sí:bi*, phonological evidence clearly militates *against* their brevity. Not only do they retain their height and tenseness, but they also cannot syncopate as short vowels do; hence *kónti sibí:h* 'you (fem.sg.) should have let him' and not **kónti s_bí:h* (< /kúnti + sibí:h/). The only reason to insist nevertheless that those vowels are 'short' lies outside the realm of phonological behaviour. It is the auditory percept that they 'sound' short, for instance when compared to the stressed vowels (underscored) in the same words, *sibí:(h)* and *sí:bi*. But to draw any conclusion from that auditory difference we would have to be sure that what we hear in *sibí:(h)* and *sí:bi* is pure 'vowel length'. This is precisely what I intend to question.

In the next section, I claim that the difference is one of prominence, not one of length.

Prominence, not length

It has long been recognised that Cairene Arabic stress assigns dramatic saliency to one single syllable per phonological word. The correlates of saliency are melodic height,[6] loudness, and duration (Mitchell, 1975, 94). In a meticulous and detailed study, Hellmuth (2006) analyses the system as a stress-accent system with postlexical intonational pitch accents. She construes pitch-accent induced salience in terms of a Low High contour tone (henceforth LH) associated to the metrical foot and eventually marking the stressed syllable.

Hellmuth's instrumental findings show how the LH melody differentially associates to syllables depending on their geometry, CVC, CV, or CVV. Her examples are *mánga* 'mango', *málek* 'king', and *má:leħ* 'salty' (noted *málik* and *má:liħ* by Hellmuth). In all three cases, the Low tone aligns with the onset (or very shortly thereafter). On CVC syllables, the High tone aligns shortly after the coda (*mánga*). In CV syllables, H aligns shortly after the middle consonant (*málik*). On CVV syllables, by contrast, H aligns a bit before the middle consonant (*ma:liħ*).

Abstracting away from fine-grained phonetic distinctions, a representation of a type familiar from the description of tone languages can be inferred from Hellmuth's results:[7]

(8) a.   b.   c.

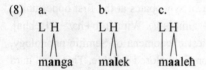

All stressed syllables in (8) are salient as against unstressed syllables. However, the configuration in (8c) stands out against the other two: the high tone is entirely absorbed by vocalic material. For easier reference, I call such a syllable *prominent* as against all other syllables. This is where pitch will raise highest, where loudness will be maximal, and duration most increased. What we hear in stressed long vowels, in other words, is *not* their phonological length but the total bundle of properties I just mentioned, and which culminate in prominence. If this is correct, a comparison between the two vowels of, for example, *sí:bi* can only tell us which is prominent and which is not; it does not tell us that the non-prominent one is short. Indeed, I claim that the two vowels of *sí:bi* or *sibí:h* differ in prominence but are equally long. For graphic convenience, I note prominence $\mathscr{P}$, where $\mathscr{P}$ stands for the configuration exemplified in (8c) and reproduced as (9a). All vowels associated with that configuration will be marked $+\mathscr{P}$, all others (unstressed long and stressed or unstressed short) $-\mathscr{P}$. This is shown in (9) with some of the examples discussed earlier. Stressed syllables are noted in bold italics. In (9f, g), I show how the vowels of *sí:bi* or *sibí:h* differ in prominence but not in length.

(9) a.   b.   c.   d.   e.   f.   g.

```
    L H
    | /\
    C V V    ma̱nga   ma̱lek   maa̱leh   katabuu̱haa    sii̱bii       siibii̱(h)
             -𝒫 -𝒫   -𝒫 -𝒫   +𝒫 -𝒫    -𝒫 -𝒫 +𝒫 -𝒫   +𝒫 -𝒫       -𝒫 +𝒫
```

On this view, $+\mathscr{P}$ vowels stand out against all others. My system thus implements the same dichotomy as in classical accounts by Watson or McCarthy but on the basis of prominence, not length. All length distinctions are preserved. In a 'short and opaque' account, it is an accident that such opaque vowels are confined to open syllables. In my proposal, there is nothing opaque about the 'short' high vowels which behave as if they were long. They *are* long (whether they be $+\mathscr{P}$ as in *sí:bi* or $-\mathscr{P}$ as in *sí:bi*) and they perfectly fit the classical Semitic pattern whereby long vowels exclusively occur in open syllables.

In the next section, I examine a prediction of my proposal.

Duals

A noun in Cairene can be singular, dual, or plural. The dual is formed by the suffixation of +eːn, for example, *kalb* 'dog', *kalbéːn* 'two dogs'. The dual suffix +éːn always carries main stress. According to the view put forward in the previous section, the prominence of +éːn will systematically result in the non-prominence of all other vowels of the noun. This can be seen in (10) where *diːn* is +𝒫 in (10a.i), but demoted to –𝒫 when appended by +éːn (10b.i).[8] My proposal being that 𝒫-marking exclusively encodes prominence and leaves all other properties of the vowels intact, I predict that vowels marked –𝒫 in (10b) will remain unchanged under dual suffixation. That is, the duals of all forms will have the exact same stem vowel as their corresponding singulars.

(10)

	a. Singular			b. Dual				
	+𝒫					–𝒫 +𝒫		
i.	/diːn/	[díːn]	'religion'	/diːn+eːn/	→	/diːneːn/	[dinéːn]	'two religions'
ii.	/nuːr/	[núːr]	'light'	/nuːr+eːn/	→	/nuːreːn/	[nuréːn]	'two lights'
iii.	/baːb/	[báːb]	'door'	/baːb+eːn/	→	/baːbeːn/	[babéːn]	'two doors'
iv.	/beːt/	[béːt]	'house'	/beːt+eːn/	→	/beːteːn/	[betéːn]	'two houses'
v.	/deːn/	[déːn]	'debt'	/deːn+eːn/	→	/deːneːn/	[denéːn]	'two debts'
vi.	/yoːm/	[yóːm]	'day'	/yoːm+eːn/	→	/yoːmeːn/	[yoméːn]	'two days'
vii.	/ṣoːt/	[ṣóːt]	'voice, vote'	/ṣoːt+eːn/	→	/ṣoːteːn/	[ṣotéːn]	'two voices, votes'

Moreover, consider a minimal pair such as *diːn*/*deːn* 'religion/debt'. Because the quantity (and therefore the quality) of stem vowels is unaffected by dual formation, the contrast will be reproduced in the dual forms, hence [dinéːn] 'two religions' versus [denéːn] 'two debts'.[9,10] Both predictions are in accordance with the facts.

My account contradicts Broselow's (1976, 18ff.). Broselow asserts that unstressed long mid vowels shorten and rise to high. Thus, she reports *yuméːn* and *bitéːn* for the duals of *yoːm* and *beːt*, respectively. As well, she predicts that /diːn+eːn/ and /deːn+eːn/ will neutralise into [dinéːn]. In both cases, this is at odds with my experience with the language, but more significantly with the information gathered in countless interviews with other native speakers. The confusion, I believe, can be traced back to Broselow's reliance (Broselow 1976, xix) on material from Lehn and Abboud's *Beginning Cairo Arabic* (Lehn and Abboud 1965). Lehn and Abboud consistently ignore the distinction emphasised by McCarthy in (3) above and in Note 4. Because their crude orthographic system makes no room for short mid vowels, the only graphic symbols available to Lehn and Abboud are *i* and *u*, respectively. Evidently, [yumé:n] or [bité:n] with initial high vowels are mere artefacts of Lehn and Abboud's inadequate notational system.[11]

Conclusion

A number of notions about vowel length and brevity in Cairene Arabic have been taken for granted for decades. Here, I have explicitly challenged one such notion, viz. 'length is what we hear in, for example, *katabu:ha*'. I have argued on the contrary that what we hear in that case is Prominence, not length. My proposal also carries an implicit challenge of most accounts of the stress assignment system of Cairene. Indeed, in most accounts *katabu:ha* has penultimate stress because of its outstanding length. In my account, the penultimate vowel of *katabu:ha* stands out (as prominent) because it carries stress.[12]

Notes

1. Note the asymmetrical role of stress in Watson's account: stress plays no role in the lengthening of vowels, but its absence plays a crucial role in their shortening.
2. The claims I make in this chapter are intended to cover non-low vowels, both front and back. But because of space limitations, the discussion has been confined to front vowels.
3. For the sake of accuracy, I follow Harrell (and many others) in representing as [e] the vowel noted [ɪ] by McCarthy. Harrell (1957, 53) describes it as (in): « Free variation from somewhat below [ɪ] to a lax [e] ». Because this issue is peripheral to the main point of this chapter, I often quote examples in both versions, for example, «...[bent] (or [bɪnt])...».
4. Recognising this difference goes a long way towards correcting an unfortunate practice which goes back to the elementary manuals of Lehn and Abboud (1965) and Abdel-Massih (1974), and still mars virtually all generative work on Cairene: these authors ignore (Lehn and Abboud) or deny (Abdel-Massih) the distinction mentioned by McCarthy. As a result, they are incapable of representing some of the most basic surface contrasts, for example, the difference between the surface vocalic melodies in, for example, [šili:h] and [zemí:l] (or [zɪmí:l]) 'colleague' both identically noted by them as CiCí:C; or in [kálbe bónni] (or [kálbɪ bónni]) 'a brown dog' versus [kálbɪ bónni] 'my dog is brown', an example adduced by Hafez (1996, 8). Note how Hafez renders the epenthetic vowel in [kálbe bónni] as [e]. So does Harrell (1957, 60) in *sette kwayyesa* 'a good lady' versus *settɪ kwayyesa* 'my grandmother is good'. On this point, see also Mitchell (1993, 128) describing /i/: "the norm is a front spread vowel, half close in, for example, Egyptian Arabic *fikr* 'idea, thought', *fíhim* 'he understood'". In (Mitchell 1990, 17), his example of a front half close vowel is French fée [fe] 'fairy'.
5. The same error is repeated in Mitchell (1962, 24), though not in Mitchell (1990; 1993).
6. On melodic height, Harrell (1957, 17–18) reports possible differences of up to one octave between the melodic height of a stressed and an unstressed vowel.
7. While this section owes much to Hellmuth (2006), the interpretation of her work is my own.
8. The careful reader will have noted that, unlike all other +𝒫 syllables, the syllable of the dual marker seems to involve a coda. In reality, word-final CVVC syllables function as penultimate open syllables CVV-C(v)# in Egyptian Arabic as in many other Semitic languages.
9. As is the case with all subtle distinctions, the [diné:n]/[dené:n] contrast will be lost in very fast speech.
10. Conversely, /di:n+na/ 'our religion' and /de:n+na/ 'our debt' do neutralise, but into [denna] (or [dɪnna]), not *[dinna]. Harrell (1957, 55) *does* note /dɪnna/ with *i* but it must be kept in mind that Harrell's examples are quoted in their 'phonemic' form (Harrell 1957, 6), *not* as they are realised on

the surface. His description of the *phonetic* form of underlying (or, in his terms, 'phonemic') /i/ in closed syllables was reproduced in Note 3.
11. Lehn and Abboud, and Abdel-Massih are actually isolated in their unfortunate practice of noting *yuméːn* and *bitéːn*. Indeed, most authors note *yoméːn* and *betéːn* with no modification of the original quality of the initial mid vowel for example, Spitta-Bey (1880, 132), Willmore (1905, 238, 322), Jomier and Khouzam (1964, 37), Mitchell (1956) on a dozen occasions, Jomier (1976, 111), Hinds and Badawi (1986, 965).
12. On this, see Fathi (in preparation).

References

Abdel-Massih, E. (1974). *Introduction to Egyptian Arabic*. Ann Arbor: Center for Near Eastern and North African Studies, University of Michigan.
Broselow, E. (1976). *The Phonology of Egyptian Arabic*. Doctoral dissertation, University of Massachusetts.
Fathi, R. (in preparation) *Stress in Cairene Arabic*.
Hafez, O. (1996). 'Phonological and morphological integration of loanwords into Egyptian Arabic'. *Égypte/Monde Arabe* (27–8), 383–410. https://doi.org/10.4000/ema.1958.
Harrell, R. S. (1957). *The Phonology of Colloquial Egyptian Arabic*. New York: American Council of Learned Societies.
Hellmuth, S. (2006). *Intonational Pitch Accent Distribution in Egyptian Arabic*, Doctoral dissertation, School of Oriental and African Studies, University of London.
Hinds, M., and Badawi, E. (1986). *A Dictionary of Egyptian Arabic*. Beirut: Librairie du Liban.
Jomier, J., and Khouzam, J. (1964). *Manuel d'arabe égyptien*. Paris: Editions Klinksieck.
Jomier, J. (1976). *Lexique pratique français-arabe*. Cairo: Institut français d'archéologie orientale du Caire.
Lehn, W., and Abboud, P. (1965). *Beginning Cairo Arabic*. Austin: The Middle East Center, The University of Texas.
McCarthy, J. (2005). 'The length of stem-final vowels in Colloquial Arabic'. In *Perspectives on Arabic Linguistics XVII–XVIII: Papers from the 17th and 18th Annual Symposia on Arabic Linguistics*, edited by M. T. Alhawary and E. Benmamoun, 1–26. Amsterdam: John Benjamins.
Mitchell, T. F. (1956). *An Introduction to Egyptian Colloquial Arabic*. Oxford: Oxford University Press.
Mitchell, T. F. (1962). *Colloquial Arabic, the Living Language of Egypt*. London: The English Universities Press.
Mitchell, T. F. (1975). *Principles of Firthian Linguistics*. London: Longman.
Mitchell, T. F. (1990). *Pronouncing Arabic 1*. Oxford: Oxford University Press.
Mitchell, T. F. (1993). *Pronouncing Arabic 2*. Oxford: Oxford University Press.
Spitta-Bey, W. (1880). *Grammatik des arabischen Vulgärdialectes von Aegypten*. Leipzig: J.C. Hinrichs'sche Buchhandlung.
Watson, J. (2002). *The Phonology and Morphology of Arabic*. Oxford: Oxford University Press.
Willmore, J. S. (1905). *The Spoken Arabic of Egypt*. London: David Nutt.

10
#sC in stereo: a dichotic-listening study of initial clusters in Cypriot Greek
John Harris and Faith Chiu

Introduction

It was once widely held as a matter of self-evident truth that any consonant cluster at the beginning of a word forms a syllable onset.[1] At least for languages that impose phonotactic constraints on initial clusters, such as English, there is little reason to doubt that this assumption is correct for sequences of rising sonority (such as in *play*, *grow*, *flow*). However, the assumption has always sat awkwardly with sequences consisting of a sibilant plus consonant ('#sC'), as in *spin*, *sting*, *skin*. One long-acknowledged reason has to do with phonological distribution: in the relevant languages, #sC is typically alone in defying virtually all the phonotactic restrictions that otherwise apply to initial clusters, such as the requirement that complex syllable onsets rise in sonority.

There is mounting evidence from various other sources that confirms the syllabically anomalous status of #sC. This evidence, which we summarise below, includes the behaviour of #sC in morphophonemic alternations, first language acquisition, and speech production. In this chapter, we turn our attention to evidence from speech perception.

Is the anomalous nature of #sC due to some property specific to sibilants or to some more general property of clusters that fall in sonority? We investigate this question by means of a dichotic-listening experiment. Previous studies using this methodology show that English listeners, when simultaneously presented with words containing different initial singleton consonants to each ear, hear certain pairs as fusing into single-word percepts, but not others. Pairs consisting of an obstruent (for example, *pay*) and a liquid (for example, *lay*) are readily fused and sequenced in the order obstruent-liquid (*play*), that is, as a complex rising onset (Cutting and Day 1975).

However, pairs consisting of [s] (*sigh*) and another consonant (*pie*) are much less likely to be fused (Chiu et al. 2016).

To understand whether sibilance uniquely accounts for the non-fusing behaviour of #sC, we need to investigate languages which, like English, impose phonotactic restrictions on word-initial clusters but which, unlike English, also allow non-rising clusters to begin with nonsibilants. Cypriot Greek fits the bill. It has a range of word-initial falling-sonority clusters that includes not only #sC but also sequences starting with nonsibilant fricatives (#fC), such as [fc] and [xt]. Morphophonemic evidence, which we detail below, indicates that #sC and #fC in Cypriot Greek pattern together and are not syllabified in the same way as rising-sonority clusters.

Native Cypriot Greek listeners were dichotically presented with pairs of nonwords containing different initial singleton consonants in varying sonority combinations and then asked to report what they heard. In line with previous studies of English, obstruent-liquid pairs were found to favour fusion and, when fused, were more likely to be sequenced as rising clusters. In contrast, neither of these biases was observed in fricative-stop pairs. Tellingly, the latter result was found for both sibilant and nonsibilant fricatives. This co-patterning is consistent with the shared morphophonemic behaviour of #sC and #fC and suggests that neither is syllabified like rising onset clusters. It also suggests that sibilance is not special and that there is some more general constraint disfavouring the syllabification of falling clusters as complex onsets.

In the next section we review the evidence against syllabifying #sC as a complex onset and consider what properties might make it syllabically anomalous. In the third section we describe the morphophonemic behaviour of initial clusters in Cypriot Greek. The fourth section summarises the methodology and general findings of previous dichotic listening experiments. In the fifth section we present our dichotic listening study of Cypriot Greek. The final section lays out our main conclusions.

#sC

Syllabifying #sC

In what follows, we will use the conventional notion of sonority to describe the various phonotactic configurations found in word-initial consonant clusters. This is purely a matter of descriptive convenience and is not meant to imply an assumption that sonority corresponds to some independent phonetic property (for differing views on this matter, see Parker 2012).

Our interest in #sC will be focused entirely on clusters of falling sonority, that is, clusters consisting of sibilant plus stop (for example, [sp, st, sk]). We will have nothing to say here about rising-sonority clusters consisting of sibilant plus sonorant, such as are found in English (for example, *slide, snide, smile*). There are clear phonological differences between these two types of cluster. For one thing, some languages permit initial sibilants to be followed by a stop but not by a sonorant.

Besides the anomalous phonological-distributional characteristics mentioned above, there are three main sources of evidence against the traditional view that #sC syllabifies as a complex onset, just like initial rising-sonority clusters.

The first piece of evidence comes from syllabically sensitive morpho-phonemic alternations that discriminate between #sC and rising clusters. Perhaps the best-known illustration comes from the behaviour of proclitics in Italian, which mould themselves to the initial syllable structure of a following stem (Davis 1990; Bertinetto 2004). The alternants occurring before #sC differ from those occurring before singleton consonants or rising clusters and more closely resemble those occurring before vowels, for example, [il seːɲo] 'the mark', [il treːno] 'the train' versus [lo spaːro] 'the shot', [l amiko] 'the friend (m.)'. Since the vowel-initial environment is a syllable rime, a reasonable conclusion is that the [s] of #sC also falls within a rime (Davis 1990; Kaye 1996). That is to say, the [s] of #sC occupies a coda at the beginning of the stem. Similar syllabically sensitive alternations and distributions that segregate #sC from rising clusters are to be found in European Portuguese (Cavaco Miguel 1993) and, as we will see below, Cypriot Greek.

A second source of evidence indicating that #sC is syllabically unlike rising clusters comes from articulographic studies of speech production. The results of one such study of Italian corroborate the morphophonemic evidence just reviewed. Using electromagnetic midsagittal articulography, Hermes et al. (2013) investigated the articulatory phasing of word-initial consonants relative to a following vowel. Their results confirm previous findings showing that rising clusters are coordinated as a unit – the C-centre effect. With #sC clusters, however, they found no C-centre effect: the presence or absence of an initial [s] (for example, *spina* versus *pina*) makes no difference to the timing of the C-centre relative to the vowel. Hermes et al. interpret this as reflecting different syllabications: rising clusters form complex onsets, while #sC clusters do not.

A third source of evidence against syllabifying #sC like rising clusters is to be found in the process of consonant-cluster simplification that occurs in the early stages of first language acquisition. The process typically acts differently on the two sorts of sequence: in rising clusters it is the second consonant that is dropped (for example, [pej] 'play'), whereas in #sC it is the second ([puwn] 'spoon') (see McLeod et al. 2001 for a review of the extensive literature).

All of the evidence just reviewed suggests a negative answer to the question of how #sC is syllabified: not as a complex onset. A positive answer is suggested by the Italian morphophonemic evidence: #sC syllabifies as a coda plus an onset. A comparison of different Romance languages provides us with further insights into this syllabification through the presence versus absence of a vowel preceding historical #sC (cf. Spanish *escuela* versus Italian *scuola*).

Other evidence suggests that coda-onset is not the only way #sC can be syllabified. The other alternative is where #sC results from the devoicing and eventual total syncope of a vowel between two consonants, as in Japanese [sukida] > [skida] 'I like it' (Tsujimura 2007) or Sesotho [sɪtulo] > [stulo] 'chair'. A reasonable analysis of this scenario is to say that the two consonants remain in different onsets separated by a silent nucleus.

Since these two ways of syllabifying #sC are independent of one another, there is nothing to prevent them both from showing up in the same language. As Monik Charette has shown (1991, 1992), this is indeed the case in French, where words with etymological #sC (for example, *sport*, *store*) exist alongside words where #sC is created by syncope of an intervening schwa (for example, [s(ə)riz] *cerise*, [s(ə)mɛl] *semelle*). A similar situation prevails in some varieties of European Portuguese (Cavaco Miguel 1993; Kaye 1996).

To summarise, the evidence reviewed above suggests word-initial consonant clusters come in three different syllabic configurations: (a) complex onset, (b) coda plus onset, and (c) onset plus silent nucleus plus onset. Configuration (a) is limited to rising clusters, while #sC can syllabify as either (b) or (c). We have expressed this three-way distinction in terms of a rather conventional notion of syllabic constituency. There are other ways of capturing the same three-way distinction, for example in terms of different dependency or licensing relations between segmental positions (for example, Lowenstamm 1996; 1999; Scheer 2004; Ségéral and Scheer 2008; Chapter 23). However we conceptualise it, what is important here is that, according to the evidence reviewed above, there is a syllabification difference between #sC and rising clusters. It is this difference that we wish to investigate further by seeing whether it also shows up in speech perception.

Is #sC special?

One of the questions addressed by the dichotic listening study described below is whether there is something uniquely special about sibilant fricatives that allows them to form the only non-rising initial clusters in many languages.

There are good grounds for viewing sibilance as bestowing an auditory perceptual privilege on a consonant that occurs word-initially before another consonant, particularly when the latter is a stop. Compared to rising clusters consisting of an obstruent followed by an approximant, falling clusters consisting of any consonant followed by a stop are in general cross-linguistically disfavoured in initial position. The most plausible explanation for this starts from the observation that the closure phase of the stop inhibits transitional acoustic cues to the identity of a preceding consonant (Ohala 1992; Steriade 1999; Wright 2004; Henke et al. 2012). If an initial consonant is to survive in this position, it is more likely to be identified by listeners if it provides them with segment-internal cues, such as we find in continuants but not in stops. Among continuants one of the most robust internal cues is frication noise. And among fricatives the most robustly cued are those where the intensity of this noise is greatest, viz. sibilants.

The relative robustness of auditory-acoustic cues to consonants before stops suggests an implicational scale of phonotactic preferences governing clusters in initial position (Steriade 1999; Wright 2004; Henke et al. 2012). If a language that places phonotactic restrictions on initial clusters allows not just sibilants to precede a stop, we can expect the next best candidates to be nonsibilant fricatives. This is exactly the situation in Cypriot Greek. The language allows us to investigate whether initial clusters beginning with nonsibilant fricatives show the same anomalous syllabification behaviour as #sC.

Word-initial clusters in Cypriot Greek

Like all Indo-European languages, Cypriot Greek has a set of rising word-initial clusters consisting of a stop or fricative followed by a liquid, for example, [tría] 'three', [kréas] 'meat', [platís] 'wide (m.)', [kléftis] 'thief'. Like some Indo-European languages, it also has initial #sC, for example, [skáfto] 'I dig', [spíθca] 'houses'. In addition to #sC, it has a limited set of #fC sequences – falling clusters where the first consonant is a nonsibilant fricative, for example, [ftoxós] 'poor', [fkó] 'to go out', [xtíz:o] 'I built', [θcó] 'two'. These combinations are summarised in Table 10.1.

Table 10.1 Word-initial consonant clusters in Cypriot Greek.

Sonority	C1	C2	Examples
Rising	Stop	Liquid	[pl, pɾ, tɾ, kl, kɾ]
Rising	Nonsibilant fricative	Liquid	[fl, fr, θl, θɾ, xl, xɾ]
Falling	Sibilant	Stop	[sp, st, sk]
Falling	Nonsibilant fricative	Stop	[ft, fc, θc, xt]

The fact that the set of #fC clusters in Cypriot Greek is rather small is important in the context of the study to be presented below. Although Cypriot Greek has a rather wider range of initial clusters than, say, English or Italian, they are still subject to quite strict phonotactic constraints. This means that Cypriot Greek is not an 'anything goes' language (Dumercy et al. 2013), like Polish or Czech for example, where word-initial clusters are largely unfettered by sonority-based phonotactic restrictions (Gussmann 2007; Orzechowska 2019). Dichotic listening experiments have shown that Czech speakers can fuse more or less any pair of initial consonants, regardless of sonority combinations (Dumercy et al. 2013). Why Cypriot Greek is of interest to us is that it provides a useful testbed for investigating whether sibilance is uniquely responsible for the syllabically anomalous behaviour of #sC. Dichotic listening studies indicate that in English, with its fairly tight phonotactic restrictions on initial clusters, #sC is less readily fusible than rising sequences (Chiu et al. 2016). With Cypriot Greek, we can test not only whether this difference is replicated but also whether it carries over to #fC. If it does, it points to [s] not being particularly special.

An initial indication that #fC and #sC are syllabically alike in Cypriot Greek is provided by the morphophonemics of proclitics, which alternate according to the phonological shape of the stems they attach to. This is illustrated by the copula [en] in (1). The basic alternant occurs before a vowel-initial stem, as in (1a). Before a singleton consonant or a rising cluster, we see partial or total assimilation of the copula-final consonant to the initial consonant of the stem, as in (1b) and (1c). Before a stem beginning with #sC, the copula-final consonant deletes, as in (1d); the same thing happens before #fC, as in (1e).

(1) a. [en árostos] 'he is sick' [en omón] 'it is raw'
    b. [em makrís] 'he is long' [es sazméni] 'it is fixed (fem.)'
    c. [ev vreménos] 'he is wet' [eŋ glaméni] 'she is tearful'
    d. [e spazménon] 'it is broken' [e skotoménos] 'he is killed'
    e. [e ftanós] 'he is silly/thin' [e xtarménon] 'it is scratched'

These alternations are strongly reminiscent of those involving Italian proclitics. Since the latter are generally agreed to be driven by syllable structure, there is good reason to assume those in Cypriot Greek are too.

Syllabic sensitivity explains the deletion of the copula-final [n] by linking it to the fact that the coda in Cypriot Greek contains at most one consonant. The [n] survives before a vowel because it can take up residence in an available onset, as in (2a). Before an onset, the *n* occupies the preceding coda, where it undergoes assimilation, as in (2b) and (2c).

(2) a. [en–omón] b. [en–makrís]>[emmakrís] c. [en–vreménos]>[evvreménos]

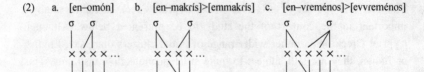

According to some analyses, all word-initial consonant clusters in Cypriot Greek syllabify as complex onsets, regardless of their sonority profile (for example, Coutsougera 2003; Armosti 2009). However, the morphophonemic evidence illustrated in (1) strongly suggests that only rising clusters syllabify this way; as shown in (2c), these behave just like singleton onsets exemplified in (2b). In contrast, if we assume that #sC syllabifies as a coda plus onset, as in Italian, we can explain why the *n* fails to survive in this environment: there is no syllabic position available to host it. As shown in (3a), the coda is already occupied by *s*. The same analysis can evidently be applied to #fC, as shown in (3b).

(3) a. [en–spazménon] > [espazménon]   b. [en–ftanós] > [eftanós]

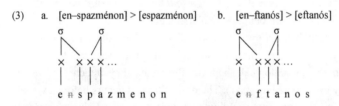

Although the analysis in (3) departs from the view that all initial clusters in Cypriot Greek are complex onsets, it nevertheless incorporates an insight provided by Armosti (2009) that some initial consonants can be moraic.[2] Under the analysis in (3), this is achieved through weight by position: being in a coda entails that the first consonant of a falling cluster bears weight.

Based on their morphophonemic behaviour, we can draw two conclusions about the syllabification of #sC and #fC in Cypriot Greek: they syllabify the same way irrespective of sibilance, and they are not syllabified like complex onsets. These facts inform our choice of stimuli in the dichotic listening study to be presented below.

Dichotic listening

The use of dichotic listening as a method for studying the syllabification of consonant clusters is originally due to Cutting and Day (for example, Cutting 1973; 1975; Cutting and Day 1972; 1975). The basic method involves simultaneously presenting listeners with different words to each ear, with the words differing only in one consonant. For example, the listener hears a word with an initial stop in one ear (for example, *pay*) and a word with an initial liquid in the other ear (for example, *lay*). Listeners then report what they hear. The results of such experiments show two noteworthy effects. Firstly, listeners sometimes report fusion: two simultaneously presented words are heard as a single percept (here *play*). Secondly, at least with English listeners, fusion typically favours a rising sonority sequence (that is, *play* rather than *[lpej]). Cutting and Day place a phonological interpretation on these effects: fusion indicates that listeners parse the two consonants as part of the same syllable onset, and sequencing reflects language-specific phonotactic constraints on consonant clusters.

Chiu et al. (2016) found that, when English listeners are dichotically presented with different singleton consonants in varying sonority combinations, they readily fuse and sequence stop and liquid pairs as rising-sonority clusters, as in Cutting (1975), Cutting and Day (1975). In contrast, listeners do not readily fuse pairs where one consonant is [s], thus corroborating evidence that #sC is not a complex onset.

Dichotic listening study of Cypriot Greek

The aim of the dichotic listening study to be presented here is to discover whether speakers of Cypriot Greek perceive #sC clusters any differently than #fC and initial rising clusters.

Method

Forty-five native speakers of Cypriot Greek completed the study (27 female, age range 19–35, mean age 22;8 years).[3] All were born and raised in Cyprus. There were no self-reports of hearing problems or speech and language disorders.

The selection of stimuli for the experiment was guided by the morphophonemic patterning described above. The pairs of consonants presented to listeners fall into the four major-class divisions shown in Table 10.2.[4] Each consonant was placed in a nonword consisting of the initial target position followed by a __VCV tail, for example, *kovi*, *lovi*, *sovi*. The tail was held constant except for one factor: the vowel following the target consonant was varied between [e] and [o]. Having a contrast between front and back vowels in this position is necessary to accommodate phonologically conditioned variation between palatal and velar realisations of dorsal consonants in Cypriot Greek. Members of each stimulus pair always contained the same vowel.

Table 10.2 Consonant pairs used in the dichotic listening study.

Major Classes	Pairs
Stop|Liquid	p|l, t|ɾ, k|ɾ
NonsibilantFricative|Liquid	f|l, θ|ɾ, x|ɾ
Sibilant|Stop	s|p, s|t, s|k
NonsibilantFricative|Stop	f|k, θ|k, x|t

The intention behind using nonwords was to stress-test fusion, as previous dichotic listening studies have shown that listeners fuse consonant pairs more readily when the fused percept is an existing word (Day 1968, reported in Cutting 1973). The decision to use a disyllabic CVCV word frame was motivated by two factors. Firstly, disyllables are by far the most frequent word size in the Cypriot Greek lexicon (Themistocleous et al. 2011). Secondly, working with disyllables rather than monosyllables greatly increases the area of usable lexical space not already occupied by existing words. Having a singleton consonant in the non-target second syllable was considered preferable to having a cluster, since the latter could potentially interfere with the fusibility of target consonant pairs in the initial syllable.

The stimuli were recorded in a sound-proof studio by a phonetically trained female native speaker of Cypriot Greek. The experiment was conducted online using Qualtrics survey software.[5] Participants, after confirming they were wearing headphones, were presented with the auditory stimuli. On each trial, participants were simultaneously presented with one nonword to each ear, with the members of each nonword pair differing only in the initial consonant, for example, *povi*, *lovi*. The nonword pairs were drawn from the set of options defined by the major-class permutations listed in Table 10.2. Participants were presented with four trials per nonword pair, counterbalanced for left versus right ear (for example, *povi* twice in one ear, twice in the other), to control for right-ear dominance in the perception of verbal stimuli (Kimura 1961).

Immediately after being presented with each stimulus pair, participants indicated which of four alternatives they had heard. For example, after hearing *povi* in one ear and *lovi* in the other, they were given the choices *povi*, *lovi*, *plovi*, or *lpovi* (see Table 10.3). The alternatives were presented visually on a computer screen in Roman spelling.[6] These forced-choice response options were designed to capture (a) whether the listener heard a fused percept (*plovi* or *lpovi*) or not (*povi* or *lovi*) and, if so, (b) the order in which the target consonants were perceived (*plovi* versus *lpovi*).

Table 10.3 Possible responses to dichotically presented nonword stimuli.

Possible responses			Examples
Fused	Cluster	Rising CC	*plovi*
		Falling CC	*lpovi*
Unfused	Singleton	Lower sonority C	*povi*
		Higher sonority C	*lovi*

Results

For reasons of space, we will limit our focus here to the question of whether the major-class affiliation of target consonant pairs influences participants' responses to the input stimuli. We analysed responses for two possible biases. Firstly, is there a bias towards hearing stimulus pairs as fused (for example, *plovi* or *lpovi*) or not (for example, *povi* and *lovi*)? Secondly, where there is a preference for fusion, is one sonority sequence preferred over the other (for example, rising in *plovi* versus falling in *lpovi*).

Figure 10.1 groups the responses according to the major-class affiliation of the target consonant pairs and shows the extent to which each class combination is perceived as fused. The percentage values given in Figure 10.1 were obtained by averaging across the three consonant pairs in each of the major-class combinations shown in Table 10.2, and across the four trials per stimulus pair per participant.

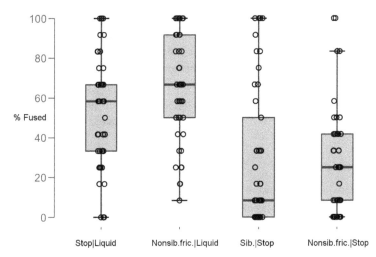

Figure 10.1 Cypriot Greek dichotic listening: participants' preference for fused percepts (%Fused) classified by the major class of pairs of input consonants.

Does major class influence the likelihood of input consonant pairs to fuse? An analysis of variance of percentage fused values establishes that this is indeed the case: $F(3, 176) = 16.904$, $p < 0.001$, $\eta p^2 = 0.224$. We followed up with paired comparisons to investigate which particular major-class combinations favour fusion more than others. Two results are of immediate relevance to the research questions we started out with. Firstly, there is no significant difference in fusion rates between Sibilant|Stop ($M = 28.333\%$, SD $= 35.060\%$) and NonsibilantFricative|Stop pairs ($M = 29.444\%$, SD $= 27.957\%$), $p = 0.771$, n.s. Secondly, neither of these fricative–stop combinations fuse anything like as much as the two obstruent–liquid combinations. Sibilant|Stop pairs fuse less readily than Stop|Liquid pairs ($M = 52.963\%$, SD $= 28.044\%$), $t(44) = -4.993$, $p < 0.001$. Sibilant|Stop pairs also fuse less readily than NonsibilantFricative|Liquid pairs (M $= 65.370\%$, SD $= 27.059\%$), t(44) $= -7.245$, $p < 0.001$. Similarly, NonSibilantFricative|Stop pairs fuse less readily than Stop|Liquid pairs, $t(44) = -5.4935$, $p < 0.001$. NonSibilantFricative|Stop pairs also fuse less readily than NonsibilantFricative|Liquid pairs, $t(44) = -8.531$, $p < 0.001$.[7]

Now let us focus on fused responses, to see whether major class biases the way the input consonants are sequenced. To this end we examined the two classes that fuse most readily, namely Stop|Liquid pairs and NonsibilantFricative|Liquid pairs (Figure 10.2).[8] In both cases, there is a clear preference for fusion into rising rather than falling clusters. This is confirmed by comparing percentages of rising versus falling responses. Fused Stop|Liquid pairs show significantly more rises ($M = 92.898\%$, SD $= 13.999\%$) than falls ($M = 7.1023\%$, SD $= 13.999\%$), $t(41) = 13.0999$, p < 0.001. The same goes for fused NonsibilantFricative|Liquid pairs: more rises ($M = 84.941\%$, SD $= 17.286\%$) than falls ($M = 15.059\%$, SD $= 17.286\%$), $t(41) = 19.861$, p < 0.001.

To sum up, participants fused Stop|Liquid and NonsibilantFricative|Liquid input pairs more readily than Sibilant|Stop and NonsibilantFricative|Stop pairs. Both Stop|Liquid and NonsibilantFricative|Liquid pairs were more readily fused as rising clusters than falling. A low rate of fusion was equally evident in Sibilant|Stop and NonsibilantFricative|Stop pairs.

Discussion

If listeners in this study were fusing input consonant pairs on the basis of what is legal as a word-initial (as opposed to syllable-initial) cluster in Cypriot Greek, we would expect no biases based on major class. This is because all four of the major-class combinations included in the study are attested in word-initial position (see Table 10.1). However, we do see major-class biases, and pretty clear ones at that, which suggests that something else is influencing the propensity

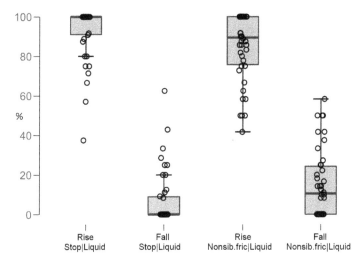

Figure 10.2 Cypriot Greek dichotic listening: participants' preference for the sonority sequencing (Rise versus Fall) of fused input consonant pairs consisting of the two major-class combinations most susceptible to fusion, Stop|Liquid and NonsibiliantFricative|Liquid.

to fuse. We believe the most plausible explanation is the one established in the earliest dichotic listening studies of Cutting and Day: listeners fuse on the basis of what is legal as a syllable-initial (as opposed to word-initial) cluster.

The intervention of syllable phonotactics would explain the difference in fusibility between obstruent-liquid pairs (Stop|Liquid and NonsibilantFricative|Liquid) on the one hand and fricative-stop pairs (Sibilant|Stop and NonsibilantFricative|Stop) on the other. Obstruent-liquid pairs are more readily fusible into rising clusters because they make good complex onsets. Fricative-stop pairs, in contrast, are less readily fusible because they do not make good complex onsets.

The relative resistance to fusion of fricative-stop pairs holds of both NonsibilantFricative|Stop pairs (for example, [x|t]) and Sibilant|Stop pairs (for example, [s|t]). This suggests that they have the same syllabification, which is consistent with the morphophonemic evidence reviewed Word-initial clusters in Cypriot Greek above. In other words, from the viewpoint of syllabification, #sC is not unique, at least in Cypriot Greek.

Conclusion

We started out here by reviewing various pieces of evidence that cast doubt on the once standard assumption that #sC is syllabified just like initial clusters of rising sonority, that is, as a complex onset. The evidence comes from morphophonemic patterning, speech production, and early phonological development. To this we can now start to add evidence from speech perception. The dichotic listening study reported on here corroborates the conclusion that #sC is not syllabified as a complex onset.

If #sC is not a complex onset, what is it? A limitation of our study is that it does not allow us to take the extra step of answering this question. At least for some languages, including Cypriot Greek itself, the morphophonemic evidence suggests #sC syllabifies as coda plus onset (however we wish to represent that). A rather different implementation of dichotic-listening methodology would be required to investigate whether this syllabification reveals itself in speech perception.

What the present study does give us, however, is yet another reason for distancing ourselves from the traditional view that any consonant cluster finding itself at the beginning of a word necessarily also finds itself at the beginning of a syllable.

Notes

1. Special thanks to Spyros Armostis for his much-valued comments and advice as well as for his practical help with the design and running of the Cypriot Greek experiment reported on here. Thanks also to Constantina Gregoriades and Gisé Tomé Lourido.
2. Armosti's (2009) focus is on initial geminates (which were not included in our study). However, he does note that these pattern morphophonemically with initial falling clusters.
3. The results from 16 other participants were discarded because they failed to complete the experiment. UCL Research Ethics Committee number LING-2013-11-12.
4. The stimulus set also included sibilant plus sonorant pairs (for example, [s|n], [s|l]), which we will not report on here. Cypriot Greek limits initial sibilant plus sonorant clusters to [zm] (sibilant plus [n] or [l] occur in a few sporadic loan words). These pairs were included only for the sake of balancing the stimulus set against one being used for a parallel dichotic study of English (where [s] plus sonorant clusters are legal, for example, *snap, slide*).
5. https://www.qualtrics.com.
6. The decision to use Roman rather than Greek writing was taken after consultation with our Cypriot Greek colleagues. While Greek writing is used for standard Greek, young Greek Cypriots typically use Roman spelling for writing Cypriot Greek, for example on social media.
7. These pair-wise comparisons remain significant when corrected for multiple comparisons.
8. Three participants, who reported no fusion of Stop|Liquid pairs, were removed from the sequencing analyses.

References

Armosti, S. (2009). *The Phonetics of Plosive and Affricate Gemination in Cypriot Greek*. Doctoral dissertation, University of Cambridge.
Bertinetto, P. M. (2004). 'On the undecidable syllabification of /sC/ clusters in Italian: Converging experimental evidence'. *Rivista di Linguistica*, 162, 349–72.
Cavaco Miguel, M. A. (1993). *Os padrões da alternâncias vocalicas e da vogal zero na fonologia portuguesa*. Doctoral dissertation, Universidade dos Açores.

Charette, M. (1991). *Conditions on Phonological Government.* Cambridge: Cambridge University Press.
Charette, M. (1992). 'Mongolian and Polish meet Government Licensing'. *SOAS Working Papers in Linguistics and Phonetics* 2, 275–91.
Chiu, F., Tomé Lourido, G., and Hödl, P. (2016). 'Are word-initial sibilant-sonorant clusters especial? Behavioural and neural correlates differentiate sonority-conforming #FR and #SR clusters in English'. Conference presentation, *OCP 13*, 13–16 January 2016, Budapest.
Coutsougera, P. (2003). 'The Cypriot Greek syllable'. *Oxford University Working Papers in Linguistics, Philology and Phonetics* 8, 1–30.
Cutting, J. E. (1973). Levels of processing in phonological fusion. *Haskins Laboratories Status Report on Speech Research* SR-34, 1–54. https://files.eric.ed.gov/fulltext/ED081295.pdf (accessed 6 February 2023).
Cutting, J. E., and Day, R. S. (1972). 'Dichotic fusion along an acoustic continuum'. *Journal of the Acoustical Society of America* 52, 175.
Cutting, J. E., and Day, R. S. (1975). 'The perception of stop-liquid clusters in phonological fusion'. *Journal of Phonetics* 3, 99–113.
Cutting, J. E. (1975). 'Aspects of phonological fusion'. *Journal of Experimental Psychology: Human Perception and Performance* 104, 105–20.
Davis, S. (1990). 'Italian onset structure and the distribution of "il" and "lo"'. *Linguistics* 28, 43–55.
Day, R. S. (1968). *Fusion in Dichotic Listening*. Doctoral dissertation, Stanford University.
Dumercy, L., Lavigne, F., Scheer, T., and Ziková, M. (2013). 'Anything goes: Czech initial clusters run against evidence from a dichotic experiment'. *Formal Description of Slavic Languages* 10, 5–7 December 2013, Leipzig.
Gussmann, E. (2007). *The Phonology of Polish*. Oxford: Oxford University Press.
Henke, E., Kaisse, E. M., and Wright, R. (2012). 'Is the sonority sequencing principle an epiphenomenon?'. In *The Sonority Controversy*, edited by S. Parker, 65–100. Berlin: De Gruyter.
Hermes, A., Mücke, D., and Grice, M. (2013). 'Gestural coordination of Italian word-initial clusters: The case of "impure s"'. *Phonology* 30, 1–25.
Kaye, J. (1996). 'Do you believe in magic? The story of s-C sequences'. In *A Festschrift for Edmund Gussmann from his Friends and Colleagues*, edited by K. Henryk and S. Bogdan, 155–76. Lublin: Wydawnictwo KUL.
Kimura, D. (1961). 'Cerebral dominance and the perception of verbal stimuli'. *Canadian Journal of Psychology/Revue canadienne de psychologie* 15, 166–71.
Lowenstamm, J. (1996). 'CV as the only syllable type'. In *Current Trends in Phonology: Models and method*, edited by J. Durand and B. Laks, 419–41. Salford: European Studies Research Institute.
Lowenstamm, J. (1999). 'The beginning of the word'. In *Phonologica 1996*, edited by J. Rennison and K. Kühnhammer, 153–66. The Hague: Holland Academic Graphics.
McLeod, S., van Doorn, J., and Reed, V. A. (2001). 'Normal acquisition of consonant clusters'. *American Journal of Speech-Language Pathology* 10, 99–110.
Ohala, J. J. (1992). 'Alternatives to the sonority hierarchy for explaining segmental sequential constraints'. *CLS: Papers from the Parasession on the Syllable*, 319–38. Chicago: Chicago Linguistic Society.
Orzechowska, P. (2019). *Complexity in Polish Phonotactics*. Berlin: Springer.
Parker, S. (ed.). (2012). *The Sonority Controversy*. Berlin: De Gruyter.
Scheer, T. (2004). *A Lateral Theory of Phonology, Volume 1. What is CVCV and why should it be?* Berlin: De Gruyter.
Ségéral, P., and Scheer, T. (2008). 'The Coda Mirror, stress and positional parameters'. In *Lenition and Fortition*, edited by J. de Carvalho Brandão, T. Scheer, and P. Ségéral, 483–518. Berlin: De Gruyter.
Steriade, D. (1999). 'Alternatives to the syllabic interpretation of consonantal phonotactics'. In *Proceedings of the 1998 Linguistics and Phonetics Conference*, edited by O. Fujimura, B. D. Joseph, and B. Palek, 205–42. Prague: Karolinum Press.
Themistocleous, C., Katsoyannou, M., Armosti, S., and Christodoulou, K. (2011). *Lexical Database of Cypriot Greek*. http://lexcy.library.ucy.ac.cy.
Tsujimura, N. (2007). *An Introduction to Japanese Linguistics*. 2nd edition. Oxford: Blackwell.
Wright, R. (2004). 'A review of perceptual cues and cue robustness'. In *Phonetically-based Phonology*, edited by B. Hayes, R. Kirchner, and D. Steriade, 34–57. Cambridge: Cambridge University Press.

11
The segholate verbs of English
Jean Lowenstamm

Introduction

Based on joint consideration of their Present, Past, and Past Participle forms, English verbs are traditionally divided into two groups of unequal size.[1] A few form their past tense and past participle by means of Ablaut (for example, *sing/sang/sung*). Those are the 'strong' verbs. 'Weak' verbs, the overwhelming majority, merely suffix +*ed* to the stem (*hoped*, *debunked*, *trespassed*, etc.). However, a third group of some 60 verbs stands out on account of two negative characteristics: the verbs of that group show neither Ablaut nor +*ed*. On the other hand, their pasts and past participles always involve a final coronal obstruent whether one shows in the present or not (*shot*, *hid*, *felt*, *rid*, *kept*, etc.).[2] Because that ubiquitous final coronal is reminiscent of +*ed*, and because of the absence of Ablaut, those verbs are viewed as a special pocket of weak verbs. They are called 'irregular' weak verbs (henceforth IWV).

Much valuable work has been devoted to that group though usually in the context of more encompassing discussions of length alternations in English, cf. Kiparsky (1982), Myers (1987), Dresher and Lahiri (1991), Minkova and Stockwell (1996), Lahiri and Dresher (1999), Lahiri and Fikkert (1999) and references therein, to mention just a few.

It is fair to say that IWV are viewed as a kind of morass, a historical residue, moreover one of modest size, and therefore of limited significance. I intend to argue, on the contrary, that they are part of a large and organised set enjoying a place of its own in the synchronic grammar of English.[3] Against the background of a comparison with the class of Semitic nouns known as segholates, I will argue that the irregular weak verbs of English are templatic.[4] In the sections that follow this introduction I will list characteristics of IWV as well as some of the questions I will attempt to answer; provide a brief introduction to segholate nouns; and lay out fairly standard assumptions about the construction of English verbs along with a proposal of my own. After this, I implement my proposal in several steps, followed by a section in which I discuss a small class of exceptions and the intriguing voicelessness of their final coronal (*built*, *bent*, etc.).

Some characteristics of IWV and related questions

IWV are all 'short'. Indeed, 'longer' verbs do not replicate their behaviour. Thus, *hit* is the past of *hit*, but *solicit could never be the past of *solicit*; *hid* is the past of *hide*, but *subsid could never be the past of *subside*, etc. The corresponding questions appear in (1).

(1) a. How is 'short' defined?
    b. Why are IWV 'short'?

One of the few solid generalisations about IWV is the exceptionless brevity of their past tense vowel in contrast with the free distribution of length in the present (*keep/kept*, *read/read*, *cut/cut*). The question in (2) therefore arises.

(2) Why is vowel length not free in past tense forms?

With respect to the final coronal present in all pasts, Myers (1987, 492) writes:

(3) There are two past tense suffixes in English, both of which happen to be coronal stops; *–t* as in *burnt*, and *–d* as in *faded*. The former is restricted to the root level, while the latter can be either root level or word level.

There is something highly intriguing with (3). Not only are the two supposedly distinct exponents of past tense almost identical, but their distributions overlap. Hence the question in (4).

(4) Are there really two past tense suffixes? And they merely *happen* to be coronal? Or have we maybe missed something?

A survey of a list of IWV reveals a massive gap: their roots exclusively end in *p* (*keep*), *t* (*hit*, *bite*), *d* (*rid*, *hide*), *m* (*dream*), *n* (*lean*), *l* (*feel*) and, in two exceptional cases, *v* (*leave*, *bereave*). Two questions arise:

(5) a. Does something in the grammar of English make it impossible for a verb whose root ends in, say, *b, g, z, f, k, s*, or *š* to be an IWV?
　　b. Is the definition of IWV sound, to begin with?

In the next section, I introduce relevant aspects of the segholate nouns of Arabic.

Segholates

The typical surface profile of segholate nouns is CVCC. Examples are given in (6).

(6) a.　　　　　　　b.　　　　　　　　c.
　　baḥr 'sea'　　　diyn 'religion'　　ḥubb 'love'
　　bint 'girl'　　　ʕuwd 'lute'　　　sadd 'dam'

Their ingredients – root and vocalic melody – are mapped onto a template as shown in (7).[5] The root in (7a) inasmuch as it contains no glide is known as 'sane'. The root in (7b) with its medial glide is dubbed 'hollow'. Finally, the biliteral root in (7c) is called 'deaf'. The latter spreads rightward according to the scheme laid out in McCarthy (1979). A low-level rule affecting all segholates from hollow roots will map *diyn* and *ʕuwd* into [dīn] and [ʕūd], respectively.

(7) a.　　　　　　　b.　　　　　　　　c.

```
      a                 i                 u
      |                 |                 |
   C V C V C V       C V C V C V       C V C V C V
    \  \   /          \  \  /            \   \/
    √B Ḥ R            √D Y N             √Ḥ B
    [baḥr]            [dīn]              [ḥubb]
```

Given the types of roots in (7) and the makeup of the template, the above configurations exhaust the set of logical possibilities.

The point of a comparison with Arabic segholates is this: Germanic roots, as Jacob Grimm had discovered (Grimm 1878), reproduce the same array: CVC_iC_j (like *baḥr*), $C\bar{V}C$ (like *dīn*), and CVC_iC_i (like *ḥubb*). *Does the presence of that array in Germanic also reflect the presence of a template?* Following Bendjaballah (2012, 2014) on German, I will argue that the IWV system, too, is template-based.

Templatic versus non-templatic English verbs

Following many, I make two assumptions. First, I assume that verbs arise as the result of the selection of a root by categorising head v, [$_{vP}$ v √P]. Second, I assume that verbs move up to Tense and left-adjoin to the head of that constituent. Depending on the content of Tense, verbs will be Present or Past. If Present, the verb comes out unsuffixed, if Past, +d (henceforth D_{Past}) is added.

My proposal is that English v comes in two versions.[6] One is the 'plain' v; it merely makes it possible for a root to play a role in the syntactic computation. The other version of v has the same effect, but it specifies in addition a condition on the material realisation of the verb: its phonetic ingredients will have to be realised within the confines of the space defined by a verbal template, [$_v$ C V C V C V], once more the same as for the segholate nouns of Arabic.

In (8), I show the representation of four verb forms, *hope, hoped, keep,* and *kept* at a point where they have left-adjoined to the head of Tense and Tense has released the exponent of its value, ø if Present, D_{Past} if Past. √HOPE has been selected by 'plain' v, and D_{Past} therefore attaches as a suffix (8b). √KĪP, by contrast, has been selected by 'templatic' v. In (8c), the root deploys over the template as indicated. In this case, the surface result unremarkably parallels that of (8a), viz. [CV̄C]. But in the Past (8d), D_{Past} must be realised *inside* the template, much as if an augmented root – √KĪP+D_{Past} – was now involved. In this case, the increased segmental load of the root thwarts the full deployment of the underlying long vowel and shortening follows,[7] [kɛpt] vs. [kiʸp] as opposed to [hoʷp]/[hoʷpt] with no shortening.[8]

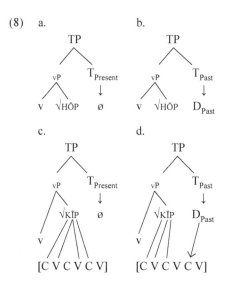

(8)

We now have answers to (1a): the template defines 'short'; (1b) 'long' roots (*solicit, subsidise*, etc.) will never pattern as IWV do because their size exceeds the capacity of the template. Their sole access to verbhood will be through selection by 'plain' *v*. Less trivial is another consequence, namely the fact that one and the same 'short' root can be selected by either version of *v*, thus making it possible for an irregular weak verb to also have a regular doublet, viz. *dreamt/dreamed, knelt/kneeled*, etc. Note moreover that there is nothing necessary in the fact that *keep* is templatic and *hope* non-templatic. Indeed, √KIP might as well have been selected by 'plain' *v*, thus giving rise to [kiʸpt], or by *both* 'plain' *v and* 'templatic' *v* giving rise to a [kɛpt]/[kiʸpt] doublet. Similarly, hypothetical [hɔpt] or the hypothetical doublet [hɔpt]/[hoʷpt] would have been as well-formed as the attested [hoʷpt].[9]

This account can be compared to an earlier one capitalising on the distinction made available by Lexical Phonology between Level 1 and Level 2 suffixation. It runs as follows: the last consonant of *keep* is extrametrical, *kee(p)*; the syllable of the stem therefore counts as open. When *t* attaches at Level 1, *t* now counts as extrametrical (*keep(t)*), and Closed Syllable Shortening must apply, yielding *kept*. On the other hand, *hoped* has a case of Level 2 attachment, and so no shortening takes place. The problem is that Level 1 attachment would have to be restricted to 'short' verbs inasmuch as 'longer' verbs, for example, *elope*, never show any shortening in the past (*[elɔpt]). In Lexical Phonology, as far as I know, this coincidence between Level 1 attachment and shortness has to be fortuitous. By contrast, it follows from my proposal that vowel shortening will take place only where the verb is templatic.

Thirteen past tense verbs, listed in (9), are derived in the manner described in (8d).

(9)   (be)reft, crept,[10] dealt, felt, heard, kept, knelt, left, lost, meant, slept, swept, wept; and three antiquated or British forms: *dreamt, leant, leapt*.

More verbs

The read/read group

A second group of verbs is exemplified by *read*, [riyd/rɛd]. That second group shares something with the first group, namely the vowel is long in the present tense, [riʸd], but short in the past. But, whereas the shortening in *kept* followed from the extra load of consonantal material incurred by the presence of D_{Past}, the past tense of *read* shows no such increase. Why does the vowel shorten nevertheless? This is my next point.

In (10a), I have given the representation of Present *read*. It is comparable to (8c). In (10b), the augmented root deploys over the template positions, thereby forcing the brevity of the vowel. The internal realisation of D_{past} will never allow an underlying long vowel to survive in the past. This answers the question in (2). In (10c), the OCP conflates radical D and D_{past}. The geminate thus created is pronounced as a simplex segment. The claim here, in other words, is that English has virtual geminates in the sense of the argument developed in Lowenstamm (1996) about germane verbal evidence involving the Danish *stöð*.[11]

(10) a.   b.   c.
      C V C V C V   C V C V C V   C V C V C V
         \ V // | | / /   \ \ V /
          RĪD   RĪD+D_{Past} RĪD
                                                                      ↓
                                                              [rɛdd] → rɛd?[12]

The fourteen past tense verbs derived in the manner just described are listed in (11).

(11) *sped, slid, chid* (archaic), *plead, shot, read, met, lit, lead, hid, fed, bred, bit, bled.*

Note that the roots of all verbs in the group just reviewed end in *t* or *d*. None of the roots of the verbs reviewed in the preceding group, (9), did. This complementary distribution, obscured by the fact that English geminates remain unpronounced and are inconsistently acknowledged by the spelling conventions in word-final position, clearly shows how that second group is just a special case of the first. For the sake of clarity, I will benchmark such inclusion relations in the format of (12).

(12) *Root type*   CV̄C
      Coronal-final roots   read, meet
      Other roots   keep, deal

A prediction is now within reach. It is the topic of the next section.

The cut/cut, rid/rid group

If a configuration such as (10c) is recognised, it cannot be confined to Past Tense verbs. Rather, because the template is the same in Present and Past, it should be observable in Present Tense verbs as well. If that is correct, there should be a group of verbs of type CVd(d) or CVt(t) in which the Present and Past are phonetically identical. That group indeed exists. It can be exemplified by means of verb *rid*.

(13) a.   b.   c.

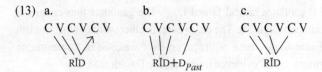

In (13a), I show how the present of *rid* is formed. Spreading is required by the imperative of template saturation. There is a positive reason for supposing that Present *rid* involves a geminate. It rests on an extension of Hammond's point: if a geminate is present in *ridding* and *ridden*, there must be one in their stem, too. The past of *rid* in (13b) involving the augmented root, no spreading of the root-final consonant is necessary in this case. The OCP kicks in, (13c), and the same form, [rɪdd], eventually surfaces for both the Present and the Past. The nineteen verbs patterning in that fashion appear in (14).

(14)   *bet, bid, cut, fit, hit, knit, let, put, quit, rid, set, shed, shit, shut, slit, spit, spread, wed, wet*.

Now is the time to try and answer the question in (4). If we place the verbs of (14) in the benchmarking frame, we can easily fill in the root type box: by the account just proposed, the roots of those verbs are of type CVC_iC_i (like Arabic *ḥubb*). But what sits in the 'Other roots' box? That is, of what larger group are the verbs in (14) the coronal-final subtype?

(15)   Root type CVC_iC_i
        Coronal-final roots   cut, rid
        Other roots   ?

At this point, spelling must be briefly discussed because it is, in reality, the sole basis on which a verb is deemed regular or irregular. Thus, if the Past Tense forms of *dab, hug, buzz* could be written *dabd, hugd, buzd*, they would be viewed as *bona fide* IWV. As it is, English spelling does not sanction final clusters such as bd#, gd#, zd# and those pasts can only be written *dabbed, hugged, buzzed*, which makes them look regular. ft# clusters are possible in English but the Past of verbs such as *puff* or *sniff* is never written *puft* or *snift*, rather *puffed* and *sniffed*. ckt# is not sanctioned by English spelling and therefore [hækt] can only be written *hacked*. Just like graphic *zz*-, and *ff*-final verbs, *ss*-final verbs never simplify under any circumstances. Thus, [hɪst] for instance will have to be written *hissed*.

Except in loanwords, *sht#* is not a possible final graphic sequence and [læšt] will have to spell *lashed*. Finally, even though *pt#* is graphically possible, [klæpt] which used to be spelled *clapt* must now be spelled *clapped*, as do most other *p*-final verbs.

Evidently, those *very* numerous monosyllabic roots with a short vowel, which I represent – as in (16a,c) – as would be done for Semitic words from biliteral roots, *are* tokens of the general pattern of which *rid*, *cut*, etc., are the special, coronal-final subpattern. Because the OCP and the silence of geminates conspire with English spelling to obscure things, I have brought out the formal parallelism between *dabbed* (16b) and *rid* (16d) with the hourglass (⧖) between the coronal obstruents in (16d) indicating that the operation of the OCP is imminent but hasn't taken place, yet.

(16)   a.   b.   c.   d.
       C V C V C V   C V C V C V   C V C V C V   C V C V C V
        \\\↗   \|| /   \\\↗   \|| /
         DAB   DAB+D$_{Past}$ RĬD   RĬD⧖D$_{Past}$
       dab, /dæbb/   *dabbed*, /dæbd/   *rid*, /rĭdd/   *rid*, /rĭdd/

Squatters and why they devoice

As pointed out, for a verb to be involved in the processes I have described, its makeup must be such that the augmented version of its root does not exceed the capacity of the template. Clearly, a CVC_iC_j root, a root consisting of three different consonants, for example, *curb*, will fit into the template *on its own*, but not what I have called its 'augmented' or 'past' version. In such cases, D_{Past} will have to be realised extratemplatically: *curbed*, etc.

Can any such verb stand a chance to force in its augmented root, nevertheless? Here, a two-faceted prediction is made. If a CVC_iC_j root is coronal-final, its last segment *will* allow D_{Past} to dock and coalesce. Such is the case of *build*, *cost*, as shown in (17). The second facet of the prediction is of course that this can only happen if the verb is templatic. If the root underlying the verb cannot fit the template as, for example, *manifest*, the past will have to be regular, that is, manifested/*manifest.

(17)   a.   b.
       C V C V C V   C V C V C V
       ||| /↑ ||/ / ↑
       COST+ D$_{Past}$ BILD+ D$_{Past}$
       cost   built

Such verbs are:

(18) *bent, built, burnt, cast, cost, hurt, learnt, lent, sent, spent, thrust.*

In this case, the content of the benchmarking frame records the fact that the only possible IWV from CVC_iC_j roots must be coronal-final.

(19) *Root type* CVC_iC_j
      Coronal-final roots   *build, cost*
      Other roots   none

The truly interesting feature of those verbs is the voicelessness of D_{Past} which systematically accompanies coalescence. This is where I attempt to answer the question in (3) and refute the notion that English has two distinct Past Tense suffixes, both of which accidentally happen to be coronal.

On the view depicted in (17a), the voicelessness of D_{Past} in *cost*, and *cast, hurt, thrust* is unsurprising. But why are the pasts of *build, bend, lend, send, spend* t–final??? Why doesn't coalescence maintain, indeed foster, voicing, yielding [bɪld], [lɛnd], etc., for both present *and* past? To put things differently, if *d* is legitimate in [$_{Present}$ bɪl _ #], why not in [$_{Past}$ bɪl _ #]?

My proposal involves two conjectures. First, I submit that D_{Past} differs in an important way from other *d*'s of English – crucially from the root-final *d* of √BILD 'build' – in being unspecified for voice. The *d* of the root, in other words, is [+ voice] whereas the *d* of D_{Past} is [? voice]. In the manner of a probe, it seeks valuation of its [voice] feature in the environment. Second, I submit that valuation of the [voice] feature of D_{Past} can only be sought (though not always found as we will soon see) in the very specific place defined by the rule in (20).

(20)   C V *C* V C V

     [voice] → [α voice] / [α voice] (X)   [D_{Past} _]

The rule in (20) formulates the idea that D_{Past} will have the same value for voice as the consonant linked to the central templatic position italicised and underscored there. The parenthesised expression represents the possible (but irrelevant) presence of a consonant attached to the same templatic position as D_{Past} as in, for example, (21c,e).

(21)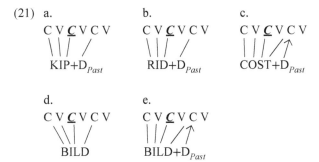

All the configurations reviewed up to this point appear in (21). The reader can verify that the value for voice of D_{Past} in (21a,b,c) is the same as in the consonant linked to the italicised templatic position in (20).[13] In (21d), I have represented the present of *build* for comparison with its past *built* (21e). The final root-coronal in (21d) is specified for voice and nothing more needs to be said. The fact that in (21e), D_{Past} does *not* find valuation of its voice feature in the adjacent radical *d* is expected, because the latter is *not* attached to the templatic position specified in (20). Rather, a sonorant is attached to that position. Why does a sonorant cause the devoicing of D_{Past}? Because of space limitations the outline of an answer only will be offered. Universally, sonorants appear to have no impact on the voice value of neighbouring segments. One interpretation of that fact is that sonorants are themselves *phonologically* unspecified for voice.[14] If this is correct, D_{Past} in (21e) will not be able to value its own voice feature according to the rule in (20), and it will simply default to [- voice] eventually devoicing the adjacent root consonant. Similar examples of post-sonorant default devoicing of D_{Past} in IWV are given in (22).

(22) *dealt, dreamt, felt, knelt, leant, meant, hurt, learnt, bent, lent, sent, spent, dwelt, spelt, smelt, spilt*.[15]

Conclusion

In this brief chapter, based on an analogy with the mode of deployment of root consonants in the class of Arabic segholate nouns, I have argued that the 60 or so IWV of English are much less irregular than might seem and that there is nothing elusive or mysterious in the form of their Past Tense morpheme.

Notes

1. I am grateful to Edoardo Cavirani, Radwa Fathi, Noam Faust, Andrew Nevins, Tobias Scheer, Yuko Yoshida, and Connor Youngberg for help and encouragement. All mistakes are my own.
2. While all verbs will eventually be reviewed, space limitations leave me no choice but to assume familiarity with the evidence. Where lists are provided, I have not distinguished between dialects of English.
3. For a radically different view, see Kaye (1995).
4. In doing so, I follow a line of research wherein morphological devices usually associated with Semitic or Afroasiatic languages can be shown to play a major role in the morphology and phonology of languages outside that family. Early efforts in that vein include the demonstration in Ségéral (1995) and Ségéral and Scheer (1998) that the vocalisation of every single Standard German strong verb is amenable to the Ablaut system argued for in Guerssel and Lowenstamm (1990; 1996) for Classical Arabic; or, closer to the point of this chapter, the argumentation in Bendjaballah (2012; 2014) whereby non-concatenative marking is shown to be similarly implemented in the verbal systems of genetically and typologically unrelated languages such as Taqbaylit Berber and Standard German.
5. Following Lowenstamm (1996) or Scheer (2004), the template is represented as a sequence of light syllables.
6. Cf. Faust (2019) for a related proposal.
7. See Lowenstamm (1996) and Scheer (2004) for general discussion and Balogné Bérces (1998) for English specifically.
8. For similar cases of templatic pressure causing vowel shortening in Chaha, see Lowenstamm (2000; 2001).
9. With two paths to verbhood, the ongoing historical change whereby IWV's tend to shift to regular weak, can be construed without having recourse to analogy.
10. The reader may wonder how *crept* or *dreamt* with their two initial consonants fit into a template with one single, initial C position. Perhaps, those clusters should be analysed as complex segments as argued in Lowenstamm (2003), [kʳɛpt], [dʳɛmt]. Alternatively, the template should perhaps include an extension, viz. [v C(C) V C V C V]. I am not really interested in pressing either point because all the phenomena to be discussed here take place elsewhere, that is, in the underscored portion of the template: [v C(C) V C V C V].
11. On Danish, see Larsen (1994). Hammond (1997) provides arguments specific to English in support of that view. He observes that because they sit in open syllables the lax stressed vowels in [hæDi] Hattie or [míni] Minnie should normally undergo tensing. The fact that they do not, he notes, follows from his claim that the intervocalic consonant is in reality a geminate.
12. The question mark records my scepticism about degemination. If degemination had any consequence, for instance if it fed or bled a process; or if it allowed for the statement of a non-trivial generalisation; or if it applied in context-specific fashion, I would accept any of that as solid evidence. As no such evidence has been produced (to the best of my knowledge), I would rather think of the geminates of English as intact albeit unpronounced. I will continue noting the pasts of read and rid as [rɛdd] and [rɪdd].
13. The voice value of D_{Past} in (21c), it is claimed, is due to s, <u>not to radical t</u>. On the same view, the voiceless member of the f/v alternation in leave/left, bereave/bereft does not result from the presence of a final t in the Past Tense. The opposite is claimed: the voicelessness of D_{Past} results from the voicelessness of the f of left or bereft.
14. See Scheer (2015a,b) for an in-depth discussion of the voice status of sonorants, including a critical review of the literature as well as the author's own views.
15. By the account I give of default devoicing of D_{Past} in the presence of a sonorant, *heard* – contrary to fact – should be pronounced as *hurt*.

References

Balogné Bérces, K. (1998). *English Syllable Structure and Vowel Shortening*. Master's dissertation, Eötvös Loránd University.
Bendjaballah, S. (2012). *La grammaire des gabarits*. Habilitation thesis, Université Paris 7.

Bendjaballah, S. (2014). 'Remarks on Nonconcatenative Affixation'. *Brill's Journal of Afroasiatic Languages and Linguistics* 6(1), 45–73. https://doi.org/10.1163/18776930-00601006.

Dresher, B. E., and Lahiri, A. (1991). 'The Germanic foot: Metrical coherence in Old English'. *Linguistic Inquiry* 22(2), 251–86. http://www.jstor.org/stable/4178721.

Faust, N. (2019). 'New reasons to root for the Semitic root from Mehri and Neo-Aramaic'. *The Linguistic Review* 36(3), 575–99. https://doi.org/10.1515/tlr-2019-2030.

Grimm, J. (1878). *Deutsche Grammatik*. Berlin: Dümmlers Verlagsbuchhandlung – Harrwitz und Gossmann.

Guerssel, M., and Lowenstamm, J. (1990). *The Derivational Morphology of the Classical Arabic Verbal System*. Unpublished manuscript, UQAM and Université Paris 7.

Guerssel, M., and Lowenstamm, J. (1996). 'Ablaut in Classical Arabic Measure I active verbal forms'. In *Studies in Afroasiatic Grammar*, edited by J. Lecarme, J. Lowenstamm, and U. Shlonsky, 123–34. The Hague: Holland Academic Graphics.

Hammond, M. (1997). 'Vowel quantity and syllabification in English'. *Language* 73(1), 1–17. https://doi.org/10.2307/416591.

Kaye, J. (1995). 'Derivations and interfaces'. In *Frontiers of Phonology: Atoms, structures, derivations*, edited by J. Durand and F. Katamba, 289–332. London: Longman.

Kiparsky, P. (1982). 'Lexical morphology and phonology'. In *Linguistics in the Morning Calm*, edited by I.-S. Yang, 3–91. Seoul: Hanshin Publishing Co.

Lahiri, A., and Dresher, B.E. (1999). 'Open syllable lengthening in West Germanic'. *Language* 75(4), 678–719. https://doi.org/10.2307/417730.

Lahiri, A., and Fikkert, P. (1999). 'Trisyllabic shortening in English: Past and present'. *English Language and Linguistics* 3(2), 229–67. https://doi.org/10.1017/S1360674399000234.

Larsen, U. B. (1994). *Some Aspects of Vowel Length and Stöd in Modern Danish*. Master's dissertation, Université Paris 7.

Lowenstamm, J. (1996). 'CV as the only syllable type'. In *Current Trends in Phonology: Models and methods*, edited by J. Durand and B. Laks, 419–43. Salford: European Studies Research Institute.

Lowenstamm, J. (2000). 'The No Straddling Effect and its interpretation: A formal property of Chaha 2nd feminine singular formation'. In *Research in Afroasiatic Grammar*, edited by J. Lecarme, J. Lowenstamm, and U. Shlonsky, 183–99. Amsterdam: John Benjamins.

Lowenstamm, J. (2001). 'The image of a segment'. In *Naturally! Linguistic Studies in honour of Wolfgang Ulrich Dressler presented on the occasion of his 60th birthday*, edited by C. Schaner-Wolles, J. Rennison, and F. Neubarth, 281–90. Torino: Rosenberg & Sellier.

Lowenstamm, J. (2003). 'Remarks on muta cum liquida and branching onsets'. In *Living on the Edge. 28 Papers in honour of Jonathan Kaye*, edited by S. Ploch, 339–65. Berlin: De Gruyter.

McCarthy, J. (1979). *Formal Problems in Semitic Phonology and Morphology*. Doctoral dissertation, Massachusetts Institute of Technology (MIT).

Minkova, D., and Stockwell, R. (1996). 'The origin of long-short allomorphy in English'. In *Advances in English Historical Linguistics*, edited by J. Fisiak and M. Krygier, 211–40. Berlin: De Gruyter.

Myers, S. (1987). 'Vowel shortening in English'. *Natural Language and Linguistic Theory* 5, 485–518.

Scheer, T. (2004). *A Lateral Theory of Phonology Volume 1: What is CVCV, and why should it be?* Berlin: De Gruyter.

Scheer, T. (2015a). 'A world without voiced sonorants: Reflections on Cyran 2014 (Part 1)'. *Studies in Polish Linguistics* 10(3), 125–51.

Scheer, T. (2015b). 'A world without voiced sonorants: Reflections on Cyran 2014 (Part 2)'. *Studies in Polish Linguistics* 10(4), 223–47.

Ségéral, P. (1995). *Une théorie généralisée de l'apophonie*. Doctoral dissertation, Université Paris 7.

Ségéral, P., and Scheer, T. (1998). 'A generalized theory of Ablaut: The case of modern German strong verbs'. In *Models of Inflection*, edited by R. Fabri, A. Ortmann, and T. Parodi, 28–59. Berlin: De Gruyter. https://doi.org/10.1515/9783110919745.28.

12
From me to [juː]: on government licensing and light diphthongs
Markus A. Pöchtrager

Introduction

This short contribution discusses the representation of English [juː] and, in a wider context, distributional asymmetries in (light) diphthongs. It picks up the line of research started in some early works in Government Phonology (GP) (Kaye et al. (KLV) 1985; 1990; Charette 1990; 1991), especially Kaye and Lowenstamm (1984) and Kaye (1985). It shows where the theoretical machinery commonly employed for light diphthongs is in need of further development. Potential for such improvement comes from two sources: On the one hand from Government Licensing (Charette 1990; 1991), and on the other from GP 2.0 (Pöchtrager 2006b; 2018; 2020; 2021a,b; Kaye and Pöchtrager 2013; Živanovič and Pöchtrager 2010). Firstly, because GP 2.0 argues that structure continues below the traditional 'segmental' level – put differently, that we have not reached the right level of granularity yet – and light diphthongs show that we need to zoom in closer. Secondly, because it takes seriously the various asymmetries between elements, and that between **I** and **U** has a role to play in (light) diphthongs, too. Frustratingly, while it seems clear in which direction we must look, the precise answers are far from obvious.

Let us begin with English. When looking at the distribution of English [j] one has to make a distinction between [j] preceded by a consonant (henceforth: Cj) and [j] not preceded by a consonant (henceforth: plain [j]). Two pieces of evidence point towards plain [j] sitting in an onset: It goes with *a* as the indefinite article (**an yard*) and, since onset and nucleus show great independence of each other, plain [j] precedes practically any vowel: *yes, yield, yip, yawn, yeast, yoke, yearn, yard, university*, etc.

This is quite different from Cj as in *queue* [kjuː], and the problem has long been known (Chomsky and Halle 1968, 192 ff.; Polgárdi 2015; Szigetvári

2016). Harris (1994, 62) takes Cj to be a branching onset in parallel to [bl] in *blue*. Thus, by the Binarity Theorem (Kaye et al. 1990) he correctly excludes *[blj], *[klj], *[trj], etc., since a constituent cannot dominate more than two positions. Cj can be dominated by a binary branching onset, while *[blj], etc., cannot. However, there is a downside: If Cj is indeed a branching onset, then why is the following vowel restricted to [uː] (or variants thereof, that is, reduction to schwa in unstressed position, lowering by *r*)? That is, why is there [kjuːt] but no *[kjeɪt], *[kjɑːt], etc.? This dependency is unexpected if onset and nuclei are independent of one another, and suggests that [j] and [uː] share a constituent, forming a complex nucleus of the kind that Kaye (1985) dubbed light diphthong.[1] Light diphthongs are attached to a single skeletal slot, hence (metrically) 'light', with the general structure given in (1a), but one of their component parts might also extend over two positions, as in the [juː] in *cute* with a long second member (1b). This is the representation that also Polgárdi (2015) assumes, though in the slightly different framework of Loose CV.

(1) a. **Structure of a light diphthong**   b. **English [juː] in *cute*, etc.**

Treating [juː] in the Cj context[2] in this way correctly predicts the lack of phonotactic restrictions between [juː] and the preceding onset, where almost all consonants are possible: [kjuːt], [mjuːt], [ljuːd], [vjuː], [hjuː], etc. (Some English varieties bar coronals, though, which I cannot go into here, but see Note 12.) But by treating [juː] as fully contained in the nucleus we lose another phonotactic generalisation: An onset preceding [juː] cannot branch. Onset and nucleus are (relatively) independent of one other, yet *[krjuːt], *[bljuː] do not exist.[3] Note that other kinds of complex nuclei, for example, heavy diphthongs, are not so restricted (*brown*, *clay*). In other words, the [j] in Cj behaves as if it belonged to onset *and* nucleus simultaneously, as assumed by Giegerich (1992, 158), who links the [j] in a word like *view* to both constituents. This captures the ambiguous constituency,[4] but fails to explain it: Why is [j] special and why in this particular way? In order to answer these questions we will have a quick look at light diphthongs in French in the next section, followed by an attempt to express the ambiguous constituency and then add on another complication in the fourth section of the chapter when looking at the other glide of English, [w], as well as French (again) and Japanese. The final section of the chapter gives a summary and discusses open issues.

A first look at light diphthongs

Within GP, light diphthongs have been studied in detail for French (Kaye and Lowenstamm 1984), Vata (Kaye 1985), and Japanese (Yoshida 1996), among others.

French has three glides that occur in light diphthongs:[5] front unrounded [j] as in *miette* [mjɛt] 'crumb', front rounded [ɥ] as in *muette* [mɥɛt] 'mute (fem.)', and [w] as in *mouette* [mwɛt] 'sea gull'. Kaye and Lowenstamm (1984) discuss various tests for their constituency, based on phonotactic restrictions to the left/right and the behaviour of determiners. For example, the definite articles *le/la* lose their vowel before vowel-initial words and thus provide clues about the nature of what follows. (2) illustrates that test for nouns beginning with [w] (examples from Kaye and Lowenstamm 1984, 136) and reveals a systematic ambiguity.

(2) a. *le watt*   [lə wa...] 'the watt'   b. *l'oie*   [lwa...] 'the goose'
         le week-end [lə wi...] 'the weekend'   *l'oint*   [lwẽ...] 'the anointed one'
         le western   [lə wɛ...] 'the western'
         le wombat   [lə wɔ̃...] 'the wombat'   *l'ouest* [lwɛ...] 'the west'

The words in (2a) behave as if they began with a consonant, those in (2b) as if they began with a vowel. The contrast is particularly stark when the vowel following [w] is identical between the two sets, as in *le watt/l'oie*. Accordingly, Kaye and Lowenstamm (1984, 136) argue that one has to distinguish between [w] in the onset and [w] as part of the nucleus, that is, a light diphthong:

(3) a. **Onset + Nucleus**   b. **Light diphthong**

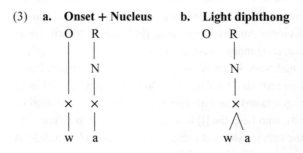

This not only explains why (3a) behaves as consonant-initial (because the onset has both a point and melody attached to it) while (3b) does not (because its onset is empty).[6] Furthermore, Kaye and Lowenstamm argue that (3b)

correctly predicts there to be restrictions on the nature of the vowel following [w], since [w] and the following vowel share a position. No such restrictions hold in (3a), where [w] and the following vowel occupy separate positions and constituents. Lastly, further support comes from words like *trois* [tʁwa] '3', where the onset branches to its (binary) maximum, and still there is room for [w]. This must mean that [w] sits in the nucleus, that is, structure (3b), but with a branching onset instead.

Government Licensing

Applying this kind of reasoning to English we can posit the following representation for *queue*, as has been done for example, by Polgárdi (2015).

(4)   English *queue* with a light diphthong

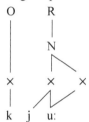

This explains why the preceding onset is quite unrestricted in quality (again, leaving the ban on coronals in some varieties aside) and also why there are restrictions on the following vowel, since the glide shares a position with (the first half of) it. However, (4) fails to explain why branching onsets cannot precede the nucleus. If we still want to stick to (4) we will need to explore in more detail under which conditions branching onsets and/or light diphthongs are possible at all.

The first question, under what conditions branching onsets are licit, is (partially) addressed by Charette's (1990; 1991) notion of Government Licensing (GL).[7] GL expresses the idea that the head of an onset needs a licence to govern a non-head position, and this licence ultimately derives from the following nuclear head. (5a) illustrates this for a case where an onset governs a complement, as in *tree*, and (5b) for an onset governing a preceding rhymal position (*winter*). The two overlap in a word like *pantry*, where the *t* governs both the preceding rhymal complement as well as the onset complement.

(5) a. **GL in *tree*** b. **GL in *winter***

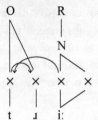 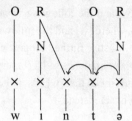

c. **GL in *pantry***

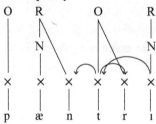

The labels *direct* and *indirect* refer to the 'flow' of dependency, which moves consistently away from the nucleus in direct GL, but changes direction in indirect GL (and skips a position, at least at the skeletal level; though see below). The difference can be illustrated by what kind of GL a final empty nucleus can dispense. French allows both direct and indirect GL by a final empty nucleus, hence *pacte* [...kt] 'pact' (direct GL) as well as *table* [...bl] 'table' (indirect GL). Final empty nuclei in English, however, only allow direct GL: *pact* is fine, but in *table* we do not find a final branching onset *bl*, but rather a sequence of onsets with an intervening empty nucleus.[8] At least in final position it seems that the possibility of indirect GL implies direct GL; a final empty nucleus appears less likely to confer indirect GL.[9]

The same asymmetry comes back before [juː]. We do not find branching onsets preceding, as mentioned before (*[krjuːt], *[bljuː]), but we do find coda-onset clusters: *endure* [ɪndjuːə], *impute* [ɪmpjuːt], *spew* [spjuː], *skew* [skjuː], etc. (Incidentally, the last two examples support yet again Kaye's (1992a) proposal that *sC* cannot be a branching onset but is fine as coda-onset.) The recurrence of this asymmetry suggests strongly, that here, too, GL is at play. In other words, just like a final empty nucleus in English, [juː] can dispense direct, but not indirect GL (6a–b).

(6) a. **Direct GL in** *impute*   b. **(No) indirect GL *[trjuː]**

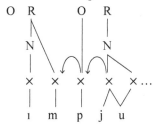 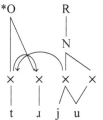

c. **Indirect GL in** *tray*

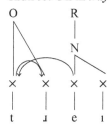

In contrast, heavy diphthongs as in *tray, cloud, ploy* (6c) do allow for direct GL. The question is, why is there such a difference in GL potential between the two types of diphthong? Given that the two structures differ in several aspects at the same time, isolating the responsible factor is tricky. (Several factors might also be interdependent.) Let us look the differences individually.

The first obvious difference between a heavy and a light diphthong is that the head of the nucleus, the ultimate source of licensing, is associated to two separate phonological expressions in the case of a light diphthong, but a single one in a heavy diphthong, as contrasted in (7).

(7) a. **N of** *queue*   b. **N of** *toy*
       with elements   **with elements**

By containing two phonological expressions (that is, two units with separate elements), the head is more complex in the light diphthong in (7a). Obviously, complexity here cannot mean counting elements in the style of Harris (1990), since the head of the nucleus (the leftmost skeletal point) is associated to the same number, two, in both (7a) and (7b). We rather want to capitalise on the complex one-to-many association between skeleton and phonological expression in (7a). But while this usage of 'complex' might seem intuitive, from a theoretical point of view it remains unclear how exactly it is relevant for GL: Charette (1990; 1991) assumes that all nuclei project to the so-called licensor projection; see also Yoshida (Chapter 13). Governing onsets (and only those) are also present at that particular projection, and it is at this level that GL takes place. But on the licensor projection the elements and the configurations in which they attach to a skeletal slot, that is, the contrast between (7a) and (7b), should be irrelevant. Above the skeleton both are identical.

The same objection can be raised against the second point of difference between (7a) and (7b), viz. the position of the weaker member of the diphthong. In a heavy diphthong this is the offglide, accurately captured in (7b), as the offglide is linked to the non-head position of the branching nucleus. In a light diphthong like [juː], on the other hand, one might deem the onglide [j] less important, the 'ultimate head' is what follows. Thus, in order to get from that 'ultimate head' to the preceding onset one would have to cross the glide and this non-local relationship is why direct GL is precluded. But note that none of this can be read off the structure in (7a). Given Charette's definition of where GL takes place and the fact that headship is defined at the skeletal level, the onglide and (at least the first half of) the following vowel are equidistant from the preceding onset, as they both associate to the leftmost skeletal position.[10]

Both points so far show that the theory is not fine-grained enough, or somewhat incomplete: It has the means to express a crucial distinction, but inadequately, since it does not allow us to derive the precise properties of the two types. The same holds true of the third difference between the structures in (7): The light diphthong in (7a) contains no **A**, while heavy diphthongs like [aʊ], [aɪ], and [ɔɪ] (7b) have **A** in the head position, and no **A** in non-head position – at least in English.[11] Within GP 2.0 (Pöchtrager 2006b; Kaye and Pöchtrager 2013), the element **A** has been under extensive scrutiny, since it differs in its behaviour from other elements. **A** seems to license more complex structures than otherwise possible, for example, Southern British English *draft*, with a long vowel (containing only **A**) followed by a coda-onset cluster (with coronal *t* also assumed to contain **A**), cf. Pöchtrager (2012; 2021b) for discussion of such super-heavy structures. The presence of **A** might also be (part of) the reason why heavy diphthongs (7b) can government license a preceding branching onset, while the light diphthong in (7a) cannot. (Not the sole reason, since *monophthongal* high vowels do allow preceding branching onsets, for example, *tree* or *true*, so **A** is only *one* ingredient.) Note again that nothing in the original definition of GL allows us to derive this in an insightful way, and there is no deeper reason why **A** of all elements should interact with GL. The best we can do at this point is state it in prose.[12]

While it is not entirely clear how exactly those factors can be made relevant, it seems clear that at least some of them impact the potential of a nucleus to dispense (direct) GL. In fact, by assuming that a lack of GL is responsible for the ungrammaticality of *[klju:], etc., another parallel emerges: English prohibits branching onsets preceding [ju:] in the same way that it disallows them before final empty nuclei, that is, we also do not find final branching onsets.[13] And as we saw before, coda-onset clusters are fine before either (*imp*[ju:]*te*, *imp*Ø). French however allows branching onsets both before (certain) light diphthongs (*trois* '3') and before final empty nuclei (*maître* 'master'); so once again the GL abilities of light diphthongs and (final) empty nuclei match up.[14] We will come back to this at the end of the concluding section of this chapter.

I and its unlike brother U

Once we broaden our view beyond [ju:], the picture becomes considerably more complex, as the quality of the onglide also plays a role. This asymmetry can already be shown in English, but will get even more important as we move on to other languages. But let us look at English first and contrast [j] to [w]. Despite both being glides, their distribution is quite different. Plain w (not preceded by a consonant) can be followed by almost any vowel (*wheat, wit, wet, wait, walk, woe*, etc., though *[wɑ:]) including [u:/ʊ] (*woo, woman*). In Cw (consonant preceding) we notice distributional restrictions on the preceding consonant: coronal obstruents *(twin, dwell, thwart)* and velars are fine *(quick, Gwen)*, but labials are not (*[pw], *[fw], etc.), and neither are sonorants. All this suggests that in words like *twin*, etc., we are dealing with branching onsets.[15] If Cw is fully contained in a branching onset, we do not expect systematic restrictions on the following vowel, which is indeed correct *(twin, tweet, twice, twang, twat)*, only with the exception of *Cw+[u:/ʊ/ʌ/aʊ], which might or might not be an accidental gap.[16] Furthermore, the ban on labials can then be construed as a general homorganicity restriction similar to why we do not find [tl/dl] as a branching onset, as is often assumed, for example, Harris (1994, 172). And finally, the lack of *[twr] or *[trw] falls out from the Binarity Theorem, imposing an upper limit of two members on constituents. Unlike [j], [w] seems to be a fine second member of a branching onset.[17]

Now, this difference between [j] (containing the element **I**) and [w] (**U**) is unsurprising, given that asymmetries between those two elements have long been noted (Charette and Göksel 1994; 1996; Denwood 1997; Goh 1997; Pöchtrager 2015; Mutlu 2017; Živanović and Pöchtrager 2010). For example, in Turkish vowel harmony (Charette and Göksel 1994; 1996; Pöchtrager 2010), **U** spreads only into a subset of the positions that **I** spreads into. Pöchtrager (2015) argues that similar **I/U**-asymmetries are found in English *heavy* diphthongs and the internal structure of Mandarin nuclei, among others.

Such asymmetries in the behaviour of **I/U** can be found in various languages and all kinds of phonological structures, including glides in light diphthongs. Kaye and Lowenstamm (1984), cf. the second section of this chapter, discuss the varying constituency of French [ɥ] and [w] (onset versus part of nucleus), but do not go into [j]. This is not accidental: While we find cases where [j] qualifies as the first member of a light diphthong after a single consonant (8a) and at least one initial case (8b), there do not appear to be cases with a preceding branching onset (8c).

(8) a. *bien* [bjɛ̃] 'well', *rien* [ʁjɛ̃] 'nothing', *mien* [mjɛ̃] 'mine', *vieux* [vjø] 'old', *pièce* [pjɛs] 'piece', *piaf* [pjaf] 'sparrow', *piaule* [pjol] 'den', etc.
b. *les yeux* [lez jø] 'the eyes'
c. *[bljɛ̃], *[kʁjø], *[trja], etc.

What sets apart [j] (**I**) from [ɥ] (both **I** and **U**) and [w] (**U**) is the lack of **U** in [j]. For a light diphthong to license a branching onset, then, it seems that **U** is needed in the first member. In fact, this same requirement can be exploited to explain (part of) the English facts: [j] does not contain **U**, so *[plj-], etc., will be out. And since [w] never occurs as the first part of a light diphthong in English, the issue of having to or not being able to license a branching onset will simply not arise. Of course this does not yet explain *why* [w] cannot act as the first member of a light diphthong, but that is an independent problem. But in any case, we do not know yet why **U** should be needed to make GL possible.

While we can identify a common restriction for the two languages, it is unclear to what extent generalisation beyond English and French is possible. Spanish makes clear that this condition might not be universal, at least if forms like *griego* 'Greek' are to be analysed as a branching onset [gr] followed by a light diphthong [je], which seems likely (Harris 1983).[18]

Let us finally turn to Japanese for another example of an **I/U**-asymmetry in glides. Japanese does not restrict C in a Cj-sequence and lacks branching onsets in general. Accordingly, Yoshida (1996, 151ff.) and

Kaye (1992b, 145ff.) take [j] as part of a light diphthong. (9) gives examples from Kaye (1992b, 148).[19]

(9) *kyaku* 'visitor', *hyaku* '100', *ryaku* 'omission', *zyama* 'hindrance', *myaku* 'pulse', etc.

Further support for a light diphthong analysis comes from the fact that front vowels are excluded after [j] (*[ji], *[je]). If [j] shares a position with another expression we do expect phonotactic restrictions. There is one important point of contrast to English, though. English plain [j] (see the introductory section of this chapter) behaves like an onset and shows no restrictions on the following vowel, while for Cj the following vowel is restricted. In Japanese, the restrictions on the following vowel hold irrespectively of whether [j] is 'plain' or post-consonantal, suggesting that both cases involve a light diphthong (preceded by an empty onset in the case of Japanese plain [j]).

As is already to be expected by now, the distribution changes when we look at the glide [w], which only precedes [a] in native Japanese words and never follows a consonant in the standard variety (*[wi], *[twa]). This suggests that [wa] is a light diphthong and unable to license even a *non-branching* onset. (Unless that non-branching onset is empty, of course.) In contrast to French, [w]-initial light diphthongs seem to be the more restricted type in Japanese.

Summing up

Table 12.1 summarises what we have seen for the three languages that we have looked at in some detail.

When presented like this, three patterns can be gleaned from Table 12.1. Firstly, French (part (a) of the table) has the most liberal system, in the sense that light diphthongs show great freedom in what onsets they are preceded by:

Table 12.1 Systematic comparison of permitted glide plus vowel sequences and structural conditions for (a) French, (b) Japanese, and (c) English. '—' indicates systematic gaps that exist independently of light diphthongs.

Onset	(a) French			(b) Japanese			(c) English		
	jV	ɥV	wV	jV	ɥV	wV	jV	ɥV	wV
Empty	yes	yes	yes	yes	—	yes	no	—	no
Non-branching	yes	yes	yes	yes	—	no	yes	—	no
Branching	no	yes	yes	—	—	—	no	—	no

empty, non-branching, or branching. The only restriction occurs with [j]-initial light diphthongs. Moving on to part (b), Japanese seems to allow a subset of the French system – on the condition that we ignore systematic gaps (such as the systematic lack of branching onsets or of the glide [ɥ] in Japanese). That is, everything that is possible in Japanese is also possible in French. English (part (c)) can then be taken as a subset of Japanese, since all that is possible in English (which is very little, in fact) is also possible in Japanese or French, unless excluded for independent reasons.

This neat pattern might well run into trouble once extended to even more languages. Spanish, for example, is even more liberal than French in that it allows branching onsets before light diphthongs ([je/we]): *griego* 'Greek', *prueba* 'test', etc. Yet at the same time it is not immediately clear that Spanish allows empty onsets preceding light diphthongs, since (at least) *plain* [j] is quite free in Spanish in what it is followed by and thus must be taken as an onset (rather than the first half of a light diphthong), that is, exactly what we saw for English in first section of the chapter. This would make it *less* liberal than French.

Secondly, in all languages in Table 12.1 a light diphthong beginning with [j] bars branching onsets, or, put differently, an **U** is needed for GL to happen. (Again, this is not true for Spanish, which is more liberal.) The reasons for this special role of **U** in GL are mysterious. For Japanese such a restriction can be stated vacuously only, as there are no branching onsets to begin with. Note in this context that the beneficial properties of **U** in a light diphthong, whatever they are, do not hold for simple onsets: [j]-initial light diphthongs in Japanese allow preceding consonants (that is, non-branching onsets with melody), [w]-initial ones do not.

Thirdly, English [juː] as a light diphthong disallows both branching onsets and empty onsets. (Allowing empty onsets would predict that there are [juː]-initial words behaving as vowel-initial; recall plain [j] from this chapter's first section. This is an interesting conjunction of onset types, whose commonality lies in being a deviation from the simple, non-branching case. Van der Hulst (personal correspondence) surmises that a similar conjunction holds for empty nuclei and branching nuclei, both deviating (but in opposite directions) from simplex, non-empty nuclei. In fact, we saw a variant of this in the section 'Government Licensing', when we looked at how English and French final empty nuclei (that is, an empty nuclear head) patterned together with light diphthongs (nuclear head complex) in their GL abilities: Either both disallowed direct GL (English), or both allowed it (French). I say 'variant' for two reasons: (i) Light diphthongs are not necessarily branching nuclei (they can be, as in English), though they are of course complex. (ii) Final empty nuclei differ from internal empty nuclei, so they cannot be lumped together as one class. Finally, let us notice that Spanish obscures the pattern considerably, in that its light diphthongs do not pattern with final nuclei with respect to GL at all. Spanish has both branching onsets (_griego_ 'Greek') and coda-onset clusters (_entiendo_ 'I understand') preceding light diphthongs, but neither can precede final empy nuclei. (Consonants preceding final nuclei are generally quite limited in Spanish; only (some) coronals and [x] occur.)

While this little survey of light diphthongs raises more questions than it answers, it illustrates how in a seemingly innocent topic such as the analysis of light diphthongs a whole series of different questions comes together: the nature of **I/U** asymmetries, the internal structure of nuclei and what counts as a deviation from the 'normal state' of a constituent, and last not least the interaction with preceding onsets. At least for the last aspect we have the established tool of GL.[20]

Notes

1. I take [jæ] in _piano_ to be immediately preceded by an unstressed syllable (and not by a consonant); similarly in _Vietnam_, _Myanmar_. I assume that those sequences do not form a light diphthong. This assumption is not absolutely crucial, since there is no guarantee that English has only one diphthong beginning with [j]. (Southern British) English has more than one (heavy) diphthong beginning with [a] (_mouse_, _mice_) and more than one ending in [ʊ] (_crow_, _crowd_). More light diphthongs might be developing, but we expect some restrictions between the two members to remain. However, the number of possibilities will pertain to the discussion of substantive conditions in the 'Government Licensing' section of this chapter.
2. '[juː] in the Cj context' sounds clumsy, but I remind the reader that talking about [juː] 'in general' would (incorrectly) lump together [uː] preceded by plain [j] and Cj. The ambiguous interpretation of [juː] illustrates a structural ambiguity in phonology, examples of which can also be found elsewhere. (French _pl_ can be a branching onset whose members remain adjacent, as in _tripler_ 'to triple'/_je triple_ 'I triple', or a sequence of two onsets which can get broken up, as in _appeler_ 'to call'/_j'appelle_ 'I call'.) I will stick to just '[juː]' in the following, urging the reader to keep this footnote in mind.
3. This does not follow from Polgárdi's (2015) account, and I cannot see a simple way to implement it in her analysis. Polgárdi does address the lack of branching onsets preceding [ju(ː)/jə] in _unstressed_ position, however, though by a different mechanism.
4. In Giegerich's proposal the single skeletal position that [j] is attached to is shared between onset and peak (his nucleus). This would be inexpressible in GP, where skeletal positions are never shared between constituents. Attaching [j] to two skeletal positions, one associated to each constituent, circumvents that problem but incorrectly predicts long [jː].
5. Scheer (Chapter 19) analyses word-internal [Cj] sequences in French _cimetière_ 'cemetary', _cafetière_ 'coffee maker', _hôtelier_ 'hotel keeper', etc., as two consecutive onsets, which behave like the (Strict CV equivalent of) branching onsets (except for when C is a lateral), instead of onset plus light diphthong. It is not clear that his arguments extend to the examples in the main text or those in (8) in the section 'I and its unlike brother U', all of which have word-initial [Cj]. There is no guarantee that constituency is constant across positions. Scheer bases his rejection of [j] as the first part of a light diphthong on the contrast between _caf_[ə]_tière_ 'coffee maker' versus _hôt_[ə]_lier_ 'hotel keeper': the former can lose schwa, the latter cannot, which is unexpected if [jV] constitutes a light diphthong and thus a source for PG in both cases. This assumes that PG is the only factor responsible for keeping a vowel silent, but as Heo (1994) has argued for Korean, adjacent consonants might play a role, too. (Which Scheer's own analysis capitalises on as well, but by different means.)

6. There is a third logical possibility that also allows for *h aspiré* as in *le héros* [lə eʁo] 'the hero', treated as a consonant despite the lack of an audible reflex (Charette 1991). In such a case there is an onset with a point (but without any melody), which is why it patterns with (3a).
7. 'Partially' because the basic substantive and formal conditions on branching onsets are given by other parts of the theory, such as the Binarity Theorem (Kaye et al. (KLV) 1990) and the Complexity Condition (Harris 1990), and/or earlier charm (Kaye et al. 1985; 1990).
8. I take 'syllabic consonants', at least in English, to be just another name for onset plus onset with an intervening, non-p-licensed (that is, realised) empty nucleus, as I am not aware of any need to make a distinction. Blaho's (2004) work on long and short syllabic consonants does not seem to contradict that view.
9. While we will look at another instance of the same asymmetry in GL potential imminently, I will leave open whether the preference for direct over indirect GL can be generalised completely independently of position and for an entire language, as in Kaye and Lowenstamm (1981) or Cyran (2010). Thai (Smyth 2002) might be problematic for such a view since it has what seem to be *bona fide* branching onsets (indirect GL, with gaps similar to English/French, that is, no **tl-*), while lacking coda-onset clusters (direct GL), except for loans.
10. Kaye (1985) assumes that the two melodic expressions associated to a single position are unordered. (This follows from the assumption that the skeleton is the only place where linear order is specified.) His proposal implies that the order in acoustic realisation must be determined by general principles of the input-output system. To my knowledge this has never been followed up or clarified. In fact, for English, an ordering *is* specified, though only indirectly so: The **U** of [juː] attaches to *two* positions in the skeleton, with the second ordered after the first, hence **I** must precede in realisation. This does not change the fact that for GL the head of the nucleus (a skeletal position) is relevant. Since that nucleus is associated to the melody of the onglide and (part of) the following vowel, the problem in the main text remains unsolved.
11. French and Japanese (see the fourth section of this chapter) do have light diphthongs containing **A**, and in French they also allow direct GL. There, other factors come into play for the GL potential, as we shall see. I will have to leave open whether there are ever heavy diphthongs without **A**, and, if yes, what their properties are; cf. Pöchtrager (2006a) for a discussion of Finnish, Pöchtrager (2015) for English and Mandarin.
12. The element **A**, which interacts with structural properties, has been replaced by structure in GP 2.0. That version of the theory holds that in general the common understanding of phonological structure has not reached the right level of granularity yet. While this does not yet explain the connection to GL, it does at least allow us to understand better the internal complexity of various kinds of diphthongs (Pöchtrager 2015). The particular structure chosen as a replacement of (old) **A** also has a bearing on [jə] as in *accurate*, one of the unstressed counterparts of [juː] and similarly lacking in direct GL potential. In GP 2.0 [ə] has the same structure (a head and a non-head) as the high vowels [i/ɪ/u/ʊ], thus explaining the parallels between [jə] and [juː]. Those high vowels still differ from schwa, in that in the former one position is empty, while in the latter both positions are empty; this expresses aperture. For details, refer to Pöchtrager (2021a).

    The replacement of old **A** by structure also has consequences for coronals, since they, too, were assumed to contain **A** (at least in some varieties of the theory): Coronals will then contain more structure (despite their purported unmarkedness, on which cf. Pöchtrager 2021b). This might explain why in some varieties of English coronals are barred from preceding [juː] just as branching onsets are: Both are too complex. Evidence for the complexity of coronal *stops* comes from the various kinds of lenition they are subject to (Pöchtrager 2016).
13. For 'syllabic consonants' as in *apple* see Note 7.
14. This does not yet explain why they match up.
15. Two comments are in order: Firstly, if [kw/gw] were treated as labiovelars (rather than as branching onsets), a separate stipulation would be needed to exclude them as part of branching onsets, in coda position and finally. That [gw] only occurs in names is surprising but possibly accidental. Secondly, loans like *reservoir* can show [w] after a labial, but it seems more likely that that word is borrowed with a light diphthong [wa], rather than containing a branching onset [vw]; cf. Fudge (1987) for more examples.
16. [swuː] does exist (*swoon, swoop*), supporting yet again Kaye's (1992a) view that *s*C is never a branching onset; see also Chapter 10.
17. I do not mean to imply that all cases of Cw are always branching onsets; velar+[w] might of course be a (mono-segmental) labiovelar in some languages. Note that treating [kw/gw] as a branching onset

in English will be problematic for Pöchtrager's (2019) requirement that branching onsets contain at least one coronal member (including *r*).
18. In the section 'Government Licensing' and, in particular, Note 10, we looked at **A** as a potentially crucial factor in the GL abilities of light diphthongs. The two light diphthongs of Spanish, [je/we], both contain **A** in their second members; but again, so does French [je], and the two languages differ in the GL abilities of [je].
19. Both authors treat forms like [tʃa] 'tea' as [t]+[ja], as commonly done for Japanese (Vance 1987; Labrune 2012; Pöchtrager 2021b).
20. … and for that we say thank [juː], Monik.

References

Blaho, S. (2004). *Syllabic Consonants in Strict CV*. Master's dissertation, Pázmány Péter Catholic University.
Charette, M. (1990). 'Licence to govern'. *Phonology* 7(2), 233–23. https://doi.org/10.1017/S0952675700001196.
Charette, M. (1991). *Conditions on Phonological Government*. Cambridge: Cambridge University Press.
Charette, M., and Göksel, A. (1994). 'Vowel harmony and switching in Turkic languages'. *SOAS Working Papers in Linguistics and Phonetics* 4, 29–56.
Charette, M., and Göksel, A. (1996). 'Licensing constraints and vowel harmony in Turkic languages'. *SOAS Working Papers in Linguistics and Phonetics* 6, 1–25.
Chomsky, N., and Halle, M. (1968). *The Sound Pattern of English*. New York: Harper & Row.
Cyran, E. (2010). *Complexity Scales and Licensing in Phonology*. Berlin: De Gruyter.
Denwood, A. (1997). *The Role of the Element I in Khalkha Mongolian Phonology*. Doctoral dissertation, SOAS, University of London.
Fudge, E. (1987). 'Branching Structure within the syllable'. *Journal of Linguistics* 23(2), 359–77.
Giegerich, H. J. (1992). *English Phonology*. Cambridge: Cambridge University Press.
Goh, Y.-S. (1997). *The Segmental Phonology of Beijing Mandarin*. Taipei: Crane Publishing Co.
Harris, J. W. (1983). *Syllable Structure and Stress in Spanish. A nonlinear analysis*. Boston, MA: MIT Press.
Harris, J. (1990). 'Segmental complexity and phonological government'. *Phonology* 7(2), 255–301.
Harris, J. (1994). *English Sound Structure*. Oxford: Blackwell.
Heo, Y. (1994). *Empty Categories and Korean Phonology*. Doctoral dissertation, SOAS, University of London.
Kaye, J. (1985). 'On the syllable structure of certain West African Languages'. In *African Linguistics: Essays in memory of M. W. K. Semikenke*, edited by D. L. Goyvaerts, 285–308. Amsterdam: John Benjamins.
Kaye, J. (1992a). 'Do you believe in magic? The story of *s+C* sequences'. *SOAS Working Papers in Linguistics and Phonetics* 2, 293–313.
Kaye, J. (1992b). 'On the interaction of theories of Lexical Phonology and theories of phonological phenomena'. In *Phonologica 1988. Proceedings of the 6th International Phonology Meeting*, edited by W. U. Dressler, H. C. Luschützky, O. E. Pfeiffer, and J. R. Rennison, 141–55. Cambridge: Cambridge University Press.
Kaye, J., and Lowenstamm. J. (1981). 'Syllable structure and markedness theory'. In *Syllable Structure and Markedness Theory*, edited by A. Beletti, L. Brandi, and L. Rizzi, 287–316. Pisa: Scuola Normale Superiore.
Kaye, J., and Lowenstamm, J. (1984). 'De la syllabicité'. In *Forme sonore du langage*, edited by F. Dell, D. Hirst, and J.-R. Vergnaud, 123–59. Paris: Hermann.
Kaye, J., Lowenstamm, J., and Vergnaud, J.-R. (1985). 'The internal structure of phonological representations: A theory of Charm and Government'. *Phonology Yearbook* 2, 305–28.
Kaye, J., Lowenstamm, J., and Vergnaud, J.-R. (1990). 'Constituent structure and government in phonology'. *Phonology* 7(2), 193–231.
Kaye, J., and Pöchtrager, M. A. (2013). 'GP 2.0'. *SOAS Working Papers in Linguistics and Phonetics* 16, 51–64.
Labrune, L. (2012). *The Phonology of Japanese*. Oxford: Oxford University Press.
Mutlu, F. (2017). *Valence and Saturation in Phonology*. Master's dissertation, Boğaziçi University.

Pöchtrager, M. A. (2006a). 'A short note on Finnish diphthongs'. In *A Man of Measure. Festschrift in honour of Fred Karlsson on his 60th Birthday*, edited by M. Suominen, A. Arppe, A. Airola, O. Heinämäki, M. Miestamo, U. Määttä, J. Niemi, K. K. Pitkänen, and K. Sinnemäki, 162–71. Turku: The Linguistic Association of Finland.
Pöchtrager, M. A. (2006b). *The Structure of Length*. Doctoral dissertation, University of Vienna.
Pöchtrager, M. A. (2010). 'Does Turkish diss Harmony?'. *Acta Linguistica Hungarica* 57(4), 458–73.
Pöchtrager, M. A. (2012). 'Deconstructing A'. Conference presentation, *MFM Fringe Meeting on Segmental Architecture*, 23 May 2012, University of Manchester.
Pöchtrager, M. A. (2015). 'Binding in phonology'. In *Representing Structure in Phonology and Syntax*, edited by H. van Riemsdijk and M. van Oostendorp, 255–75. Berlin: De Gruyter.
Pöchtrager, M. A. (2016). 'It's all about size'. In *70 Snippets to Mark Ádám Nádasdy's 70th Birthday*, edited by P. Szigetvári. Department of English Linguistics, Eötvös Loránd University. http://seas3.elte.hu/nadasdy70/pochtrager.html (accessed 8 February 2023).
Pöchtrager, M. A. (2018). 'Sawing off the branch you are sitting on'. *Acta Linguistica Academica* 65(1), 47–68.
Pöchtrager, M. A. (2019). 'Zárlatok és kezdetek'. [What's in a cluster?] *Általános Nyelvészeti Tanulmányok* 31, 205–32.
Pöchtrager, M. A. (2020). 'Tense? (Re)lax! A new formalisation for a controversial contrast'. *Acta Linguistica Academica* 67(1), 53–71.
Pöchtrager, M. A. (2021a). 'English vowel structure and stress in GP 2.0.' In *Perspectives on Element Theory*, edited by S. Bendjaballah, A. Tifrit, and L. Voeltzel, 157–83. Berlin: De Gruyter.
Pöchtrager, M. A. (2021b). 'Towards a non-arbitrary account of affricates and affrication'. *Glossa* 6(1), 61, 1–31. https://doi.org/10.5334/gjgl.1116.
Polgárdi, K. (2015). 'Vowels, glides, off-glides and on-glides in English: A Loose CV analysis'. *Lingua* 158, 9–34.
Smyth, D. (2002). *Thai. An essential grammar*. London: Routledge.
Szigetvári, P. (2016). 'The curious case of Cj clusters in English'. *The Even Yearbook* 12, 93–105. Budapest: Department of English Linguistics, Eötvös Loránd University.
Vance, T. (1987). *An Introduction to Japanese Phonology*. New York: SUNY Press.
Yoshida, S. (1996). *Phonological Government in Japanese*. Faculty of Asian Studies Monographs. New series; no. 20. Canberra: The Australian National University.
Živanovič, S., and Pöchtrager, M. A. (2010). 'GP 2.0 and Putonghua, too'. *Acta Linguistica Hungarica* 57(4), 357–80.

13
Licensor tier and culminativity
Yuko Yoshida

Introduction

A lexical word cannot have more than one primary stress or pitch accent (after Hyman 2006).[1] This chapter aims to provide a unified account for such culminativity of a word domain, in relation to the licensors and licensed nuclear positions.[2] Licensed nuclear positions include an empty nucleus observed in vowel-zero alternation. Both stress/pitch accent and vowel-zero alternation are the manifestation of licensing operating at the licensor projection (Charette 1990) proposed in relation to vowel-zero alternations (VZA), for example, in French.

The headship of a domain culminates at the projection where all the licensors are present. That accounts for why the weak member of a branching constituent and empty nucleus receives no word accent. In Japanese, a nuclear position is obligatorily filled by an element, unlike in a language where VZA occurs at an empty nuclear position: there is silence when such a position is licensed, while an unlicensed empty nuclear position (in French) is interpreted variously as [œ] in non-final positions and [ɛ] in final accented position. In Japanese, as in the case of Tangale (Charette 1990) a nucleus filled with element(s) loses phonetic interpretation at a licensed position. High Vowel Devoicing (HVD) is an instance of such non-interpretation of the licensed positions and does not in fact involve a deletion (structural change).

Headedness of a melodic expression contributes to the bifurcating phonetic interpretation of the same element(s) (Yoshida 2019). A headed element is projected to the Licensor Tier (LT): for example, an element |I| on LT manifests phonetically as [i], while non-headed |I| is not projected to LT and would be devoiced. The |I| element on LT is phonetically interpreted as [i] and, when licensed, the same element may not be fully interpreted as [i].

Accent location is determined at the tier of licensors, namely the LT, where the heads of various domains at all levels are projected. The VZA equivalent in Japanese, HVD, rarely occurs when the nuclear position bears the word accent, and unaccented high vowels, /i/ and /u/ are typically subject to devoicing (Vance 1987; Yoshida 2013). Stress facts lend support for the interaction of heads at LT, in particular, in languages such as English that show quantity sensitivity in stress assignment (Hayes 1995). In morphologically simplex English nouns, for example, heavy syllables attract word stress, thus the head member of a branching nucleus and a head nucleus of a branching rhyme preceding its complement are stressed: the head member is on LT and so visible to stress/accent assignment.

Problems

An accented position and its melodic content are intricately related in many languages and Japanese is no exception. In this chapter, I would like to focus on issues of pitch-accent in Japanese and stress in English, in particular related to quantity sensitivity.

For a noun without lexical marking, the default position for pitch accent in Standard Japanese (and some other dialects) is the antepenultimate nucleus with full melodic content (Yoshida 1999).

(1) a. [mɯ ɾá sa ki]   'purple'
    b. [ho to tó gi sɯ]   'mountain cuckoo'

In Standard Japanese, two high-vowels, namely /i/ and /u/, are subject to devoicing, which strongly relates to accent: accented high-vowels are unlikely to be devoiced, and in the assignment of accent, devoiced high-vowels are ignored: they are transparent (2a,b). A high vowel is subject to devoicing when flanked by voiceless consonants. Note that [ɸ] represents a voiceless bilabial fricative, to be distinguished from /ø/, an empty nucleus, which is central to the issues in this chapter.

(2) a. [na ná ɸɯ̥ ɕi gi]   'seven wonders'
    b. [boo é kị̊ ɕoo]   'trading company'

In traditional analyses geminate consonants are counted as one 'mora' (Haraguchi 1991); however, that 'mora' behaves in a unique way in the assignment of pitch accent. The default accent location is antepenultimate in Standard Japanese, as noted above, and a geminate consonant is counted when it appears within the last three 'moras' (3a), but that 'mora' itself is not accented (3b) (Yoshida 1999).

(3) a. [i bɯ ɾi gá k ko]   'smoked pickles'
    b. [ma tsɯ bó k kɯ ɾi]   'pine cone'

In the framework of Government Phonology (GP), we can simply say that the empty nuclear position that separates the two O slots in a geminate consonant takes part in the counting of nuclei, but is not accented (as an empty nucleus cannot take an accent, cf. Yoshida 1999).

The second member of a vowel sequence, namely a long vowel or a diphthong, is also avoided in accent assignment. Within a branching nucleus (4a), the first position is the licensor of the two, thus the head of the constituent domain only is the candidate for the word-domain head.

(4) a. [ɸɯ ɾá wa a]   'flower'
    b. [ɾé e da a]   'radar'

What the three types of examples above reflect is that a nuclear position without full phonetic interpretation cannot be accented in the word domain. Such positions are licensed, and licensed nuclear positions cannot be projected to the Licensor Projection (LP) (Charette 1990).

Theoretical development

Licensing of a given domain should operate in a regular manner for a speaker to manage processing in a given utterance. Considering the generalisations above in the section 'Problems', the phonological processes observed are the instances of licensing at a projection where licensors of domains are projected (Yoshida 2019). Here, we will focus on how these accent facts are related to the LP proposed for vowel-zero alternation.

Licensor Projection (LP)

Charette (1990) proposed the LP as a means of shedding light on vowel zero alternation in French. This projection is of course responsible for other phonological phenomena, and the attempt in this chapter is to develop the theoretical implications of determining the head position of a phonological domain, to formalise previous work and to propose the LT. One of the manifestations of licensing between two adjacent nuclei is Proper Government (PG), which regulates vowel-zero alternations. PG results in non-interpretation of the licensed nuclear position, which Charette proposed as a development of PG discussed by Kaye (1987).

(5) **Proper Government (PG)**
    a. The governor may not itself be governed.
    b. The domain of PG may not include a governing domain.

To discuss PG (5), we first confirm what a governing domain refers to. Government is an instance of licensing (Charette 1990, 1991), and I develop the concept of a licensing tier within Strict CV (Lowenstamm 1996) in this chapter. Government of a licensing domain can be expanded to that of a phrase (Yoshida 1999) and can be found also within a constituent (Kaye et al. (KLV) 1985, 1990) as shown in (6). This is shown with an arrow.

(6)   a.   O   b.   N   c.   R

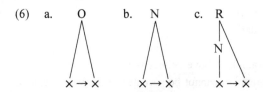

The LP (Charette 1990) is a tier where all the licensors are projected. These are the head nucleus of an inter-nuclear licensing relation (6a), the head of a branching onset, which itself is an intra-constituent governing domain (6b), and the non-nuclear head that governs its preceding rhymal complement (6c). This is shown in (7).

(7) a.

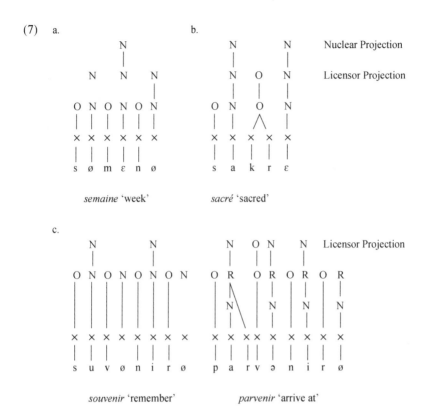

semaine 'week'   *sacré* 'sacred'

c.

souvenir 'remember'   *parvenir* 'arrive at'

This chapter extends the context of licensing from relations operating in a phonological domain of a CV pair and between 2 Vs of the consecutive CV pair to those at work in a word domain, which designates the head position of the word domain. Phonological domains often extend to those of phrases, that is, merged domains of different syntactic categories (Yoshida 1999); however, we limit our discussion to those of nouns in isolation for brevity.

Accent assignment and licensed positions: towards a non-diacritic approach to the headedness of an element

The focus here will first be on the accent location of the Japanese words examined in (2)–(4). The default accent location is antepenultimate, and some sets exhibit pre-antepenultimate accent (Yoshida 1999). The viewpoint in this chapter is that the pre-antepenultimate V position is the head of the entire word domain. V-slots that qualify as the head of the word domain have to be a licensor at the lower level and will be projected to the LT.

Apparent diphthongs or monophthongs involve sequences of V positions. In Standard Japanese, like in many other varieties, the two V positions contract licensing relations, namely the initial position of that sequence licenses the second one. In other words, we do not need to postulate an extra tier of skeletons (x-slots) and what effectively works is the LT. For the vowel sequences question, the initial V position is the head that will be projected to that tier. The second position within the apparent branching nucleus is a licensee of the initial position and thus not projected to the LT. The licensor of the word domain projects to what we now call the LT, and thus the second position never attains the status of the licensor of the word domain as it is licensed itself. Except for certain varieties of Japanese such as Kansai Japanese (Yoshida 2019), we hardly ever obtain a lexical item that places an accent on the second member of what can be perceived as a diphthong or a long monophthong, and they belong to separate CV pairs, not a branching constituent.

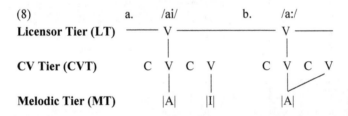

(8) a. /ai/   b. /a:/

This analysis of apparent monophthongs and diphthongs finds a support in the pitch pattern of Kansai dialect: the second member of the consecutive nuclear material can be accented. In this case the second V is not licensed and is projected to the LT, which can be the head of the domain, the accented position.

In Japanese, devoiced high vowels, an intervening nuclear position within a geminate and the second member of the long vowels are licensed. Licensed positions are not projected to the LT. The first structure we investigate is a devoiced high vowel, which is more typical in Standard Japanese than in many western dialects, for example, the Osaka dialect. The difference manifests in the actual pronunciation as well: /u/ in the Osaka dialect is pronounced as lip-rounded [u], and in the Standard as [ɯ]. The devoicing of the back vowel is far less frequent in Osaka Japanese than in Standard Japanese. That is due to the floating melodic content |U| in Standard Japanese (Yoshida 1999, 2019), and that does not allow the nucleus to project to the LT due to general principles of association and projection. Thus, the accent does not land on that nucleus.

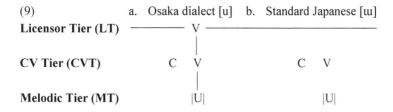

This line of analysis provides an explanation as to why some western dialects of Japanese locate accents on a so-called moraic nasal /N/, on which we do not normally find accents in Standard Japanese. The GP view is that the moraic nasal /N/ is a nasal element for the onset and an empty nucleus (Yoshida 1990) unlike other standard approaches, and in fact, /N/ involves the element |U| (Yoshida 1999, 2019).[3] In the Osaka dialect, an accent can land on the so-called moraic nasal /N/, which rarely happens in other eastern dialects including Standard Japanese, which is a hybrid variety based on the Tokyo dialect. As was proposed in Yoshida (2019), a headed expression of this element |U| projects itself to the LT. Though the representations of /N/ involve a nasal element associated to the onset positions (Yoshida 1991, 1999), similar to the distinction of [u] (Osaka) and [ɯ] (Standard Japanese), the representations of /N/ (10) below differentiate Osaka /N/ with the headed |U| and Standard Japanese /N/ with a floating (non-headed) |U|. Only headed |U| can be projected to LT to serve as the prosodic head of the word domain (see Yoshida 2019 for more detailed discussion).

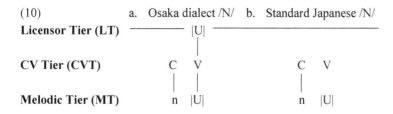

The headed |U| is projected to LT; however, non-headed |U| is not, which results in a /N/ which cannot bear an accent.

Now we turn to geminates. A geminate 'consonant' counts in the count of Vs, but it cannot be the site of a pitch accent. This is another instance of a nuclear position not being projected to the licensor projection or licensor tier. This can be easily explained from a Strict CV point of view if we assume that a geminate consonant involves a consonant linked to two onset or Consonant positions sandwiching an empty V. For example, loan words, which also have accents on the antepenultimate V, will count the empty V between the geminate consonant. The two examples below are from Italian loans, *ricotta*

'ricotta cheese' and *(Ponte) Vecchio* 'old (bridge)'. The former has a geminate consonant /tt/ and that part counts as one unit for accent assignment. Yoshida (1999) defined the empty V to be counted at the nuclear projection for accent assignment; however, we might want to focus on the fact that the onsets surrounding that empty nucleus form a licensing domain, and the licensor onset is projected to the LT. That's exactly where the licensor of the word domain is selected, the antepenultimate licensor on that tier. When the antepenultimate licensor coincides with the geminate licensor, the accent shifts towards the left as in /bekkio/ (11b). We refer also to the LP (Charette 1990) organised into the representation with LT. The LP includes the licensor of the geminate consonant: here I assume that a head-final geminate embracing an empty nucleus is governed by the following filled nucleus. C slots do not serve as an accent bearer, and this suggests that the determination of an accent bearing slot works on a different tier. The LT only accommodates the licensor nuclei, or those that license in various forms such as PG that hold between the nucleus enclosed between the geminate consonants and the nucleus that follows it.

(11) Geminates

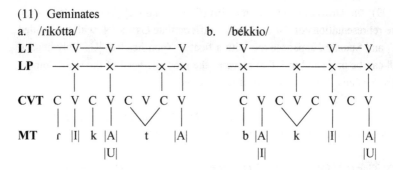

We have demonstrated how empty nuclei interact in accent assignment in Japanese along with the necessity of the LT.

The reason we count nuclei to assign the word accent, but we need to refer to a different tier, LT, is to actually choose the nucleus that can be the licensor of the domain, as the head of the entire prosodic domain. So the nuclear positions which are not projected to LT are not candidates for the domain head.

The phenomenon of course is not a language particular matter and what is happening in other languages, for example in English, lends support to the presence of a LT.

Theoretical implication for English word stress

English stress on 'branching constituents'

LT along with the idea of properly representing empty nuclei can explain why branching constituents attract stress in English. A large class of English nouns are proparoxytonic when the penultimate syllables contain a non-branching rhyme. When the penultimate syllable contains a branching constituent, either branching nucleus or rhyme, English nouns are paroxytonic. (There are also nouns with lexical stress like *Kentúcky* or *medúlla*.) Most examples are from Halle and Vergnaud (1987).

(12) **Proparoxytonic – Antepenultimate Stress**
 América   cínema   óctopus

(13) **Penultimate Stress when it has:**
 i) *a branching nucleus*   ii) *a branching rhyme*
 aróma   agénda
 balaláika   amalgam

English word stress exhibits sensitivity to constituent structures as the above examples show, and stress locations prove to be highly predictable, by counting the 'syllables'. The last syllable of English nouns is extrametrical (Hayes 1981; Halle and Vergnaud 1987), and thus the word-final rhyme is invisible to stress assignment. But that invisible rhyme *is* included in the count of nuclei to determine the third nucleus from the last. Here we'd like to focus on what we are actually counting. This comes down to identifying what a 'syllable' is, and we interpret this in terms of onsets and nuclei contracting licensing relations. In standard GP, as well as Strict CV theory, a nucleus is allowed to be empty, and both phonetically realised nuclei and empty nuclei are subject to counting. In the count of nuclei to determine stress/accent assignment, filled nuclei are equal to empty nuclei (Ulfsbjorninn 2014; Faust and Ulfsbjorninn 2018).

Here are some representations to illustrate what the interpretations look like. We follow Strict CV theory in assuming that apparent branching constituents are in fact a sequence of two CV pairs. A position may be empty, analysed as a null vowel in Burzio's terms (Burzio 1994).

(14) apparent penultimate stress

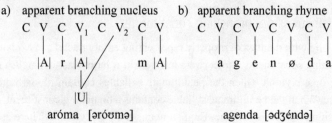

a) apparent branching nucleus

b) apparent branching rhyme

aróma [əróʊmə]

agenda [ədʒéndə]

Both (14a) and (14b) illustrate that counting the nuclei says we place a stress on the third V from the last, so the count of nuclei is crucial for the accent placement, and this is the case for the word class above, which does not need to be treated as exceptional from the antepenultimate stress. Antepenultimate accent in Latin is discussed in Scheer and Szigetvári (2005). (14b) shows that the penult is an empty nucleus, which is counted for the stress assignment. The empty position is licensed by the preceding nucleus which carries word stress, which is projected to LT. We also see tonic lengthening in (14a), as the following section explicates.

Apparently short vowels are underlyingly long vowels

Compare *aróma* [aróʊmə] and *aromátic* [arəmátik]. This stress found on *aróma* [aróʊmə] tells us that the stress accented nucleus is projected to LT, and that nucleus now licenses an extra V that follows it, to form a diphthong. These vowels must occupy 2 independent CVs, namely, CV_1CV_2. (Different analyses are possible; see, for example, Balogné Bérces and Ulfsbjorninn's proposal in Chapter 8.) Also note that loan words with final open syllables have a strong tendency of being paroxytonic: *banána* (from Wolof), *basmáti* (from Hindi), *pláza* (from Spanish), *mojíto* and *barracúda* (from American Spanish). Occurrences of antepenultimate stress are lower, as in *cínema* in (12). The word *aroma* itself is a loan from Greek via Latin into English. Loan word accentuation of this type marks the penultimate vowel as the head of the domain; thus the nucleus is projected on the LT, which means that the position should have a headed expression on the melodic tier. The position is a licensor and will license a CV which is inserted to its right (Scheer 2004).

Strict CV theory assumes that the stress means an insertion of a CV (Scheer 2004), for example, Italian tonic lengthening, and when the nucleus is stressed, that nucleus licenses the inserted nuclear position. The stress is on the penultimate in words like *aróma*, and the stressed CV licenses a now inserted CV pair of the CV_1CV_2. Considering the LT, it finds the nucleus of CV_1 while licensed position CV_2 is not recognised. As for the melodic material, the element from CV₁ spreads to its licensee CV₂, as the manifestation of the licensing relationship, which is realised as the second member of a monophthong, or a diphthong, [ʊ].

The phonetic interpretation of CV₁CV₂ reduces to a single vowel such as [ə] in [arǝmátik]. Those vowels won't be realised as long when licensed by another nucleus, as in the case of arǫmátic [arǝmátik] where the stress location is determined by the morphology. The position is licensed; thus they are not headed and so the vowel is realised as reduced.

The strong tendency of branching constituents to attract word stresses in fact comes from the nature of those constituents contracting licensing within themselves. The two classes distinguished above, namely branching nucleus and branching rhyme, can now be conflated into one category – that of a CV position in a licensing relation. Without the extrametricality of the rightmost constituent (Hayes 1980), we can readily conclude that the head of a sequence of consecutive Vs will attract the word accent.

Antepenultimate stress and 'lengthening'

Note that words with heavy 'penultimate syllables' place the accent on the fourth nuclear position from the last as seen in *gladiolus* [gladióʊləs]. One might still emphasise that the syllable generalisation is necessary. However, we are to refute this apparent advantage of a syllable in favour of CVCV, that is, the head part of the branching nucleus will take the role of the word accent. Recall the Japanese examples, which demonstrated how the licensor projection worked. At the same time, if a vowel sequence involving a long vowel or diphthong is found in the antepenultimate nuclear point, the one that licenses another position is chosen as the head nucleus of the word domain, the CV₁ of the CV₁CV₂. The head of the word domain in English manifests as the stressed nucleus.

When the antepenult falls on the licensed position of the branching constituent, namely a vowel position/nucleus, we predict correctly that the stress will fall on the nucleus/vowel to the left, as in *gladiolus* [gladióʊləs]. The number of Vs are counted, however, and if the antepenultimate V coincides with a licensed position, that is, the second member of a diphthong or a monophthong, the stress will be on the one to the left. The LT is where the headship of a word domain is determined, where the licensed members are not projected.

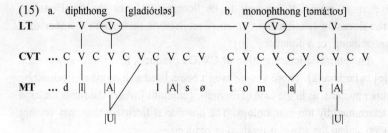

Consider the case of apparent penultimate stress, as in *tomáto* or *aróma* as opposed to antepenultimate *cínema*. When a 'penult stress' is observed, the stressed vowel appears as a long vowel to form a licensing domain [a:] and [oʊ], resulting in the word placing the stress on the third nuclear point from the right edge. Compare *aróma* [aróʊmə] and *aromátic* [arəmátik]. A word like *tomato* provides divergent responses when placing stress on the word medial /a/. In British English, it is pronounced [təmá:toʊ], the medial vowel is lengthened, and in American English, it is generally pronounced [təméɪtoʊ]. In both cases, the stressed vowel is long: monophthong [a:] and diphthong [eɪ] both form progressive licensing domains.

Remaining questions regarding the vowel length include the unstressed final nuclear sequence of *tomato*. GP assumes that the English domain-final nuclei are parametrically licensed, which means that a word can end with a consonant in English. Most vowel-final words in English are of foreign origin, which are incorporated into the above parametric setting. In a language whose domain-final nucleus is not licensed, for example, Japanese, the final nuclei must be filled, thus loanwords from English obtains an element |U| for that position as in *hamu* 'ham' (Yoshida 2003). In English, to obtain the licensed final-nucleus, the word-final filled vowel becomes a licensor, thus projecting to LT. The proposal given by Scheer (2004) and extended here predicts that we license an extra CV pair to the right of a final syllable. In words with a word-final diphthong, which has an |I| element or |U| element, for example, [təmá:toʊ], manifests as the result of those elements spreading onto the Cs, leaving the following V empty and licensed by virtue of being domain-final. However, I also have in mind words that end in /ə/ like [bəná:nə]. The same CV insertion applies to have a totally empty CV, with no melody spreading onto that C. It is necessary to examine this in more detail in the future.

Conclusion

This chapter pursued the possibility of the LT, a tier that controls stress/accent placement in phonological system, motivated by the LP (Charette 1990).

The argument is based on examples in Japanese and English. Further investigation on stress and accent should focus on other languages as well as on larger prosodic domains in English.

Notes

1. I would like to express my huge gratitude towards Geoff Williams for discussions, invaluable comments and improving the manuscript. Remaining errors are mine alone.
2. Some of the main abbreviations used in this chapter: LT = Licensor Tier; HVD = High Vowel Devoicing; LP = Licensor Projection; PG = Proper Government; NP = Nuclear Projection; MT = Melodic Tier; CT = Constituent Tier.
3. Youngberg (2021) offers an alternative view where /N/ is either a nasal vowel in Standard Japanese or a syllabic nasal in Kansai Japanese, but this may hinder capturing some facts, for example, realisation of /N/ as the labial consonant [m] in emphatic pronunciation in both varieties.

References

Burzio, L. (1994). *Principles of English Stress*. Cambridge Studies in Linguistics 72. Cambridge: Cambridge University Press.
Charette, M. (1990). 'Licence to govern'. *Phonology* 7(2), 233–53. https://doi.org/10.1017/S0952675700001196.
Charette, M. (1991). *Conditions on Phonological Government*. Cambridge: Cambridge University Press.
Faust, N., and Ulfsbjorninn, S. (2018). 'Arabic stress in strict CV, with no moras, no syllables, no feet and no extrametricality'. *The Linguistic Review* 35(4), 561–600.
Gussmann, E., and Harris, J. (2002). 'Word-final onsets'. *UCL Working Papers in Linguistics* 14.
Halle, M., and Vergnaud, J.-R. (1987). *An Essay on Stress*. Cambridge, MA: MIT Press.
Hayes, B. (1980). *A Metrical Theory of Stress Rules*. Doctoral dissertation, Massachusetts Institute of Technology (MIT).
Haraguchi, S. (1991). *A theory of stress and accent*. Berlin: Foris.
Hayes, B. (1995). *Metrical Stress Theory*. Chicago: University of Chicago Press.
Hyman, L. (2006). 'Word-prosodic typology'. *Phonology* 23, 225–257.
Kaye, J. (1987). 'Government in phonology. The case of Moroccan Arabic.' *Linguistic Review* 6(2), 131–160.
Kaye, J., Lowenstamm, J., and Vergnaud, J.-R. (1985). 'The internal structure of phonological representations: A theory of Charm and Government'. *Phonology Yearbook* 2, 305–28.
Kaye, J., Lowenstamm, J., and Vergnaud, J.-R. (1990). 'Constituent structure and government in phonology'. *Phonology* 7(2), 193–231.
Lowenstamm, J. (1996). 'CV as the only syllable type'. In *Current Trends in Phonology: Models and method*, edited by J. Durand and B. Laks, 419–41. Salford: European Studies Research Institute.
Scheer, T. (2004). *A Lateral Theory of Phonology, Volume 1: What is CVCV, and why should it be?* Berlin: Mouton de Gruyter.
Scheer, T. (2012). *A Lateral Theory of Phonology, Volume 2. Direct interface and one-channel translation*. Berlin: De Gruyter.
Scheer, T., and Szigetvári, P. (2005). 'Unified representations for stress and the syllable'. *Phonology* 22(1), 37–75.
Ulfsbjorninn, S. (2014). *A Field Theory of Stress: The role of empty nuclei in stress systems*, Doctoral dissertation, SOAS, University of London.
Vance, T. (1987). *An Introduction to Japanese Phonology*. Albany, New York: SUNY Press.
Yoshida, S. (1990). 'A government-based analysis of the "mora" in Japanese'. *Phonology* 7, 331–5.
Yoshida, Y. (1999). *On Pitch Accent Phenomena in Standard Japanese*. The Hague: Holland Academic Graphics.
Yoshida, Y. (2003). 'Licensing Constraints to let'. In *Living on the Edge: Festschrift for Jonathan Kaye*, edited by S. Ploch, 449–64. Berlin: De Gruyter.

Yoshida, Y. (2013). 'Accents and vowel devoicing in bimoraic Yamato words'. *Communicare* 2, 21–41.
Yoshida, Y. (2019). 'Pitch accent on /N/ in Osaka and Kyoto Japanese'. *KLS Selected Papers* 1, 185–97.
Youngberg, C. (2021). 'Representing the moraic nasal in Japanese: Evidence from Tōkyō, Ōsaka and Kagoshima'. *Glossa* 6(1), 1–36. https://doi.org/10.5334/gjgl.1099.

Part 3
Emptiness, schwa, and epenthesis

14
Emptiness, schwa, and epenthesis: a brief introduction
Connor Youngberg

Introduction

This part of the book focuses on the study of epenthetic vowels, vowels defined as schwa, and the study of empty constituents or positions in phonological structure. Broadly speaking, we can view epenthesis as a process that affects morphologically complex words or as a repair for loanwords that breaks up illicit, banned, or unfavourable consonant or vowel sequences by inserting a vowel or consonant respectively (Kenstowicz and Kisseberth 1979; Hall 2011). Schwa can be loosely defined as a central vowel like [ə] or [œ] which alternates with zero in some languages. French is one such language, having a stable vowel [œ] as in [bœf] 'beef' and an alternating vowel [œ] as in [ʃœvø ~ ʃvø] 'hair' which is phonetically identical in word-medial context, but which exhibits divergent phonological behaviour (Anderson 1982; Charette 1991).[1] This schwa is often transcribed [ə] to differentiate its status, exemplifying a different phonological identity to stable [œ] which never varies.

Emptiness in phonology and Government Phonology

Emptiness in phonology has a more complicated story and has been recognised to various degrees within the literature. The variability of certain vowels in phonological studies has led directly to the recognition of the potential of emptiness. To account for the alternating behaviour of what we identify as French schwa above, Anderson (1982) proposed that schwa is an empty nucleus which is realised as [œ]. Within Government Phonology (GP) (Kaye et al. (KLV) 1990; Charette 1991) schwa vowels, syncope, and epenthesis are in fact interrelated phenomena, and it is proposed that a) epenthetic vowels and schwa vowels are instantiations of empty nuclei, whose existence and silence is heavily regulated, b) empty nuclei are found word medially at sites of vowel-zero alternations and within certain consonant clusters, and c) that word-final 'codas' are onsets preceding an empty nucleus (Kaye et al. 1990; Kaye 1990a,b; Charette 1990, 1991; Harris 1994; Gussmann 2002). Empty nuclei remain silent or are realised as a vowel such as [œ] in French or [ə] in English based on the medial or final position of the nucleus and the relevant conditions licensing their silence. Word-final empty nuclei are licensed by a parameter which is ON or OFF, being permitted in English /kæt_/ [kæt] 'cat' but absent in Japanese and subject to epenthesis, e.g. [gasɯ] for English *gas* (petrol).

(1) **English and Japanese final nuclei**

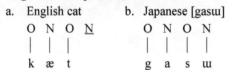

a. English cat
O N O N
| | |
k æ t

b. Japanese [gasɯ]
O N O N
| | | |
g a s ɯ

In the word-medial context, empty nuclei are licensed to remain empty and silent by their following nuclear constituent. This does not come for free and is possible if and only if the following nucleus has a phonetic interpretation or contains a segment (Kaye 1990a, b; Charette 1991). If this fails, the nucleus is realised phonetically. This licensing is called Proper Government (PG) within the GP literature. Kaye (1990a) shows that this regulates alternations in the occurrence of Moroccan Arabic [ɨ] in verbal forms of roots like /ktb/, such as [ktɨb] 'he/she writes' and [kɨtbu] 'they write' (Kaye 1990a). In short, Kaye claims that [ɨ] is the realisation of an empty nucleus which is not properly governed and thus phonetically realised; epenthesis is explained not by reference to consonant clusters, but to the status of the following nucleus as shown below. PG is shown with a solid arrow, while the failure of government is shown with a crossed arrow.

(2) **Moroccan Arabic verbal alternations**

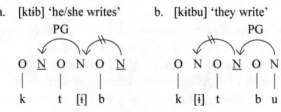

a. [ktɨb] 'he/she writes'
PG
O N O N O N
| | |
k t [ɨ] b

b. [kɨtbu] 'they write'
PG
O N O N O N
| | | |
k [ɨ] t b u

PG can also be said to regulate the appearance and disappearance of schwa (or alternating [œ]) in words like *cheveux* 'hair' [ʃœvø~ʃvø] or in clitic groups within French phrases such as *envie de te le demander* (Charette 1991, 199). This phrase may be maximally realised as [ãvi dœ tœ lœ dœmãde], but the vowel [œ] in each morpheme within the clitic group may be syncopated in a strictly alternating pattern, giving possible grammatical realisations such as [ãvi d tœ t dœmãde] or [ãvi dœ t lœ dmãde] but never *[ãvi d t l dœmãde]. Charette (1991) explains that this can be accounted for through PG, which gives rise to the on-off nature of epenthesis.

Epenthesis can be correlated to the occurrence and avoidance of certain consonant clusters. This is recognised early in Kenstowicz and Kisseberth's (1979) study of Yowlumne or Yawelmani epenthesis and syncope. Investigation of the interlinked relation between consonant clusters and epenthesis has led to a wealth of proposals examining the exact reasons for the conspiracies outlined by Kenstowicz and Kisseberth. Let us briefly consider French.

While above schwa in French is characterised as an alternating vowel, Charette (1991) points out that some vowels realised as [œ] never alternate with zero in specific cluster contexts, namely following a cluster of rising sonority or falling sonority word medially like *brebis* 'sheep' [bʁœbi], *[brbi] and *parvenir* 'reach' [paʁvœniʁ] *[paʁvnir]. The link between epenthesis or schwa and consonant clusters is considered by Charette (1990, 1991, 1992, 2003, 2018) in languages such as French, Polish, Mongolian, and Tangale and the author proposes that the realisation (or lack thereof) of empty nuclei is directly linked to the existence of consonant clusters in the surrounding environment due to licensing requirements within phonological constituents. In a close examination of the relation between nuclei and their preceding onsets, Charette (1990, 1991) proposes that Government Licensing (GL) is a relation where a nucleus licenses not only the preceding onset, but also its ability to branch and form either a branching onset or coda-onset cluster. In short, a full nucleus can license the maximal syllable in a language, but languages will be forced to choose how empty nuclei are dealt with following a consonant cluster. In French, empty nuclei are typically unrealised in light syllable contexts like *semaine* 'week' [smɛn ~ sœmɛn]. Word medially, schwa *must* be realised following a branching onset like *brebis* 'sheep' [bʁœbi], *[bʁbi] and following a coda-onset like *parvenir* 'reach' [paʁvœniʁ] *[paʁvniʁ]. This is because this empty nucleus must be realised and not silenced and licensed by PG so that it can government license its onset. However, Charette (1991) shows that conditions are not the same in word-final context in French words like *quatre* [katʁ] 'four', with different parameter settings regulating word-final and word-medial nuclei. Word-medial and word-final full and empty nuclei may thus be seen as having different potential. Charette (1991, 1992) also shows that the potential of empty nuclei to license clusters differs not only in different varieties of French, but also cross-linguistically in Portuguese (Charette 1991, 141), Polish, Mongolian (Charette 1992), Laurentian and Continental French (Charette 2003), and Acadian French (Charette 2018). Further work on the role of licensing of empty constituents, consonant clusters, as well as parametrical variation and licensing potential in GP approaches includes, but is not limited to, work from Harris (1992, 1994, 1997), Lowenstamm (1996), Gussmann (2002, 2007), Kula (2002), Scheer (2004, 2012) and Cyran (2010). More recently, empty nuclei have been combined with Turbidity Theory by Cavirani and van Oostendorp (2017) and Cavirani (2022).

Emptiness, schwa, and epenthesis in this volume

The contributions in this part of the book contain experimental, descriptive, and theoretical works on epenthesis and vowel-zero alternations which consider not only representational and theoretical analyses, but also enlightening studies of epenthetic vowels and consonants focusing on empirical results. Many of the contributions are influenced by the Government Phonology analyses mentioned above, others focus on improving our understanding of epenthesis in specific languages with careful considerations of data.

Some chapters overlap with topics discussed elsewhere in this book, but are placed here as they invoke emptiness and its effects within a word structure. For example, Kula (Chapter 18) discusses consonant cluster occurrence in Bantu languages, crucially invoking the power of nuclei to license clusters and silence an empty nuclear position in languages lacking tell-tale vowel-zero alternations showing PG activity. Likewise, Cavirani (Chapter 15) and Scheer (Chapter 19) discuss consonant-glide sequences in French, paralleling nicely with Pöchtrager (Chapter 12), though Cavirani and Scheer place more emphasis on the link between empty or realised nuclei and consonant-glide sequences compared to Pöchtrager's focus on the profiles and composition of these sequences.

A brief summary of the chapters

Cavirani (Chapter 15) examines consonant-yod (*Cj*) sequences in French words like *cimetière*, building on Charette (2003) using Optimality Theory style computation and Turbidity Theory to improve our understanding of epenthesis and gliding in Laurentian and Continental French. Turning to Brazilian Portuguese, Cristófaro Silva (Chapter 16) considers the role of final empty nucleus in Brazilian Portuguese and implements empty nuclei to better understand stress patterns. In an experimental study, Kenstowicz (Chapter 17) examines the epenthetic vowels of Connemara Irish, their realisation, and their syllabification. Such data crucially provides important empirical clarification on the status of epenthesis vowels in Connemara Irish.

Turning to the question of consonant clusters and licensing, Kula (Chapter 18) examines Meinhof's Law in Bantu languages from a GP point of view, arguing that restrictions and variations on NC cluster realisation are linked to licensing potentials of nuclei, with NC cluster alterations and lack of *NC1VNC2 arising as a result of the competing government licensing demands from nuclei to NC clusters, which must govern the empty nucleus within.

Scheer (Chapter 19) examines the effects of consonant-glide sequences in French varieties, echoing Cavirani, but with a careful eye on what structures may be posited for *Cj* sequences, focusing on the governing and licensing possibilities and their implications. This part of the book concludes with a study from Szigetvári (Chapter 20), who neutrally examines plosive-zero alternation within consonant clusters in English in words like *prince* [prin(t)s]. He presents results from a new survey of English speakers and considers resultant problematic implications for analyses framed within GP.

Note

1. Schwa in French is much more complex than the broad and simplified picture given here. Its realisation and behaviour varies in the speech of different speakers, generations, speech registers, and French varieties. I refer the reader to Anderson (1982) and Charette (1991) for their discussion of the relevant data and Detey et al. (2016) for one recent overview of French variation.

References

Anderson, S. (1982). 'The analysis of French schwa; or how to get something from nothing'. *Language* 58(3), 534–73.
Cavirani, E. (2022). 'Silent lateral actors: the role of unpronounced nuclei in morpho-phonological analyses'. *The Linguistic Review* 39(4), 615–653. https://doi.org/10.1515/tlr-2022-2099.
Cavirani, E., and van Oostendorp, M. (2017). 'On silent markedness'. In *Beyond Markedness in Formal Phonology*, edited by B. Samuels, 101–20. Amsterdam: John Benjamins.
Charette, M. (1990). 'Licence to govern'. *Phonology* 7(2), 233–54.
Charette, M. (1991). *Conditions on Phonological Government*. Cambridge: Cambridge University Press.
Charette, M. (1992). 'Mongolian and Polish meet Government Licensing'. *SOAS Working Papers in Linguistics and Phonetics* 2, 275–91.
Charette, M. (2003). 'Empty and pseudo-empty categories'. In *Living on the Edge: 28 Papers in Honour of Jonathan Kaye*, edited by S. Ploch, 465–79. Berlin: De Gruyter.
Charette, M. (2018). 'The internal TR clusters of Acadian French: a hint from schwa'. In *Sonic Signatures*, edited by G. Lindsey and A. Nevins, 18–32. Amsterdam: John Benjamins.
Cyran, E. (2010). *Complexity Scales and Licensing in Phonology*. Berlin: De Gruyter.

Detey, S., Durand, J., Laks, B., and Lyche, C. (2018). *Varieties of Spoken French*. Oxford: Oxford University Press.
Gussmann, E. (2002). *Phonology: Analysis and Theory*. Cambridge: Cambridge University Press.
Gussmann, E. (2007). *The Phonology of Polish*. Oxford: Oxford University Press.
Hall, N. (2011). 'Vowel Epenthesis'. In *The Blackwell Companion to Phonology*, edited by M. Oostendorp, C. J. Ewen, E. Hume, and K. Rice. Oxford: Blackwell. https://doi.org/10.1002/9781444335262. wbctp0067.
Harris, J. (1992). 'Licensing inheritance'. *UCL Working Papers in Linguistics* 4, 359–406.
Harris, J. (1994). *English Sound Structure*. Oxford: Blackwell.
Harris, J. (1997). 'Licensing Inheritance: An integrated theory of neutralisation'. *Phonology* 14(3), 315–70.
Kaye, J. (1990a). '"Coda" licensing'. *Phonology* 7(1), 301–30. https://doi.org/10.1017/S0952675700001214.
Kaye, J. (1990b). 'Government in phonology. The case of Moroccan Arabic'. *The Linguistic Review* 6(2), 131–60. https://doi.org/10.1515/tlir.1987.6.2.131.
Kaye, J., Jean Lowenstamm, and Vergnaud, J.-R. (1990). 'Constituent structure and government in phonology'. *Phonology* 7(2), 193–231.
Kenstowicz, M. J., and Kisseberth, C. W. (1979). *Generative Phonology: Description and theory*. New York: Academic Press.
Kula, N. C. (2002). *The Phonology of Verbal Derivation in Bemba*. Lublin: LOT Publications.
Lowenstamm, J. (1996). 'CV as the only syllable type'. In *Current Trends in Phonology: Models and method*, edited by J. Durand and B. Laks, 419–41. Salford: European Studies Research Institute.
Scheer, T. (2004). *A Lateral Theory of Phonology, Volume 1. What is CVCV and why should it be?* Berlin: De Gruyter.
Scheer, T. (2012). *A Lateral Theory of Phonology, Volume 2. A non-diacritic theory of the morphosyntax-phonology interface*. Berlin: De Gruyter.

15
Turbid government
Edoardo Cavirani

Introduction

Government Phonology (henceforth GP) was developed around the 1980s, when the power of transformational rules was being drastically reduced both in phonology and in syntax.[1] The structural description of rules was gradually simplified, until it definitively disappeared. This resulted in the formulation of very basic rules that apply freely, minimally, and cyclically until the affected representation complies with the requirements of well-formedness constraints, which, in turn, gained an increasingly important role.

In syntax, this tendency is witnessed by Government and Binding (GB; Chomsky 1981, 1982, 1986), where, for example, movement was formalised in terms of a very simple rule – *Move α* – that applies freely, its result being controlled by constraints such as barriers, Empty Category Principle (ECP), and, more recently, by the Minimalist Program (Chomsky 1995), where the free application of the one and only structure-building operation – *Merge* – is checked against interface constraints.

In phonology, the anti-rule movement produced autosegmental phonology (Goldsmith 1976). Also in this case, well-formedness constraints on representations took a prominent role, as the application of a very simple rule associating the autosegments to the skeleton was triggered and controlled by constraints such as the Well-Formedness Condition, the Obligatory Contour Principle, and the No-Crossing-Line Convention.

From this moment on, phonological research developed along two parallel lines. On the one hand, the rule has been totally dismissed, the whole computational burden being taken by a system of constraints, which can be absolute, as in Declarative Phonology (Scobbie et al. 1996), or violable, as in Optimality Theory (Prince and Smolensky 1993). On the other hand, frameworks such as GP and its descendants (for example, strict CV; Lowenstamm 1996; Scheer 2004) shifted the focus on the representational component, retaining a system of absolute constraints modelled on GB – c-command, Minimality Condition, Projection Principle, Structure Preservation, ECP, and Proper Government (PG) – and a sort of informally described association rule (Scheer and Kula 2018).

In this chapter, I address two of the constraints that GP inherited from the 1980s – ECP and PG – as well as the computational component, namely the operation linking melodic elements to root nodes (for further discussions of ECP and PG see Cristófaro Silva (Chapter 16) and Rennison (Chapter 6), for the No-Crossing-Line Convention). By analysing an alleged case of ECP violation, I aim at showing that such a violation is only apparent, and that PG can be retained in its original form, that is, absolute, exceptionless, and local. This is allowed by a redefinition of the association operation in terms of Turbidity Theory, an approach to input-output mapping that decomposes the autosegmental symmetrical relation between melodic elements and root nodes into two independent relations: projection and pronunciation. This makes it possible to distinguish between truly empty nuclei, which show no melodic content, and silent non-empty nuclei, which only lack the pronunciation relation (Cavirani and van Oostendorp 2017, 2019; Cavirani 2022). The empirical ground against which these hypotheses are tested is represented by sequences of two unpronounced nuclei in French (Charette 2003). Crucially, these sequences are argued to violate the ECP, which requires that each word-internal empty nucleus must be properly governed by a following non-empty nucleus. I argue that this ECP violation is only apparent, as the second of these two silent nuclei is not really empty: it is endowed with phonological content, which, though, is not pronounced. Crucially, by virtue of reaching a sufficient amount of representational complexity, it is entitled to properly govern the preceding empty nucleus (for a different account of similar data see Scheer, Chapter 19).

Besides eliminating apparent cases of ECP violation, the refinement of the empty category typology provides a solution to a set of interrelated formal issues of PG, such as the unclear relation between representational complexity and lateral strength, the dubious status of parametrically determined lateral strength, and the behaviour of yers, which, despite being pronounced, cannot govern a preceding empty nucleus, nor another yer.

On some formal issues of PG

One of GP's most renowned trademarks is empty nuclei. Something similar was already around in the early 1980s (Anderson 1982; Spencer 1986), but it is only in GP that such a device receives a thorough formalisation (Scheer and Cyran 2018). This parallels what happened in syntax, where, although the debate on empty elements can be traced back to the outset of generative grammar (see Cavirani and van Oostendorp 2017 for references), empty categories become a pretty standard theoretical device with the development of GB. In GB, the distribution of these categories is taken care of by PG, which *licenses* the empty categories/traces left back by movement only if governed/bound by an antecedent. PG allows for the recovery of the semantic content of the trace, and the derivation of a well-formed syntactic representation. Inspired by the Structural Analogy hypothesis (Anderson 1985, 1992; den Dikken and van der Hulst 2020), Kaye et al. (1990) introduce PG in phonology. As in syntax, PG is meant to account for the distribution and empty categories, which in phonology usually translates in nuclei that are part of the phonological representation but receive no phonetic interpretation: empty nuclei (ENs). Also in this case, what is at stake is the well-formedness of representations containing empty categories: ENs need to be given the right to stay silent, namely, they need to be (p-)licensed. In GP, this is granted via PG, which is dispensed by a phonetically realised nucleus occurring in the following syllable. Something different needs to be said about final empty nuclei (FENs), as they are not followed by any audible nucleus. FENs are thus argued to be parametrically licensed. Besides FENs, two other special cases were recognised: ENs that are enclosed within an interconsonantal governing domain (for example, coda-onset sequences) or precede a s+C word-initial cluster (where they are *magically* licensed). The latter two cases have been addressed by strict CV, which gets rid of GP prosodic constituents and of the non-proper form of government, such as the one holding in an interconsonantal domain and the one involved in magic licensing. As a result, the theory gains in elegance and simplicity.

However, as recently pointed out, for example, by Bafile (2020), strict CV seems to show some difficulties in accounting for patterns such as the one shown by Finale Emilia dialect, where segmentally similar consonant clusters are repaired via epenthesis in some forms but not in others. For instance, a form such as /ˈsalØsØ/ 'willow' results in [ˈsalɐs], where an epenthetic [ɐ] fills in the rightmost EN. The very same cluster, though, emerges as it is in /ˈdolØsØ/ 'sweet': [ˈdols]. Here, the first EN stays silent, despite being followed by another EN. In strict CV, the difference between the two forms has been related to a representational difference between the leftmost ENs: whereas the one of the latter form is *really* empty, the alternating one is represented as a N with a floating melodic content (/ɐ/), which gets associated to N, thus phonetically interpreted, only if not properly governed. As discussed by Bafile (2020), an important ingredient of such an analysis is a stipulation that says that 'final empty nuclei can only govern nuclei that do not possess any floating melody in the lexicon' (Scheer 2004, 644). Thus, it seems that it is necessary to distinguish between truly empty and empty-cum-floater N, or, as suggested by Bafile (2020), retreat from the bold EN-proliferating positions of strict CV towards the safer standard GP shores, where the difference between [ˈsalɐs] and [ˈdols] is due to the fact that only the former displays an EN, whereas in the latter, lateral and sibilant represent a coda-onset sequence. In her view, the problem is that 'the formalism of strict CV theory and its conception of empty nuclei is not able to properly characterise the distinction between 'true' empty nuclei and alternating empty nuclei' (Bafile 2020, 103).

In line with what Bafile (2020) observed, I argue that it is necessary to develop a more adequate formalisation of the various types of ENs. Differently from her, though, I do not take position with respect to whether GP offers more adequate tools than strict CV. Rather, I propose a refinement of the representational technology that is compatible with both theories and improves on a few interrelated drawbacks, such as a) the arbitrary and diacritic-like character of the parametrised government strength of FENs, b) the inconsistent relation between representational complexity and government strength, and c) the *visibility* of empty-cum-floater N, aka *yers*.

The problem in c) should already be quite evident: floaters are by definition unassociated melodic primes, and it is thus unclear why a given floater should be considered private property of a specific root node before some phonological operation (linking/spreading) introduces the relevant association relation. At the level of underlying representation, namely prior to phonological computation, ENs are just ENs, and a following EN shouldn't be able to discriminate whether there is some melodic prime floating around or not. On the other hand, if there is a floater, and that floater is aligned with a specific N, then it would be hard to conceptualise the latter differently from any other filled N.

This brings us to b), namely the inconsistent relation between the representational complexity of N and its governing strength. In GP, government strength is traditionally assumed to be proportional to representational complexity, as governees cannot be more complex than governors, where complexity is a function of the number of elements making up the segment (Harris 1990). Building on this, Cyran (2008, 2010) develops a licensing strength scale, where a three-way distinction is made between full vowels, schwas, and ENs. This scale is related to the distribution of onsets (T), complex onset (TR), and coda-onset (RT) sequences. For instance, he observes that full vowels can be preceded by (that is, they can *license*) T, RT, and TR clusters, schwa by T and RT clusters, and FENs only by (a subset of)

T. As claimed by Cyran (2008), 'the status of schwa in this scale is symbolic, and simply means that it represents a "prosodically weaker context than a full vowel". A precise definition of schwa for the purpose of this scale is a matter of further research'. I refer the reader to Cavirani and van Oostendorp (2017, 2020) for the development of a theory that attributes the different behaviour of full vowels and schwas to differences in terms of the elements' internal complexity. Details aside, it is important in this context to stress that the scale just referred to rests on the representational difference between the relevant segments, irrespective of whether they are pronounced or not. This, together with the assumption that empty-cum-floater Ns are representationally more complex that ENs, would predict that the former can properly govern the latter, no matter if they are not pronounced.

Note, though, that the pervasive direct relation between representational complexity and governing strength breaks down in word-final position, as rather than from the former, the latter is traditionally argued to follow from the setting of an ad hoc parameter. Some languages have this parameter turned on, so their FENs can properly govern. Others have it off, so their FENs cannot govern a preceding EN. This is a potential problem, as such a parameter looks like a diacritic, namely as something that is not encoded in the module-specific phonological vocabulary. In this sense, it looks like a betrayal of the autosegmental mantra inspiring GP-related frameworks, according to which, given the right representation, a process would follow. This encourages translating such a diacritic in more appropriate phonological, representational terms. This would allow us to tie the governing strength of FENs to their representational complexity, and the variation in FEN government strength across and within languages to representational variation, namely to the lexicon.

This brings us to a crucial aspect of the hypothesis defended so far. I argued that (i) it is necessary to provide a formalism that enables us to distinguish between various kinds of EN; (ii) empty-cum-floater Ns are suspicious objects, and (iii) we should possibly not give up the direct relation between representational complexity and government strength, which would in turn allow us to get rid of FEN parameters. As I will discuss below, the key to bringing all these pieces together is a formal and explicit distinction between *phonetic* and *phonological* emptiness. The necessary formal tools enabling such distinction are provided by Turbidity Theory (TT). In what follows, TT will be introduced, and applied to a case of so-called pseudo-emptiness in French (the section below on 'Pseudo-emptiness and turbid government in Canadian French'). As will be shown, this development also allows for a more adequate formalisation of empty-cum-floater N, and a solution to their alignment and visibility problem.

A turbid solution

Turbidity Theory (Goldrick 2001; van Oostendorp 2008; de Castro-Arrazola et al. 2015) is an optimality theoretic approach to faithfulness based on containment, which assumes an input-output relationship whereby the former is contained in the latter. The containment assumption of TT provides the tools to formally express the difference between *phonetic* and *phonological* emptiness mentioned above. These tools are the two different relations linking melodic content to root nodes that derive from splitting the symmetric autosegmental relation traditionally assumed by GP-based models. Rather than assuming that if an element α is associated to a root node ×, × is associated to α, TT assumes two asymmetric relations: a projection relation expressing the lexical affiliation between melodic primes and root nodes, and a pronunciation relation expressing the fact that a set of melodic primes is phonetically interpreted in a specific root node. Graphically, these relations are represented by two arrows: one from the root node to the melodic prime for the projection relation, and one from the melodic prime to the root node for the pronunciation relation. This is illustrated in (1), below, where representations are given that show no melodic content and no relation ($×_1$), only the projection relation ($×_2$), or both the projection and pronunciation relation ($×_3$). The former represents an EN, the latter a full N, and the middle one an empty-cum-floater N (henceforth eN).

(1) $×_1$ $×_2$ $×_3$
      ↓   ↕
      |A| |A|
   Ø   Ø   [a]

In TT, projection relations are part of the lexical representation of a morpheme, and cannot be altered because of containment and Consistency of Exponence (van Oostendorp 2008). On the other hand, the pronunciation relations can be modified in the input-output mapping process. This results from the pressure exerted by structural constraints holding on surface representations. I argue that the ECP and the related PG can be conceived of as structural constraints evaluating the well-formedness of a surface phonological representation. Assuming a direct relation between representational complexity and government strength, PG would behave like a constraint favouring surface representations where a nucleus lacking the pronunciation relation is followed by one which is representationally no less complex.[2] For this to work, TT relations must be included in the calculation of representational complexity, together with the number of elements.

In (1), complexity would decrease from right to left. The rightmost nucleus is the most complex, and is endowed with a full government potential. The middle nucleus is slightly less complex, but it contains phonological material, so it can exert PG. The leftmost nucleus is phonologically empty, and cannot govern.

Phonetically, the melodic content of the full N is faithfully interpreted, as expected. The phonetic interpretation of the other two Ns depends on their environment. If followed by a proper governor, they can stay silent, otherwise they are interpreted according to their phonological content: ENs are assigned a default vowel (usually the less marked vowel of the language), while eNs have their melodic content interpreted.

This approach provides a solution to the issues mentioned in the previous section. The problems of the visibility and the alignment of floaters in eNs vanishes, as there is no floater to start with. What was considered a floater, is now a melodic prime projected by a root node. As such, it is integrated in the phonological representation, and it can thus be seen by the following N, which can discharge its government power. If the latter is missing, the melodic content of an eN is given the chance to be heard: it gets its pronunciation relations and becomes audible. As for the parametrically determined government strength of FENs, this can now be transparently related to representational complexity. This implies a distinction between FEN and FeN: the former is phonologically empty, and cannot properly govern a preceding EN/eN, whereas the latter is endowed with some phonological content, and can properly govern a less complex N occurring on its left.[3]

Another issue that can be solved by such an approach is represented by apparent sequences of ENs, namely cases in which an EN seems to properly govern another EN. This possibility is in principle excluded by the ECP. However, French seems to show such unexpected sequences, which leads Charette (2003) to loosen the otherwise absolute binarity and locality principles of GP. In what follows, I provide a TT-based solution that allows for keeping such principles (a different analysis of these data can be found in Scheer, Chapter 19 of this book).

Pseudo-emptiness and turbid government in Canadian French

In her account of vowel-glide alternation in French, Haworth (1994) introduces pseudo-empty categories, namely positions that share their melodic content with an adjacent position. This is shown in (2) with the representation of *confié* [kõf'je] 'confided'. Due to OCP, the |I| element of the penultimate N spreads to the following onset empty position, whereas the N itself, being properly governed by the word-final N, is silent. By virtue of having some lexically defined melodic content, pseudo-empty categories resemble our eN, whose melodic content manages to escape government and gets interpreted in the adjacent consonantal position.

(2)

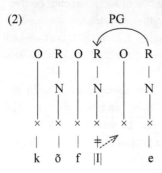

Note that, as the spreading of |I| depends on the availability of a following onset, in the Lexicon, the pseudo-empty N in (2) seems to rather correspond to a full N: before the concatenation of the past participle suffix *é*, |I| belongs exclusively to the stem final N. It is not shared with any following onset, as there is none. It is only after suffixation that the configuration is created by which (i) PG can take place, resulting in |I| delinking, and (ii) the OCP is violated, thereby triggering |I| spreading. Crucially, given that the pseudo-empty N can be silenced by PG, it must be different from a full N. One could thus represent it as a yer, but, because of the problems of yers discussed in the preceding section, it is possibly preferable representing the pseudo-empty N in (2) as eN (hence, in what follows I will refer to pseudo-empty N as eN).

As shown in (3a), in the Lexicon, whereas all the other segments have both the projection and the pronunciation relation, the final N of the root *kõfi* lacks the pronunciation one. The pronunciation of its melodic content is negotiated once this form is fed to the phonological module. If it is not followed by a proper governor, it gets its pronunciation relation and is phonetically interpreted.[4] On the other hand, as shown in (3b), if it is followed by a proper governor, it must keep silent. In such a case, if there is an adjacent empty position, its melodic content can spread to that position. This is formally expressed by the introduction of a pronunciation relation linking the element to the relevant root node.

(3) a.　　　　　　　　b.

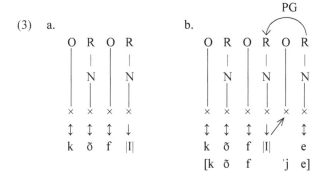

Charette (2003) moves from Haworth (1994) and considers cases in which a properly governed eN is preceded by an EN, namely cases that show two silent nuclei in a row, violating ECP. She compares Continental and Quebec French, and identifies two structures, which differ with respect to the consonant surrounding the EN. If the EN is preceded by a 'potential onset governor' (that is, the first segment of a complex onset) and followed by a 'potential onset governee' (that is, the second segment of a complex onset), the two consonants do not enter in a (onset-to-onset) governing relationship. In this case, the EN cannot be properly governed and needs to be phonetically interpreted. See, for example, *atelier* [atəl'je], where the EN occurring between *t* and *l* cannot be properly governed by the eN, which is itself properly governed by the following full N and surfaces as a glide.[5] Conversely, if the EN is preceded by a 'potential onset governee' and followed by a 'potential onset governor', the two consonants either do not enter into a governing relationship and the EN behaves as in the previous case, as in Quebec French *cimetière* [simət'jɛr], or they do enter in a governing relationship. In this case, the EN is properly governed, as in Continental French *cimetière* [simt'jɛr]. Thus, the presence of a governing relationship between the two consonants flanking an EN seems to be a condition for ENs to be properly governed by a following eN. Another condition should hold, though, namely the presence of an external proper governor. This is because, 'if one were to argue that onset-to-onset government alone was responsible for the p-licensing of the [relevant EN], it would still remain a mystery why this condition plays no role in other contexts', namely why i) 'a p-licensed [EN] is never a proper governor regardless of the consonants surrounding the empty governee', and ii) 'an unlicensed nucleus can always be a proper governor whether or not the empty nucleus is contained within an onset-to-onset governing domain' (Charette 2003, 476).

The problem with this hypothesis is deciding whether the relevant EN – for example, the one occurring between *m* and *t* in (4) – is properly governed by the following eN (which is in turn properly governed and surfaces as a glide), or by the full N further to the right – for example, (4)'s /ɛ/.

(4)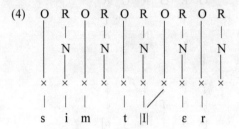

One possibility is that 'the proper government of a [eN] does not exhaust the governing potential of its proper governor [and that the] latter can therefore [...] properly govern two nuclei' (Charette 2003, 466). Alternatively, one could argue that 'a p-licensed [eN] act as a proper governor and assure the p-licensing of [a EN]' (Charette 2003, 474). In her paper, she starts exploring the latter option, but she eventually settles on the former.

Both options come with their own problems. Assuming that a full N properly governs the eN as well as the preceding EN 'implies relaxing the condition on strict adjacency between proper governor and governee' (Charette 2003, 476) and the binarity principle according to which a proper governor can only govern one empty position. On the other hand, 'claiming that a p-licensed position can act as a proper governor forces us to relax the conditions on what constitutes a proper governor [...] How could therefore any other type of p-licensed position be different? The condition is on p-licensing in general, not on the type of p-licensed category' (Charette 2003, 476). Crucially, I argue that p-licensed positions can in fact differ from each other in terms of complexity, and that it is the latter that determines what governs what. As claimed throughout the chapter, this grounds on the possibility of distinguishing between two asymmetric root-melody relations, which can enter the calculation of complexity. Once this is taken into consideration, Continental French *cimetière* [simt'jɛr] can be represented as in (5).

(5)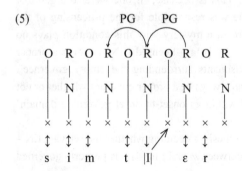

In (5), the full N /ɛ/ properly governs the preceding eN. Accordingly, the latter is assigned no pronunciation relation and keeps silent, whereas its melodic content spreads to – that is, is pronounced on – the following empty onset. Crucially, as the eN is representationally more complex than the preceding EN, it can discard its PG power on the latter, which gets no phonetic interpretation.[6] Note that, as in the original analysis of Charette (2003), the presence of an external eN proper governor is not enough for the silencing of the relevant EN, as it would be impossible teasing apart the behaviour of forms where EN is properly governed (for example, *cimetière* [simt'jɛr]) and that of forms where PG does not apply (*atelier* [atəl'je]). Thus, a further condition referring to the possibility of the consonants flanking the relevant EN to create an interconsonantal governing domain is necessary in the analysis proposed in this chapter too. I leave the refinement of the interaction between this condition and the lateral actorship of eNs to future work, and I refer the reader to Scheer (Chapter 19) for an analysis building solely on interconsonantal government.

Conclusion

In this contribution, I moved from a proposal put forward by Charette (2003), who suggests that, in order to account for some cases of sequences of silent Ns, we need to (i) relax the condition on strict adjacency between proper governor and governee, and (ii) give up on the binarity principle that allows a proper governor to govern only one empty position, and I suggested that such a departure from standard GP assumptions can be avoided by exploiting the representational possibilities provided by Turbidity Theory. More specifically, I proposed that the formal distinction between 'really' empty nuclei (ENs) and silent nuclei endowed with some phonological content (eNs) granted by Turbidity Theory allows for maintaining a tight correlation between representational complexity and lateral actorship. In particular, I maintained that, given that eNs are more complex than ENs, the former can properly govern the latter even if it is itself properly governed. Provided we accept the extra condition concerning the governing domain established by the two consonants flanking the EN preceding an eN, this crucially allows for accounting for sequences of silent nuclei without departing from strict adjacency and binarity.

Notes

1. This work is supported by the FWO Marie Skłodowska-Curie Actions – Seal of Excellence Postdoctoral Research Grant Nr. 12Z7520N. I would also like to thank Jean Lowenstamm, Radwa Fathi, and Tobias Scheer for useful comments.
2. See Polgárdi (1999), Harris and Gussmann (2002), Cavirani (2015) for attempts at translating GP mechanisms into constraints, and Brandão de Carvalho (2021) for a discussion of this possibility.
3. The (lack of) pronunciation of FeN can be taken care of by a constraint ranking where a constraint favouring CV sequences, for example, NoCoda, dominates a constraint penalising unparsed melodic content, for example, Parse or Pronounce. Due to space limitations, it is not possible to discuss this point further, but see Harris and Gussmann (2002) for a similar approach.
4. This happens, for example, in the present tense, where the element gets faithfully interpreted. As an example, see 1sg *confie*, pronounced as [kɔ̃'fi]. In such a case, one might assume an EN/eN 1sg marker. As this is not more complex than the root-final eN, the latter cannot be properly governed, and it gets phonetically interpreted.
5. Following Charette (2003), I assume that the glide corresponds to the phonetic interpretation of an eN silenced under PG, despite the fact that the paper provides no evidence supporting the hypothesis that the relevant piece of melodic content is doubly linked.
6. Charette (2003, 475) raises a further question, namely whether a properly governed pseudo-empty N can govern license the head of an onset-to-onset governing domain. Her answer is positive, which we can take as representing further support for the lateral actorship of eN.

References

Anderson, J. (1985). 'Structural analogy and dependency phonology'. *Acta Linguistica Hafniensia* 19(2), 5–44.
Anderson, J. (1992). *Linguistic Representation: Structural analogy and stratification*. Berlin: De Gruyter.
Anderson, S. (1982). 'The analysis of French schwa: Or, how to get something for nothing'. *Language* 58, 534–73.
Bafile, L. (2020). 'Vowel-zero alternations in government phonology and Strict CV theory'. *Studi e Saggi Linguistici* 57(2), 83–113.
Brandão de Carvalho, J. (2021). 'Representation vs derivation: the case for a modular view of phonology'. *Radical: A Journal of Phonology* 1, 292–327.
Cavirani, E. (2015). *Modeling Phonologization: Vowel reduction and epenthesis in Lunigiana dialects*. Doctoral dissertation. Utrecht: LOT Publications.
Cavirani E. (2022). 'Silent lateral actors: the role of unpronounced nuclei in morpho-phonological analyses'. *The Linguistic Review* 39(4), 615–53.
Cavirani, E., and van Oostendorp, M. (2017). 'On silent markedness'. In *Beyond Markedness in Formal Phonology*, edited by B. Samuels, 101–20. Amsterdam: John Benjamins.
Cavirani, E., and van Oostendorp, M. (2019). 'Empty morphemes in Dutch dialect atlases: Reducing morphosyntactic variation by refining emptiness typology'. *Glossa* 4(1), 1–22.
Cavirani, E., and van Oostendorp, M. (2020). 'A theory of the theory of vowels'. *Morpheme-internal Recursion in Phonology*, edited by K. Nasukawa, 37–56. Berlin: De Gruyter. https://doi.org/10.1515/9781501512582-003.
Charette, M. (2003). 'Empty and pseudo-empty categories'. In *Living on the Edge: 28 Papers in Honour of Jonathan Kaye*, edited by S. Ploch, 465–79. Berlin: De Gruyter.
Chomsky, N. (1981). *Lectures on Government and Binding: The Pisa Lectures*. Dordrecht: Foris.
Chomsky, N. (1982). *Some Concepts and Consequences of the Theory of Government and Binding*. Boston, MA: MIT Press.
Chomsky, N. (1986). *Barriers*. Boston, MA: MIT Press.
Chomsky, N. (1995). *The Minimalist Program*. Boston, MA: MIT Press.
Cyran, E. (2008). 'Consonant clusters in strong and weak positions'. In *Lenition and Fortition*, edited by J. de Carvalho, T. Scheer, and P. Ségéral, 447–81. Berlin: De Gruyter.
Cyran, E. (2010). *Complexity Scales and Licensing in Phonology*. Berlin: De Gruyter.

de Castro-Arrazola, V., Cavirani, E., Linke, K., and Torres-Tamarit, F. (2015). 'A typological study of vowel interactions in Basque'. *Isogloss* 1(2), 147–77.

den Dikken, M., and van der Hulst, H. (2020). 'On some deep structural analogies between syntax and phonology'. *Morpheme-internal Recursion in Phonology*, edited by K. Nasukawa, 57–116. Berlin: De Gruyter. https://doi.org/10.1515/9781501512582-004.

Goldrick, M. (2001). 'Turbid output representations and the unity of opacity'. In *NELS 30*, edited by M. Hirotani, A. Coetzee, N. Hall, and J.-Y. Kim, 231–26. Amherst, MA: GLSA.

Goldsmith, J. (1976). *Autosegmental Phonology*. Doctoral dissertation, Massachusetts Institute of Technology (MIT).

Harris, J. (1990). 'Segmental complexity and phonological government'. *Phonology* 7(2), 255–300.

Harris, J., and Gussmann, E. (2002). 'Word-final onsets'. *UCL Working Papers in Linguistics* 14, 1–42.

Haworth, E. (1994). 'The trouble with French glides'. *SOAS Working Papers in Linguistics* 4, 53–70.

Kaye, J., Lowenstamm, J., and Vergnaud, J.-R. (1990). 'Constituent structure and government in phonology'. *Phonology* 7(1), 193–231.

Lowenstamm, J. (1996). 'CV as the only syllable type'. In *Current Trends in Phonology: Models and methods*, edited by J. Durand and B. Laks, 419–41. Salford: European Studies Research Institute (ESRI).

Polgárdi, K. (1999). 'Constraint ranking, government licensing and the fate of final empty nuclei'. In *Phonologica 1996*, edited by J. Rennison and K. Kühnhammer, 167–82. The Hague: Holland Academic Graphics.

Prince, A., and Smolensky, P. (1993). *Optimality Theory: Constraint interaction in generative grammar*. Oxford: Blackwell.

Scheer, T. (2004). *A Lateral Theory of Phonology, Volume 1: What is CVCV, and why should it be?* Berlin: De Gruyter.

Scheer, T., and Cyran, E. (2018). 'Syllable structure in Government Phonology'. In *The Routledge Handbook of Phonological Theory*, edited by S. J. Hannahs and A. R. K. Bosch, 262–92. London: Routledge.

Scheer, T. and Kula, N. C. (2018). 'Government phonology: Element theory, conceptual issues and introduction'. In *The Routledge Handbook of Phonological Theory*, edited by S. J. Hannahs and A. R. K. Bosch, 226–261. London: Routledge.

Scobbie, J., Coleman, J., and Bird, S. (1996). 'Key aspects of declarative phonology'. In *Current Trends in Phonology: Models and methods*, edited by J. Durand and B. Laks, 685–710. Salford: European Studies Research Institute.

Spencer, A. (1986). 'A non-linear analysis of vowel-zero alternations in Polish'. *Journal of Linguistics* 22, 249–80.

van Oostendorp, M. (2008). 'Incomplete devoicing in formal phonology'. *Lingua* 118(9), 1362–74.

16
Word-final onsets: a Brazilian Portuguese case study
Thaïs Cristófaro Silva

Introduction

This chapter considers word-final onsets in Brazilian Portuguese (BP). It intends to support the view that word-final consonants are syllabified as onsets followed by an empty nucleus (Kaye 1990, Charette 1991, Harris 1994, Lowenstamm 1996, Piggott 1999, Harris and Gussmann 2002).[1] In order to understand how word-final consonants are syllabified in BP we have to consider how post-tonic zero-vowel alternation currently takes place in BP. Both BP and European Portuguese (EP) traditionally had a restricted set of word-final consonants: /S, R, N, l/. Consider (1).

(1) Word-final consonants in Portuguese

	Orthography	EP	BP	*	Gloss
/S/	mês	[meʃ]	[mes]	*[meʃɨ] or *[mesi]	'month'
/R/	mar	[maɾ]	[mah]	*[maɾɨ] or *[mahi]	'sea'
/l/	sal	[saɫ]	[saw]	*[saɫɨ] or *[sawi]	'salt'
/N/	tom	[tõ]	[tõ]	*[tõɨ] or *[tõi]	'tone'

The first column in (1) lists the consonant that occurs word-finally. The second column lists the orthography for each word. The third and fourth columns list the data from EP and BP respectively. The fifth column indicates that in these examples a word-final vowel does not occur, be it in EP or in BP. The last column presents the gloss. Notice that if a final vowel were to occur it would be different in EP and BP. EP has [ɨ] and BP has [i] as vowels that manifest when an empty nucleus is spelled out. Notice also that /S/ and /R/ have specific surface forms in EP and BP.[2] The lateral is vocalised in BP and /N/ triggers vowel nasality in both varieties. Our discussion is restricted to /S/ and /R/.

In order to account for the word-final consonants in Portuguese, it has been proposed that word-final nuclei are parametrically licensed (Miguel 1993). Some languages, like English or French license word-final nuclei and a number of consonants occur word-finally (Kaye 1990; Charette 1991). However, the restricted number of word-final consonants illustrated in (1), may posit a problem to Portuguese, as some other word-final consonants may appear word-finally where zero-vowel alternation is observed (Miguel 1993, Assis 2017). Consider (2).

(2) Word-final zero-vowel alternation in Portuguese

	Orthography	EP	BP	Gloss
/s/	doce	['dosɨ] ~ ['dos]	['dosi] ~ ['dos]	'sweet'
/ʃ/	lanche	['lãʃɨ] ~ ['lãʃ]	['lãʃi] ~ ['lãʃ]	'snack'
/ɾ/	pare	['paɾɨ] ~ ['paɾ]	['paɾi] ~ ['paɾ]	'stop'
/l/	vale	['valɨ] ~ ['val]	['vali] ~ ['val]	'valley'
/n/	cone	['kõnɨ] ~ ['kõn]	['kõni] ~ ['kõn]	'cone'

The examples in (2) illustrate cases of word-final zero-vowel alternation in EP and BP, where words end in sibilants, taps, laterals, or nasals. Other consonants may also occur word-finally in EP and BP.[3] What is important to observe is that in (2) a word-final vowel may occur, whereas in (1) a word-final vowel is not allowed.

It appears that EP and BP accept any consonant in word-final position when a zero-vowel alternation occurs. Word-final consonants in Portuguese, like in other languages, seem to have appeared as a consequence of unstressed vowels weakening and loss (Kager 1989, 2007). Whereas vowel weakening and loss has been documented in EP for a long time (Mateus 1974; Mateus and Andrade 2002), BP is at a stage where vowel weakening, reduction, and loss has only been recently reported (Leite 2006; Dias and Seara 2013; Albano and Meneses 2015; Assis 2017; Freitas 2019).

A question we posited is how to interpret the facts presented in (1) and (2), which present word-final onsets. Do both cases reflect the same phenomenon, or do they express different phonological interpretation? In order to address this question, we will take into consideration the notion of Proper Government and the Empty Category (Kaye 1990, Kaye et al. (KLV) 1990; Charette 1991; Harris 1994; Lowenstamm 1996; Harris and Gussmann 2002) to analyse zero-vowel alternation in Portuguese and explain the facts illustrated in (1) and (2). In the next section of this chapter we consider empty nuclei in EP. After that, we consider empty nuclei in BP where we propose an account for zero-vowel alternation and also explain the different sets of word-final onsets.

Empty nuclei in European Portuguese

A number of works have considered zero-vowel alternation in EP (Barbosa 1965; Mateus 1974; Andrade 1996; Mateus and Andrade 2002). Miguel (1993, 2003a,b) specifically adopted the Government Phonology framework. In order to account for word-final consonants that cannot be followed by a vowel, as shown in (1), Miguel (1993) assumed that word-final nuclei are parametrically licensed, and thus not phonetically manifested.

Miguel's (1993) work also explains the zero-vowel alternation in pretonic position in EP by assuming that Proper Government operates from right-to-left. Her analysis accounts for the similar pronunciations of the verbs *superar* 'to overcome' and *soprar* 'to blow' in EP, as shown in (4).

(4) Proper Government in pretonic position in EP

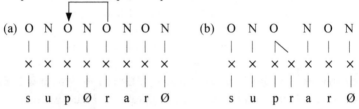

Both words in (4) are pronounced as [suˈpɾaɾ] in EP. In (4a) we have the word *superar* where the primarily stressed nucleus filled with the vowel [a] properly governs the nuclear position to its left, which then does not have phonetic content. In (4b) the *soprar* presents a branching onset. Notice that in both diagrams the word-final nuclei are not phonetically manifested as they are parametrically licensed. However, EP also presents zero-vowel alternation in post-tonic position. Consider (5).

(5)

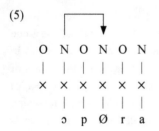

Miguel (1993) proposed that zero-vowel alternation in post-tonic medial position is accounted for by Proper Government which, in this case, operates from left-to-right as shown in (5). A problem her analysis faces concerns the direction of Proper Government, which is assumed to be language specific rather than variable (Kaye et al. 1990; Charette 1991). Whereas Miguel's (1993, 2003a) analysis proposes that in pretonic position Proper Government operates from right-to-left, in post-tonic position it operates from left-to-right. Miguel's analysis faces further problems in cases where a word-final consonant occurs (cf. 1, 2). Consider (6).

(6)
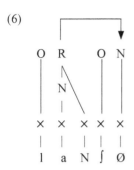

The representation in (6) illustrates the word *lãs* [lãʃ] 'wool (pl.)' and *lanche* [lãʃ] 'lunch' in EP. Notice that, the word *lãs* belongs to examples in (1) where the vowel is not manifested, whereas the word *lanche* belongs to examples in (2) where zero-vowel alternation occurs. According to Miguel's (1993, 2003) analysis the empty nucleus is parametrically licensed word-finally, thus not explaining the difference between *lãs* and *lanche* as shown in (6). Her analysis faces two problems: the variable direction of Proper Government and word-final onsets (cf. 1, 2). In the next section we consider empty nuclei in BP with the aim of understanding how word-final onsets can be explained in cases similar to (1) and (2).

Empty nuclei in Brazilian Portuguese

Word-final onsets in BP have been traditionally assumed to be restricted to the same consonants as in EP: /S,R,l,N/. Examples in (1) illustrated cases where the word-final onset in preceded by a primarily stressed vowel. Consider (7).

(7) Word-final consonants in Portuguese

		Orthography				**Gloss**
a.	/S/	*lápis*	[ˈlapis]	~	[ˈlaps]	'pencil'
b.	/R/	*açúcar*	[aˈsukah]	~	[aˈsuka]	'sugar'
c.	/l/	*fóssil*	[ˈfɔsil]	~	[ˈfɔsiw]	'fossil'
d.	/N/	*viagem*	[viˈaʒẽj]	~	[viˈaʒi]	'tone'

Examples in (7) show that word-final onsets filled with any of the consonants /S,R,l,N/ may be preceded by an unstressed vowel. Cases like in (7a) tend to have the post-tonic vowel deleted (Cantoni 2009; Soares 2016). Cases similar to (7b) tend to have the final onset deleted (Oliveira 1997; Huback 2006). In (7c) either a lateral or a posterior glide may occur. Cases as in (7d) tend to be subject to nasal diphthong reduction (Schwindt and De Bona 2017). We will focus on cases like (7a) as the discussion of cases (7b–d) would take us away from the purpose of this chapter. Consider (8).

(8) Word-final consonants followed by a sibilant

	Orthography				Gloss
a.	cheques	[ˈʃɛkis]	~	[ˈʃɛks]	'cheques'
b.	aves	[ˈavis]	~	[ˈavs]	'birds'
c.	clubes	[ˈklubis]	~	[ˈklubs]	'clubs'
d.	jegues	[ˈʒɛgis]	~	[ˈʒɛgs]	'donkeys'

Examples in (8) are plural forms. They represent a recurrent pattern in BP where a post-tonic high front vowel may be deleted when followed by a word-final sibilant (Cantoni 2009; Soares 2016). Data in (8) are accounted for by a sequence of two adjacent nuclei: *cheques* /ʃɛkØsØ/. Notice that assimilation does not take place between the consonants, as they are not adjacent since an empty nucleus intervenes between them. The word-final empty nucleus is accounted for as being parametrically licensed. Regarding the medial nucleus we suggest that it is governed by the preceding stressed vowel defining a metrical governing domain. We will develop this proposal in the following pages, after considering other properties of post-tonic non-final vowels in BP. Consider (9).

(9) Series of empty nuclei[4]

	Orthography	Final vowel		Final Consonant	Gloss
a.	hóspede	[ˈɔspidʒi]	~	[ˈɔspdʒ]	'guest'
b.	hipótese	[iˈpɔtʃizi]	~	[iˈpɔtz]	'hypothesis'
c.	hélice	[ˈɛlisi]	~	[ˈɛls]	'propeller'

Examples in (9) present words where two high front vowels occur in post-tonic position. The high front vowels may be deleted, so that a sequence of consonants occur. These words are nouns which can have a plural form where a final sibilant is added as a plural marker, leading to a sequence of three post-tonic empty nuclei: *hóspedes* /ˈɔspØdʒØsØ/ 'guests' (cf. 9a). In order to understand sequences of two and three post-tonic empty nuclei we have to consider penultimate stressed words. Consider (10).

(10) Antepenultimate stressed words
     Orthography   **Gloss**
   a. *xícara*   ['ʃikara] ~ ['ʃikra]   'cup'
   b. *córrego*   ['kɔhegu] ~ ['kɔhgu]   'stream'
   c. *básico*   ['baziku]   ['bazku]   'basic'

Data in (10) show that the vowel which follows the primarily stressed vowel in antepenultimate stressed words can be deleted (Amaral 1999; Ribeiro 2007). In order to account for the zero-vowel alternation shown in (10) we will consider Segundo's (1994) proposal for antepenultimate stress assignment in BP. Consider (11).

(11) Antepenultimate stress template in BP

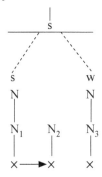

The diagram presented in (11) illustrates the metrical template for antepenultimate stressed words in BP (Segundo 1994, 157). The primarily stressed nucleus (N_1) metrically governs locally (N_2), and also governs (N_3). The binary foot is formed by the metrical domain which projects (N_1) and (N_3), as only the projected nuclei are accessible to the metrical structure. According to Segundo (1994, 160) 'metrical structure is not aware of the existence of two nuclear positions under the primary stress node when it is constructed'. We suggest that her proposal is in accordance with Kager's (1989, 2007) proposal for the interaction of the metrical domain and syllabification. Thus, one expects that syllable structure and metrical structure will be related.

Segundo (1994) argues that as a governee (N_2) should not branch, and this is the case in BP. Words such as *lirismo or *cólheita are not allowed in BP, as the former would have a post-tonic branching rhyme and the latter would have a post-tonic heavy diphthong. However, words as lirismo 'lyrism' and colheita 'crop' occur, where penultimate stress is observed. She also observes that as a governor (N_1) presents a greater number of different vowels than (N$_2$) and also that there is a relationship between vowel quality in (N$_1$) and (N$_2$).

Notice that a primarily stressed nucleus in antepenultimate stressed words may have a branching rhyme, as in *fósforo* 'phosphorus' or *círculo* 'circle', but it may not have a branching nucleus: *géologo or *cáotico. This is because, primary stress in BP must be assigned to the final, penultimate or antepenultimate vowel, but not to the fourth-to-last vowel. Thus, *geólogo* 'geologist' and *caótico* 'chaotic' are good words in BP.[5] The reason why branching nuclei are not allowed in primarily stressed positions in antepenultimate stressed words is that such a position governs the nuclear positions to its right, as shown in (11).

The proposal we have presented accounts for the intermediate nuclear position in antepenultimate stressed words not being manifested, as in *hóspede* 'guest' (cf. 9) and *xícara* 'cup' (cf. 10), as well as plural forms with three post-tonic empty nuclei as in *hóspedes* 'guests', as shown in (12), since any post-tonic medial position may be metrically governed.

(12)

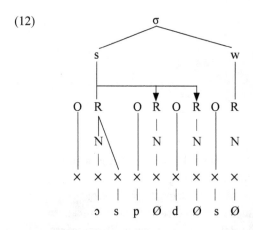

We still have to account for zero-vowel alternation in word-final position in BP (cf. 2). Consider (13).

(13) Word-final zero-vowel alternation in Brazilian Portuguese

	Orthography				Gloss
/p/	*jipe*	[ˈʒipi]	~	[ˈʒip]	'jeep'
/g/	*sangue*	[ˈsãgi]	~	[ˈsãg]	'blood'
/f/	*bife*	[ˈbifi]	~	[ˈbif]	'beef'
/v/	*chave*	[ˈʃavi]	~	[ˈʃav]	'key'
/ʃ/	*peixe*	[ˈpejʃi]	~	[ˈpejʃ]	'fish'
/ʒ/	*hoje*	[ˈoʒi]	~	[ˈoʒ]	'today'

Data in (13) illustrate cases where a high front vowel is deleted word-finally. Assis (2017) considered cases where /s,ʃ,z,ʒ,f,v,p,b,t,d,k,g,m,n/ occurred word finally in BP, where a word-final vowel occurred or not.[6] We have to explain why a vowel may or may not occur in cases like (13) but a vowel is not allowed to occur after some word-final consonants, as illustrated in (1). We suggest that any post-tonic nuclear position filled with a high front vowel may be metrically governed by a preceding governor nucleus, so that it is not phonetically manifested. This proposal is similar to Segundo's (1994). Consider (14).

(14) Licensed and metrically governed word-final empty nuclei

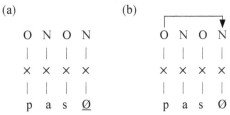

The diagram in (14a) illustrates the representation of the word *paz* 'peace', which presents a word-final empty nucleus that is parametrically licensed, and for the purpose of illustration is underlined in (14a). The diagram in (14b) illustrates the representation of the word *passe* 'entry ticket' where the nuclear position filled with the primarily stressed vowel in (14b) metrically governs the word-final nuclear position, which may or may not be manifested.

The proposal we presented accounts also for a sequence of two and three post-tonic nuclei (cf. 12). A word-final empty nucleus may be either parametrically licensed or it may be metrically governed by the nuclear position which bears primary stress. Any post-tonic medial nuclear position (cf. 9, 10) may also be metrically governed. If the post-tonic position is not metrically governed, then the vowel is phonetically manifested. The metrical foot is formed by the primarily stressed vowel which is projected to the metrical structure and the word-final nucleus. The metrical governing domain we proposed, which is based on the interaction of the metrical domain and syllabification, offers a unified account of word-final onsets in BP and also accounts for zero-vowel alternation in post-tonic position, be it medial or final (Segundo 1994; Kager 1989, 2007).

We posited the question whether cases in (1) and (2) reflect the same phenomenon, or they express different phonological interpretation. Our proposal suggests that cases where a vowel is not manifested (cf. 1)

are accounted for by the parametrical licensing of the word-final nucleus. Cases which display zero-vowel alternation in post-tonic positions are accounted for by metrical governing relations where an empty nucleus may or may not be phonetically manifested. Thus, cases like those in (1) and (2) are phonologically interpreted in different ways. This proposal offers a better analysis than the one proposed by Miguel (1993, 2003a), which assumed that cases in (1) and (2) had similar phonological interpretations, although they characterise different phenomena.

A number of issues may be raised as this system of vowel-zero alternation develops. Some of the parametrically licensed word-final empty nuclei in Portuguese undergo segmental change of the final consonant as the plural is added: *mar* [mah]*x*[maɾis] 'sea(s)' and *mês* [mes]*x*[mezis] 'month(s)'.[7] Notice that word-final consonants that may present a post-tonic vowel do not display similar segmental changes: *torre(s)* [toh]*x*['tohs] 'tower(s)'. It will also be interesting to observe how zero-vowel alternation develops in pretonic position in BP and see whether a phonetically motivated process of vowel weakening and loss may become a productive phonological phenomenon (Napoleão de Souza 2014; Nascimento 2016).

Conclusion

This chapter considered word-final onsets in Brazilian Portuguese (BP) offering evidence for word-final empty nuclei. It also considered how post-tonic empty nuclei in BP are phonologically represented. Word-final consonants in BP have different representations in cases where a word-final nucleus must not be spelled out (cf. 1), and cases where zero-vowel alternation occurs (cf. 2). We proposed that a metrical governing domain operates from the primarily stressed vowel to the post-tonic nuclear positions to its right. Thus, post-tonic zero-vowel alternation in BP is accounted for by metrical governing relations that are established at the level of lexical representation. A word-final post-tonic nucleus that is parametrically licensed is not phonetically manifested (cf. 1). Otherwise, zero-vowel alternation takes place under metrical governing relations (cf. 2). Our proposal explains why in BP some word final empty nuclei will not be spelled out (cf. 1) whereas others will display zero-vowel alternation (cf. 2). It appears that BP is at a developmental stage where it formerly preferred word-final filled nuclei whereas now it tends to favour word-final empty nuclei.

Notes

1. I would like to thank Yuko Yoshida, Connor Youngberg, and Florian Breit for their dedication to organising this volume. I would also like to thank CNPq (PQ-311934/2020-0) and FAPEMIG (PPM-X-00702-18).
2. BP may also present an alveopalatal sibilant in some dialects, as Rio de Janeiro, for words like 'mês'. It may also present a tap in some dialects, as São Paulo, for words like 'mar'. The examples were transcribed as in the variety of Belo Horizonte (state of Minas Gerais).
3. There are restrictions as to whether a vowel may or may not occur depending on whether a branching onset or a heterosyllabic cluster precedes the nucleus which may not be manifested. This issue is not relevant to the present discussion. Please refer to Miguel 1993.
4. In words like *hóspede* and *hipótese* the second-to-last vowel may be pronounced with a high vowel, as shown in (9) or with a mid-vowel, as in ['ɔspedʒi] and [i'pɔtʃezi]. We adopted the high vowel as it is relevant to the current discussion.
5. The only exception is the word *náutico* 'nautical'.
6. Assis (2017) did not consider the rhotics /R,ɾ/ which alternate in verbal morphology, palatals /ʎ,ɲ/ which tend to be vocalised, and the lateral /l/ which is vocalised word-finally.
7. The lateral undergoes more specifically changes: sal [saw]ːr[sajs] 'salt (pl.)'. To discuss these cases would take us away from the purpose of the current chapter. The nasal /N/ does not display any segmental changes as the nasal vowel just receives the plural morpheme: /soNS/ [sõs] 'sounds'.

References

Albano, E., and Meneses, F. (2015). 'From reduction to apocope: Final poststressed vowel devoicing in Brazilian Portuguese'. *Phonetica* 72, 121–37.
Amaral, M. (1999). *As proparoxítonas: teoria e variação*. Doctoral dissertation, Pontifical Catholic University of Rio Grande do Su (PUCRS).
Andrade, A. (1996). 'Reflexões sobre o 'e mudi' em português europeu'. *Actas do Congresso Internacional sobre o Português* (vol. 2), Lisbon, 303–44.
Assis, A. (2017). *A emergência de consoantes finais no Português Brasileiro na microrregião de Araguaína/Tocantins*. Doctoral dissertation, Federal University of Minas Gerais.
Barbosa, J. M. (1965). *Études de Phonologie Portugaise*. Lisbon: Junta de Investigaciones do Ultramar.
Cantoni, M. (2009). *Categorização fonológica e representação mental: uma análise da alternância entre [ks] e [s] à luz de modelos de uso*. Master's dissertation, Federal University of Minas Gerais.
Charette, M. (1991). *Conditions on Phonological Government*. Cambridge: Cambridge University Press.
Dias, E., and Seara, I. (2013). 'Redução e apagamento de vogais átonas finais na fala de crianças e adultos de Florianópolis: uma análise acústica'. *Letrônica* 6(1), 71–93.
Freitas, M. (2019). *A redução segmental em sequências #(i)sC no português brasileiro*. Master's dissertation, Federal University of Minas Gerais.
Harris, J. (1994). *English Sound Structure*. Oxford: Blackwell.
Harris, J., and Gussmann, E. (2002). 'Word-final onsets'. *UCL Working Papers in Linguistics 14*. http://roa.rutgers.edu/files/575-0203/575-0203-HARRIS-0-0.PDF (accessed 14 February 2023).
Huback, A. P. (2006). 'Cancelamento do (r) final em nominais: uma abordagem Difusionista'. *Scripta* 9(18), 11–28.
Kager, R. (1989). *A Metrical Theory of Stress and Destressing in English and Dutch*. Doctoral dissertation, University of Utrecht.
Kager, R. (2007). 'Feet and metrical stress'. In *The Cambridge Handbook of Phonology*, edited by P. Lacy, 195–228. Cambridge: Cambridge University Press. https://doi.org/10.1017/CBO9780511486371.010.
Kaye, J. (1990). '"Coda" licensing'. *Phonology* 7(1), 301–30. https://doi.org/10.1017/S0952675700001214.
Kaye, J., Lowenstamm, J., and Vergnaud, J. (1990). 'Constituent structure and government in Phonology'. *Phonology* 7(1), 193–231. https://doi.org/10.1017/S0952675700001184.
Leite, C. (2006). *Seqüências de (oclusiva alveolar + sibilante alveolar) como um padrão inovador no português de Belo Horizonte*. Master's dissertation, Federal University of Minas Gerais.

Lowenstamm, J. (1996). 'CV as the only syllable type'. In *Current Trends in Phonology: Models and methods*, edited by J. Durand and B. Laks, 419–41. Salford: European Studies Research Institute.
Mateus, M. H. (1974). *Aspectos da Língua Portuguesa*. Lisbon: Centro de Estudos Filológicos.
Mateus, M. H., and Andrade, E. (2002). *The Phonology of Portuguese*. Oxford: Oxford University Press.
Miguel, M. A. C. (1993*)*. *Os padrões das alternâncias vocálicas e da vogal zero na fonologia Portuguesa*. Doctoral dissertation, University of the Azores.
Miguel, M. A. C. (2003a). 'As estruturas silábicas e a redução vocálica no Português Europeu'. *Revista de Estudos da Linguagem, Belo Horizonte* 11(1), 95–118.
Miguel, M. A. C. (2003b). 'Regência de núcleos vazios'. In *Razões e Emoção. Miscelânea de estudos em homenagem a Maria Helena Mira Mateus, Vol. 2*, edited by I. Castro and I. Duarte, 73–94. Lisbon: Imprensa Nacional-Casa da Moeda.
Napoleão de Souza, R. (2014). 'The emergence of syllable structure? Data from gradient vowel reduction in Brazilian Portuguese'. *Proceedings of the Tenth High Desert Linguistics Society Conference*. Albuquerque: HDLS. https://napoleaodesouzacom.files.wordpress.com/2018/07/napoleacc83o-de-souza-2014-the-emergence-of-syllable-structure-data-from-gradient-vowel-reduction-in-brazilian-portuguese.pdf (accessed 14 February 2023).
Nascimento, K. (2016). *Emergência de Padrões Silábicos no Português Brasileiro e seus Reflexos no Inglês Língua Estrangeira*. Doctoral dissertation, Ceará State University.
Oliveira, M. A. (1997). 'Reanalisando o processo de cancelamento do (r) em final de sílaba'. *Revista de Estudos da Linguagem, Belo Horizonte* 6(2), 31–58.
Piggott, G. L. (1999). 'The right edge of words'. *The Linguistic Review* 16, 143–85.
Ribeiro, D. (2007). *Alçamento de Vogais Postônicas não Finais no Português de Belo Horizonte – Minas Gerais: uma abordagem difusionista*. Master's dissertation, Pontifical Catholic University of Minas Gerais (PUCMINAS).
Schwindt, L. C., and De Bona, C. (2017). 'Lexical frequency effects on reduction of final nasal diphthongs in Brazilian Portuguese'. *ReVEL, edição especial* 14. http://www.revel.inf.br/files/b3c33d8aa3915193ef94cdbef2abd8fc.pdf (accessed 14 February 2023).
Segundo, S. (1994). *Stress and Related Phenomena in Brazilian Portuguese*. Doctoral dissertation, SOAS, University of London.
Soares, V. H. (2016). *Encontros consonantais em final de palavra no português brasileiro*. Master's dissertation, Federal University of Minas Gerais.

17
A note on the svarabhakti vowels in Connemara Irish
Michael J. Kenstowicz

Introduction

The svarabhakti (epenthetic vowels) in Scottish Gaelic (SG) were first described in detail in a series of studies by Carl Borgstrøm (1937, 1940, 1941) based on fieldwork in the 1930s with speakers from the island of Barra and later from Skye and Ross-shire.[1] Borgstrøm postulated a contrast in the syllabic affiliation of segmentally identical morpheme-internal VCV sequences such as *marbh* [ma.rav] 'dead' versus *aran* [ar.an] 'bread'. As indicated by the orthography, the CV.CVC structures such as *marbh* contained an etymologically inserted copy vowel while the CVC.VC structures such as *aran* contained an 'organic' vowel that displayed the more reduced range of vowel contrasts that were possible in unstressed syllables. Borgstrøm reported that the epenthetic vowel of structures like *marbh* [ma.rav] displayed a stress prominence equivalent to the first vowel while organic CVC.VC structures like *aran* [ar.an] had a strong-weak falling contour. Given that SG has regular word-initial accent, the equal stress would support the idea that V1 and V2 are both constituents of the first syllable in the svarabhakti CV.CVC structures; and by bearing stress they would protect V2 from the reduction of phonological contrasts found in unstressed short syllables. Borgstrøm also indicated that native speakers judge the CV.CVC structures as monosyllabic, providing additional evidence for the contrast with disyllabic organic stems. The svarabhakti contrast was subsequently documented by other researchers for more Scottish dialects (Oftedal 1956).

Kenstowicz and Kisseberth (1979) called attention to this unusual contrast in light of the (re)introduction of formal models of syllabification into generative grammar. In general, when grammatical junctures are controlled for, languages have predictable syllable parsing. The SG data stood as a significant challenge to this thesis. This is especially remarkable because the postulated CVCC inputs to the epenthesis are not in general manifested in any of the svarabhakti stems' range of surface alternants. Over the intervening forty years the SG svarabhakti contrast has been the subject of numerous studies that have largely corroborated Borgstrøm's original observations and taken up the challenge they pose for models of prosody. These studies approach the issue from a variety of theoretical perspectives and include, among others, Clements (1986), Hind (1996), Bosch and de Jong (1997), Ladefoged et al. (1998), Bosch (1998), Smith (1999), Hall (2006), Hammond et al. (2014), Iosad (2015), Stanton and Zukoff (2018), and Morrison (2019).

Experimental results bearing on the SG svarabhakti contrast can be briefly summarised as follows. Bosch and de Jong (1997) report some observations on 102 CVRVC structures excerpted from recordings of conversations with an elderly Barra Gaelic speaker. The most significant of their findings concern the durations of the first and second vowels of the VCV strings as well as their pitch contours. V1 was found to be longer in the organic sequences compared to svarabhakti ones while V2 had the opposite duration profile. As the authors observe, the first observation makes sense under Borgstrøm's proposal that the copy vowel extends V1 and shares its stress; but the 'backwards' VC.V parsing of organic sequences would naturally tend to shorten the tautosyllabic V1, contrary to their finding. Bosch and de Jong also identified an F0 contrast between the two structures. Organic CVCVC sequences had a falling pitch contour starting at V1 while in epenthetic structures the F0 peak tended to fall at the onset of V2. Ladefoged et al. (1998) collected and analysed data from 11 elderly native speakers from the Lewis dialect. They confirm Borgstrøm's discovery that the svarabhakti sequences are judged as monosyllabic and document a falling pitch contour for organic *ballag* [pal^{y}ak] 'skull' versus a sustained rising one for *balg* [pal^{y}ak] 'belly' comparable to Bosch and de Jong's Barra speaker. Ladefoged and colleagues also suggest an alternative to Borgstrøm's analysis of the contrast as a difference in the affiliation of the medial consonant; they suggest that the svarabhakti sequence remains a monosyllable with the copy vowel simply extending the articulation of the stressed V1 through the sonorant consonant. On this proposal *ballag* parses as disyllabic V.CV while svarabhakti *balg* constitutes a single syllable with two vocalic sonority peaks. This structure expresses the native speaker perception of svarabhakti sequences as monosyllables directly. Finally, Hammond et al. (2014) investigated the svarabhakti contrast in several psycholinguistic judgement tasks with 18 SG native speakers (dialects not indicated). In one experiment speakers matched VCV sequences extracted from a corpus of spoken words like epenthetic [ara] of *bargan* 'bargain' versus the organic [ara] of *marag* 'blood pudding' with forced choice VCC versus VCVC orthographic sequences. Speakers distinguished among the excerpted VCV stimuli at the margins of statistical significance ($p > (|z|) = 0.04$). Acoustic analysis of the stimuli confirmed earlier findings of differences in vowel length and pitch contour on the basis of which the subjects were presumably forming their judgements. Hammond et al. (2014) also conducted finger tapping tests of syllable count that found svarabhakti sequences to have less positive disyllable syllable responses compared to the organic structures. The speakers' judgements were not categorical, however. Based on this observation the authors conclude that the svarabhakti vowels are present in the native speaker's phonological consciousness and hence should not be treated as excrescent vowels as suggested by Hall (2006).

The svarabhakti vowels have also been documented and analysed for various dialects of Modern Irish. Studies include Noyer (1990), Ní Chiosáin (1991), and Cyran (1996). Carnie (1994), Ní Chiosáin (1999), and Fullwood (2013) focus on the particular consonant clusters that allow or disallow the epenthesis. In Irish distinctions among unstressed short vowels have been significantly curtailed compared to SG. In general, they are transcribed with schwa and are subject to considerable variation as a function of the surrounding consonants – in particular the co-articulatory effects of palatalisation and velarisation. Nevertheless, the svarabhakti contrast exists in the orthography reflecting an historical sound change: *dorn* [tʌrən] 'fist' versus *doras* [tʌrəs] 'door'. Due to the vowel reduction Irish lacks the tell-tale copy-vowel sequences that mark the svarabhakti structures in SG and so raises the question of whether or not the orthographic distinction is merely a relic of the language's history with no synchronic grammatical validity. An important observation that motivates drawing a phonological distinction between the svarabhakti and organic VCV sequences is the phenomenon of inflectional palatalisation. For many noun stems an oblique or plural form is marked by the insertion of palatalisation on the final consonant or consonant cluster of the stem. Due to the strong co-articulatory effect of palatalisation on preceding vowels, the distinction between the citation and inflected forms of such words is quite noticeable. Svarabhakti sequences show palatalisation effects across the entire sequence while organic sequences confine palatalisation to the stem-final rhyme: *doirn* [tʌrʲɪnʲ] versus *dorais* [tʌrɪʃ].

Assuming that the inflectional palatalisation as well as the orthographic difference provide sufficient grounds for postulating a phonological contrast between organic and svarabhakti VCV sequences, many of the same phonological and phonetic questions posed by the contrast in Scottish Gaelic carry over into Irish. Are the svarabhakti vowels copies of the stem vowel so that a syntagmatic correspondence holds between them that is simply masked by unstressed vowel reduction? Do the vowels in the VCV sequences differ in duration and pitch as a function of the orthographic and corresponding palatalisation distinction? Finally, are there in fact consistent differences in palatalisation that justify drawing the distinction between the organic and svarabhakti sequences in the first place? In this note we address these questions based on data collected from a native speaker of the Connemara dialect of Galway in West Central Ireland.

Methods

Our data were collected from a female native speaker originating from Leitir Móir (Lettermore), a rural Connamara Gaeltacht in West Central Ireland. While residing in Boston, she makes frequent trips back to Galway to visit family and friends and has taught the Irish language and the traditional song repertoire for many years. The data for this study were recorded in a sound proof booth using professional equipment. Our corpus consists of c. 300 nouns elicited in list format over the course of three months in 2014. Many nouns were recorded as pairs with the citation form followed by the inflected form with stem-final palatalisation as reflected in the orthography. Several sets of words were constructed to investigate the questions noted above.

Our data replicate most of the restrictions on the VRC sequences found to govern the svarabhakti vowels in SG and earlier studies of Irish. First, epenthesis is restricted to clusters formed by a liquid or nasal: *arm* [arəm] 'army', *calm* [k^{h}aləm] 'calm', *banbh* [panəf] 'piglet', but *cosc* [k^{h}ʌsk] 'restraint'. Second, it is blocked in homorganic clusters (geminate integrity): *gorm* [kʌrəm] 'blue', *binb* [pinəp] 'venom', but *dord* [tʊrt] 'buzz'. Third, it is also blocked before a voiceless stop (realised with preaspiration): *lorg* [lʌrək] 'trace' but *cearc* [k^{hj}ar^{h}k] 'hen' and *dorcha* [tʌrəxə] 'dark'. Finally, epenthesis does not occur if the preceding vowel is long or a diphthong: *léargas* [le:rgəs] 'insight', *téarma* [t^{h}e:rmə] 'term', *ailb* [a:lp] 'alb'. In this case, our speaker had a few words that violated this restriction: *táirge* [t^{h}a:rəkə] 'product'.

Set 1

The first set of words were designed to investigate the duration and vowel quality correlates of the organic versus (orthographic) epenthetic stems. Twenty-five nouns of each type were recorded in citation and palatalised inflected forms. The data were analysed in Praat (Boersma and Weenink 2019). Praat textgrids were constructed to segment the VCV intervals based on visual inspection of the wave forms and the spectrograms. Praat scripts collected duration measurements for the vowels (V1 and V2) as well as the average values for their first and second formants.

(1)

CVCVC			CVCC		
citation	palatalised	gloss	citation	palatalised	gloss
dollar	*dollair*	dollar	*dorn*	*doirn*	fist
donas	*donais*	misfortune	*corn*	*coirn*	horn
doras	*dorais*	door	*calm*	*cailm*	calm
córam	*córaim*	quoram	*carn*	*cairn*	pile
asal	*asail*	donkey	*arm*	*airm*	army
camall	*camaill*	camel	*banbh*	*bainbh*	piglet
camas	*camais*	cove	*bolb*	*boilb*	caterpillar
calar	*calair*	cholera	*bolg*	*boilg*	belly
capall	*capaill*	horse	*colg*	*coilg*	sword
córas	*córais*	system	*colm*	*coilm*	dove
dochar	*dochair*	harm	*dearg*	*deirg*	red
domhan	*domhain*	world	*fearg*	*feirg*	anger
foras	*forais*	foundation	*gorm*	*goirm*	blue
galar	*galair*	disease	*lorg*	*loirg*	trace
iarann	*iarainn*	iron	*marbh*	*mairbh*	dead
imeall	*imill*	border	*scolb*	*scoilb*	chip
inneall	*innill*	engine	*scorn*	*scoirn*	disdain
iomas	*iomais*	intuition	*tarbh*	*tairbh*	bull
ionad	*ionaid*	place	*tolg*	*toilg*	sofa
ionadh	*ionaidh*	surprise	*borb*	*boirb*	fierce
solas	*solais*	light	*dealg*	*deilg*	thorn
eolas	*eolais*	knowledge	*dealbh*	*deailbh*	statue
ladar	*ladair*	ladle	*fearg*	*feirg*	anger
sionnach	*sionnaich*	fox	*leanbh*	*linbh*	child
uasal	*uasail*	noble	*ainm*	*ainm*	name

The notch plots in Figure 17.1 show the distributions for the duration measures of the V1 and V2 vowels as a function of their status as organic (CVCVC) versus svarabhakti (CVCC) sequences. Comparing the two plots it is obvious that the durations of the stressed V1 vowels are significantly greater than V2 for both stem types. Within each plot the durations for V1 and V2 are somewhat shorter for the svarabhakti stems. But a linear regression found no significant difference for either V1 or V2: F-statistic: 0.9031 on 1 and 98 DF, $p = 0.3443$ for V1; and F-statistic: 1.438 on 1 and 98 DF, $p = 0.2333$ for V2. We conclude that unlike in SG, the organic and svarabhakti sequences are not significantly different in terms of their vowel lengths.

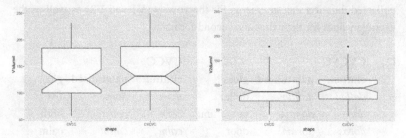

Figure 17.1 Duration (in ms) of first (left plot) and second (right plot) vowels of the svarabhakti (CVCC) and organic (CVCVC) stems.

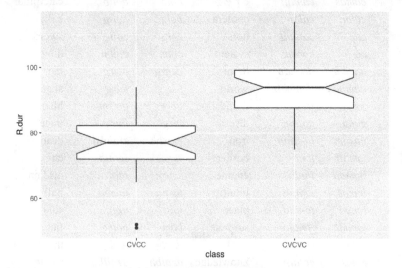

Figure 17.2 Duration (in ms) of the medial nonrhotic sonorant consonant in svarabhakti (CVCC) and organic (CVCVC) stems.

The plots in Figure 17.2 show the duration of the medial sonorant in the two types of VCV sequences. The rhotic [r] was excluded from this calculation since its segmentation from the surrounding vowels was less clearcut compared to the lateral and nasals. In this case, there is a significant difference with the sonorant from the svarabhakti CVRC stems being shorter (F-statistic: 26.12 on 2 and 57 DF, $p < 0.001$).

The plot in Figure 17.3 shows the F1*F2 distribution of the reduced V2 stem vowels as a function of the organic versus svarabhakti classification. It is clear that there is no overall separation between the two stem types as indicated by the overlapping confidence intervals. Both types show an inverse relation between the first and second formants such that as F1 decreases, F2

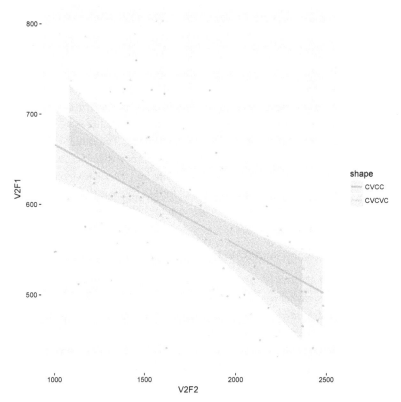

Figure 17.3 First (y axis) and second (x axis) formant values (in Hz) for the second (reduced) vowel in svarabhakti (CVCC) and organic (CVCVC) stems.

increases. This distribution suggests that there is just a single tongue body target for these unstressed reduced vowels whose height and backness is presumably determined by the surrounding consonants.

In sum, it appears that the Modern Irish neutralisation of vowel contrasts in unstressed syllables has wiped out any length and timbre distinctions in the vowels that might have existed between the organic and svarabhakti sequences comparable to what has been documented for SG. On the other hand, the duration of medial sonorant itself may help to distinguish the two stem types.

Set 1: pitch

We also investigated the F0 contours for the svarabhakti stems and compared them with the corresponding CVCVC disyllables and CVCC monosyllables. Forty-two words of each type were selected for analysis. We chose organic words where the medial consonant is a sonorant in order to better match the svarabhakti stems. The VCV intervals were marked in the Praat textgrids and then submitted to the time normalised F0 analysis in Prosody Pro (Xu 2013). The analysis window was set to 15 sections and the program extracted average F0 values for each sector. These were then averaged across the 42 samples for each word type. The results are displayed in the chart below. The chart suggests that in the svarabhakti stems the F0 peak is reached considerably earlier compared to the organic disyllables, which have a flatter more sustained summit that drops off at the start of the second syllable. The earlier F0 peak in the svarabhakti sequences mimics what is found in monosyllables, which also begin falling at roughly the midpoint of their (single) vowel. This pitch contour is quite different from what has been found for SG where it is the svarabhakti stems that display the delayed peak reached at the onset of the copied vowel.

Set 2: inflectional palatalisation

We recall that the major motivation for drawing a synchronic distinction between the svarabhakti and organic sequences in Irish is their contrasting behaviour under inflectional palatalisation. This process palatalises the stem-final consonant or consonant cluster in certain oblique/plural forms of a lexically determined class of nouns. For organic CVCVC stems just the final consonant seats palatalisation. But in svarabhakti CVRC stems, both the R

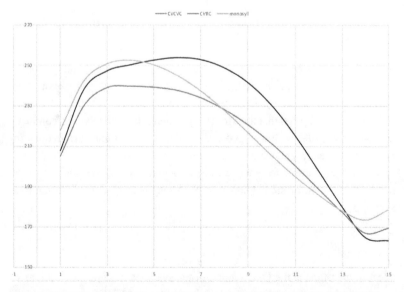

Figure 17.4 F0 plots of time-normalised organic (CVCVC), svarabhakti (CVRC) and monosyllabic stems.

and the final C are palatalised even though on the surface they are separated by
a schwa that at least phonetically is no different from the underlying reduced
vowel in the organic CVCVC stems. Examples of the two types appear below.

(2) | citation | | inflected | | gloss |
|---|---|---|---|---|
| calar | [kʰalər] | calair | [kʰalərʲ] | cholera |
| donas | [tʌnəs] | donais | [tʌnəʃ] | misfortune |
| foras | [fʌrəs] | forais | [fʌrəʃ] | foundation |
| colm | [kʰʌləm] | coilm | [kʰʌlʲəmʲ] | dove |
| banbh | [panəf] | bainbh | [panʲəfʲ] | piglet |
| gorm | [kʌrəm] | goirm | [kʌrʲəmʲ] | blue |

In order to corroborate this distinction two additional sets of words were
constructed. The first consisted of CVRC svarabhakti stems with a medial
lateral or nasal paired with a comparable number of organic stems with a
medial nasal or lateral (N = 13 in each case). Stems in [r] were excluded
because of difficulties in accurately segmenting the consonant from the
surrounding vowels. The second and larger set included [r] but restricted the
stressed initial vowel to /a/ or /o/. The presence or absence of palatalisation on
the medial consonant was then inferred on the basis of its presumed effect on
the F2 value of the preceding vowel.

The plot in Figure 17.5 from the data in the first set clearly establishes
that the medial sonorant in the svarabhakti stems is palatalised and hence
distinct from the comparable consonant in the organic CVRVC stems.

The plots in Figure 17.6 show the distribution of the F2 values for V1
in the second set of noun stems that include the sonorant [r]. They suggest
that in the basic citation form context there is no significant difference as a
function of stem shape (CVCC svarabhakti versus CVCVC organic). This
point was corroborated by linear regression (F-statistic: 1.716 on 1 and 50 DF,
$p = 0.1962$). On the other hand, in the 'derived' context of stem-final palatalisation the F2 of the first stem vowel was significantly greater (F-statistic:
35.94 on 1 and 43 DF, $p < 0.001$).

In sum, the data confirm the observation from the earlier literature that
the medial sonorant consonant in the svarabhakti stems is palatalised while the
corresponding consonant in the organic CVCVC stems is not even though in
both cases these consonants are separated from the stem-final consonant by a
full-fledged schwa vowel. In combination with suggestive differences in the
duration of the medial consonant and its contribution to the F0 pitch contour
observed in sections 'Set 1' and 'Set 1: pitch' of this chapter, they indicate that
the svarabhakti vowels are not just a relic from the history of the language but
also a synchronic reality which should be expressed by the grammar.

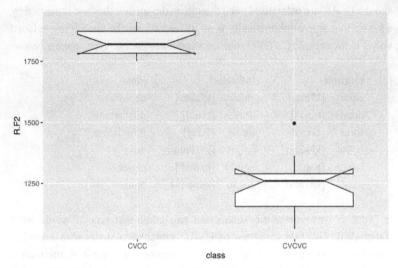

Figure 17.5 Second formant values (in Hz) of the medial sonorant consonant in svarabhakti (CVCC) and organic (CVCVC) stems.

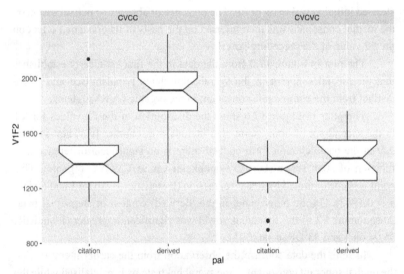

Figure 17.6 Second formant values (in Hz) of the initial vowel in citation (left side) and inflected palatalised form (right side) of svarabhakti (CVCC) and organic (CVCVC) stems.

Discussion and conclusion

To summarise the results of this study, we investigated the phonetic reflexes of the svarabhakti vowels in the speech of a native speaker of Connemara Irish. Our speaker consistently distinguished the underlying VRC versus disyllabic VCVC sequences in terms of inflectional palatalisation. But unlike in SG, the vowels of the two structures were not distinguished by surface phonetic duration or quality. We did, however, uncover a distinction in the duration of the medial sonorant, which was shorter in the svarabhakti stems. We also found suggestive evidence that the svarabhakti stems had an earlier pitch fall compared to the organic VCV sequences. Finally, when informally quizzed for intuitions of syllable count, our speaker did not clearly distinguish the two sequences – sometimes counting them as one syllable and at other times as two.

The literature on the svarabhakti contrast in both Scottish Gaelic and Modern Irish has seen a variety of proposals on how to account for the distinction. As far as the generalisations uncovered in this study are concerned, we believe the most straightforward analysis would assign the factors enumerated above at the derivational stage that precedes epenthesis. At this stage *doras* [tʌ.rəs] 'door' would be represented as disyllabic while *dorn* [tʌ.rən] 'fist' would be parsed as a bimoraic monosyllable /torn/. Inflectional palatalisation over the stem-final syllable rhyme targets the entire VRC sequence in *dorn* but just the final VC in *doras*. This monosyllabic stage provides a natural way to distinguish the duration and pitch differences as well. In /torn/ the medial sonorant shares its mora with the final consonant and hence will see its portion of the duration accorded to the mora reduced. Finally, the bimoraic stressed syllable of /torn/ could also seat both tones comprising the *HL pitch accent accounting for the earlier pitch fall compared to disyllabic *doras*.

It almost goes without saying that one must be very cautious in drawing any conclusions based on data from a single speaker. But we think it is fair to conclude that the questions posed here and the generalisations derived, tentative though they may be, certainly merit further investigation.

Note

1. Thanks to Anton Kukhto and an anonymous reviewer for helpful comments and to Mairin Keady for sharing her language.

References

Boersma, P., and Weenink, D. (2019). *Praat: Doing phonetics by computer*. Computer software, Version 6.1. https://www.praat.org.
Borgstrøm, C. (1937). 'The dialect of Barra in the Outer Hebrides'. *Norsk Tidsskrift for Sprogvidenskap* 8, 71–242.
Borgstrøm, C. (1940). *A Linguistic Survey of the Gaelic Dialects of Scotland. Vol. 1: The dialects of the Outer Hebrides*. Oslo: Aschehoug.
Borgstrøm, C. (1941). *A Linguistic Survey of the Gaelic Dialects of Scotland. Vol. 2: The dialects of Skye and Ross-shire*. Oslo: Norwegian Universities Press.
Bosch, A. (1998). 'The syllable in Scottish Gaelic dialect studies'. *Scottish Gaelic Studies* 18, 1–22.
Bosch, A., and de Jong, K. (1997). 'The prosody of Barra Gaelic epenthetic vowels'. *Studies in the Linguistic Sciences* 27(1), 1–15.
Carnie, A. (1994). 'Whence sonority? Evidence from epenthesis in Modern Irish'. *Papers in Phonology and Morphology* 21, 81–108.
Clements, G. N. (1986). 'Syllabification and epenthesis in the Barra dialect of Gaelic'. In *The Phonological Representation of Suprasegmentals*, edited by K. Borgers, H. van der Hulst, and M. Mous, 317–36. Dordrecht: Foris.
Cyran, E. (1996). 'Licensing properties of nuclei and principle ranking in Irish'. *The Linguistic Review* 13, 1–31.
Fullwood, M. (2013). 'The perceptual dimensions of sonority-driven epenthesis'. General Examination Paper, MIT Department of Linguistics.
Hall, N. (2006). 'Cross-linguistic patterns of vowel intrusion'. *Phonology* 23, 387–429.
Hammond, M., Warner, N., Davis, A., Carnie, A., Archangeli, D., and Fisher, M. (2014). 'Vowel insertion in Scottish Gaelic'. *Phonology* 31, 123–53.
Hind, K. (1996). 'The structure of epenthesis in Gaelic'. *Journal of Celtic Linguistics* 5, 91–119.
Iosad, P. (2015). 'Pitch accent and prosodic structure in Scottish Gaelic: Reassessing the role of contact'. In *New Trends in Nordic and General Linguistics*, edited by M. Hilpert, J.-A. Östman, C. Mertzlufft, M. Rießler, and J. Duke, 28–54. Berlin: De Gruyter.
Kenstowicz, M., and Kisseberth, C. (1979). *Generative Phonology: Description and theory*. New York: Academic Press.
Ladefoged, P., Ladefoged, J., Turk, A., Hind, K., and Skilton, J. (1998). 'Phonetic structures of Scottish Gaelic'. *Journal of the International Phonetic Association* 28, 1–41.
Morrison, D. (2019). 'Metrical structure in Scottish Gaelic: Tonal accent, glottalization, and overlength'. *Phonology* 36, 391–432.
Ní Chiosáin, M. (1991). *Topics in the Phonology of Irish*. Doctoral dissertation, University of Massachusetts.
Ní Chiosáin, M. (1999). 'Syllables and phonotactics in Irish'. In *The Syllable: Views and facts*, edited by H. van der Hulst and N. Ritter, 551–75. Berlin: De Gruyter.
Noyer, R. (1990). 'Secondary epenthesis and stress in Munster Irish'. *Proceedings of the Harvard Celtic Colloquium* 10, 1–23.
Oftedal, M. (1956). *A Linguistic Survey of the Gaelic Dialects of Scotland, Vol. 3: The Gaelic of Leurbost, Isle of Lewis*. Oslo: Aschehoug.
Smith, N. (1999). 'A preliminary account of some aspects of Leurbost Gaelic syllable structure'. In *The Syllable: Views and facts*, edited by H. van der Hulst and N. Ritter, 577–630. Berlin: De Gruyter.
Stanton, J., and Zukoff, S. (2018). 'Prosodic identity in copy epenthesis: Evidence for a correspondence-based approach'. *Natural Language & Linguistic Theory* 36, 637–84.
Xu, Y. (2013). *ProsodyPro: A Praat script for large-scale systematic analysis of continuous prosodic events*. Computer software. http://www.homepages.ucl.ac.uk/~uclyyix/.

18
Domino effects and licensing chains in government licensing: sequential NC clusters in Bantu

Nancy C. Kula

Introduction

Co-occurrence restrictions in sequential nasal-consonant clusters (henceforth NC clusters) in Bantu is a well-known phonotactic effect owing to Meinhof (1932) and thus appropriately christened Meinhof's Law (ML). Meeussen (1962) and Schadeberg (1982, 1987) provide descriptions and discussion. Various works in the phonological literature provide different analyses (Herbert 1986; Katamba and Hyman 1991; Kula 2006; Peng 2007). ML is akin in nature to Japanese *Rendaku* (Ito and Mester 1986; Nasukawa 2012) but differs from it, as while there is no restriction on the adjacency of the segments involved in *Rendaku*, some notion of adjacency is required in ML. In its most general form, ML can be characterised as a process that disallows a sequence of two voiced obstruents within NC clusters, that is, *NCvNC where both Cs are voiced.

From a Government Phonology (GP)/Element Theory perspective, I have argued that the restriction *voiced NCvNC is explainable by licensing relations as defined in a phonological domain (Kula 2002, 2006). Most of what follows here is based on that work highlighting the central argument that the restriction results from the failure of government licensing (as defined in Charette 1990, 1991) to apply, when there are competing licensing roles within a phonological domain, here consistent with a prosodic word. Another way of framing the question is, how many 'government licenses' can be offered within one interconnected domain? If this approach is on the right track, then it also, although only tangentially, brings us full circle to confirming the representations of N+C sequences as clusters in the Bantu languages that show ML, and begins to touch on how word maximality may be defined.

ML sound patterns across Bantu

A short overview of ML is given here, with further details accessible in the various works cited. In its simplest form the rule changes the first or second NC cluster in a sequence of two, depending on the language, to either a simple homorganic nasal or a nasal geminate. There is variation as to whether the trigger can also be a simplex nasal (for example, as occurs in Luganda, Kikuyu, and Umbundu) that we discuss only briefly here. (1), below, gives examples from Luganda (Ashton et al. 1954; Cole 1967), Lamba (Doke 1922) and Bemba (van Sambeek 1955). (1a,b) shows that the process only affects voiced NCs (N-l → /nd/ in 1b), with voiceless ones (1c) showing no simplification. (2) gives a fuller set of data from Bemba to fully illustrate the pattern within one language.[1] In (2d–e) we see that the process also does not apply when one of the two NCs is voiceless irrespective of its position, and (2f) shows the significance of adjacency with no ML applying when the two voiced NCs are not adjacent.

(1) a. N-genda   → nenda   'I go'   *ngenda   (Luganda)
     b. iN-lembo   → inembo 'tattoo'   *indembo (Lamba)
     c. N-tampa   → ntampa 'I begin' *nampa   (Bemba)

(2) ML in the Bemba perfective (-ile ending)
     a. n-βó:mbele → mó:mbel-e   *mbó:mbele 'I have worked'
     b. n-la:ndile → na:ndil-e   *nda:ndile 'I have spoken'
     c. n-tampile   → nta:mpile   *na:mpile   'I have started'
     d. n-pá:ŋgile → mpá:ŋgil-e *má:ŋgile   'I have made'
     e. n-lu:ntwiile → ndu:ntwiile *nu:ntwiile 'I have bumped'
     f. n-βéleŋgele → mbéle:ŋgel-e *méle:ŋgele 'I have read'

We can thus summarise the markedness relations of sequential NCs as in (3) below:

(3) root
     a. C_1VC_2-   voiceless   voiceless   most unmarked
     b. C_1VNC_2-   voiceless   voiceless
     c. C_1VNC_2-   voiceless   voiced
     d. NC_1VNC_2-   voiceless   voiceless
     e. NC_1VNC_2-   voiceless   voiced
     f. NC_1VNC_2-   voiced   voiceless
     *g. NC_1VNC_2-   voiced   voiced   most marked

Licensing chains: the domino effect

I will assume Strict CV in the following discussion (Lowenstamm 1996) and assume, following Scheer (2004), that government and licensing are the relations that define the syntagmatic relations between Cs and Vs to generate surface linear order building on standard GP work (Kaye et al. (KLV) 1990). The starting point is the licensing principle mandating that all positions within a phonological domain have to be licensed, apart from the head, which is itself the source of licensing potential, usually a dominant nucleus – V position in current currency. To recap and recast standard assumptions (Charette 1990, 1991) the head V position licenses all other V positions in the domain, which in turn license the C positions in their CV pairs. The precise manner in which such licensing applies is nicely exemplified in Harris' (1997) Licensing Inheritance Principle as given in (4).

(4) *Licensing inheritance principle*
A licensing position inherits its autosegmental licensing potential from its licensor.
Prosodic licensing and autosegmental licensing
Prosodic licensing sanctions the presence of positions at different levels of projection from the skeletal tier upwards. Autosegmental licensing determines the melodic content of a particular position.

The domino effect of the LIP and licensing through a domain as discussed above is exemplified in (5) below. Assuming V_1 to be the head, it licenses V_2 and then V_3 by domino effect. V positions then license C positions in their CV pairs:

(5) V- and C-licensing

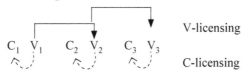

We can refine this idea to distinguish (i) the licensing of positions versus (ii) a position acquiring licensing potential so that it can itself be a licensor. Thus, in (5) all positions are dually licensed to be licit entities and are further licensed to license either melodic material (autosegmental licensing) or processes. Further, maximising this idea, we will assume that every process/activity within a phonological domain must be licensed in some way.

This in a way takes to heart what is already implied in the *non-arbitrariness* fundamental principle in KLV (Kaye et al. 1990, 194), requiring a non-arbitrary relation between a phonological process and the context in which it occurs. This then, coming back to ML, raises the question of licensing potential. How much licensing potential does a position have, and can we in some way, think of this potential as deteriorating as more licensing tasks are performed, so that a saturation point when no more licensing can be done is reached? This is the basic idea pursued here.[2] ML seems like good ground to test this idea as it offers us the phonotactic refinement given in (3) where voiceless only and a voiced-voiceless mix of NCs is acceptable but two voiced NCs is not. So that it is not just about the complexity of having two NCs. In addition, the locality restrictions also suggest proximity to potential licensors as playing a role.

Types of licensing and their relations

Before getting to the analysis, we need to make a few more assumptions in the context of enriched licensing (see also discussion in Cyran 2010 on this). I will assume three types of licensing as categorised below and also that they move from being universal and across the board to being more language specific, which we can capture by parameter. Type I involves licensing positions which every language will do. Type II and III are both going to involve parametric choices, with the former focused on the licensing of constituents while the latter deals with content both in terms of melody and processes. There is a natural hierarchy only in the sense that we assume a phonology needs positions which can then interact to create different syllable structure complexities and which themselves host melody that interacts in different ways. This is captured in (6) below, with (6b) giving an example of how syllable complexity emerges as different licensing relations are allowed in a language. The contrast between the presence of TR versus RT clusters in a language, for example, follows from which licensing relations are allowed in Type II licensing.

(6) a. Type I » Type II » Type III

Basic (universal) *Less basic* *Language specific*
position licensing government licensing licensing processes
V positions licensing gov. licensors licensing changes in
C positions p-licensing melodic structure

b. CV » CC (TR) » CC (RT) » (processes)

In (7) we see that V-licensing, that is, licensing that emanates from a V position, can be either local in targeting other V positions or non-local interacting with C positions within its CV unit.

(7)
    a. V-licensing ⟨ within its domain (nuclear level) – local licensing
                      outside its domain (CV level)   – non-local licensing

    b. local licensing » non-local licensing

We can thus trace a licensing path in some language (x) with positive parameter settings as yielding the licensing hierarchy in (8):

(8)   Hierarchy of licensing functions in a domain:
local licensing » non-local licensing » licensing government licensors » government licensing » p-licensing » licensing processes $\{p^1...p^n\}$

NC simplification as a result of licensing demand

The process of NC simplification or ML that we have seen applies in a context that involves consonant hardening (l→d, b→b) and voicing. In fact, these two processes cannot be told apart in such cases (see examples in (2)) as the result of hardening is a voiced obstruent. But other Bantu languages allow us to distinguish these are two separate processes when post-nasal voicing applies to voiceless obstruents. Considering NC simplification in examples like (2b) we can capture the process as in (9) below. Following assumptions on the commutability of nasality and voicing as now accepted in Element Theory (see, for example, Nasukawa 1998; Botma et al. 2011), voicing is treated as the sharing of the |L| nasal element in the nasal prefix with the following sonorant /l/ (|?| must also be shared from the nasal to effect hardening). za representation of voicing is simplified here for presentation purposes and is represented as a change of head from a headed |L̲| in the nasal prefix to a non-head |L| in the resulting voiced obstruent.[3] A process that Charette and Göksel (1998) refer to as 'switching'. We assume a government relation between C_2 and C_1 that renders the intervening V position inert.

(9)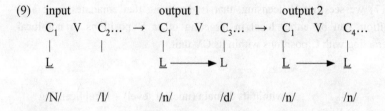

The input is the nasal with |L| head in C_1, which spreads to C_2 to result in voicing (or at least should), but then output 2 is the final form where nasal |L| spreads but fails to change its head status. ML or NC simplification therefore amounts to the failure of head switching (or failure to assume a different structural position allowing a voicing interpretation). The central question is thus why 'switching' should fail to take place? And importantly how can we represent this failure?

Licensing restrictions have been expressed in GP with respect to undergoers being unable to be triggers. Thus Charette 1991 argues that properly governed positions may not themselves be proper governors, and similarly Szigetvári and Dienes (1999) showed that governed positions may not themselves govern. On the back of these restrictions I argue in Kula (2006) that there are also restrictions on triggers so that *triggers may not be multiple triggers*. In this respect governors and proper governors may not be multiple governors and proper governors, respectively.[4] I revise this idea here and cast it firstly as parametric and secondly as defining additional kinds of licensing that present demands on a head nucleus. We can thus consider that NC clusters require to be licensed by drawing on: Type I licensing of constituents, government licensing to define the NC sequence, and that Vs will need to be licensed to perform each of these different tasks.

Under this reasoning we can account for ML/NC simplification as resulting from the inability of one V position, amidst other competing licensing demands, to multiply license government that is needed to maintain an NC cluster. We assume the head V position in a Bantu verb is the root V position which may in full verb forms be preceded by TAM markers. This position of the head is crucial, indeed supported by the patterning of ML where it is sandwiched between the two NC sequences. Recall that we are assuming that all relations and processes must be licensed in some way and therefore in this context only a domain head V can inherently be a government licensor and any other V position needs to specifically be licensed to be a government licensor apart from other licensing, in particular local/basic Type I licensing that sanctions the existence of constituents. The ungrammaticality of (11) then follows from the inability of V_2 to both license government licensing in V_4 and simultaneously directly government license C_2 to then govern C_1 to create the NC cluster.

(11) *NCvNCv...

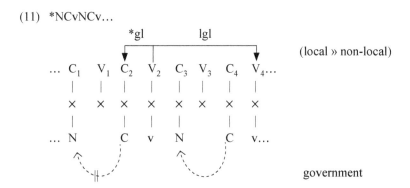

(local » non-local)

government

The other licensing relations involved in this representation are touched on below, but so then here the failure of V_2 to government license C_2 results in simplification. This would be the Bemba case in the examples in (2) where local licensing precedes non-local licensing for government licensing. We must assume that this choice is parametric because in languages like Kwanyama (Bantu, Namibia) (Schadeberg 1982) it is the second NC in a sequence that simplifies, as (12) shows, but also it is the nasal rather than the C that is lost. There are a few assumptions we need to make to get this, but space precludes further discussion (see Kula 2006).

(12) ML in Kwanyama: ngombe → ongobe 'cattle'

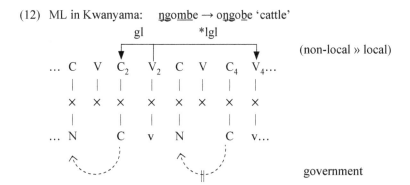

(non-local » local)

government

The reason why only the restriction on triggers does not capture the distribution, that is, that a government licensor (a V position) cannot also be a licensor of government licensing in another V, is because not all sequences on NCs are disallowed. Two voiceless, or one voiced and the other voiceless are allowed. These cases would need both clusters to be government licensed and we assume that they are as in (13).

(13) ML w Voiceless NCs (example 1c):   ntampa → ntampa 'I start'
    *nampa

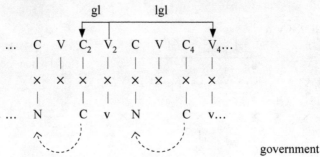

The motivation then for *NCvNC when the two NCs are voiced is to do with the additional licensing of voicing. Recall that this involves a process of |L| spreading from the nasal to the obstruent, treated here as involving 'switching' which fails to be licensed to take place under licensing demands. This is not the case in (13) and so both clusters can be successfully licensed.

The other well-known pattern in ML/NC simplification is cases where the rule applies before a simplex nasal as in Luganda (also referred to as the Ganda Law). We can relate this to a co-occurrence restriction that bars a non-head |L| in the presence of a headed |L|. In the current discussion, this is to express that 'switching' fails to be licensed in the presence of an |L|-head in the domain. This is a mirror image of the process involved in the general version of ML and can be regarded as within expected parametric variation, expressed in the following co-occurrence restrictions:

(14) ML1: presence of 'switching' in a domain bars another application of 'switching'
ML2: presence of an |L| head in a domain requires any other |L| to also be head.

A final point to consider is why there is no simplification when the two voiced NCs are not adjacent, as example (2f) shows, that is, *NCvNCv with voiced obstruents but NCvCvNCv also with voiced obstruents is grammatical. The argument is that in (15) the head V_2 is not directly involved in licensing the government licensing of the following voiced NC cluster because it is not immediately adjacent to it. V_2 only licenses V_3 on its right to exist as a constituent, V_3 then licenses V_5 which licenses government licensing, the constituent, and |L| head switching to allow the voiced obstruent. V_3 is itself not a government licensor and as such has enough licensing capacity to pass on to V_5. This implies that it is more about how much licensing a particular

V position is able to sanction, here V_2 which is hence relieved when no NC immediately follows, and not so much about the overall amount of licensing available to a domain. Naturally, the amount of licensing in a domain is impacted upon by having restrictions on what a single V can do, but only in this indirect way.

(15) Grammatical NCvCvNCv (Bemba *mbelenga* 'I read')

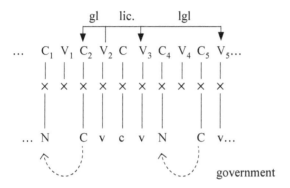

To summarise, we account for ML/NC simplification as the failure of government to take place because the potential governing head fails to be licensed to be a governor. More specifically this must be interpreted as the failure to license 'switching' under |L| spreading from the nasal to the stem-initial position. Under this view we can then explain why voiceless NC's never undergo ML – switching never has to be licensed in these clusters. Similarly, a sequence of voiced and voiceless NCs is also possible because switching is only licensed once in the voiced NC. It is crucial that the same V position is implicated in the licensing of switching, since if it is not, simplification does not occur as seen in examples where the two NCs are not immediately in sequence. This explains why place assimilation is still seen to apply.

Defining saturation points

A natural consideration to finally make is whether licensing within a domain can be defined globally and by so doing feed into the possibility of defining limits on word size in language, given the possibility of word minimality and possibly maximality effects. This would require us to consider licensing saturation points that define restrictions on word size per language, defined over the whole phonological domain/V positions.

The distinction made between more basic and less basic licensing functions would help us distinguish between less marked and more marked structure. This means that simple syllable structures that only require basic licensing, such as a CV language type, require less licensing than languages with CC clusters that also need Type II licensing. A characterisation of saturation over a domain must therefore oppose the syllable structure type with licensing potential in relation to domain size. This is depicted in (16) where SS stands for syllable structure complexity, LP for licensing potential, and DS for domain size.

(16) Defining saturation points
    a.   SS (x)   LP (z)   DS (licensing path) (y)
        (i)   increase   increase   decrease
        (ii)   decrease   decrease   increase
    b. (i) $z = x+y$ where $z = (x-1) + (y+1)$
        (ii) $LP = SS\downarrow + DS\uparrow$ or $LP = SS\uparrow + DS\downarrow$
        (iii) $z = k$?

In (16a, (i)) increasing the complexity of SS also increases the LP needed to license such structure in which case LP will be depleted quicker from the greater demand resulting in a shorter (but more complex) licensing path and hence a shorter phonological domain. The converse relation holds for (16a, (ii)); a decreased complexity in SS requires less LP to be sanctioned, and thus can accommodate more structure which means an increase in phonological domain size. The question for the characterisation of licensing saturation, expressed in (16b, (iii)), is whether we can equate LP to a constant (k) and, further, whether such a constant should be deemed universal.

Under such a view of licensing saturation we could regard ML as resulting from a saturation point being reached in the resolution of an increase in SS complexity (the need to license voiced NCs) which implies more licensing functions that demand increased LP.

Conclusion

Licensing Inheritance suggests that licensing potential is spread in varying degrees in a phonological domain: recessive V positions depend on preceding V positions for their licensing tasks. It is argued here that because of this, a V position that has itself licensed a preceding or following C position to be a governor cannot also license another V position for the same task. By virtue of its own action, a government licensor has depleted its licensing potential for further tasks of the same nature, termed here as licensing saturation. This failure to license government after depletion of licensing potential has been interpreted as the failure to license 'switching' in NC clusters in Bantu that then gives rise to the ML/NC simplification effects. The analysis requires the treatment of licensing as of three different types that stand in an implicational relation – giving explanation to why CV is the simplest syllable type.

An alternative version of licensing saturation, which assumes an upper limit on licensing potential, draws a relation between syllable structure complexity and phonological domain size, so that a flat licensing path has more potential for increased phonological domain size than one where clusters must be licensed. It remains to be seen whether there is empirical evidence to support such a view.

Notes

1. The initial N- represents the 1stsg. subject marker and $(i)N$- the Class 9/10 noun class marker. Consonant hardening in (1b) also applies in (2a–b) and is a regular standard process in this context.
2. This follows Kula (2006). In recent OT work this idea is very similar to Zimmermann (2018).
3. My assumption is that element geometries, building on dependency relations, is what captures the interpretation of |L| as nasality, voicing, or low tone. See Kula (2002), Botma (2004), Liu and Kula (2020) for discussion. 'Switching' will be used as a shorthand for this.
4. In earlier versions of GP this was, for government, expressed at the constituent level by having binary branching structures so that a governor could only govern one dependent.

References

Ashton, E. O., Mulira, E. M. K., Ndawula, E. G. M, and Tucker, A. N. (1954). *A Luganda Grammar*. London: Longmans, Green and Co.
Botma, B. (2004). *Phonological Aspects of Nasality*. Doctoral dissertation, University of Amsterdam.
Botma, B., Kula, N. C., and Nasukawa, K. (2011). 'Features'. In *Continuum Companion to Phonology*, edited by N. C. Kula, B. Botma, and K. Nasukawa, 33–63. London: Continuum.
Charette, M. (1990). 'License to govern'. *Phonology* 7, 223–53.
Charette, M. (1991). *Conditions on Phonological Government*. Cambridge: Cambridge University Press.
Charette, M., and Göksel, A. (1998). 'Licensing constraints and vowel harmony in Turkic languages'. In *Structure and Interpretation: Studies in phonology*, edited by E. Cyran, 65–88. Lublin: Wydawnictwo KUL.
Cole, D. T. (1967). *Some Features of Ganda Linguistic Structures*. Johannesburg: Witwatersrand University Press.
Cyran, E. (2010). *Complexity Scales and Licensing in Phonology*. Berlin: De Gruyter.
Doke, C. M. (1922). *The Grammar of the Lamba Language*. London: Longmans, Green and Co.
Harris, J. (1997). 'Licensing Inheritance: An integrated theory of neutralisation'. *Phonology* 14, 315–70.
Herbert, R. K. (1986). *Language Universals, Markedness Theory and Natural Phonetic Processes: Trends in linguistics*. Berlin: De Gruyter.
Ito, J., and Mester, A. (1986). 'The phonology of voicing in Japanese: theoretical consequences for morphological accessibility'. *Linguistic Inquiry* 17(1), 49–73.

Katamba, F., and Hyman, L. (1991). 'Nasality and morpheme structure constraints in Luganda'. In *Lacustrine Bantu Phonology: Afrikanistische Arbeitspapiere* 25, edited by F. Katamba, 175–211. Cologne: University of Cologne.

Kaye, J. D., Lowenstamm J., and Vergnaud, J.-R. (1990). 'Constituent structure and government in phonology'. *Phonology* 7, 193–231.

Kula, N. C. (2002). *The Phonology of Verbal Derivation in Bemba*. Utrecht: LOT dissertations 65.

Kula, N. C. (2006). 'Licensing saturation and co-occurrence restrictions in structure'. *Linguistic Analysis* 32(3–4), 366–406.

Liu, X, and Kula, N. C. (2020). 'Recursive representations for depressor effects'. In *Morpheme-internal Recursion Structures in Phonology*, edited by K. Nasukawa, 143–80. Berlin: De Gruyter.

Lowenstamm, J. (1996). 'CV as the only syllable type'. In *Current Trends in Phonology: Models and methods. Vol. 2*, edited by J. Durand and B. Laks, 419–41. Salford: European Studies Research Institute (ESRI).

Meeussen, A. E. (1962). 'Meinhof's Rule in Bantu'. *African Language Studies* 3, 25–9.

Meinhof, C. (1932). *Introduction to the Phonology of Bantu Languages*. Berlin: Dietrich Reimer.

Nasukawa, K. (1998). 'An integrated approach to nasality and voicing'. In *Structure and Interpretation: Studies in phonology*, edited by E. Cyran, 205–26. Lublin: Wydawnictwo KUL.

Nasukawa, K. (2012). *A Unified Approach to Nasality and Voicing*. Berlin: De Gruyter.

Peng, L. (2007). 'Gemination and anti-gemination: Meinhof's Law in Luganda and Kikuyu'. *UPenn Working Papers in Linguistics* 13(1), 309–22.

Schadeberg, T. C. (1982). 'Nasalization in Umbundu'. *Journal of African Languages and Linguistics* 4, 109–32.

Schadeberg, T. C. (1987). 'Silbenanlautgesetze im Bantu'. *Afrika und Übersee* 70, 1–17.

Scheer, T. (2004). *A Lateral Theory of Phonology. Vol. 1: What is CVCV, and why should it be?* Berlin: De Gruyter.

Szigetvári, P., and Dienes, P. (1999). 'Repartitioning the skeleton: VC Phonology'. Unpublished manuscript, Eötvös Loránd University.

van Sambeek, J. (1955). *A Bemba Grammar*. London: Longmans, Green and Co.

Zimmermann, E. (2018). 'Gradient Symbolic Representations in the Output: A case study from Moses Columbian Salishan stress'. In *Proceedings of NELS 48*, edited by S. Hucklebridge and M. Nelson, 275–84. Amherst, MA: GLSA.

19
CəCj in French
Tobias Scheer

Charette's analysis of CəCj

Charette (1998, 171–3; 2003, 471–5) wonders why schwa may be left unpronounced in [CəCj] *cimetière (cim'tjère)* 'cemetery', but not in [CəCj] *atelier* (**at'ljer*) 'workshop' (this pattern is also analysed by Cavirani in Chapter 15).[1] In these articles (173/473ff.), Charette ascribes the contrast to the type of CC cluster created if schwa were left out: schwa may only drop if this cluster is a good coda-onset sequence in Standard Government Phonology (GP) (Kaye et al. (KLV) 1990; Charette 1991). This amounts to any cluster which exists in intervocalic position and is different from a branching onset (obstruent-liquid TR) and a bogus cluster (tl, dl). In the [CəCj] pattern, though, the cluster created by the non-pronunciation of schwa ([mt] in *cim'tière*) cannot be a coda-onset sequence since it encloses a schwa in the lexicon and resyllabification is prohibited in Government Phonology (Kaye et al. 1990, 221). Therefore, Charette argues, the CCs at hand are in fact onset-onset clusters that afford a right-headed onset-to-onset government whose definition is the same as the one that holds within coda-onset sequences: any intervocalic cluster that exists in the language qualifies except TR and bogus [tl, dl].

(1) **CəCj** (Charette 1998, 2003)
   a. *cimetière*   b. *atelier*

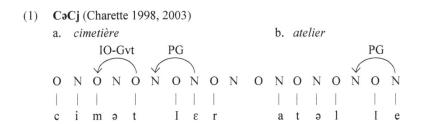

Thus in *cim'tière* under (1a), the [m] and the [t] are onsets and [t] governs [m], thereby circumscribing the empty nucleus enclosed which for that reason is rightfully empty: [møtøjV] is well-formed since both empty nuclei are taken care of, the first by onset-onset government, the second by government from the following V. In **at'lier* under (1b) on the other hand, being bogus, [t] and [l] are unable to establish interonset government and therefore schwa cannot drop when followed by another empty nucleus: *[tøløjV] is ill-formed because the first empty nucleus is neither governed nor enclosed in a governing domain (while the second empty nucleus is governed by the following V as before).

Charette's analysis of [CəCj] is thus based on the management of the CC cluster that is left when schwa remains unpronounced, knowing that it encloses an empty nucleus and is followed by another empty nucleus in all cases: in Charette's analysis, [Cj] identifies as /Cøj/ whose empty nucleus is governed.[2]

Charette's earlier analysis of CəCj

Both data and analysis presented in the previous section have changed since Charette (1991, 115ff.) first studied [CəCj]. In 1991, she compares Quebec and Parisian French, reporting that while schwa is always realised in the former (*cim[ə]tière, at[ə]lier*), it may remain (or actually is) unpronounced in the latter (*cim'tière, at'lier*). That is, Charette does not make any difference between the *cimetière* type and the *atelier* type.

The contrasting behaviour of the two types had been observed by 1991, though, but as far as I can see only by Dell (1973, 262ff.) for Parisian French: schwa may be left out in the *cimetière* type, but not in the *atelier* type. In her 1998 and 2003 articles, Charette acknowledges this difference also for Quebec French: she now reports that schwa may or may not be realised in the *cimetière* type, while (as in Parisian French) it is mandatory in the *atelier* type.

Regarding the analysis, in 1991 Charette argues that schwa cannot drop in Quebec French because the following Cj is a branching onset 2a, but that it may be left out in Parisian French since the yod belongs to a complex (light) nucleus 2b (see Pöchtrager's Chapter 12 on light diphthongs in general and in French).

(2) **CəCj** (Charette 1991, 115ff.)

a. *Quebec French* (schwa mandatory)

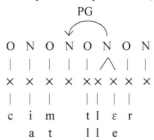

b. *Parisian French* (schwa may be left unpronounced)

Under (2a), the nucleus containing schwa cannot be reached by government from the following nucleus since in Standard GP government cannot jump over a branching onset (Charette 1991, 113ff.). Therefore, the ungoverned nucleus must be realised and schwa is pronounced. By contrast under (2b), only a single consonant separates the schwa-containing and the following nucleus: the yod is part of the latter. Thus nothing prevents government falling on the nucleus containing schwa, which therefore may be left unpronounced.

As was mentioned, this analysis is based on incorrect data: in both varieties, there is a crucial difference between the *cimetière* type and the *atelier* type of words. But the analytic options are interesting: in [CəCj], schwa is mandatory when the yod belongs to a branching onset, while it may be left out in case the yod belongs to a complex nucleus. This contrasts with the analysis discussed in the previous section where [Cj] identifies as two independent onsets. Also note that in Charette's 1991 analysis, the syllabic status of the [Cj] cluster is responsible for the behaviour of schwa, while in her 1998/2003 analysis the syllabic identity of the CC cluster drives schwa deletion. It will be shown in the ensuing section 'Empirical situation' that the former is correct.

Syllabic identity of Cj

Complex nucleus

The complex nucleus analysis is a consequence of the incorrect data that Charette's 1991 analysis was based on: it accounts for the pattern where schwa in [CəCj] can be dropped no matter what (which is what Charette thought occurs in Paris). It may therefore be discarded.

This is particularly clear when considering cases such as *cafet-ière* (schwa may be dropped) and *hôtel-ière* (schwa must be realised) where the yod and the following vowel belong to a suffix (the morphological structure of *cimetière* and *atelier* is less clear): the syllabic identity of the suffix-initial [jV] sequence must be the same in both types of words since the [jV] belongs to the same morpheme. If it identified as a complex nucleus, it should be able to govern the preceding schwa in both types of words – but this is not the case.

Branching onset

The branching onset analysis of [Cj] is impossible in Standard GP where resyllabification is prohibited (Kaye et al. 1990, 221; Charette 1991, 222, note 1): whatever the lexical identity of the yod in the suffix *-ière*, it would need to become the second element of a branching onset, whose first element is the root-final consonant, a simple onset in the lexicon. In other words, a branching onset made of items from two different morphemes is impossible in Standard GP.

In this context, let us consider the parallel between [əTRV] and [əCjV] that Charette (1991, 116ff.) makes explicit. In her 1991 analysis, the reason why in Quebec French schwa cannot drop in *la s[ə]crétaire* 'the secretary' (əTRV) and *at[ə]lier* (əCjV) is the same: its nucleus cannot be reached by government, which is blocked by the following branching onset (TR in the former, Cj in the latter case) (see 2a).

In French, word-internal clusters of three consonants always involve a coda followed by a branching onset [C.TR] (*perdre* 'to lose', *arbre* 'tree', *filtre* 'filter', *mercredi* 'Wednesday', etc., Dell 1995, 10–17). Therefore, knowing that the yod is indeed a consonant (rather than part of a complex nucleus, see the previous section), the [Cj] in [C'Cj] (*cim'tière*) can only be a branching onset. That is, [C'Cj] from /CəCj/ and [C'TR] from /CəTR/ should instantiate the same syllabic pattern: a coda followed by a branching onset.[3]

Given this situation, not pronouncing schwa in [CəCj] sequences should be just as fine as leaving it out in [CəTR] clusters: speakers who can pronounce [C'TR] should also be able to pronounce [C'Cj].

Empirical situation

In her 1998/2003 articles, Charette mentions ten words that illustrate the [CəCj] pattern: four where schwa can be dropped ([mtj] *cimetière*, [ftj] *cafetière*, [nbj] *canebière*, [ntj] *canetière*) and six where it cannot. Among the latter, four have a bogus cluster [dl+j], [tl+j] (*hôtelière, atelier, chandelier, dentellière*), one shows [ʃl+j] (*bachelier*) and one appears with [ml+j] (*sommelier*). Given her analysis, Charette must say that [ʃl] and [ml] are not possible coda-onset (and thus interonset) sequences. She does not discuss the issue, but supporting evidence is the fact that these clusters do not occur in intervocalic position in French.[4]

Looking at a broader record of words instantiating [CəCj], it appears that the CC cluster created by the putative loss of schwa does not bear any responsibility for the (non-)pronunciation of schwa. Rather, the pattern is governed by the consonant *following* schwa: if this consonant is the lateral [l], schwa cannot be left out. If this consonant is different from the lateral, schwa may be dropped.

This is shown under (3), where [CəCj] clusters produced by the suffix *-ier/-ière* appear.[5] The lexical record for [CəC]-*ier/-ière* should be near exhaustive and may contain a number of words that natives are unfamiliar with. In case speakers encounter a word that they do not know, they will treat it as a new lexical item, that is, as a nonce word, and that does not appear to alter the grammaticality judgements reported below.

(3) **CəC-ier/-ière**

a. $C_1 \partial C_2 j$ where $C_2 \neq l$

b	s	*gibecière*	'gamebag'	n	t	*lunetier*	'glasses maker'
f	t	*buffetier*	'shopkeeper'		t	*panetier*	'bread keeper'
	t	*cafetier*	'café tenant'		t	*panetière*	'bread cupboard'
	t	*cafetière*	'coffee maker'		t	*robinetier*	'tap maker'
l	t	*giletier*	'waistcoat maker'	v		*chènevière*	'hemp field'
	t	*giletière*	'watch chain'	p	t	*papetier*	'paper maker'
	t	*molletière*	'puttee'	r	t	*charretier*	'carter'
	t	*muletier*	'donkey keeper'		t	*ferretier*	'farrier hammer'
	t	*pelletier*	'furrier'		t	*jarretière*	'garter'
	t	*pelletiérine*	'type of dewormer'	ʃ	t	*guichetier*	'counter clerk'
	t	*toletière*	'oar reenforcer'	t	n	*centenier*	'centurion'
m	t	*cimetière*	'cemetery'	v	t	*buvetier*	'barkeeper'
n	b	*canebière*	'hemp field'		t	*louvetier*	'wolf hunter'
	t	*bonnetier*	'bonnet maker (masc.)'		t	*savetier*	'cobbler'
	t	*bonnetière*	'bonnet maker (fem.)'	z	n	*dizenier*	'commander of 10 men'
	t	*canetière*	'silk worker'		t	*gazetier*	'gazette owner'
	t	*chaînetier*	'chain maker'		t	*noisetier*	'hazel tree'
	t	*grainetier*	'seed merchant'	s	v	*sansevière*	'sansevieria (bot.)'

b. $C_1 \partial C_2 j$ where $C_2 = l$

d	l	*chandelier*	'candle stick'	t	l	*coutelier*	'cutler'
m	l	*chamelier*	'camel caravan driver'		l	*hôtelier*	'hotel keeper'
	l	*sommelier*	'wine waiter'		l	*râtelier*	'rack'
n	l	*cannelier*	'cinnamon tree'		l	*dentellière*	'lacemaker'
	l	*tonnelier*	'cooper'	s	l	*chancelier*	'chancellor'
	l	*tunnelier*	'tunnel borer'		l	*pincelier*	'brush box'
p	l	*chapelier*	'hat-maker'		l	*vaisselier*	'dresser'
r	l	*bourrelier*	'harness-maker'		l	*ficelier*	'trickery-using person'
ʃ	l	*bachelier*	'bachelor'		l	*boisselier*	'wooden objects merchant'
	l	*échelier*	'ladder'		l	*muselière*	'muzzle'
	l	*richelieu*	'type of shoe'		l	*oiselier*	'bird-seller'
t	l	*atelier*	'workshop'		l	*roselière*	'reed bed'
	l	*batelier*	'ferryman'				

Grammaticality judgements by seven native speakers from mainland France that were born and brought up North of the Loire were collected. Only speakers were selected who could leave out schwa in CəTR *la secrétaire* 'the secretary': this made sure that negative judgements of a particular item were not due to the impossibility for schwa to be left out before branching onsets (see section above, 'Branching onset': a number of speakers of Northern varieties cannot leave out schwa before TR). The speakers selected were asked to say for each word whether a pronunciation without schwa is possible, bizarre but possible, or impossible.

Results are unambiguous: items under (3b) where yod is preceded by the lateral were overwhelmingly judged impossible by all speakers, while items under (3a) where a consonant different from the lateral precedes yod were overwhelmingly said to be possible. Details are as follows. 32 [CC+j] words (3a) and 15 [Cl+j] words (3b) were tested ([CCC+j] and [Cs+j] were not included, the latter because of possible [s+C] effects). Participants had one vote for each word where schwa was left out, to be chosen among 'possible', 'bizarre but possible', and 'impossible'. With seven participants, for any given word each of the three possible votes scores between zero and seven. The average score of 'possible' for [CC+j] was 4.88, against 0.4 for [Cl+j]. Conversely, 'impossible' scored 0.94 with [CC+j], against 5.27 with [Cl+j] (scores for 'bizarre' were comparable: [CC+j] at 1.19, [Cl+j] at 1.33). The contrast between [CC+j] and [Cl+j] is thus very strong, in the direction predicted.

The same contrast appears when looking at percentages: 69.6 per cent of responses for [CC+j] items were 'possible' (156 of 224), against only 5.7 per cent for [Cl+j] items (6 of 105). This difference is of course highly significant ($\chi^2 (1, N = 224) = 116,89, p<.00001$). Conversely, 13.4 per cent of votes were on 'impossible' for [CC+j], against 75.2 per cent for [Cl+j]. The difference is also highly significant ($\chi^2 (1, N = 224) = 123,42, p <.00001$).

The blame is on the lateral

The testimony of words suffixed by *-ier/-ière* under (3) shows that it is not the cluster type preceding yod that governs schwa loss in [CəCj] (as held by Charette 1998/2003), but rather the [Cj] cluster following schwa (as argued by Charette 1991): schwa may be dropped when followed by any consonant plus yod, except if this consonant is the lateral.

Note that Charette's (1998, 173; 2003, 473ff.) generalisation according to which schwa can be dropped if the CC in [CəCj] makes a good coda-onset sequence is also contradicted by [rl] (*bourrelier*) and [sl] (*vaisselier*) where schwa is mandatory, although the clusters at hand are good coda-onset sequences in French, as shown by *merle* 'blackbird', *arlequin* 'harlequin', *(avoir la) berlue* 'being blind', *dirlo* 'director', *horloge* 'clock', *hurler* 'to yell', etc., for [rl] and *islam* 'Islam', *Islande* 'Iceland', *législatif* 'legislative', etc., for [sl].

Given the parallel with [CəTR] where TR is a good branching onset (see section 'Branching onset'), the generalisation suggests that yod can engage with any preceding consonant to form a branching onset, except with the lateral: speakers who can drop schwa in [CəTR] (*la s'crétaire* 'the secretary') can also leave it out in [C_1əC_2j], provided that C_2 is not the lateral (*cim'tière*). In other words, any [Cj] sequence is a good branching onset, except [lj] which is not.

Charette (1991) was thus right in identifying the syllabic status of [Cj] in [CəCj] as the driving force of schwa deletion. She did not identify the distributional pattern that decides whether schwa may be left out or not, though: schwa may be dropped when followed by any consonant plus yod, except if this consonant is the lateral. Has this generalisation gone unnoticed in the literature on [Cj] in French, then?[6] No: Dell (1973, 262) incidentally notes that he will not address the question why schwa cannot be deleted when followed by a liquid and yod ('La seconde question que nous laisserons de côté est le maintien de schwa lorsqu'il est suivi d'une liquide et d'un yod'). As far as I can see, he is the only author who has understood that schwa deletion in [C_1əC_2j] is blocked when C_2 is the lateral. But since he says that he will not pursue this question, the pattern remains largely unillustrated in his book. It may thus be the case that the data in the section 'Empirical situation' are the first empirical demonstration of the generalisation at hand.

Finally, note that Dell's statement also includes [rj] clusters: he says that schwa cannot drop in [C_1əC_2j] if C_2 is a liquid, that is [r] or the lateral (note that [C_1əC_2]-*ier*/-*ière* under (3a) does not appear to produce any cases with C_2 = [r]). It takes some argument to see that Dell is right (a piece of evidence are conditionals like *donn-er-i-ez* 'you (pl.) would give' or *huil-er-i-ez* 'you (pl.) would oil' where schwa cannot be dropped: **donn'rjez*, **huil'rjez*), but [rj] clusters represent an intricate pattern in French that cannot be examined here for lack of space.

Analysis based on branching onsets

It was mentioned in section 'Branching onset' that Charette's 1991 analysis where [Cj] in [CəCj] is a branching onset in Quebec French is impossible in Standard GP since this would require resyllabification, which is prohibited in this theory: in *cafet-ière* for example, the lexically simplex onset containing the root-final consonant would have to become a complex onset in order to accommodate the yod coming from the suffix.

As we have seen, though, the pronunciation of schwa in [CəCj] depends on whether the following [Cj] cluster does (all [Cj] except [lj]) or does not ([lj]) qualify as a branching onset. In Strict CV (Lowenstamm 1996; Scheer 2004), a branching onset identifies as a TR cluster belonging to two onsets whose solidarity is due to an infrasegmental relation (⇐ in 4a) (Scheer 2004, §64; Brun-Trigaud and Scheer 2010). The empty nucleus enclosed does not require government because it is silenced by this infrasegmental relation. Being therefore ungoverned, it is itself a good governor and governs the preceding schwa. This is shown under (4a) for [tj] in *guichet-ier* where schwa may be left unpronounced.

(4)   **CəCj in Strict CV**
       a. [Cj] branching onset: schwa governed   b. [lj] no branching onset: schwa ungoverned

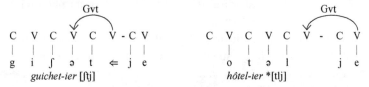

guichet-ier [ʃtj]   hôtel-ier *[tlj]

By contrast under (4b), government cannot reach schwa because [lj] is not a good branching onset: the nucleus enclosed needs to be governed and therefore cannot be a governor itself. Thus schwa is pronounced.

Note that the issue of resyllabification does not arise in Strict CV since there are no branching constituents and there is no coda constituent (or post-rhymal complement): under (4a), the suffix-initial yod makes a branching onset with the root-final [t] by establishing an infrasegmental relation (⇐).

Conclusion

The [CəCj] pattern is but a piece of the [Cj] puzzle in French, and the preceding pages have studied only a facet of that piece. Some other aspects and pieces are the following. Why is it that *diérèse*, that is, expanding [j] into [ij], allows schwa to remain unpronounced in conditionals (*vous donn-er-i-ez* [dɔn'rije] 'you (pl.) would give'), but not in [Cəl]-*ier* (*hôtel-ier* *[ot'lije])? How come [Rlj] from /Rlj/ is possible (*perl-ier* [rlj] 'pearl, adj.', *vous parl-iez* 'you (pl.) talked'), but not when [Rl] encloses a schwa /Rəlj/ (**bourr'lier* 'saddler')? Why can schwa be absent in *vous vous atteliez* (*att'liez* [tlj]) 'you took care of', but not in *atelier* (**at'lier* *[tlj]) 'workshop' (Klein 1992, 39)?

Why is [Tlj] well-formed when created by *-i-ons/-i-ez* (*vous boucl-i-ez* [klj] 'you (pl.) surround / bring to an end'), but impossible when originating in other suffixes (*boucl-ier* *[klj] 'shield') (Dell 1972, 73)? How come that *-i-ons/-i-ez* can occur without [i] after [Tl] (*vous boucl-i-ez* [klj] 'you (pl.) surround / bring to an end'), but not after [Tr] (*vous plâtr-i-ez* [trij] *[trj] 'you (pl.) plaster') (Dell 1972, 73; Tranel 1987, 121; Klein 1992, 23ff.)? I pursue these issues elsewhere.

And there is also something to be understood about the whole [Cj] pattern in Quebec French. Recall the parallel between [CəTR] and [CəCj] ('Branching onset' section): it holds indeed for the variety described in the article (unmarked Northern mainland or Parisian speakers), but Quebec French is different. Here the branching onset [Cj] (*cim'tière*) allows for the preceding schwa to be dropped, but regular branching onsets TR (obstruent-liquid) do not: *la s'crétaire* 'the secretary' and *le s'cret* 'the secret' are possible in Paris, but not in Quebec French (Charette 1991, 102–4). So what does that mean? The existence of two different types of branching onsets in Quebec French, or in any other language for that matter, would be unsettling.

Notes

1. Most French words that appear in this chapter are listed in the section 'Empirical situation' where glosses are provided. Elsewhere, glosses only appear for words that are not mentioned in this section.
2. In fact, following Haworth (1994), [Cj] in Charette's analysis is a C followed by an I element that branches on both the following nucleus and the following onset: [Cj] is realised when the /i/ of /CijV/ is governed by the following V. This is to account for the fact that based on an invariant underlying /ij/, the i is unpronounced (governed) when preceded by a single consonant as in *abricot-ier* [abʁikotje] 'apricot tree', but realised when preceded by a TR cluster that requires the presence of a vowel to its right, as in *sucr-ier* [sykrije] 'sugar bowl'.
3. This description also holds for Charette's 1998/2003 analysis where, recall from the opening of this chapter, the CC cluster of [CCj] (*cim'tière*) identifies as two onsets, which however have the exact same distribution as coda-onset clusters. On this take, if the C'C from /CəCj/ in *cimetière*-type words can form an onset-onset governing domain, the same should be true for C'C from /CəTR/ in *la secrétaire* 'the secretary'.
4. Except when resulting from schwa deletion as in *éch'ler* 'to climb on a ladder' for [ʃl] and *gromm'ler* 'to mutter', *jum'ler* 'to twin' for [ml]. But that does not count since the members of the cluster are lexically separated by a schwa.
5. In French, [Cj] clusters are produced by a number of word types, which fall into cases where the yod belongs to the root and others where it originates in a suffix. In the former category, items occur whose [Cj] i) may (*li-er* 'to join', *ni-er* 'to deny') or ii) may not (*copi-er* 'to copy', *unifi-er* 'to unify') be word-initial. The latter group is made of three suffixes: iii) *-ier /-ière* (*abricot-ier* 'apricot tree', *chemis-ier* 'blouse'), iv) *-ien* (*alsac-ien* 'Alsatian', *brésil-ien* 'Brazilian') and v) 1pl. *-i-ons*, 2pl. *-i-ez* (imperfect *nous batt-i-ons* 'we beat', subjunctive *que nous batt-i-ons* 'that we beat', conditional *nous batt-er-i-ons* 'we would beat').
   Group i) of course cannot produce [CəCj] items, which also appear to be absent in groups ii) and iv). Group v) does create [CəCj], but only with [rj] (C'rj). This is because there are no roots ending in [Cə] to which imperfective/subjunctive *-i-ons*, *-i-ez* could be added, and conditional *-i-ons*, *-i-ez* only attach to infinitives, which always end in *-r*. When belonging to the first group of verbs in *-er*, the *-e-* appears as schwa in the conditional, hence producing [Cərj] as in *vous aimər-i-ez* (*aimer* 'to love'). In this case, schwa may be dropped if the following yod expands into [rij] (a pattern called *diérèse*: *ram'rijez* (*ramer*

'to row'), *fil'rijez* (*filer* 'to push off'), *donn'rijez* (*donner* 'to give'), but must be pronounced if followed by rj (**ram'rjez*, **fil'rjez*, **donn'rjez*) (Tranel 1981, 285ff., Klein 1992, 23, Dell 1973, 263).

In sum, thus, only iii) *-ier /-ière* produces [CəCj] sequences.

6. Relevant work includes Dell (1972, 1973), Morin (1979 [1971]), Lyche (1979), Tranel (1981, 64–6, 1987, 115–21), Kaye and Lowenstamm (1984), Klein (1992), Rizzolo (1999), Durand and Lyche (1999), and Côté (2018).

References

Brun-Trigaud, G., and Scheer, T. (2010). 'Lenition in branching onsets in French and in ALF dialects'. In *Development of Language through the Lens of Formal Linguistics*, edited by P. Karlík, 15–28. Munich: Lincom.

Charette, M. (1991). *Conditions on Phonological Government*. Cambridge: Cambridge University Press.

Charette, M. (1998). 'Empty and pseudo-empty categories'. *SOAS Working Papers in Linguistics and Phonetics* 8, 167–76.

Charette, M. (2003). 'Empty and pseudo-empty categories'. In *Living on the Edge. 28 papers in honour of Jonathan Kaye*, edited by S. Ploch, 465–79. Berlin: De Gruyter.

Côté, M.-H. (2018). 'Glissantes et diphtongues en français laurentien'. *Cahiers de l'ILSL* 56, 41–59.

Dell, F. (1972). 'Une règle d'effacement de i en français'. *Recherches Linguistiques de Vincennes* 1, 63–88.

Dell, F. (1973/1985). *Les règles et les sons*. 2nd edition. Paris: Hermann.

Dell, F. (1995). 'Consonant clusters and phonological syllables in French'. *Lingua* 95, 5–26.

Durand, J., and Lyche, C. (1999). 'Regard sur les glissantes en français: français standard, français du Midi'. *Cahiers de Grammaire* 24, 39–65.

Haworth, E. (1994). 'Prevocalic C-Glide sequences in French'. *SOAS Working Papers in Linguistics and Phonetics* 4, 53–70.

Kaye, J., and Lowenstamm, J. (1984). 'De la syllabicité'. In *Forme Sonore du Langage*, edited by F. Dell, D. Hirst, and J.-R. Vergnaud, 123–59. Paris: Hermann.

Kaye, J., Lowenstamm, J., and Vergnaud, J.-R. (1990). 'Constituent structure and government in phonology'. *Phonology* 7, 193–231.

Klein, M. (1992). *Vers une approche substantielle et dynamique de la constituance syllabique. Le cas des semi-voyelles et des voyelles hautes dans les usages parisiens*. Doctoral dissertation, Université Paris 8.

Lowenstamm, J. (1996). 'CV as the only syllable type'. In *Current Trends in Phonology: Models and methods. Vol. 2*, edited by J. Durand and B. Laks, 419–41. Salford: European Studies Research Institute.

Lyche, C. (1979). 'Glides in French: questions for natural generative phonology'. *Lingua* 49, 315–30.

Morin, Y. C. (1979/1971). 'Computer experiments in generative phonology: low-level French phonology'. In *Natural Language Studies No. 11*, edited by K. C. Hill. Ann Arbor, MI: Department of Linguistics at the University of Michigan.

Rizzolo, O. (1999). 'La formation des adjectifs dérivés en -ien en français'. Mémoire de DEA, Université de Nice-Sophia Antipolis.

Scheer, T. (2004). *A Lateral Theory of Phonology. Vol.1: What is CVCV, and why should it be?* Berlin: De Gruyter.

Tranel, B. (1981). *Concreteness in Generative Phonology. Evidence from French*. Oakland, CA: University of California Press.

Tranel, B. (1987). *The Sounds of French. An introduction*. Cambridge: Cambridge University Press.

20
The prince and the nymph: interconsonantal plosive-zero alternation in English
Péter Szigetvári

Introduction

Some cluster types of English are variably pronounced with or without a plosive in the middle.[1] Examples include *prince* [prin(t)s],[2] *nymph* [nim(p)f], *month* [mən(t)θ], *lynx* [liŋ(k)s], *strength* [streŋ(k)θ], *prompt* [prom(p)t], *instinct* [ínstiŋ(k)t], etc. The status of these plosives is not clear: are they 'underlying' or 'lexical', or are they 'superficial', 'emergent', 'ephemeral', or 'phonetic' phenomena? Or perhaps some are 'underlying', others 'superficial'? Are they (independent) segments at all? Or maybe they form 'affricates' together with the following fricative, at least where such a fricative is available? This is what the present chapter concerns itself with, but let me admit right away that no definite answers will emerge. Our first question has to be much simpler: what is the environment where these plosives alternate? Descriptions, dictionaries, and native speakers do not fully agree on the data.

The title of this chapter tries to be neutral: I am not talking about inserted or deleted plosives, but about plosives that alternate with zero in interconsonantal position. Dictionaries do not indicate these plosives uniformly. The online Merriam-Webster dictionary (henceforth MW)[3] applies the most obvious method: parenthesising the plosive, as I have above. The Longman Pronunciation Dictionary (Wells 2008, henceforth LPD) distinguishes between 'insertable' plosives which are marked by a raised symbol (for example, *prince* [prinᵗs]) and 'deletable' ones which are set in italics (for example, *chintz* [tʃin*t*s]). Fourakis and Port (1986) have found a slight durational difference between the two types. But even if this difference is real, native speakers may make it on orthographical grounds: the [t] is not indicated in the spelling of *prince*, but it is in the spelling of *chintz*. In any case, LPD seems to use a raised symbol for the plosive in exactly those words where it is not shown in the spelling and an italic one in those where it is shown, suggesting that the former is superficially inserted, the latter is underlying and deleted (some further examples: *Simpson* [símpsən] versus *Simson* [símᵖsən]; *century* [séntʃərij] versus *censure* [séntʃə], etc.). What raises some doubt about separating the two types is that the variation occurs in both directions: a [t] may be inserted between [n] and [s], and the [t] may be deleted between [n] and [s]. This makes sense if one either (i) denies that the output of this process is a pattern that is phonotactically more desirable than the input (since either [nts] or [ns] is 'better' phonotactically than the other, but not both) or (ii) claims that 'insertion' and 'deletion' are two names for the same process here, 'underlyingly' either both *prince* and *chintz* contain [t] or neither does so. In case (ii), the only difference between these two words is in their prevocalic part, their postvocalic portion is identical, so the two words are either [prins] and [tʃins], or [prints] and [tʃints].

The phenomenon

Some of the existing descriptions of this phenomenon are rather anecdotal and often mention it merely as an argument for some hypothesis of phonological representation (Clements 1987; Harris 1994; Kiss 2002). Therefore we must first identify the environments where the alternation takes place. In doing so, I will limit the phenomenon to alternations that occur between two consonants that are within a morpheme. Variable plosives occur in word-final position in compounds or before a suffix, as in *breaststroke* [bres(t)#strəwk], *dumped* [dəm(p)#t] or *thinks* [θiŋ(k)#s]. This kind of variation, however, does not directly concern us here, since these plosives are variable only when followed by an obstruent, but, in any case, a consonant in the next morph, without which they are stable: the emboldened plosive is obligatory in *breastwork*, *jumping*, or *thinking*. In other words, the plosive is undoubtedly not inserted, but deleted in these cases. I also ignore the type of variation witnessed in *often* [of(t)ən], since it does not occur between (nonsyllabic) consonants and it is lexical, that is, unpredictable (cf. *chieftain* [tʃíjftən] with no alternation).

Neighbouring segments

A variable plosive occurs much more commonly before a fortis fricative or plosive, than before a lenis one as shown in (1). Note that [ð] does not occur after a consonant within a morpheme at all, but even if it did, the prediction is that no plosive could turn up before it. We do find a plosive before [z] in (1b) and (1d) and [ʒ] in (1c), more on which below. Grammaticality judgements are those of LPD, I do not distinguish the 'insertable' and the 'deletable' plosives.

(1) **Alternating plosives before fortis and lenis fricatives**
    fortis   **lenis**
  a. *triumphal* [trajə́m(p)fəl]   *triumvir* [trajə́mvə]
     warmth [wóːm(p)θ]   —
     Gimson [gím(p)sən]   *crimson* [krímzən]
  b. *infant* [ín(t)fənt]   *inventory* [ínvəntrij]
     anthem [án(t)θəm]   —
     cancel [kán(t)səl]   *Bermondsey* [bə́ːmən(d)zij]
  c. *mensural* [mén(t)ʃərəl]   *lingerie* [lán(d)ʒərij]
  d. *length* [léŋ(k)θ] (also [lén(t)θ])   —
     angst [áŋ(k)st]   *anxiety* [aŋ(g)zájətij]
     anxious [áŋ(k)ʃəs]   —
  e. *empty* [ém(p)tij]   *lambda* [lámdə]
  f. *extinct* [ikstíŋ(k)t]   *kingdom* [kíŋdəm][4]

The data in (1) are representative of the consonants between which the alternation of plosives takes place. I only include clusters beginning with a nasal, although in an earlier discussion of this phenomenon, Clements (1987) also mentions [l]. However, LPD does not indicate this plosive in any word containing an [l]+fortis fricative cluster,[5] and MW only have it in some of the candidates: *else*, *waltz*, *health*, and *Welsh* (note the alternative spelling *Welch*), but not in other similar words like *pulse*, *salsa*, *ulcer*, *filth*, *stealth*, etc. The apparent rarity of the alternation between [l] and a fortis fricative may be due to the spread of L-vocalisation: the words affected contain [w] instead of [l] for an increasing number of speakers.

We find very few environments where a lenis plosive alternates: [n_z] (as in *Bermondsey*, in (1b)), [n_ʒ] (as in *lingerie*, in (1c)), and [ŋ_z] (as in *anxiety*, in (1d)). Although my aim is to not distinguish between cases where the plosive is 'underlying' and others where it is not, it is noteworthy that in all three words, as well as in others like them (*Windsor* [wín(d)zə], *Lindsey* [lín(d)zij], *plunge* [plən(d)ʒ], *orange* [órin(d)ʒ], etc.) the plosive *is* indicated in the spelling. In fact, the alternation of [nʒ] and [ndʒ] may be analysed as one of the affricate [dʒ] with the fricative [ʒ], rather than that of the plosive [d] and zero. For example, MW, which does not use standard IPA transcriptions, has [-jə-] (=[-dʒə-]) versus [-zhə-] (=[-ʒə-]), and only in *lingerie*, not it *plunge* or *orange*. The [dʒ]~[ʒ] alternation is a feature of recent French loanwords, irrespective of the preceding nasal (cf. *garage* [gáːraːʒ]~[gáridʒ], *genre* [ʒónrə]~[dʒónrə]). Neither the LPD, nor MW marks an optional plosive in words where the spelling shows [nz][6] (like *bonanza, lens, stanza*). Nevertheless, citing Fourakis and Port (1986), Clements does mention the possibility of a [d] before the [z] in words like *lens, dens, dells* (1987: 34). The alternation of a lenis plosive is vanishingly rare after a noncoronal nasal, even in cases where the orthography indicates one. The labial [b] never alternates: *ambsace* [éjmzejs], *lambda* [lámdə]; but we do find an exception in LPD for the velar [g]: *anxiety* [aŋ(g)zájətij], the plosiveful version labelled as 'non-RP'. In what follows, I ignore the possible alternation after [l] or before a lenis obstruent, and concentrate only on that which occurs after a nasal and before a fortis obstruent.[7]

As already stated, in the vast majority of cases the variable plosive occurs before a fortis obstruent. Its place of articulation is that of the preceding nasal as shown in (1a) and (1e) for labials, (1b–d) for coronals and (1d) and (1f) for velars, the obstruent that follows does not influence its place. So after [m] the alternating plosive is uniformly [p], after [n] it is [t], after [ŋ] it is [k], irrespective of whether the following obstruent is [f], [θ], [s], [ʃ], as in (1a–d) or [t], as in (1e–f). This means that the plosive appearing between the nasal and the following fricative shares its place of articulation and its noncontinuancy with the nasal, and its fortisness (and obstruency) with the following obstruent. I will return to the preplosive alternation in below.

Stress

All the words in (1) contain a stressed vowel right before the nasal+fricative cluster in which the alternating plosive is located. Yet it is not the status of the preceding vowel that matters, but that of the following one. The alternation equally occurs after an unstressed vowel, as long as the alternation site is not followed by a stressed vowel: *triumph* [trájəm(p)f], *entrance* [éntrən(t)s], *larynx* [láriŋ(k)s].[8] The data in (2), taken from dictionaries, show that there is no alternation before a stressed vowel. Here I mark not only main or 'primary' stress (the tonic), but also the full vowel following, which, as these data show, also counts as stressed.

(2) **Alternating plosives and stress**
not before stressed vowel   **before stressed vowel**
symphony [sím(p)fənij]   *symphonic* [simfónik]
nymph [ním(p)f], *nymphet* [ním(p)fət]   *nymphet* [nímfèt]
Gimson [gím(p)sən]*   *Gimsonian* [gimsə́wnijən]*
plimsoll [plím(p)səl]   *plimsoll* [plímsə̀wl]
Sam(p)son [sám(p)sən]   *Samsung* [sámsə̀ŋ]*

infant [ín(t)fənt]
synthesis [sín(t)θəsis]
prince [prin(t)s]
insolent [ín(t)sələnt]
sensual [sén(t)ʃ(u)wəl]
conscious [kón(t)ʃəs]
jinx [dʒín(k)s]

confess [kənfés]
synthetic [sinθétik]
princess [prìnsés]
insect [ínsèkt]
ensure [inʃúː]
Kinshasa [kinʃáːsə]
—

All the data in (2) are agreed on by LPD and MW, except for the words marked '*', which are LPD-only pronunciations, missing from MW. The word *princess* appears as [prín(t)səs] in MW, with the alternating plosive, before an unstressed vowel. MW adds the variant in (2), [prìnsés], without a plosive before the stressed vowel, with the label 'usually British'. However, the two dictionaries differ in their judgements of the variant [prínsès]: MW does not indicate a [t] in it, as we would expect based on, for example, *insect*, which has the same stress pattern. Somewhat surprisingly, LPD does indicate a plosive here ([prín(t)sès]), at least for British English. In its American variants, LPD conforms to the pattern in (2): [prín(t)səs], [prínsès]. It is not clear to me if this is a real difference between the two accents, or simply a typographical error.

The cluster [ŋks] in *jinx* and other words of its kind corroborates the hypothesis that the distribution of the alternating plosive is related to stress. While [ŋks] occurs word finally (for example, *Bronx*, *lynx*, *sphinx*) and, rarely, before an unstressed vowel (for example, *Banksy*, *pinxit*), we do not find this cluster in any word before a stressed vowel. Etymologically, the [k] of an [ŋks] cluster cannot be epenthetic: [ŋ] is a recent development in English, which did not occur before [s], except where a velar plosive, alternating in present-day English, intervened. So it is not only that a plosive is not inserted in a hypothetical [ŋs] cluster before stress, but the plosiveful [ŋks] cluster does not exist in this environment either.[9] We find a similar situation with [mps]: it occurs word finally (for example, *glimpse*, *mumps*) and before an unstressed vowel (mostly in names, for example, *Dempsey*, *Empson*). I have found a single example with [mps] before a stressed vowel, *pálimpsèst*, which is a learned word, and possibly the pronunciation is influenced by the spelling.[10]

However, in addition to *princess*, there are further words in LPD that are transcribed with an unexpected plosive, like *menthol* [mén(t)θòl] or *samphire* [sám(p)fàjə]. MW does not indicate a plosive in either of these words. To try to figure out what's going on, I decided to ask native speakers.

A survey

I conducted a simple survey on alternating plosives. To do this, I set up a website at http://seas.elte.hu/epenthesis, which offered a randomly ordered list containing 50 words, each containing a nasal+fortis fricative cluster. Each word was given in standard spelling and a transcription in which a plosive homorganic with the nasal was printed in red between the nasal and the fricative. The participants were mostly phonologists and other linguists, recruited through the MFM list (the mailing list of the Manchester Phonology Meeting) and the Linguist List. They were asked to mark each item with one of three options, 'yes' if they thought the word was possible with the plosive, 'no' if they thought it was not, and 'dunno' if they could not decide. I recorded the answers from 8 November to 7 December 2019. Statistics about the participants are provided in (3).

(3) **The survey participants**

- Number of participants: 191, of which self-declared native speakers: 182.
- Age ranges: under 30: 33; 30–50: 91; 50–70: 44; over 70: 14; did not say: 9.
- Came via: MFM list: 137; Linguist List: 38; friend: 6; other: 10.

I did not expect the judgements to be influenced by the informant's dialect, so I did not ask for this bit of information. The differences between LPD and MW in *príncèss*, *ménthòl*, or *sámphìre* suggest that this may have been a mistake.

It is obviously not easy to decide by introspection whether a plosive is possible or not in a given word. The results of the survey show not what the participants produce, but what they believe they produce, or even worse, what they believe they should be producing. Even with these restrictions in mind, the results are surprisingly uncategorical. For rarer words, over 40 per cent of participants gave a 'dunno' answer. Many participants shared their concerns and dilemmas after giving their judgements. When preparing the survey, I carelessly labelled the plosives as epenthetic, which resulted in some concerned comments, especially in the case of *anxious* and *palimpsest*. Even though the plosive is claimed by many to be 'underlying' in these words (obviously a claim based on spelling/etymology), 8 and 17 participants, respectively, deemed it impossible to have a [k] and [p] in them.

The results

The results are ordered by the ratio of yes and no answers in the first column of Table 20.1. If this ratio is greater than 1, there were more participants who said they could imagine the plosive in that word than who said they could not; if it is less than 1, there were fewer such participants. Thus we have a ranking list of words (environments) from most to least favourable for containing a plosive between the nasal and the fortis fricative. In the last two columns I mark the view of LPD and MW on these plosives. The two dictionaries have different strategies. LPD *never* marks an obligatory plosive between a nasal and a fricative; these plosives are either in italics (when present in the spelling) or in a raised index (when absent from the spelling).[11] The first case I mark with a tick (✓), the second with a percent sign (%). I use the cross (✗) to mark words where no plosive is indicated at all. MW only marks one type of alternation (here labelled %), in this column the tick marks a plosive which is obligatorily present according to MW (only in *avalanche*). Words with a dash are not listed in the relevant dictionary.

The words in Table 20.1 were not meant to be representative of words containing nasal+fortis fricative clusters; instead I aimed at including an example for each possible segment combination both with and without a stressed vowel following. No neat cut-off point that separates words in which the plosive is acceptable and unacceptable emerged from the answers. Nevertheless, words with plosive alternation in LPD and MW tend to appear at the top of Table 20.1, and words without at the bottom.

The name *Banff* contains a [t] in LPD ([ban^{t}f]) with potential labial assimilation ([bam^{p}f]), while MW has assimilation variant only; this is marked by an asterisk. Several participants mentioned this assimilation in other [nf] clusters, while LPD does not indicate any such possibility.[12]

Some discussion

The two words which were mostly deemed acceptable with the plosive are those whose spelling suggests that the plosive is lexical ('underlying'): *anxious* and *palimpsest*. The words least likely to have an alternating plosive contain [nf]. While it is true that this is a nonhomorganic cluster, words containing another nonhomorganic cluster, [ŋθ], came out at the top of the list. Homorganicity apparently is not (always?) a relevant factor in the likelihood of plosive alternation.

Stress, on the other hand, appears to be relevant, as the dictionary data collected in (2) show. However, as it has been noted MW does not, but LPD does have some examples that have a plosive before a stressed vowel,

Table 20.1 The results of the survey.

Yes/No	Yes	Dunno	No	Word		LPD	MW
23.750	181 (95%)	2 (1%)	8 (4%)	anxious	áŋ(k)ʃəs	✓	%
8.111	140 (73%)	34 (18%)	17 (9%)	palimpsest	pálim(p)sest	✓	%
6.692	166 (87%)	1 (1%)	24 (13%)	length	léŋ(k)θ	%	%
4.824	156 (82%)	3 (2%)	32 (17%)	lengthen	léŋ(k)θən	%	%
4.222	145 (76%)	11 (6%)	35 (18%)	prince	prín(t)s	%	%
3.850	147 (77%)	5 (3%)	39 (20%)	avalanche	ávəlaːn(t)ʃ	✓	✓
3.524	142 (74%)	9 (5%)	40 (21%)	nymph	ním(p)f	%	%
3.409	143 (75%)	6 (3%)	42 (22%)	warmth	wóːm(p)θ	%	%
2.593	133 (70%)	6 (3%)	52 (27%)	ancient	éjn(t)ʃənt	%	%
1.879	119 (62%)	9 (5%)	63 (33%)	Samsonite	sám(p)sənajt	%	—
1.649	116 (61%)	4 (2%)	71 (37%)	emphasis	ém(p)fəsis	%	%
1.639	113 (59%)	9 (5%)	69 (36%)	sensual	sén(t)ʃwəl	%	%
1.325	101 (53%)	14 (7%)	76 (40%)	nympho	ním(p)fəw	%	%
1.209	100 (52%)	9 (5%)	82 (43%)	comfort	kə́m(p)fət	%	%
1.133	65 (34%)	68 (36%)	58 (30%)	samphire	sám(p)fajə	%	✗
1.067	91 (48%)	14 (7%)	86 (45%)	censor	sén(t)sə	%	%
1.051	78 (41%)	38 (20%)	75 (39%)	penchant	pón(t)ʃən	%	%
0.979	88 (46%)	14 (7%)	89 (47%)	symphonic	sim(p)fónik	✗	✗
0.827	83 (43%)	9 (5%)	99 (52%)	anthem	án(t)θəm	%	%
0.788	78 (41%)	14 (7%)	99 (52%)	philanthropist	filán(t)θrəpist	%	%
0.731	72 (38%)	20 (10%)	99 (52%)	mentholated	mén(t)θəlejtid	%	%
0.696	75 (39%)	9 (5%)	107 (56%)	month	mə́n(t)θ	%	%
0.659	52 (27%)	60 (31%)	79 (41%)	Plimsoll	plím(p)səl	%	%
0.636	54 (28%)	53 (28%)	84 (44%)	Plimsoll	plím(p)səwl	✗	✗
0.621	69 (36%)	11 (6%)	111 (58%)	menthol	mén(t)θol	%	✗
0.565	50 (26%)	53 (28%)	88 (46%)	amaranthine	ámərán(t)θajn	%	✗
0.465	38 (20%)	70 (37%)	83 (43%)	Gramsci	grám(p)ʃij	—	—
0.436	33 (17%)	83 (43%)	75 (39%)	Gomshall	góm(p)ʃəl	✗	—
0.406	54 (28%)	5 (3%)	132 (69%)	amphibian	am(p)fíbijən	✗	✗
0.396	36 (19%)	63 (33%)	92 (48%)	benthos	bén(t)θos	%	✗
0.377	49 (26%)	10 (5%)	132 (69%)	Samsung	sám(p)suŋ	✗	—
0.371	50 (26%)	7 (4%)	134 (70%)	anthology	an(t)θóləʒij	✗	✗
0.322	37 (19%)	42 (22%)	112 (59%)	Honshu	hón(t)ʃuw	✗	✗
0.296	41 (21%)	14 (7%)	136 (71%)	synthetic	sin(t)θétik	✗	✗
0.283	24 (13%)	79 (41%)	88 (46%)	Jamshid	dʒám(p)ʃijd	✗	✗
0.257	37 (19%)	13 (7%)	141 (74%)	philanthropic	filən(t)θrópik	✗	✗
0.246	30 (16%)	37 (19%)	124 (65%)	Kinshasa	kin(t)ʃáːsə	✗	✗
0.234	35 (18%)	9 (5%)	147 (77%)	conceive	kən(t)síjv	✗	✗
0.231	34 (18%)	8 (4%)	149 (78%)	insect	ín(t)sekt	✗	✗
0.228	34 (18%)	7 (4%)	150 (79%)	circumcise	sə́ːkəm(p)sajz	✗	✗
0.212	33 (17%)	5 (3%)	153 (80%)	infant	ín(t)fənt	%	✗
0.177	27 (14%)	13 (7%)	151 (79%)	circumcision	sə́ːkəm(p)síʒən	✗	✗
0.159	25 (13%)	9 (5%)	157 (82%)	Williamson	wíljəm(p)sən	✗	✗
0.146	22 (12%)	12 (6%)	157 (82%)	insure	in(t)ʃóː	✗	✗
0.135	20 (10%)	29 (15%)	142 (74%)	Banff	bán(t)f	%	*
0.103	18 (9%)	6 (3%)	167 (87%)	himself	him(p)sélf	✗	✗
0.091	15 (8%)	8 (4%)	168 (88%)	conference	kón(t)frəns	✗	✗

(Table continued overleaf)

Table 20.1 (continued)

Yes/No	Yes	Dunno	No	Word		LPD	MW
0.049	8 (4%)	26 (14%)	157 (82%)	*infarct*	ín(t)faːkt	✗	✗
0.036	5 (3%)	25 (13%)	161 (84%)	*confab*	kón(t)fab	✗	✗
0.031	5 (3%)	2 (1%)	184 (96%)	*confess*	kən(t)fés	✗	✗

though this is never main ('primary') stress: *menthol* [mén(t)θòl], *samphire* [sám(p)fàjə]. The survey partly supports the role of stress: the words at the top of the scale do not have stress after the alternation site, those at the bottom do. Nevertheless, native speakers also provide us with some surprising judgements, for example, the relatively high ranking of a plosive before the main stress in *symphonic* [sìm(p)fónik]. Although MW (though not LPD) sees a clear difference between *menthol* (only [-nθ-]) and *mentholated* [-n(t)θ-], the participants of this survey do not: *menthol*, with 69 yes responses, fared only slightly worse than *mentholated*, which had 72. The categorical difference in both LPD and MW between the two variants of *Plimsoll* [plím(p)səl] and [plímsə̀wl] is also nonexistent according to the current survey. The absence of *conference* *[kóntfrəns], however, is corroborated; more than twice as many participants ruled out this form than the plosive in a similar position in *infant* [íntfənt] (also cf. LPD's *infra* [ín(t)frə]).

It can generally be stated that native speakers accept the alternating plosive less readily than dictionaries. The yes/no ratio sinks under 1 well before the possibility of alternation disappears from LPD or MW.

Theoretical considerations

Although there is no categorical distinction between the possible appearance of a fortis plosive between a nasal and a fortis fricative, stress does seem to play a role: the plosive occurs significantly more rarely when a stressed vowel follows the cluster than otherwise, that is, when an unstressed vowel follows or at the end of a word. This state of affairs is odd. It is a well-known fact about natural languages that more contrasts are available before a vowel than at the end of a word (for example, Steriade 1999; Ségéral and Scheer 2001), and more contrasts are available before a stressed vowel than before an unstressed one (for example, Harris 1997; Cyran 2010). Possibly for the same reason, more complex clusters are available before a stressed vowel (cf. Government Licensing, Charette 1991, 1992) than otherwise. If the [nts] in *concert* [kóntsət] is a three-member consonant cluster and this three-member cluster cannot occur if the following vowel is stressed, as in *concept* [kónsèpt], then this does not comply with the observations made by Charette: the second, unstressed vowel of *concert* licenses a more complex cluster than the second, stressed vowel of *concept*. An additional problem with the three-consonant-cluster analyses is theory internal to Government Phonology and its forks: with the restricted possibilities of building syllables, a nasal+plosive+fricative cluster can hardly be analysed. The nasal+plosive part cannot be parsed as a coda in this framework, and the plosive+fricative part cannot be parsed as an onset. The third option, an empty nucleus somewhere in the cluster is also not likely in this situation, since this empty nucleus would not be present in the plosiveless alternant. Inserting a 'syllable', that is, an onset and the following (empty) nucleus in the representation is a highly dispreferred scenario in this theory.

Treating the [ts] in *concert* as an affricate seems to solve the syllabification problem of Government Phonology, but it is not an acceptable solution for other reasons. In this case the number of 'segments' does not increase in the change from [ns] to [nts], so government licensing is not affected and parsing is possible with the nasal being a coda, the affricate an onset. Nevertheless, a fricative turning into an affricate is fortition, and we do not expect fortition to occur word finally and before an unstressed vowel to the exclusion of a stressed vowel. Furthermore, while [ts] or [tʃ] could be analysed as affricates, most other clusters resulting in this process, [ps], [pʃ], [pθ], [tf], [ks], [kʃ], [kθ], can hardly be.

A nasal+fricative cluster, like [ns], is more marked (that is, less common cross-linguistically) than a nasal+plosive or nasal+affricate cluster, like [nt] or [nt͡s] (where, despite the current practice of the IPA, I use a ligature symbol for the 'affricate' to distinguish it from a three-member [nts] cluster). The questions are (i) whether the three-member cluster [nts] could be analysed as less marked than [ns], and (ii) whether the three-member [nts] cluster can be seen as distinct from a two-member [nt͡s] cluster in any sense. I am not sure what the right answers to these questions are.

Nasal+plosive clusters

I conclude this chapter with a phonotactic consideration of the status of the alternating plosives. Such a plosive is found not only before a fricative, but also before another plosive or affricate. In this case the nasal is always noncoronal, [m] or [ŋ], while the plosive or affricate is coronal, [t] or [tʃ]. The plosive alternating between a nasal and another plosive seems to be insensitive to stress. Such a plosive is indicated by both LPD and MW before a stressed vowel, even with the main stress. This alternation, however, never occurs before a lenis plosive; what is more, an earlier plosive is lost before a lenis plosive: *Camden* < *camp+den* versus *Hampton* < *hām+tūn*. Further examples are listed below, with a labial nasal in (4a), a velar one in (4b).

(4) **Alternation before a plosive**

	not before stressed vowel	before stressed vowel
a.	*prompt* [prom(p)t]	*Comptometer* [kòm(p)tómitə]
	dreamt [drem(p)t][13]	*asymptote* [ásim(p)tə̀wt]
	empty [ém(p)tij]	*asymptotic* [ásim(p)tótik]
	Sumter [sə́m(p)tə]	
	sumptuous [sə́m(p)tʃəs]	
	temptress [tém(p)trəs]	*temptation* [tèm(p)téjʃən]
b.	*succinct* [səksíŋ(k)t]	*cunctation* [kə̀ŋ(k)téjʃən]
	Langton [láŋ(k)tən]	*punctilio* [pə̀ŋ(k)tílijəw]
	sanctum [sáŋ(k)təm]	*sanctorum* [sàŋ(k)tóːrəm]
	juncture [dʒə́ŋ(k)tʃə]	*tinctorial* [tìŋ(k)tóːrijəl]

The pretonic alternation of a plosive appears to be more common within a nasal+plosive than within a nasal+fricative cluster. It is noteworthy that in this case, the three-member cluster with the plosive in the middle comprises two subclusters, both of which are less marked (more common) than the two-member cluster without the plosive in the middle. Thus, while the nonhomorganic nasal+plosive [mt] or [ŋt] clusters are not commonly encountered in English, all the more so since they are optionally split by another plosive, the clusters resulting from the presence of this plosive, [mp] and [pt], [ŋk] and [kt], are common. This is why the nasal in this alternation is always noncoronal and the stable plosive coronal. The appearance of a plosive in a homorganic nasal+plosive cluster would result in a geminate, which is ruled out in English (*[mpp], *[ntt], *[nttʃ], *[ŋkk]), while the appearance of a coronal plosive in a coronal nasal+noncoronal plosive cluster would yield the unattested [tp] ([ntp]) or the rare [tk] ([ntk]) subcluster. Note that the rare occurrences of [np] and those of [nk] are predominantly before a stressed vowel (for example, *Kanpur* [kánpóː], *incline* [inklájn]).

Conclusion

English words containing a nasal followed by an obstruent often contain a plosive between the two consonants. This alternation occurs predominantly before a fortis, rather than a lenis obstruent. In the case of fricatives, the alternation is much more common before an unstressed vowel or word finally than before a stressed vowel. The alternation before a plosive, on the other hand, is not sensitive to stress, but it exclusively occurs before a fortis plosive, never before a lenis one. A theory explaining these facts is badly needed.

Notes

1. First of all, I would like to thank Momo for the kindness I (and obviously so many of us) have experienced from her in the past decades. I'm grateful to Connor Youngberg for the invitation and both him and Florian Breit for all the support they provided in this enterprise. Ádám Nádasdy was the first reader; I thank him for his useful comments and suggestions. My research is sponsored by NKFIH grants #139271 and #142498. I am also grateful to George Soros.
2. I use the simple symbols [i], [e], [a], [ə], [o], and [u] to represent the vowels of English. In the present chapter nothing hinges on this choice; my symbols can be replaced by more serious-looking ones of the reader's preference (for example, [ɪ], [ɛ], [æ], [ʌ], [ɔ]/[ɒ], or [ʉ]/[ɵ]/[ʊ], respectively).
3. https://merriam-webster.com (accessed January 2020).
4. There is no truly monomorphemic example for [ŋd].
5. For *waltz* LPD has [wols], [woːls], [wolts], [woːlts]; curiously not the usual [wolˢ] or [wolts]. For *Helmholtz, schmaltz, Schultz* there is no [t]-less form in either the LPD or MW. LPD also contains *Torvalds* [tóːvalts], [tóːvaldz]. Here the *lenis*, but not the fortis plosive is marked as variable, which constitutes a unique case.
6. Note that [nʒ] does not have a standard orthographical representation in English. The letter *g* or *j* is [ʒ] in some recent French loans (like *lingerie* or *jupe*), but then it is also often [dʒ] in the same words. Other instances of [ʒ] occur only intervocalically, as a result of the palatalisation of [z], spelled *s* or *z* (*pleasure* [pléʒə], *azure* [áʒə]).
7. A plosive (this time always lenis) also appeared earlier between a nasal and another sonorant: OE *crymlan* > ME *crymblen* 'crumble', OE *cynrēd* > ModE *kindred*. This process is not active any more, we do not find any alternation in this environment in either direction: *omelette* [óm(*b)lət], *general* [dʒén(*d)rəl], *assembly* [əsém*(b)lij], *hundred* [hʌ́n*(d)rəd].
8. The second vowel of *triumph* and *larynx* is probably not unstressed. We do not normally find an unstressed vowel before word-final [mp], [mf], [ŋk] clusters. Also note that LPD, which uses different symbols for stressed and unstressed schwa, ʌ and ə, respectively, transcribes *triumph* as [ˈtraɪ ʌmᵖf], though it cannot indicate the difference in *larynx*, because, somewhat inconsistently, it uses the same ɪ for both the stressed and the unstressed vowel in this case. See Szigetvári (2017, 270f.) for further discussion.
9. Apart from a variant pronunciation of *anxiety*, [ŋgz] does not exist either.
10. The word *metempsychosis* is [métempsàjkə́wsis] in LPD. This may also be a spelling pronunciation. In MW we find the expected contrast: [mətém(p)sikə́wsis]~[métəmsàjkə́wsis].
11. Thus we find an italic plosive in *glimpse* [glimps], although etymologically this [p] is epenthetic; the word was earlier spelled *glimse*.
12. The contrast of [nf] and [mf] is also brought up in *Modern Family* S02E10: at 4:06 Phil Dunphy is at great pains explaining the pronunciation of his name to his father-in-law. This issue reoccurs on several occasions in the series.
13. Although *dreamt* consists of two morphemes, it is different from *dumped* [dʌ́m(p)t], since the [p] is obligatory in *dump*, but missing in *dream*.

References

Charette, M. (1991). *Conditions on Phonological Government*. Cambridge: Cambridge University Press.
Charette, M. (1992). 'Mongolian and Polish meet government licensing'. *SOAS Working Papers in Linguistics* 2, 275–91.
Clements, G. N. (1987). 'Phonological feature representation and the description of intrusive stops'. In *Papers from the 23rd Annual Regional Meeting of the Chicago Linguistic Society*, edited by A. Bosch, B. Need, and E. Schiller, 29–50. Chicago: Chicago Linguistics Society.
Cyran, E. (2010). *Complexity Scales and Licensing in Phonology*. Berlin: De Gruyter.

Fourakis, M., and Port, R. (1986). 'Stop epenthesis in English'. *Journal of Phonetics* 14, 197–221. https://doi.org/10.1016/s0095-4470%2819%2930658-8.
Harris, J. (1994). *English Sound Structure*. Oxford: Blackwell.
Harris, J. (1997). 'Licensing Inheritance: An integrated theory of neutralisation'. *Phonology* 14, 315–70. https://doi.org/10.1017/s0952675798003479.
Kiss, Z. (2002). 'Complexity effects in nasal–continuant clusters'. *The Even Yearbook* 5, 57–76.
Ségéral, P., and Scheer, T. (2001). 'Le Coda-Miroir'. *Bulletin de la Société de Linguistique de Paris* 96, 107–52.
Steriade, D. (1999). 'Alternatives to syllable-based accounts of consonantal phonotactics'. In *Proceedings of the 1998 Linguistics and Phonetics Conference: Item order in language and speech*, edited by O. Fujimura, B. D. Joseph, and B. Palak, 205–45. Prague: Karolina Press.
Szigetvári, P. (2017). 'English stress is binary and lexical'. In *Sonic Signatures*, edited by G. Lindsey and A. Nevins, 263–76. Amsterdam: John Benjamins. https://doi.org/10.1075/lfab.14.c15.
Wells, J. C. (2008). *Longman Pronunciation Dictionary*. 3rd edition. London: Pearson/Longman.

Part 4
Prosodic structure and recursion

21
Prosodic structure and recursion: a brief introduction
Connor Youngberg and Florian Breit

Recursion in syntax and phonology

While recursion is a well-accepted feature of language within generative syntax, within phonology its existence and, if it exists, the role it might play continue to be keenly debated (see, for example, Vogel 2012; Martínez-Paricio and Kager 2015; Nasukawa 2020 and contributions therein). An early example from Government Phonology (GP) is the 'matrix calculus' of Kaye et al. (1985), who proposed that elements such as |A, I, U| undergo post-phonological spell-out into phonetic feature matrices of the type familiar from SPE (Chomsky and Halle 1968). To achieve this, they proposed what is essentially an asymmetric recursive algorithm which fuses feature matrices representing each element's phonetic substance, selectively retaining feature values from head or operator. The approach faced significant challenges (Coleman 1990a, 1990b; Kaye 1990) and has given way to a more atomistic view in modern Element Theory (ET), which maps elements to patterns in the acoustic signal (Lindsey and Harris 1990; Harris and Lindsey 1993). For all intents and purposes, following work in GP has adhered to the view that phonology is essentially recursion-free.

Recursive approaches to prosodic structure

More recently, there have been a number of proposals which submit that both melodic and prosodic representations involve recursion to varying degrees. Likely the three most prominent proponents of this view in the GP/ET-tradition are GP 2.0 (Pöchtrager 2006; Živanović and Pöchtrager 2010), Radical CV Phonology (RCVP; van der Hulst 2020), and Precedence-free Phonology (PfP; Nasukawa 2014; Nasukawa and Backley 2015).

GP 2.0

GP 2.0 posits that there is a strong and inherent connection between certain 'anomalous' elements and their prosodic behaviour. Namely, |A, H, ʔ| compared to |U, I, L| show both a more restricted distribution (for example, |ʔ| is argued to never plausibly occupy nuclei) and are frequently linked to length phenomena (for example, [V:sC] sequences in British English must have |A| in either V or C). The fundamental proposition of GP 2.0 is that |A, H, ʔ| are not melodic primes, but the result of pure structure. Compare the two approaches to the Pulaar continuant-stop alternation under pluralisation as in [lefol] 'pennant' → [lep:i] 'pennants' in (1), where GP 2.0 is able to capture the three factors of suffixation, fortition, and gemination all as a single structural alternation, namely an additional projection of the head ×O.

(1) a. Lateral (~Standard GP)   b. Embedded (GP 2.0)

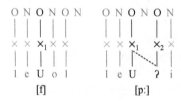
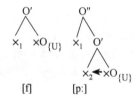

Precedence-free Phonology

Not dissimilar in seeking a more unified explanation of prosody and melody, PfP also makes use of recursive embedding but proposes that by retaining the melodic primes as the primary combinatory unit and combining these more freely into larger embedded structures we can dispense with certain lateral relations and prosodic categories. This approach is illustrated in Chapter 22, where Backley and Nasukawa set out an analysis of French nasal vowels and Japanese moraic nasals without reliance on feet, syllables, or segments as distinct phonological categories.

Radical CV Phonology

RCVP again pursues many similar aims to GP2.0 and PfP by the means of structure. However, both the stated aim and assumptions of the approach differ somewhat. First, RCVP is much more strongly rooted in Dependency Phonology (Anderson and Ewen 1987) than other current work. Second, it pursues a radical reductionism whereby only two feature primitives (the units C and V) are assumed. Recursively combining these two units in specific dependency configurations, RCVP posits that sufficient structural restrictiveness then permits the relevant categories to be read off these configurations. While early on the central focus of this approach was on melodic categories, van der Hulst has proposed many further developments of the theory which capture much prosodic structure by further expanding the structures of C and V units. Especially when expanded to complex prosodic structure, as in van der Hulst's Chapter 23, RCVP makes the case not only for the maximisation of structure in order to reduce melodic or prosodic complexity, but for extensive recursivity inside phonology as a powerful explanatory device.

References

Anderson, J., and Ewen, C. (1987) *Principles of Dependency Phonology*. Cambridge: Cambridge University Press.
Chomsky, N., and Halle, M. (1968). *The Sound Pattern of English*. New York: Harper & Row.
Coleman, J. (1990a). 'Charm theory defines strange vowel sets'. *Journal of Linguistics* 26(1), 165–74.
Coleman, J. (1990b). 'Vowel sets: a reply to Kaye'. *Journal of Linguistics* 26(1), 183–7.
Harris, J., and Lindsey, G. (1993). 'There is no level of phonetic representation'. *UCL Working Papers in Linguistics* 5, 354–73.
Kaye, J. (1990). 'The strange vowel sets of Charm theory: The question from top to bottom'. *Journal of Linguistics* 26(1), 175–81.
Kaye, J., Lowenstamm, J., and Vergnaud, J.-R. (1985). 'The internal structure of phonological elements: a theory of Charm and Government'. *Phonology* 2, 305–28.
Lindsey, G., and Harris, J. (1990). 'Phonetic interpretation in generative grammar'. *UCL Working Papers in Linguistics* 11, 53–70.
Martínez-Paricio, V., and Kager, R. (2015). 'The binary-to-ternary rhythmic continuum in stress typology: Layered feet and nonintervention constraints'. *Phonology* 32(3), 459–504.
Nasukawa, K. (2014). 'Features and recursive structure'. *Nordlyd* 41(1), 1–19.
Nasukawa, K. (ed.). (2020). *Morpheme-internal Recursion in Phonology*. Berlin: De Gruyter. https://doi.org/10.1515/9781501512582.
Nasukawa, K., and Backley, P. (2015). 'Headship as melodic and prosodic prominence'. In *pS-prominenceS: Prominences in Linguistics*, edited by A. De Dominics, 59–75. Conference proceedings. Viterbo: Disucom Press.
Pöchtrager, M. A. (2006). *The Structure of Length*. Doctoral dissertation, University of Vienna.
van der Hulst, H. (2020). *Principles of Radical CV Phonology: A theory of segmental and syllabic structure*. Edinburgh: Edinburgh University Press.
Vogel, I. (2012). 'Recursion in phonology?' In *Phonological Explorations: Empirical, theoretical and diachronic issues*, edited by B. Botma and R. Noske, 41–62. Berlin: De Gruyter. https://doi.org/10.1515/9783110295177.41.
Živanović, S., and Pöchtrager, M. A. (2010). 'GP 2, and Putonghua too'. *Acta Linguistica Hungarica* 57(4), 357–80.

22
Nasal vowels in French: a precedence-free approach
Phillip Backley and Kuniya Nasukawa

Introduction

It is estimated that about one fifth of the world's languages use nasality contrastively in vowels.[1] In French, Portuguese, Yoruba, and Punjabi, for instance, oral and nasal vowels are lexically distinct, for example, Punjabi /lũː/ 'hair', /luː/ 'heat wave' (Bhatia 1993, 337). By contrast, languages which do not belong in this group – English, Italian, Hawaiian, Persian, and countless others – have no such contrast. Instead, they tend to display contextual nasalisation, where nasality is systematically realised on vowels in the context of nasal consonants, as in English *calm* /kɑːm/ [kɑ̃ːm].

The focus here is not on context-dependent nasalisation but on contrastive nasal vowels, and specifically, those in French. French nasal vowels (henceforth FNVs) have been treated extensively in the literature and the data are already familiar to many. In this chapter, however, we take the novel approach of analysing FNVs using a version of the Element Theory model called Precedence-free Phonology or PfP, in which melodic structure is built around (vertical) head-dependency relations rather than (horizontal) sequences of segments. We begin by describing the history of FNVs and their distribution in modern French. Two analyses of FNVs are then presented, firstly, one using a standard derivational approach and, in the next section, another using a PfP approach. Finally, we draw parallels between our PfP analysis of FNVs and a PfP account of the Japanese mora nasal.

FNVs and their historical development

Regarding the status of FNVs,[2] a point of contention concerns whether they should be treated as lexical or derived (Tranel 1981, 3ff.). The lexical view taken in Martinet (1971, 143) and Trubetzkoy (1967, 130ff.) treats FNVs as distinct phonemes with their own nasality feature, allowing them to contrast with oral vowels. On the other hand, the derived view taken in Dell (1970) and Schane (1968) sees FNVs not as single segments but as sequences of an oral vowel plus a nasal consonant. In a PfP approach, the question of whether FNVs are derived or not is irrelevant because PfP is a non-derivational model.

The historical development of FNVs is thought to have gone through the stages in (1).[3] Note that, although scholars disagree over precisely when these changes took place, this issue is not important to the present discussion, which is concerned with how to represent the melodic changes themselves.

(1)
		stage 1 (Old French)	stage 2 (Middle French)	stage 3 (Modern French)
a.	*lande* 'moor'	[lãndə]	[lãdə]	[lãd]
b.	*bon* 'good'	[bɔ̃n]	[bɔ̃]	[bɔ̃]
c.	*dame* 'lady'	[dãmə]	[damə]	[dam]

In stage 1 there was no contrast between oral and nasal vowels. Presumably, however, vowel nasalisation took place as a coarticulatory effect, as in [landə]>[lãndə] 'moor'. Then in stage 2 a nasal consonant deleted after a nasalised vowel, as in [bɔ̃n]>[bɔ̃] 'good'. Also, nasalised vowels were denasalised before intervocalic /n, m/ and these nasal consonants were retained, giving the pattern [dãmə]>[damə] 'lady'. Finally, stage 3 saw the loss of word-final /ə/, leading to modern forms such as *lande* [lãd] and *dame* [dam]. The two patterns of FNV distribution in present-day French are illustrated in (2).

(2) a. **Non-alternating (nasal)**
    sombre [sɔ̃bʁ]   'dark'
    lande [lãd]   'moor'
    cinquante [sɛ̃kãt]   'fifty'

  b. **Alternating (nasal ~ oral)**
    bon [bɔ̃] ~ *bonne* [bɔn]   'good' (masc. ~ fem.)
    paysan [peizã] ~ *paysanne* [peizan]   'peasant' (masc. ~ fem.)
    maison [mɛzɔ̃] ~ *maisonnette* [mɛzɔnɛt]   'house' ~ 'little house'

The difference between the two patterns corresponds to a difference in the way the historical nasal consonant was syllabified in Old French. In the (2a) pattern, the nasal (which has since elided) was followed by an obstruent, which places it in a rhymal complement position, as in (3a). By contrast, in the (2b) pattern the original nasal was morpheme-final (in uninflected words). Using the syllabification system set out in Charette (1991) and later employed in Harris and Gussmann (1998), this places it in the onset of a final 'dull' syllable, as in (3b).

(3)   a. *sombre* /sɔn.bʁə/ 'dark'   b. *bon* /bɔ.n/ 'good'

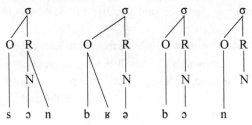

First, consider the words in (4). Like *sombre* [sɔ̃bʁ], they have a non-alternating nasal vowel. Historically, they contained a nasal consonant in a syllable 'coda' (rhymal complement).

(4)   **Non-alternating (nasal) pattern**
    lande   [lɑ̃d]   'moor'
    donc   [dɔ̃k]   'therefore'
    ensemble   [ɑ̃sɑ̃bl]   'together'
    singe   [sɛ̃ʒ]   'monkey'

There is nothing unusual about the pronunciation of these words in modern French, since they have been shaped by the kinds of phonetic effects and/or phonological changes that show up in many languages. For phonetic reasons (that is, coarticulation), the vowels in (4) are produced with nasal resonance because they precede historical nasal consonants. And for phonological reasons (that is, preservation of melodic/segmental properties), these historical nasals were free to elide because nasality appears on the neighbouring vowel. The nasal place property is also preserved, since the nasal was homorganic with the following obstruent, for example, [n] in *lande*, [ŋ] in *donc*, [m] in *ensemble*. Notice that the loss of this coda consonant leads to a less marked syllable structure – a frequent driver of diachronic change cross-linguistically.

Next, consider the words in (5). Like *bon* [bɔ̃], their vowels alternate between nasal and oral. Historically, as uninflected words they had a final nasal consonant syllabified as in (3b).

(5) **Alternating (nasal/oral) pattern**

a.	*Nasal vowel*			b.	*Oral vowel*		
	brun	[bʁœ̃]	'brown (masc.)'		*brune*	[bʁyn]	'brown (fem.)'
	chien	[ʃjẽ]	'dog (male)'		*chienne*	[ʃjɛn]	'dog (female)'
	tient	[tjẽ]	'(he) holds'		*tiennent*	[tjɛn]	'(they) hold'
	tiens	[tjẽ]	'(I) hold (indic.)'		*tienne*	[tjɛn]	'(I) hold (subjunc.)'

Again, there is nothing unusual about the modern pronunciation of the (5a) words. As in (4), they display vowel nasalisation as a coarticulatory effect, allowing the final nasal consonant to elide without losing nasality altogether. At first glance, the loss of this final consonant appears to result in a loss of contrastive information, since its place specification is not shared by neighbouring sounds, unlike in (4). On this point, however, Azra (2000) notes that in words such as *bon*, *chien*, etc., the final nasal is invariably dental, so the nasal's place property is already non-distinctive. On this basis, nasal consonant elision in (4) and in (5a) may be treated in parallel, with both changes resulting in a less marked syllable structure – the loss of a coda consonant in (4) and the loss of a domain-final consonant in (5a).

Representing FNVs (derivational approach)

First, consider the difference between the non-alternating vowels in (4) and the alternating vowels in (5). As (3) shows, they differ in syllable structure. And we suggest that this accounts for their distinct phonological behaviour. The vowels in (4) are domain-internal, so their phonological and morphological environments never alter. This makes them impervious to external influences, and consequently they do not alternate. By contrast, the vowels in (5a) are domain-final, so their environment can change as a result of suffixation. Here the focus is on cases where suffixation causes an oral vowel to appear in the stem (following the (5b) pattern) rather than a nasal vowel (following the (5a) pattern).

Modern French distinguishes between nasal vowels (Ṽ) and sequences of an oral vowel plus a nasal consonant (VN). In nouns and adjectives, they mark different genders: masculine forms end in Ṽ (*chien*, *brun*) and feminine forms in VN (*chienne*, *brune*). In some verbs Ṽ and VN distinguish singular versus plural: singular 3 forms (*il tient* [tjẽ] 'he holds') end in Ṽ while plural 3 forms (*ils tiennent* [tjɛn] 'they hold') end in VN. And Ṽ versus VN can also separate indicative mood (*je tiens* [tjẽ] 'I hold') from subjunctive mood (*je tienne* [tjɛn] 'I may hold') in some present tense verb forms.

The difference is typically explained by referring to a 'schwa morpheme' which, as a suffix, triggers phonological effects that encode grammatical features of the kind just described. However, not all scholars agree on how schwa should be represented in French. We choose to reject earlier treatments of schwa (for example, Schane 1968) which rely on a degree of abstractness to capture vowel alternations in purely melodic (segmental) terms. Instead, we focus on the prosodic properties of schwa. Our approach follows Anderson (1982), which treats French schwa as a melodically unspecified (empty) nucleus. That is, we see schwa as a prosodic entity rather than a segmental one.

To account for the nasal/oral alternations in (5), we assume that unspecified schwa can exist as an independent morpheme. To show how this schwa morpheme is used, we turn to the forms in (5b) and outline their morphological structure in (6b). Note that schwa is transcribed here as /ə/, even though it may be phonetically silent in French or may be realised with a [œ] quality.[4]

(6) a. *brun* /bʁyn/ [bʁœ̃] 'brown (masc.)'
    chien /ʃjɛn/ [ʃjɛ̃] 'dog (male)'
    tient /tjɛn/ [tjɛ̃] '(he) holds'
    tiens /tjɛn/ [tjɛ̃] '(I) hold (indic.)'

   b. *brune* /bʁyn/ + /ə/ [bʁyn] 'brown (fem.)'
    chienne /ʃjɛn/ + /ə/ [ʃjɛn] 'dog (female)'
    tiennent /tjɛn/ + /ə/ [tjɛn] '(they) hold'
    tienne /tjɛn/ + /ə/ [tjɛn] '(I) hold (subjunc.)'

The words in (6a) have nasal vowels, and they illustrate the rule of consonant deletion in French, which removes word-final consonants. It applies unless the consonant is followed by a vowel-initial word within the same phrase. So, final /n/ in *brun*, *chien*, *tient*, and *tiens* deletes when the word is pronounced in isolation. Again, the nasality associated with final /n/ is preserved by being phonetically realised on the stem vowel, producing a nasal vowel. That is, the lexical sequence VN is interpreted as Ṽ. Expressed in derivational terms, vowel nasalisation is shown in (7). Note that the deletion rule in (7b) actually targets prosodic structure, not segmental structure, since it deletes the onset of the word-final syllable.

(7) a. *brun* /bʁyn/ (lexical)   b. *brun* [bʁœ̃] (realisation)

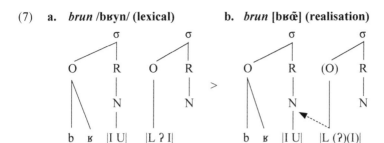

To be phonetically realised, the nasality represented by |L| must associate to another position. In this case it attaches to the preceding nucleus to create a nasal vowel.[5] While the nasality element |L| reassociates to the nucleus, the occlusion element |ʔ| also present in /n/ cannot reassign because in French (and most other languages) |ʔ| does not appear in a syllable nucleus.

Now consider the words in (6b), which contain the schwa morpheme and are realised with an oral vowel. Their final schwa is silent because this vowel is nothing more than an empty nucleus (which, in French, may be left uninterpreted – see section below, 'PfP structures in French'). Yet although no vowel sound is pronounced, the prosodic structure of the schwa morpheme remains intact. And this structure protects the final /n/ of *brune* from deletion since it is not in the final syllable of the word. The stem /bʁyn/ is therefore unchanged: the oral vowel remains oral and the final /n/ avoids deletion, as (8) shows.

(8) a. *brune* /bʁyn + ə/   b. *brune* [bʁyn]

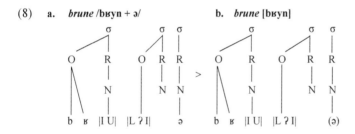

Although these analyses depart from some traditional accounts of FNVs (for example, Schane 1968), they are nevertheless 'conventional' by virtue of their derivational approach. In the next section we contrast this with an alternative analysis based on the representational approach PfP.

Representing FNVs (PfP approach)

Representations in PfP

In PfP, phonological representations do not refer to precedence relations (that is, linear ordering) between structural units, the aim being to eliminate redundancy (Anderson 1987; Backley 2021; Backley and Nasukawa 2020; Nasukawa 2011, 2014, 2015, 2016, 2017ab, 2020; Nasukawa and Backley 2015, 2017).[6] And because PfP does not treat precedence as a formal property, representations do not include timing units such as skeletal positions, CV units or Root nodes. From this it also follows that the unit 'segment' has no formal status. Instead, segments and the precedence relations between them are viewed as the phonetic outcome of externalisation.

In PfP, elements are the only structural units permitted in phonological representations. Unlike in other element-based approaches, however, elements in PfP have a dual function: they represent melodic properties in the usual way and they also project onto higher structural levels where they behave as organising units. That is, they function as prosodic constituents, taking the place of traditional prosodic units such as 'nucleus', 'mora', 'syllable', and 'foot'.

In PfP, the unit corresponding to a nucleus is represented by a single element from the set of resonance elements {|A|, |I|, |U|}. The choice is parametric, the chosen element reflecting the phonetic quality of a language's baseline resonance. For example, English uses |A| (realised as [ə] in its acoustically weak form), Fijian chooses |I| (realised as weak [ɨ]), and Japanese selects |U| (realised as [ɯ]) (Nasukawa 2014). We propose that French is like English in having |A| as its base element. By itself, the base element is pronounced as a weak or non-contrastive vowel. By contrast, full vowels have more complex structures in which the base element takes one or more elements as dependents. Example structures for full vowels are given in (9bcd), all with |A| as their base element. Note that the base element functions as the head of each expression.

(9) **Vowel representations in PfP** (Nasukawa 2020, 15)
    a. [ə]   b. [i]   c. [u]   d. [a]

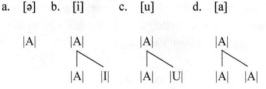

(9a) is a minimal structure containing only the base element |A|. Recall that the base element functions as a prosodic unit equivalent to a nuclear position, so (9a) has the properties of an empty nucleus, that is, a nuclear position with no dependent (melodic) structure. Predictably, it behaves as a default or non-contrastive vowel which may serve as a reduced vowel or as an epenthetic vowel in loanwords. This vowel is usually transcribed as /ə/, but its non-contrastive status means that its phonetic quality can vary, for example, [ə] in English, [ə]~[œ] in French.

By contrast, (9b–d) have complex structures in which the base element has dependents. Dependent elements are incorporated into the structure using a syntax-like Merge operation (Nasukawa 2017a). The elements |I|, |U|, and |A| are present as dependents in (9b), (9c), and (9d) respectively, and in each case the acoustic pattern of the dependent element overrides the baseline resonance from the base element |A| to give the full vowels [i], [u], and [a]. What this shows is that the phonetic realisation of a head-dependent structure is largely determined by the relative prominence of its dependent element(s). This is formalised as in (10).

(10) **The Principle of Phonetic Realisation of Head-Dependency Structure**
(Nasukawa 2014, 2015, 2016, 2017a,b; Nasukawa and Backley 2015, 2017, 2018)

Dependents, which are not necessary for structural well-formedness, are phonetically more salient in terms of their modulated carrier signal than heads, which are important for building structure.

In the mapping between phonology and phonetics, the prominence of dependents is attributed to the relatively larger modulations of the carrier signal with which these elements are realised phonetically.[7] This applies not only in structures with two elements but also in more complex structures with further levels of embedding.

PfP structures in French

Using the PfP architecture, (11) gives representations of the melodic units that are relevant to the analysis of FNVs.

(11) a. [n]   b. [nə]

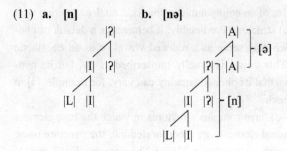

As already mentioned, we assume that the base element is |A|. This is because the default vowel in French can be pronounced [ə], which is the baseline resonance produced by realising the base element |A| on its own, that is, without dependent structure (see 9a). By contrast, [n] in (11a) has the relatively complex structure |ʔ I L|. These elements combine via the Merge operation mentioned earlier, creating a hierarchical structure in which each element occupies a different level of embedding. Comparing (9a) and (11a) reveals that the basic split between consonants and vowels is expressed in PfP by a difference in their base element: vowels take their base element from the resonance set {|A|, |I|, |U|} while consonants choose from the non-resonance set {|H|, |ʔ|}. In the case of nasal consonants, the base element is |ʔ| (Nasukawa and Backley 2018), so the expression in (11a) is a nasal consonant rather than a nasal vowel. In (11a) the base element |ʔ| has two dependents: |L| adds nasal resonance[8] and |I| provides the dental place specification for [n].

By merging the vowel expression [ə] in (9a) with the consonant expression [n] in (11a) we get the syllable-sized unit in (11b). The Merge operation creates a head-dependent relation between the vowel domain and the consonant domain, and this relation then determines how the overall structure is externalised. Externalisation is formalised by a Principle of Precedence (Nasukawa et al. 2019) which states that lower (that is, more deeply embedded) melodic structure is phonetically realised before higher melodic structure. Therefore, the (dependent) C-domain precedes the (head) V-domain when a syllable-sized unit such as (11b) is pronounced, giving the default CV pattern rather than VC.[9] It is not possible to realise the vowel and consonant expressions in (11b) simultaneously, because each requires different articulatory gestures. So, a staggered phonetic realisation is necessary.

FNVs (nasal vowel alternant)

In principle, (11b) can be realised as the CV sequence [nə]. But when this structure is word-final in French, only [n] is pronounced. This is because French belongs to the set of languages allowing words to end phonetically in a consonant. In Government Phonology this behaviour is captured by the Domain-Final Empty Nucleus Parameter (Kaye et al. (KLV) 1990; Charette 1991; Harris 1994), which controls whether a word-final or morpheme-final empty nucleus is pronounced or not. The same pattern is expressed in PfP by the parameter in (12) which, to be consistent with the aims of PfP, avoids referring to linear ordering between melodic units.

(12) **The Ultimate Head Parameter (UHP)**[10]

The highest base element in a morphological domain is p-licensed[11] if it has no vocalic dependents. [OFF/ON]

So, because the UHP is set to ON in French,[12] the vowel of (11b) is silent when it appears word-finally (see (5b) above). In this respect, French differs from languages such as Zulu and Japanese, in which words must end phonetically in a vowel because the UHP is set to OFF. In these systems, the highest base element must be audible even when it has no vocalic dependents, in which case it is pronounced as a default vowel. For instance, the base element in Japanese is |U|, which is phonetically realised as [ɯ], for example, *geemu* [geːmɯ] 'video game'.

Consider now the words in (6a), repeated here as (13). Each has a nasal vowel which alternates with an oral vowel (when the schwa morpheme is added, as in (6b)). We assume that, for each word, the stem is phonologically identical in both alternants, and that this stem has a final consonant. Here, phonological forms are shown within slashes.

(13) *brun*   /bʁyn/   [bʁœ̃]   'brown (masc.)'
    chien   /ʃjɛn/   [ʃjɛ̃]   'dog (male)'
    tient   /tjɛn/   [tjɛ̃]   '(he) holds'
    tiens   /tjɛn/   [tjɛ̃]   '(I) hold (indic.)'

From the preceding discussion it follows that forms such as /bʁyn/ have structures in which the highest base element is p-licensed by the UHP, so its vocalic portion is not phonetically realised. (In traditional parlance, the final consonant precedes a silent 'nucleus'.) This is shown in (14a).

(14) a. /bʁyn/ b. [bʁœ̃]

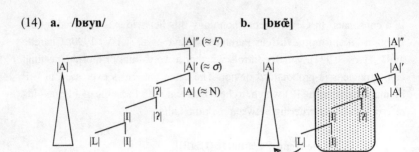

Also, recall from the section 'Representing FNVs (derivational approach)' that French has a consonant deletion rule which 'deletes the onset position in the final syllable of a word'. In PfP terms, this involves removing the consonant expression that is a dependent of the highest base element, as in (14b). When structure is deleted in this way, we expect all of its associated elements to be lost. But in the case of nasal consonants, |L| (nasality) remains and is realised by merging with the stem vowel, as indicated by the arrow in (14b).

A perceptual reason can be offered for why |L| survives, given that nasality is a defining property of the original /n/, and by extension, of the entire stem. If nasality were lost entirely, this would impact the perceptibility of the masculine form *brun*. Moreover, the importance of nasality to the identity of /n/ is reflected in phonological structure. In PfP, elements combine by forming chains of head-dependent relations, resulting in hierarchical structures of the kind in (14). At the top of each vertical structure is a base element, which has a prosodic role, that is, important for structure-building but not for expressing contrasts (since its acoustic properties are overridden by those of dependent elements). On the other hand, elements positioned lower in the hierarchy show the opposite characteristics, that is, unimportant for structure (for example, they do not support dependents) but important in melodic terms because they represent salient acoustic properties (Nasukawa 2017b; Backley 2021). In other words, the more deeply embedded an element is, the greater its acoustic prominence and its linguistic significance will be. It is no coincidence that |L| is the terminal element in the structure for /n/ in (14): as the lowest element in the hierarchy it is a defining property of nasal consonants.

FNVs (oral vowel alternant)

Consider now the words in (6b), repeated here as (15). They have the same stems as the words in (14) but are suffixed with the schwa morpheme to express feminine gender in *brune* and *chienne*, plural in *tiennent*, and subjunctive mood in *tienne*.

(15) *brune*   /bʁyn/ + /ə/   [bʁyn]   'brown (fem.)'
    chienne /ʃjɛn/ + /ə/   [ʃjɛn]   'dog (female)'
    tiennent /tjɛn/ + /ə/   [tjɛn]   '(they) hold'
    tienne   /tjɛn/ + /ə/   [tjɛn]   '(I) hold (subjunctive)'

These suffixed forms have the oral vowel alternant shown in (5b), so a phonological analysis must explain why a VN sequence (cf. Ṽ) is pronounced in the context of the schwa morpheme. We propose that VN in [bʁyn], [tjɛn], etc., results from the way morphological concatenation operates between stem and suffix. Following Nasukawa (2020), we claim that when a suffix is added it becomes the head of the new morphological domain. So the schwa morpheme in (16) occupies the highest level in the concatenated structure. Note that the schwa morpheme itself is melodically empty and phonetically silent: it is empty because it has no lexical melodic properties (/ə/ corresponds to a bare base element |A|), and it is silent by virtue of the UHP (being the highest base element in the morphological domain, |A| is p-licensed).

(16) **/bʁyn + ə/ [bʁyn]**

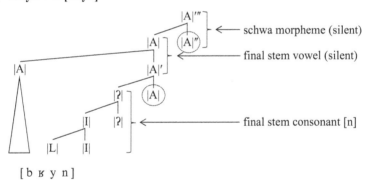

In (16) there are two vocalic base elements (circled) with no dependent vowel elements. And because both are highest in their respective morphological domains (that is, stem, suffix), both are silent following the UHP. (Informally, each one is a final empty nucleus.) So, when the suffixed form is pronounced it ends phonetically in a consonant [n]. Unlike in (14b), however, [n] is not targeted by the consonant deletion rule as it is no longer 'word-final', that is, not a dependent of the highest base element in the word. This is because, after suffixation, the highest base element is that of the schwa morpheme. Nasality is therefore realised on the consonant, and there is no need for it to migrate to the stem vowel. The result is an oral vowel in (16) which alternates with the nasal vowel in (14b).

The mora nasal in Japanese

Finally, we observe a parallel between the French nasal vowel in (14b) and the Japanese mora (or syllabic) nasal. Although the literature on Japanese phonology has not made much of the idea that Japanese could have nasal vowels,[13] it has been noted in the element-based literature that similarities do exist between nasal vowels and syllabic nasals (Yoshida S. 1991, Yoshida Y. 1995, Youngberg 2021). From a PfP perspective, the two have much in common both structurally and phonetically – so much so, that we propose to treat them as equivalents. Following Nasukawa (2004) and Nasukawa and Backley (2017), the Japanese mora nasal is represented as in (17). In hoN [hõ] 'book', the vowel and the mora nasal N merge phonetically to produce the nasal vowel [õ] (Yoshida 1996). This echoes the merging effect observed in French, as shown in (14b).

(17) hoN [hõ] 'book'

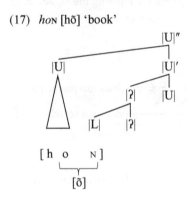

In the Japanese case, the mora nasal N is typically described as 'placeless' because it has no lexical place specification. Accordingly, it is represented as a simplex structure containing only |L| for nasality. Yet this renders it highly unstable as a consonant – in general, nasals seem to require a place specification in order to be realised as consonants. So, as an avoidance measure |L| merges with the vowel o and the two are realised simultaneously as [õ].

This analysis of the mora nasal allows a simplified explanation of certain phonological patterns in Japanese. One concerns a dialect difference between standard (Tokyo) Japanese and two regional dialects, Oogami and Kagoshima. Nouns which end in the sequence nu (for example, inu 'dog') in Tokyo Japanese are realised with a mora nasal [N] in the Oogami and Kagoshima dialects (for example, iN 'dog'). This is usually explained by saying that the final vowel u is lost and the dental nasal n changes into a placeless mora nasal N. In PfP, however, it can be captured by referring to the same deletion rule that was proposed for French and illustrated in (14b), where the place element |I| and the occlusion element |?| are suppressed. (18a) shows the structure for Tokyo Japanese, while (18b) represents the non-standard form.

(18) a. *inu* /inu/ [inɯ]   b. *iN* /iN/ [iũ]

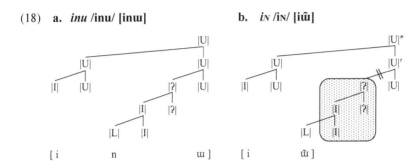

What happened in the Oogami and Kagoshima dialects, shown in (18b), is similar to the historical process which led to the emergence of FNVs, shown in (14b). In Japanese, consonant deletion took place but again |L| survived, perhaps for the same perceptual reasons that were mentioned above. And importantly, the remaining structure comprising the base element |U| and nasal |L| is almost identical to the structure of the mora nasal in (17).[14] In Japanese, this structure can be interpreted as it is – unlike in French, there is no need for |L| to merge with a neighbouring vowel. The resulting sound is [ũ], a nasalised reflex of the default vowel [ɯ]. Although this sound is conventionally described as a mora nasal, we redefine it here as a nasal vowel [ũ]. After all, it has the phonological structure of a nasal vowel as given in (18b), and when pronounced it has the phonetic characteristics of a nasal vowel.

Summary

We have analysed familiar data in an unfamiliar context, the representational approach called PfP. In some respects, PfP may seem unorthodox, yet it reveals how a small set of elements, together with a standard notion of head-dependency, has the potential to integrate melody and prosody into a single representation and offer new insights into the nature of the phonological grammar. We look forward to seeing further developments in the way elements can enrich our understanding of phonological patterning.

Notes

1. This work was supported by the following MEXT/JSPS KAKENHI grants: Grant-in-Aid for Scientific Research on Innovative Areas #4903 (Evolinguistics) Grant Number JP20H05007, Grant-in-Aid for Scientific Research (S) Grant Number JP19H05589 and Grant-in-Aid for Scientific Research (A) Grant Number JP19H00532 and Grant-in-Aid for Scientific Research (C) Grant Number JP22K00513. In writing this chapter, we hope to express something of the considerable intellectual debt we owe to Monik Charette. She was the first person to show us (both authors) that phonology could be different from the way it was presented in standard textbooks. And Monik managed to do this by rousing our curiosity, rather than by simply teaching us. The fact that we are still curious about phonology today says a great deal.
2. The data presented here come from standard (that is, Parisian or Continental) French. For a discussion of the patterns in other varieties of French, see Charette (2003) and references therein.
3. For discussion, see for example Ruhlen (1973), Hajek (1997), and Azra (2000).
4. French also has a contrastive vowel /œ/, with which the schwa vowel overlaps phonetically. However, the two vowels differ in phonological behaviour (Anderson, 1982, 538), suggesting that they have distinct representations.
5. Cross-linguistically, nasalisation occurs more readily on non-high vowels than on high vowels (Hajek 1997, 116ff.). Reflecting this, the set of FNVs excludes the high vowels */ĩ/, */ỹ/, and */ũ/. This tendency also relates to the observation that nasalisation can have a lowering effect on target vowels, as appears to happen in (7b). This is not shown in the melodic representation of (7b), as lowering is not relevant to the present discussion.
6. In another approach that also aims to eliminate representational redundancy, Raimy (2000) and Samuels (2009) represent phonological properties without referring to asymmetric relations (for example, dependency) between units.
7. Harris (2009) argues that the carrier signal makes it possible for linguistic messages to be heard whereas the energy in a modulated carrier signal contains linguistically contrastive properties that enable listeners to recognise morphemes/words. Furthermore, Ohala (1992), Ohala and Kawasaki-Fukumori (1997), Traunmüller (1994; 2005), and Harris (2006; 2009) claim that the carrier signal in speech manifests itself as a schwa-like quality characterised by an absence of converging formants in its periodic signature. According to Harris (2006; 2009), the size of the modulations of this carrier signal are then defined in terms of acoustic attributes such as periodicity, amplitude, spectral shape, fundamental frequency, and duration/timing.
8. In PfP the |L| element represents two categories of sounds: when it cooccurs with |H| it is interpreted as obstruent voicing, but when no |H| is present the |L| element contributes nasality (Nasukawa and Backley 2018).
9. To allow for the existence of a small number of languages (for example, Kaqchikel) where the preferred syllable type is VC rather than CV, it has been proposed that the Principle of Precedence is parametric (Nasukawa et al. 2019).
10. This is an adaptation of the Ultimate-head Parameter introduced in Onuma (2015, 136).
11. Expressed in PfP terms, 'p-licensed' describes an empty vocalic domain which is not phonetically realised. (An empty vocalic domain has a base (head) element but no melodic (dependent) elements.)
12. Evidently, French changed its parametric setting for the BHP from OFF to ON before the start of the Modern French period. This is clear from Middle French forms such as *lande* [lãdə] 'moor' in (1a), in which a default [ə] (that is, baseline resonance) is pronounced.
13. The exception here is Nakano (1969). We are grateful to one of the editors for pointing this out.
14. Although (17) has an additional layer of structure containing |ʔ|, this does not affect phonetic interpretation: as the base element of the consonantal domain, |ʔ| functions as a prosodic unit (that is, an onset constituent) rather than as a melodic unit.

References

Anderson, J. M. (1987). 'The limit of linearity'. In *Explorations in Dependency Phonology*, edited by J. M. Anderson and J. Durand, 199–220. Dordrecht: Foris.

Anderson, S. R. (1982). 'The analysis of French schwa: Or how to get something for nothing'. *Language* 58(3), 534–73.

Azra, J.-L. (2000). 'Emergence and evolution of French nasal vowels'. In *Historical Linguistics 1995. Volume I: General issues and non-Germanic languages. Selected papers from the 12th International Conference on Historical Linguistics*, edited by J. C. Smith and D. Bentley, 1–22. Amsterdam: John Benjamins.

Backley, P. (2021). 'Elements and structural head-dependency'. In *Perspectives in Element Theory*, edited by S. Bendjaballah, A. Tifrit, and L. Voeltzel, 9–31. Berlin: De Gruyter. https://doi.org/10.1515/9783110691948-002.

Backley, P., and Nasukawa, K. (2020). 'Recursion in melodic-prosodic structure'. In *Morpheme-internal Recursion in Phonology*, edited by K. Nasukawa, 11–35. Berlin: De Gruyter.

Bhatia, T. K. (1993). *Punjabi: A cognitive-descriptive grammar*. London: Routledge.

Charette, M. (1991). *Conditions on Phonological Government*. Cambridge: Cambridge University Press.

Charette, M. (2003). 'Empty and pseudo-empty categories'. In *Living on the Edge. 28 papers in honour of Jonathan Kaye*, edited by S. Ploch, 465–79. Berlin: De Gruyter. https://doi.org/10.1515/9783110890563.465.

Dell, F. (1970). *Les règles phonologiques tardives et la morphologie dérivationnelle du français*. Doctoral dissertation, Massachusetts Institute of Technology (MIT).

Hajek, J. (1997). *Universals of Sound Change in Nasalization*. Oxford: Blackwell.

Harris, J. (1994). *English Sound Structure*. Oxford: Blackwell.

Harris, J. (2006). 'The phonology of being understood: Further arguments against sonority'. *Lingua* 116(10), 1483–94. http://dx.doi.org/10.1016%2Fj.lingua.2005.07.009.

Harris, J. (2009). 'Why final devoicing is weakening'. In *Strength Relations in Phonology*, edited by K. Nasukawa and P. Backley, 9–46. Berlin: De Gruyter.

Harris, J., and Gussmann, E. (1998). 'Final codas: Why the West was wrong'. In *Structure and Interpretation in Phonology: Studies in phonology*, edited by E. Cyran, 139–62. Lublin: Folium.

Kaye, J., Lowenstamm, J., and Vergnaud, J-R. (1990). 'Constituent structure and government in phonology'. *Phonology* 7, 193–231.

Martinet, A. (1971). *La prononciation du français contemporain: Témoignages recueillis en 1941 dans un camp d'officiers prisonniers*. 2nd edition. Geneva: Librairie Droz.

Nakano, K. (1969). 'A phonetic basis for the syllabic nasal in Japanese'. *Onsei no kenkyū* 14, 215–28.

Nasukawa, K. (2004). 'Word-final consonants: Arguments against a coda analysis'. *Proceedings of the 58th Conference, Tohoku English Literary Society*, 47–53.

Nasukawa, K. (2011). 'Representing phonology without precedence relations'. *English Linguistics* 28, 278–300.

Nasukawa, K. (2014). 'Features and recursive structure'. *Nordlyd* 41(1), 1–19.

Nasukawa, K. (2015). 'Recursion in the lexical structure of morphemes'. In *Representing Structure in Phonology and Syntax*, edited by M. van Oostendorp and H. van Riemsdijk, 211–38. Berlin: De Gruyter. https://doi.org/10.1515/9781501502224-009.

Nasukawa, K. (2016). 'A precedence-free approach to (de-)palatalisation in Japanese'. *Glossa* 1(1). 9. 1–21. http://dx.doi.org/10.5334/gjgl.26.

Nasukawa, K. (2017a). 'Extending the application of Merge to elements in phonological representations'. *Journal of the Phonetic Society of Japan* 21, 59–70.

Nasukawa, K. (2017b). 'The phonetic salience of phonological head-dependent structure in a modulated-carrier model of speech'. In *Beyond Markedness in Formal Phonology*, edited by B. Samuels, 121–52. Amsterdam: John Benjamins.

Nasukawa, K. (2020). 'Linearisation and stress assignment in Precedence-free Phonology: The case of English'. *Radical: A Journal of Phonology* 1, 239–91.

Nasukawa, K., and Backley, P. (2015). 'Heads and complements in phonology: A case of role reversal?' *Phonological Studies* 18, 67–74.

Nasukawa, K., and Backley, P. (2017). 'Representing moraicity in Precedence-free Phonology'. *Phonological Studies* 20, 55–62.

Nasukawa, K., and Backley, P. (2018). '|H| and |L| have unequal status'. *Phonological Studies* 21, 41–8.

Nasukawa, K., Backley, P., Yasugi, Y., and Koizumi, M. (2019). 'Challenging universal typology: Right-edge consonantal prominence in Kaqchikel'. *Journal of Linguistics*, 55(3), 611–41. https://doi.org/10.1017/S0022226718000488.

Ohala, J. J. (1992). 'Alternatives to the sonority hierarchy for explaining segmental sequential constraints'. *CLS: Papers from the Parasession on the Syllable*. Chicago: Chicago Linguistic Society, 319–38.

Ohala, J. J., and Kawasaki-Fukumori, H. (1997). 'Alternatives to the sonority hierarchy for explaining segmental sequential constraints'. In *Language and its Ecology: Essays in memory of Einar Haugen*. Trends in Linguistics. Studies and Monographs Vol. 100, edited by S. Eliasson and E. H. Jahr, 343–65. Berlin: De Gruyter.
Onuma, H. (2015). *On the Status of Empty Nuclei in Phonology*. Doctoral dissertation, Tohoku Gakuin University.
Raimy, E. (2000). *The Phonology and Morphology of Reduplication*. Berlin: De Gruyter.
Ruhlen, M. (1973). 'Nasal vowels'. *Working Papers on Language Universals* 12, 1–36. Stanford, CA: Stanford University.
Samuels, B. (2009). 'The third factor in phonology'. *Biolinguistics* 3(2), 355–82.
Schane, S. A. (1968). *French Phonology and Morphology*. Boston, MA: MIT Press.
Tranel, B. (1981). *Concreteness in Generative Phonology: Evidence from French*. Oakland, CA: University of California Press.
Traunmüller, H. (1994). 'Conventional, biological, and environmental factors in speech communication: A modulation theory'. *Phonetica* 51, 170–83.
Traunmüller, H. (2005). 'Speech considered as modulated voice'. Unpublished manuscript, Stockholm University. https://researchgate.net/publication/250390908.
Trubetzkoy, N. S. (1967). *Principles of Phonology*. 4th edition. Göttingen: Vandenhoeck & Ruprecht.
Yoshida, S. (1991). *Some Aspects of Governing Relations in Japanese Phonology*. Doctoral dissertation, SOAS, University of London.
Yoshida, S. (1996). *Phonological Government in Japanese*. Canberra: Australian National University.
Yoshida, Y. (1995). *On Pitch Accent Phenomena in Japanese*. Doctoral dissertation, SOAS, University of London. https://doi.org/10.25501/SOAS.00033572.
Youngberg, C. (2021). 'Representing the moraic nasal in Japanese: evidence from Tōkyō, Ōsaka and Kagoshima'. *Glossa* 6(1), 63. https://doi.org/10.5334/gjgl.1099.

23
Recursive syllable structure in RCVP
Harry van der Hulst

Introduction

In van der Hulst (2010) I suggested that a case can be made for recursion in syllable structure, a proposal that develops a suggestion in Smith (1999; 2003) and other work. This idea runs counter to the usual statement that there are no 'syllables inside syllables', or that phonology at large is not recursive, except where it copies recursive syntactic structure. In van der Hulst (2010; 2020) I focus on recursion in the rhyme of the syllable, which allows embedded syllables, to capture trochaic and dactylic feet. In this chapter, I explore recursion in the onset, which will be justified with reference to 'excessive' consonant clusters that exceed the option of maximally having an obstruent followed by a sonorant consonant. I show that a dependency approach does not require the adoption of empty nuclei to accommodate excessive clusters, while it does explain the maximal complexity of such clusters.

Syllable structure in RCVP

Four core positions

I will briefly discuss the way in which RCVP represents 'core' syllable structure (based on van der Hulst 2020; see van der Hulst 2021 for a synopsis). Faithful to the basic premise of RCVP, the syllable itself is a combination of the C and V units, which, if no further splitting applies, delivers the 'strict' CV syllable structure that all languages have. If languages exceed this minimal CV syllable, this results from splitting the C and/or V unit, which produces binary branching onsets and rhymes, respectively:

(1) a. syllabic positions

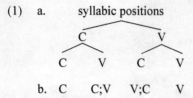

b. C   C;V   V;C   V

While the four-way division as such implies no linearisation (see the section 'Linear order in the lexicon is limited'), when combined into a syllable structure, linear sequencing will be dictated by some version of the well-known 'Sonority Sequencing Generalisation', according to which the sonority level rises towards the nucleus and then descends:

(2) a. syllabic positions, linearised

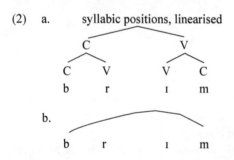

b.

    b   r   ɪ   m

A proper dependency representation of a syllable structure that contains all four syllabic categories is as follows (adding convenient unit labels for each construction and for each of the four segmental positions, although the labels have no formal status: they are just used for convenience when I refer to syllabic units):

(3) a.

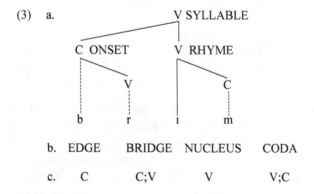

b.   EDGE   BRIDGE NUCLEUS CODA

c.   C   C;V   V   V;C

I assume a strict dependency model, which means that there is no 'constituent structure'.[1]

In 'classical' Government Phonology (GP) (Kaye et al. (KLV) 1990), it was assumed that a syllable with four positions represents the universally maximal expansion of a syllable that can occur freely (that is, word-internally, as well as at the word beginning and end, although the edges may allow 'extra segments'[2]). This would once more seem to indicate that there is, in fact, a maximal two-way split that universally limits the degree of complexity within each domain, whether a segment-internal element class or a structural unit like the syllable.[3] Whereas element groups represent paradigmatic dimensions and the syllables represent the syntagmatic dimension, the structural possibilities are the same, indeed structurally analogous. It is significant that both dimensions, whether paradigmatic or syntagmatic, are subject to the same system of categorisation as captured by the C/V syntax of RCVP.

The four syllabic positions are very restricted in terms of which segment types can occupy them. In fact, the C/V encoding of the syllabic positions defines the major classes of the segments that they allow. The onset head (C) only allows obstruents, while the rhyme head (V) only allows vowels. The two dependent positions (C;V, V;C) are reserved for sonorant consonants. It is interesting that the C/V structure for the onset dependent is C;V, while the structure for the coda is V;C. This suggests that the onset dependent is 'stronger', that is, more C-like than the coda position, which comes out as weaker (and more 'sonorant'). That sonorant consonants are phonetically stronger in the onset than the rhyme is empirically shown by the difference, for example in English, between liquids in the onset and in the coda, where the latter have a much weaker constriction. The difference between the bridge and the coda position, apart from having an effect on the phonetic implementation of sonorant consonants, also provides a basis for the fact the latter often only allow a subset of sonorant consonants, such as the liquid. That said, the coda position can also be limited to a subset, such as only nasals; see van der Hulst (2020, §4.3.3).[4]

Sonorant onsets and syllabic sonorants

Let us now turn to the obvious point that it is not the case that only obstruents can appear in the edge position. Sonorant consonants can also form onsets by themselves and in that case, they occupy the edge position. Likewise, we must be able to represent syllabic consonants, which means that the nucleus must be able to contain consonantal segments. To address these necessities, in (4a) and (4b) I propose two different structures for sonorant consonants when they occur as onset heads and as onset dependents:

(4)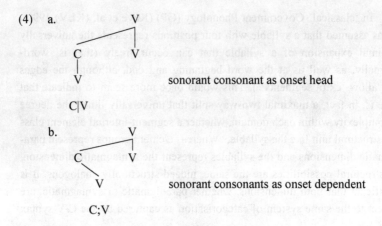

a. sonorant consonant as onset head

b. sonorant consonants as onset dependent

In both cases V is dependent on C and yet the syllabic position will reflect the difference between V being subjoined or adjoined to C. In (4a) I represent the former structure notationally as C|V, indicating that V is subjoined to C, rather than being adjoined as in (4b). The essential difference between X|Y and X;Y is that the latter leads to a linear order of both nodes, while the former does not.

Likewise, there are two different structures for syllabic sonorant consonants and coda sonorant consonants:

(5)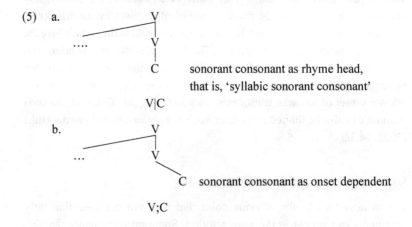

a. sonorant consonant as rhyme head, that is, 'syllabic sonorant consonant'

b. sonorant consonant as onset dependent

The distinction between subjunction and adjunction has already been used in the representation of the syllable as a whole (see 3), in which the V node is subjoined to itself so that the onset and the coda can be dependents at two different levels.[5] I refer to Böhm (2018) for a discussion of the distinction between adjunction and subjunction and the legitimacy of both in a dependency approach.[6]

We have to recognise that some languages may impose restrictions that narrow down even this restricted set of options for each syllabic position. Indeed, there are languages that disallow high-sonority consonants (specifically liquids and glides) in the onset head position; see Gordon (2016), Smith (2003), and Flack (2007). If, for example, only nasals are allowed as onset heads, we have to specify that only sonorant consonants that exhaustively contain C in their *manner* class are allowed, in other words, the most C-like sonorant consonants.

Linear order in the lexicon is limited

Anderson (1987) questions the necessity of specifying the linear order of segments in the lexicon, if segments are organised in a syllabic structure. The argument is that an onset that groups an obstruent and a sonorant consonant will necessarily order these two consonants in that order if we assume that linear order can be predicted from the Sonority Sequencing Generalisation. The same point applies to segments that form a rhyme. Golston and van der Hulst (1999) accept this point, stating that if lexical representations are syllabified, the linear order of segments is predictable. These authors cite various arguments for why syllable structure is present in lexical representations, both linguistic and psycholinguistic. In the RCVP model, I will therefore also assume that segments within a syllabic unit are not linearly ordered.[7] The linear order of onset and rhyme can also be predicted given that the rhyme contains the sonority peak. Formally, the way in which the syllabic distribution of segments is stored amounts to specifying the syllabic affiliation for each segment in terms of a syllabic C/V specification and the unordered grouping of segments into onsets rhyme and syllable units:

(6)   C   C;V   V   V;C
      ((b   r)   (ɪ   m))

Given that major class distinctions are interpretations of syllabic positions and given that segments in the lexicon are syllabified – meaning they come with a piece of syllable structure – there is no need for an independent layer of major class specifications; the piece of syllabic structure that segments 'wear on their sleeves' *is* the major class specification. In the present framework, it does not make sense to think of the syllabic specification as being specified 'in the root node' of segments (as proposed in McCarthy 1988), or elsewhere. Given that segment-internal manner specifications are the head of the segmental structure, it will be those specifications that are projected upwards and will be visible on the root node of the segmental structure, so that they can interact directly with the syllabic affiliation specification. Thus, the syllabic specification is independent of the segmental structure and one can think of the metaphor 'wearing on their sleeve' as referring to an association relation.

(7) C   C;V   V   V;C   (syllabic affiliation)
     :   :   :   :
     b   r   ɪ   m   (segmental structure)

In RCVP, in conclusion, syllable structure is not a projection of segmental structure. Rather, it is specified on a separate 'tier' in association with the segmental structure.

Empirical issues

The proposal in the previous section makes very strong predictions about the maximal complexity of syllables and which segment types can occur in syllabic positions. Both onset and rhyme can be maximally binary branching. In addition, we disallow onsets consisting of two obstruents, two sonorant consonants, and sonorant consonant followed by an obstruent. We also disallow obstruents to function as nuclei and as codas. A similarly strict view was adopted by proponents of 'classical' GP. But this approach obviously faces a host of empirical problems.

For example, this position requires a reconsideration of so-called syllabic obstruents in Tashlhiyt Berber (see Dell and Elmedlaoui 2002) and other languages (see Bell 1978). It also needs to deal with the fact that in languages such as English and Dutch obstruents would appear to occur in codas almost as freely as sonorant consonants. Finally, consideration should be given to numerous cases in which consonant clusters in apparent onsets are not a sequence of an obstruent followed by a sonorant consonant, but two obstruents (Morelli 1999; Kreitman 2008), or cases in which the number of onset consonants exceeds two, as, Polish (Cyran and Gussman 1999) and Georgian (Chitoran 1998; Toft 1999; Butskhrikidze 2002; Ritter 2006)

Closer to home (for me at least), in English and Dutch, the left edge can have triconsonantal structures of a limited variety. They have to start with [s] followed by an obstruent + liquid cluster (see Trommelen 1983; van der Hulst 1984; Fudge 1987). On the right edge, we find so-called superheavy rhymes containing a tense vowel followed by a consonant, or a lax vowel followed by two consonants.[8] Classical GP deals with such problematic cases by postulating empty nuclei, but van der Hulst (2020) argues against the use of empty structural positions (both segment-internally, such as 'empty class nodes', and in syllabic structure). In the following section, I will propose solutions for these types of empirical issues which will draw on allowing recursivity in onset structure. Unfortunately, I will not be able to offer detailed analyses for all of them.

Recursive syllable structure

Previous views

In van der Hulst (2020) I discuss the possibility of recursion in syllable structure, here understood as the possibility of embedding syllables inside syllables; that is, self-embedding tail recursion. A commonly held view in theoretical linguistics is that the formal organisation of phonology is fundamentally different from that of syntax, one manifestation of this idea being that recursion does not exist in phonology, except where phrasal phonology 'copies' recursive syntactic structure to some extent.

> Recursion consists of embedding a constituent in a constituent of the same type, for example a relative clause inside a relative clause [...]. This does not exist in phonological structure: a syllable, for instance, cannot be embedded in another syllable (Pinker and Jackendoff 2005, 10).

> ... syllabic structure is devoid of anything resembling recursion (Bickerton 2000).

It should be noted that discussions about phonological structure and recursion are always carried out in a constituency-based approach. I have adopted a dependency approach which does not involve constituency. Nevertheless, it seems to me that the issue of recursion can also be addressed in a dependency approach.

It is well known that several linguists have pushed for structural analogies between syllable structure and sentence or phrasal structure (Kuryłowicz 1948; Pike and Pike 1947; Fudge 1987):

(8) a.   syllable   b.   sentence

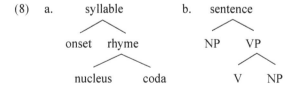

More recent claims to the same effect can be found in Levin (1985), Carstairs-McCarthy (1999), and Völtz (1999), among others. Whatever the merit of these parallels, no mention is made in these works of a potential further parallelism that would involve recursion. Most writers, while acknowledging that phonotactic structure is constituency-based (and referring to an X-bar(ish) organisation of syllables), propose that phonological (often called 'prosodic') constituency is 'strictly layered', which means that no constituent contains a constituent of the same type. This explicitly bars (self-embedding) recursion. With reference to 'higher' phonological/prosodic structure, recursion *has* been recognised, but here it is then said to reflect the recursive structure of syntax, at least to some extent (Ladd 2008; Wagner 2005; van der Hulst 2010; Hunyadi 2010).[9] Limiting recursion in phonology to units that have morphosyntactic structure is tantamount to saying that no recursion will be found *within* morphemes (or simplex words), where whatever structure exists cannot be a mapping from morphosyntactic structure. A recent collection of studies (Backley and Nasukawa 2020), however, tackles the question of morpheme-internal recursion head on. In this volume den Dikken and van der Hulst (2020) offer an extensive demonstration of parallels between morpheme-internal phonological and syntactic structure.

However, some phonologists – whose proposals differ in several ways that will not concern us here – have argued that syllable structure can display recursion (Smith 1999, 2003; Garcia Bellido (2005); van de Weijer and Zhang 2008; van der Hulst 2010). The present chapter builds on van der Hulst (2010).

The point of departure is the syllabic model that was introduced in (3). The crucial idea in van der Hulst (2010) is that the coda position can form an entire syllable, making the coda the recursive node in syllable structure, just like the complement position in an X-bar-type organisation. Adopting the C/V dependency notation, the proposal in van der Hulst (2010) is that the structure for the traditional notion is a trochaic foot in (9a) can be recast as the structure in (9b) with significant explanatory gain. This is illustrated with the Dutch word *káno* 'canoe':[10]

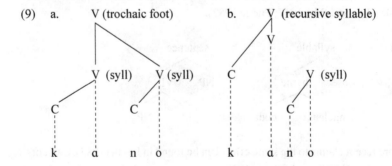

The embedding of syllables inside syllables does not have to stop here. A full structure of a so-called dactylic 'ternary foot', sometimes referred to as a 'superfoot' (as in English *vanity*), displays degree-2 embedding.

(10)   V   (recursive syllable, 2 degrees)

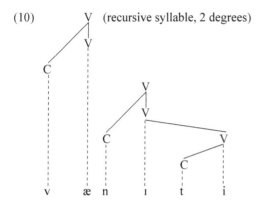

This structure is a perfectly legitimate object also in, for example, English *Winnipesaukee*, *hippopotamus*. An interesting consequence of this proposal is that it is now immediately clear why in poetic rhyme the initial onset is ignored, but not the second (or indeed the third, in forms like *sanitsy~vanity*). The initial consonant of such structures is external to the whole sequence that forms the rhyming unit in the proposal made here. The recursive structures capture the special position of the initial onset, as opposed to the other more deeply embedded onsets (which must be identical). In the structures proposed here the rhyming subpart of the string forms a unit, which is not the case in a traditional foot structure in which all syllables are separate units, as in (9a).

Recursive rhymes revisited

This proposal in (9b) and (10) faces two problems that went unnoticed in van der Hulst (2010). Firstly, the recursive node (the coda) is a 'bare' C position in a 'closed' syllable that has no embedded syllable, while it seemingly must be a V position, when the coda is an embedded syllable. The second problem is that the matrix syllable can itself be a 'closed syllable', as in a word like [tɛmpo] (in either English or Dutch), which would seem to imply 'double occupancy' of the coda position.

To solve both problems, I propose in van der Hulst (2020, §3.2.5) that the embedded syllable is the 'complement' of the C node in the case of [tɛmpo] (as in 11b), while it is *subjoined* to the C node in the absence of a coda consonant:

(11) a.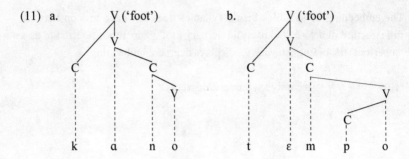

The embedded syllable is thus a C-type syllable, which accounts for its less prominent status in comparison to the head matrix syllable.[11]

Here I consider an alternative for (11a), while adding some further examples for (11b):

(12) a.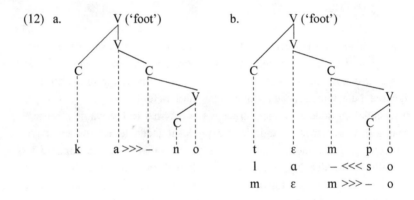

In (12a), the '>>>' indicate 'virtual gemination of the 'long' vowel. Under (12b) I also added the examples *lasso* and *menno*, which both have a virtual geminate for the so-called 'ambisyllabic' consonant (as proposed in van der Hulst 1985; 2003), albeit with different headedness. While the coda position in (3) calls for sonorant consonants, it was noted in the section 'Empirical issues' that in languages such as Dutch and English, obstruents can also make an appearance in a rhyme headed by a lax vowel. But if the syllabic position encodes the major class of segments, then the coda position simply cannot dominate an obstruent. I therefore locate the obstruent as an onset within the embedded syllable which produces a right-headed virtual geminate (even in word-final position):

(13) a.

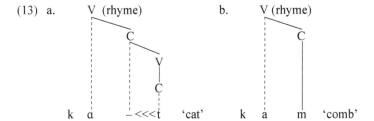

   b.

When a lax vowel is followed by a sonorant consonant, this consonant can occupy the coda position. When there is a following vowel, this creates a left-headed virtual geminate, as shown in (12b). In van der Hulst (2008) it is shown that diminutive allomorphy in Dutch is different for syllables with a lax vowel ending in a sonorant consonant or in an obstruent: *katje* versus *kammetje*, with the syllable ending in a sonorant taking the so-called long form *-etje*; see van der Hulst (2008, 1,295) for details.

The difference between the stressed vowel in *kano* and *lasso* is that the former is a tense [a], which can occur in an 'open syllable', whereas the latter is a lax [ɛ], which requires a closing consonant which is the left half of a virtual geminate. With respect to stress, tense vowels behave as light, whereas lax vowels (occurring in a close syllable) are heavy; see van der Hulst (1984).

We can extend the degree of embedding and accommodate more cases, all with initial stress. The following list of Dutch words is representative of the various syllable structures that need an account:

(14) a. *lasso*   'lasso'
     b. *menno*   (proper name)
     c. *kano*   'canoe'
     d. *tempo*   'tempo'
     e. *la*   'drawer'
     f. *lam*   'lamb'
     g. *raam*   'window'
     h. *sambal*   'Indonesian spice'
     i. *dominee*   'minister'
     j. *almanak*   'almanac'
     k. *atlas*   'atlas'
     l. *spelonk*   'grotto'
     m. *grotesk*   'grotesque'

(15)

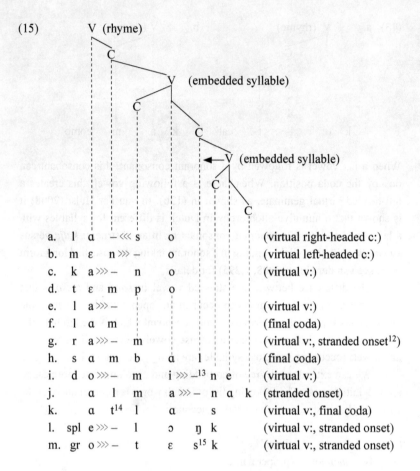

a.	l	ɑ	–‹‹‹ s	o					(virtual right-headed c:)
b.	m	ɛ	n ››› –	o					(virtual left-headed c:)
c.	k	ɑ ››› –	n	o					(virtual v:)
d.	t	ɛ	m	p	o				
e.	l	ɑ ››› –							(virtual v:)
f.	l	ɑ	m						(final coda)
g.	r	ɑ ››› –	m						(virtual v:, stranded onset[12])
h.	s	ɑ	m	b	ɑ	l			(final coda)
i.	d	o ››› –	m	i ››› –[13]	n	e			(virtual v:)
j.		ɑ	l	m	ɑ ››› –	n	ɑ	k	(stranded onset)
k.		ɑ	t[14]	l	ɑ	s			(virtual v:, final coda)
l.	spl	e ››› –	l	ɔ	ŋ	k			(virtual v:, stranded onset)
m.	gr	o ››› –	t	ɛ	s[15]	k			(virtual v:, stranded onset)

It would seem that the coda unit (the 'complementiser') can have a complement, but there appears to be no 'need' for a specifier. However, this may be a limitation for internal specifiers only, if we allow a specifier position at the highest level (not indicated in (15)) for 'rising' diphthongs like [ja, wo], etc. Perhaps this option can also be used for so-called short diphthongs which are also typically rising. If, then, only internal specifiers for codas are not needed, this is perhaps just an instance of dependent units displaying a simpler structure than head units; see Dresher and van der Hulst (1998).

Recursive onsets

In this section I will propose that the notion of recursivity can also do work for us in the onset unit of the syllable.[16] For onsets I propose the following, which is largely parallel to the rhyme structure in (15). For starters, for the onset we could have a (word-initial) specifier position for, among others, [s]:

(16) Examples of word-initial onset clusters[17]
    a.   pl   (Dutch: *plek* 'place')
    b.   sp   (Dutch: *spin* 'spider')
    c.   spl   (Dutch: *splinter* 'splinter')
    d.   sl   (Dutch: *slak* 'snail')
    e.   kn   (Dutch: *knie* 'knee')
    f.   pt   (Hungarian: *ptózis* 'ptosis', *dzéta* 'zeta')
    g.   zdźbw   (Polish: *źdźbwo* 'blade [of grass]')
    h.   g^{v}prck^{v}n (Georgian: *gwprckwni* 'you peel us'
          mts'^{v}rtn   *mts'wrtneli* 'trainer')
    i.   crm   (sesquisyllables in Kammu: [cr.mɔɔl] 'sowing season')

The structure in (17) can accommodate all cases in (16):[18]

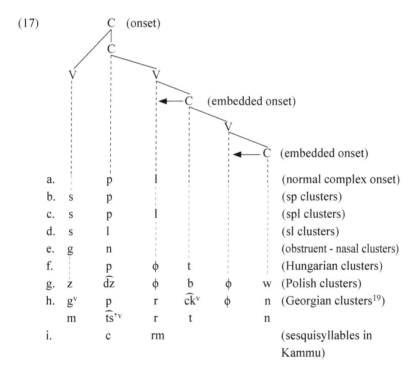

Again, we do need an internal specifier for C except at the highest level, so maybe this is a general constraint. But V also does not have/need an (internal) specifier, due to reduced complexity in dependent units, of which the onset is itself a case.

The structure in (17) suggests an appeal to empty nuclei, which van der Hulst (2020) has tried to ban. However, empty nuclei can be circumvented by subjoining V under C (in a sense making a 'vertical' CV unit) as indicated by the left-pointing arrow.

Iambic feet

The proposal for recursion in syllable structure provides an alternative to the representation of so-called trochaic (SW) and dactylic (SWW) feet that has been proposed in Metrical Theory. This theory has also made use of iambic feet and various proposals for a complete foot typology have been proposed. Here I will not discuss how RCVP can be applied to 'iambic' foot types, apart from saying that as proposed in van der Hulst and Ritter (1998) so-called iambic feet can be analysed as super syllables, with a C adjunct to the left of the head syllable:

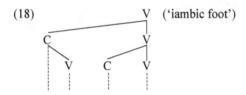

(18)   V   ('iambic foot')

This then is more like the original iambic foot structure, although I would argue that the unit as a whole is just another kind of extension of core syllable structure, in this case with a left-adjunction structure, as suggested in den Dikken and van der Hulst (2020, §4.3).

Why recursion is less pervasive in phonology

The central thesis of van der Hulst (2010, 2020, and much previous work), following Dependency Phonology's notion of Structural Analogy, is that phonology and syntax have recourse to the same computational system, that is, that both modules are maximally analogous. This thesis goes beyond the claim that both phonology and syntax build hierarchical structures. This claim is commonly made (though not supported by all linguists) with the proviso that the nature of the hierarchical organisation is fundamentally different with phonology adhering to 'strict layering', while syntax displays recursive structure. Accepting that recursion is available to phonology does not entail that phonology will display the same amount of recursive structure as morpho-syntax. The kinds of structures that are employed in both modules do not exist in a vacuum, but rather are formed to accommodate the substances that these structures are grounded in. There is a simple reason for why recursion in phonology is less pervasive. If we accept the fact that semantic, conceptual structure (Anderson would say 'conceptual *substance*') is inherently recursive, we expect morphosyntax to be isomorphic to this semantic, conceptual structure as much as is possible. Phonological structure accommodates phonetic-perceptual substance, which arguably is not inherently recursive. Rather, as the result of motoric actions, it is essentially sequential and rhythmic. This may lead to the view that phonology is 'flat' (see Scheer 2013), perhaps only displaying recursion when expressions are morphosyntactically structured. But recursion in phonology is limited even in this case because there is a 'flattening force' that causes disrhythmic structures that contain lapses (sequences of weak units, 'SWWW...') to flatten by breaking up into smaller rhythmic units (that is, SW SW), as shown in Giegerich (1985). This in itself shows that phonological structure is not entirely flat. After all, if there is rhythmic structure this means that the units (syllables, words, etc.) display a structure in which certain units are 'subordinated' to others. Standard metrical phonology has chosen to formally represent this 'subordination' by grouping units into binary, headed constituents. The crucial point of van der Hulst's (2010) proposal was that subordination can also be encoded in terms of embedding, which then establishes a perfect formal parallel with recursion in syntax. The same flattening force that limits phonological recursion in morphosyntactically complex expressions, also prevents more than three levels of recursion in monomorphemic units. A sequence of four syllables is therefore not structured as a quaternary 'foot' which would have a dysrhythmic sequence 'SWWW' that does not match the rhythmic structure of a quadrisyllabic sequence. Indeed, a string of four CV units is likely to display an alternating rhythmic structure (SWSW), which suggests the presence in the structure of two consecutive units, each with level embedding. Beyond the 'magic number' 3, unbounded recursion gives in to rhythm in phonology.

Conclusions

In conclusion, the argument that recursion is unique to morphosyntax is not compelling. It is a manifestation of a syntactico-centric way of thinking that a computational device that the human mind has would only apply within one component of the grammar. It is simply not reasonable to claim that the mental power to combine units that themselves are the product of combining (thus allowing self-embedding as a logical option) is limited to grammar, let alone to one component in the grammar. In this chapter, I have shown that by allowing recursion in syllable structure, we can account for recurrent phenomena that involve the phonological dimension of language. Recursivity in the rhyme provides a rationale for the type of poetic rhyme that refers to the stressed vowel and everything that follows in a 'foot', but traditional foot structure provides no formal basis for the rhyming sequences. What I have added in this chapter is the idea that recursivity can also be applied to onset structure, allowing precisely the maximal complexity that has been observed for languages with excessive onsets (such as Polish and Georgian), although a more detailed account of these and other cases is certainly called for. I conclude that recursion in phonology is real, and its results are revealing.

Notes

1. I here ignore the claim in GP that the syllable unit as such is not required. Rather, in GP there is a lateral licensing relation between the onset and the rhyme unit which requires them to always occur together. Perhaps there is a resemblance between seeing all syntagmatic relations in terms of dependency and seeing them in terms of lateral licensing, as discussed by Scheer (2013), among others.
2. These extra segments of course need an account. GP opts for allowing extra syllables with empty nuclei. I propose an alternative account in the section 'Recursive onsets'.
3. Here I will not discuss the RCVP theory of segmental structure; see van der Hulst (2020) for a full account and van der Hulst (2021) for a summary.
4. For a discussion of the representation of long vowels, diphthongs, and geminates, see van der Hulst (2020, § 4.5).
5. I will also invoke this distinction in the section 'Recursive onsets', where I discuss recursion in onset structure.
6. In the syntactic plane, Anderson (2011) uses the subjunction structure to represent category conversion in the lexicon, for example, from noun to verb or vice versa.
7. I will leave open here whether we can extend the elimination of linear order above the level of the syllable, although it is easy to see that syllables forming a foot can also be ordered, given that the foot type is fixed for the language as a whole.
8. In English and Dutch, a further word-final syllabic unit (called the 'appendix') is possible. I will not discuss this unit, an additional rhymal adjunction, here (see Fudge 1987; van der Hulst 1984).
9. The claim of strict layering which prevents recursion was 'officially' abandoned in later work in prosodic phonology, albeit that the driving force behind recursive structures in prosody is still morphosyntax (see Selkirk 2011).
10. The representation of both syllables requires a V node in (9a), which seemingly goes against the expectation that V heads take C dependents, and vice versa. The same issue arises in (9b). I address this issue below.
11. Several other 'solutions' to the problem of double occupancy are discussed and rejected in den Dikken and van der Hulst (2020), which explore a somewhat different development of van der Hulst (2010). This article proposes to 'enlighten' phonology with the introduction of a parallel to the syntactic notion of 'light v', an idea that is not adopted here.
12. I am here accepting the proposal in Polgárdi (1998) that word-finally a 'stranded' onset is permitted.
13. The virtually long versions of tense vowels are only required in stressed syllables, which must have a branching rhyme as proposed in Trommelen (1983) and Lahiri and Koreman (1988). This means that the second unstressed open syllable in (15i and 15j) does not need a virtual geminate vowel. Instead, the following (also unstressed) syllables can be subjoined under the preceding C position, which is indicated by the left-pointing arrow in the tree structure in (15).
14. Note that I have placed an obstruent in coda which overrides the prohibition. This is due to the fact that lax vowels are subcategorised for occurring with coda consonant.
15. Here the occurrence of [s] in the coda position is strictly speaking irregular given that this position is reserved for obstruents. The reason for allowing this obstruents is as in the previous footnote.
16. Here I develop ideas that were presented in a talk at *The form of structure, the structure of form – Three days of linguistics for Jean Lowenstamm*, January 15–17, 2015, University Paris Diderot – Paris 7.

17. Dutch (16a–e): Trommelen (1983); van der Hulst (1984). Hungarian (16f): Törkenczy and Siptár (1999). Polish (16g): Cyran and Gussmann (1999). Georgian (16h): Toft (1999); Butskhrikidze (2002); Ritter (2006). Kammu (16i): Svantesson (1983); van der Hulst and Ritter (1998).
18. I suspect that the word-initial vowel in Arrernte (Green 1999) may also find an account in this onset model, with the vowel occupying the specifier position and the following consonant(s) being the onset, which Green argues to be missing in this language.
19. The unit 'ck' is a so-called *harmonic* cluster which I here analyse as a complex segment (Butskhrikidze 2002, 103). The written <w> is analysed as a secondary articulation (Butskhrikidze 2002, 93).

References

Anderson, J. M. (1987). 'The limits of linearity'. In *Explorations in Dependency Phonology*, edited by J. M. Anderson and J. Durand, 169–90. Dordrecht: Foris.
Anderson, J. M. (2011). *The Substance of Language. Volume I: The domain of syntax; Volume II: Morphology, paradigms, and periphrases; Volume III: Phonology–syntax analogies*. Oxford: Oxford University Press.
Backley, P., and Nasukawa, K. (eds). (2020). *Morpheme-internal Recursion in Phonology*. Berlin: De Gruyter.
Bell, A. (1978). 'Syllabic consonants'. In *Universals of Human Language, Volume 2*, edited by J. Greenberg, 153–202. Stanford, CA: Stanford University Press.
Bickerton, D. (2000). 'Calls aren't words, syllables aren't syntax. Review of Carstairs-McCarthy on Language-Origins'. *Psycoloquy* 11(114). https://www.cogsci.ecs.soton.ac.uk/cgi/psyc/newpsy?11.114 (accessed 19 February 2023).
Böhm, R. (2018). 'Just for the record: Dependency (vs. constituency) for the umpteenth time – A concise guide for the confused with an appended how-(not)-to-read Tesnière's *Éléments*'. In *Substance-based Grammar: The (ongoing) work of John Anderson*. Studies in Language Companion Series 204, edited by R. Böhm and H. van der Hulst, 261–310. Amsterdam: John Benjamins.
Butskhrikidze, M. (2002). *The Consonant Phonotactics of Georgian*. Doctoral dissertation, University of Leiden.
Carstairs-McCarthy, A. (1999). *The Origins of Complex Language. An inquiry into the evolutionary beginnings of sentences, syllables and truth*. Oxford: Oxford University Press.
Chitoran, I. (1998). Georgian harmonic clusters: phonetic cues to phonological representation. *Phonology* 15: 121–41.
Cyran, E., & Gussmann, E. (1999). 'Consonant clusters and governing relations: Polish initial consonant sequences'. In *The Syllable: Views and facts*, edited by H. van der Hulst and N. A. Ritter, 219–49. Berlin: De Gruyter.
Dell, F., and Elmedlaoui, M. (2002). *Syllables in Tashlhiyt Berber and in Moroccan Arabic*. Dordrecht: Kluwer.
den Dikken, M., and van der Hulst, H. (2020). 'On some deep structural analogies between syntax and phonology'. In *Morpheme-internal Recursion in Phonology*, edited by P. Backley and K. Nasukawa, 57–114. Berlin: De Gruyter.
Dresher, E., and van der Hulst, H. (1998). 'Head-dependency in phonology: Complexity and visibility'. *Phonology* 15, 317–52.
Flack, K. G. (2007). *The Sources of Phonological Markedness*. Doctoral dissertation, University of Massachusetts Amherst.
Fudge, E. (1987). 'Branching structure within the syllable'. *Journal of Linguistics* 23(2), 359–77.
Garcia-Bellido, P. (2005). 'The morphosyntax and syntax of phonology: The svarabhakti construction in Spanish'. *Estudios de Lingüística del Español* 22. https://raco.cat/index.php/Elies/article/view/195615 (accessed 19 February 2023).
Giegerich, H. J. (1985). *Metrical Phonology and Phonological Structure*. Cambridge: Cambridge University Press.
Golston, C., and van der Hulst, H. (1999). 'Stricture is structure'. In *The Derivational Residue in Phonological Optimality Theory*, edited by B. Hermans and M. van Oostendorp, 153–74. Amsterdam: John Benjamins.
Gordon, M. K. (2016). *Phonological Typology*. Oxford Surveys in Phonology and Phonetics 1. Oxford: Oxford University Press.

Green, G. (1999). 'Arrernte: A language with no syllable onsets'. *Linguistic Inquiry* 30(1), 1–25.
Hunyadi, L. (2010). 'Cognitive grouping and recursion in prosody'. In *Recursion and Human Language*, edited by H. van der Hulst, 343–70. Berlin: De Gruyter.
Kaye, J., Lowenstamm, J., and Vergnaud J.-R. (1990). 'Constituent structure and government in phonology'. *Phonology Yearbook* 7, 193–231.
Kreitman, R. (2008). *The Phonetics and Phonology of Onset Clusters: The case of Modern Hebrew*. Doctoral dissertation, Cornell University.
Kuryłowicz, J. (1948). 'Contribution a la theorie de la syllabe'. *Bulletin de la Société Polonaise de linguistique* 8, 80–114.
Ladd, D. R. (2008). *Intonational Phonology*. 2nd edition. Cambridge: Cambridge University Press.
Lahiri, A., and Koreman, J. (1988). 'Syllable weight and quantity in Dutch'. *West Coast Conference on Formal Linguistics* 7, 217–28.
Levin, J. (1985). *A Metrical Theory of Syllabicity*. Doctoral dissertation, Massachusetts Institute of Technology (MIT).
McCarthy, J. J. (1988). 'Feature Geometry and dependency: A review'. *Phonetica* 43, 84–108.
Morelli, F. (1999). *The Phonotactics and Phonology of Obstruent Clusters in Optimality Theory*. Doctoral dissertation, University of Maryland at College Park.
Pike, K. L., and Pike, E. V. (1947). 'Immediate constituents of Mazateco syllables'. *International Journal of American Linguistics* 13(2), 78–91.
Pinker, S., and Jackendoff, R. (2005). 'The faculty of language: What's special about it?' *Cognition* 95, 201–36.
Polgárdi, K. (1998). *Vowel Harmony: An account in terms of government and optimality*. Doctoral dissertation, Leiden University.
Ritter, N. A. (2006). 'Georgian consonant clusters: The complexity is in the structure, not the melody'. *The Linguistic Review* 23(4), 429–64.
Scheer, T. (2013). 'Why phonology is flat: The role of concatenation and linearity'. Paper presentation, *11th Rencontres du Réseau Phonologique Français*, Nantes, 1–3 July 2013.
Selkirk, E. (2011). 'The syntax–phonology interface'. In *The Handbook of Phonological Theory*, 2nd edition, edited by J. Goldsmith, J. Riggle, and A. Yu, 435–85. Oxford: Blackwell.
Smith, N. S. H. (1999). 'A preliminary account of some aspects of Leurbost Gaelic syllable structure'. In *The syllable: Views and Facts*, edited by H. van der Hulst and N. Ritter, 557–630. Berlin: De Gruyter.
Smith, N. S. H. (2003). 'Evidence for recursive syllable structures in Aluku and Sranan'. In *Recent Development in Creole Studies*, edited by D. Adone, 31–52. Tübingen: Max Niemeyer Verlag.
Svantesson, J. (1983). *Kammu Phonology and Morphology*. Lund: Gleerup.
Toft, Z. (1999). 'Grunts and gutturals in Georgian: An investigation into initial consonant clusters'. *SOAS Working Papers in Linguistics* 9, 275–97.
Törkenczy, M., and Siptár, P. 1999. 'Hungarian syllable structure: Arguments for/against complex constituents'. In *The Syllable: Views and Facts*, edited by H. van der Hulst and N. A. Ritter, 249–84. Berlin: De Gruyter.
Trommelen, M. (1983). *The Syllable in Dutch: With special reference to diminutive formation*. Dordrecht: Foris.
van der Hulst, H. (1984). *Syllable Structure and Stress in Dutch*. Dordrecht: Foris.
van der Hulst, H. (1985). 'Ambisyllabicity in Dutch'. In *Linguistics in the Netherlands*, edited by H. Bennis and F. Beukema, 57–67. Dordrecht: Foris.
van der Hulst, H. (2003). 'Dutch syllable structure meets Government Phonology'. In *A New Century of Phonology and Phonological Theory: A festschrift for Professor Shosuke Haraguchi on the occasion of his sixtieth birthday*, edited by T. Honma, M. Okazaki, T. Tabata, and S. Tanaka, 313–43.Tokyo: Kaitakusha.
van der Hulst, H. (2008). 'The Dutch diminutive'. In *Trends in Prosodic Phonology*, edited by C. Ewen, H. van der Hulst, and N. Kula. *Lingua* 118(9), 1288–306.
van der Hulst, H. (2010). 'A note on recursion in phonology'. In *Recursion and Human Language*, edited by H. van der Hulst, 301–42. Berlin: De Gruyter.
van der Hulst, H. (2020). *Principles of Radical CV Phonology – A theory of segmental and syllabic structure*. Edinburgh: Edinburgh University Press.
van der Hulst, H. (2021). 'A guide to radical CV Phonology, with special reference to tongue root and tongue body harmony'. In *Perspectives on Element Theory*, edited by S. Bendjaballah, A. Tifrit, and L. Voeltzel, 111–56. Berlin: De Gruyter.

van der Hulst, H., and Ritter, N. A. (1998). 'Kammu minor syllables in Head-Driven Phonology'. In *Structure and Interpretation: Studies in Phonology*, edited by E. Cyran, 163–83. Lublin: Folium.

Völtz, M. (1999). 'The syntax of syllables: why syllables are not different'. In *Phonologica 1996*, edited by J. Rennison and K. Kühnhammer, 315–21. The Hague: Holland Academic Graphics.

Wagner, M. (2005). *Prosody and Recursion*. Doctoral dissertation, Massachusetts Institute of Technology (MIT).

Weijer, J. van de, and Zhang, J. (2008). 'An X-bar approach to the syllable structure of Mandarin'. Lingua 118, 1416–28. https://doi.org/10.1016/j.lingua.2007.09.006.

Subject Index

Page numbers with 'n' refer to notes.

|A| *see* elements, |A|
ambisyllabicity 264

coarticulation 239, 240–1
codas 3–4, 20–1, 29, 74, 93, 96n8, 100–4, 110, 128, 135, 136n9, 136n15, 157, 163–4, 209, 212, 214–16, 217n3, 228, 240–1, 256–8, 260, 262–6
complement 15, 34, 38, 40–2, 46, 235, 245 *see also* rhyme
consonants
   in general 4–5, 13–14, 16, 19, 22–7, 29, 34, 42, 51, 73–5, 83, 85, 93, 98–110, 116, 120–1, 124–6, 133, 140–1, 145–6, 155–9, 169–71, 174–8, 186–7, 190–5, 212–16, 220–1, 246–9, 263
   consonant deletion 242, 248, 251
   consonant hardening 201, 207n1
   see also onsets
constituency 3–5, 73–5, 131, 147–9, 155, 158, 163, 185, 200, 202, 216, 244, 269
contour tone *see* tone
culminativity 139
CVCV *see* Strict CV

delaryngealisation 51–5
dependent *see* complement
devoicing 5, 49, 51, 101, 119, 121 *see also* final obstruent devoicing; High Vowel Devoicing
dIp *see* elements, |I|

edge element *see* elements, |?|
Element Theory 2, 5, 13–17, 20, 22, 33–47, 52, 197, 235, 238
   formalised 37–42

elements
   antagonism 16, 33, 44–5, 47
   definitions of 15
   in general 2, 4–6, 13–15, 34, 37, 61, 68n4, 130, 162, 164, 236, 244, 251
   |A| 20, 30n7, 30n8, 60–2, 65–8, 129, 130, 236, 244, 246
   |ATR| 60–2
   |H| 5, 45, 61
   |h| 37
   |I| 20, 26–9, 65, 129, 131–3, 168, 244
   |L| 5, 45, 61, 62, 201–5, 243
   |R| 61
   |U| 20, 61–2, 66–8, 129, 131–3, 244, 251, 252n8
   |?| 13, 201, 236, 243
   see also Element Theory
emptiness
   in general 3–4, 80, 155, 165
   of nuclei 80, 128, 155, 165
   of onsets 3–4, 133–4, 171
Enhancement 52–59
epenthesis 155–9, 163, 186–8, 224
ET *see* Element Theory

Feature Theory 14
Features (unary) *see* elements
final empty nuclei (FEN) 81–3, 128, 131, 134, 156, 163–7, 181–2
final obstruent devoicing 49
formal grammar 35
formalisation 33–47, 162–5

generative capacity 37, 46–7
government 2, 16, 74, 141–2, 156, 162–8, 176, 210–12
government licensing 74, 124, 127–30, 157, 197–207, 228

Government Phonology 2–5, 13, 19, 33,
   60, 73, 77, 124, 127, 139, 155, 161,
   174, 197, 235
   see also GP 2.0; Strict CV
GP *see* Government Phonology
GP 2.0 124, 235

|H| *see* elements, |H|
harmony *see* vowel harmony
head 34, 40–1, 43, 204
high element *see* elements, |H|
high tone *see* tone
High Vowel Devoicing 139–40

|I| *see* elements, |I|
incomplete neutralisation *see*
   neutralisation, incomplete
interconsonantal government 163, 171,
   209–10
interonset government *see*
   interconsonantal government
irregular verbs 112–22

|L| *see* elements, |L|
l-vocalisation 19–30, 221
Language Specific Phonetics 50, 52, 58
laryngeal licensing 50, 52, 54
licensing 2, 50–4, 80–4, 129, 141,
   147–50, 156–7, 164, 182, 197,
   199–207
Licensing Constraints 17, 33, 42, 44, 46,
   62, 67
   formalised 42–5
Licensor Tier 139, 144–5
low element *see* elements, |L|
low tone *see* tone
LSP *see* Language Specific Phonetics

mAss *see* elements, |A|
melody *see* elements; Element Theory
merge 38–42, 245–50
mora(s) 73, 77, 140–1, 244

nasal vowels 238–49
nasalisation 238–9, 241–2
nasality 5, 174, 201–2 *see also*
   nasalisation

neutralisation 49, 191
   incomplete 49, 52, 54, 58
no-crossing constraint 60
nuclei 3, 16, 51, 74, 125, 128, 130–2,
   134, 141–7, 155–8, 162–4, 169–71,
   176–82, 210, 255, 260, 267 *see also*
   vowels

Obligatory Contour Principle 28, 116,
   118–19, 161, 168
onsets 3–4, 20–1, 74–5, 78–9, 83, 85,
   93, 98–105, 109–10, 124–35, 142,
   145–7, 151, 156–7, 163–6, 168–71,
   174–8, 181–3, 186, 209–12, 214–17,
   228, 240, 242, 248, 255–61, 263–67
   see also consonants
operator *see* complement
Optimality Theory 4, 161

p-licensing 44, 170, 200–1, 247, 249 *see
   also* government, licensing
PfP *see* Precedence-free Phonology
phonetic interpretation 54–8, 235
phonetics 49–50, 52–3, 104–10, 188–95,
   245
plosives 219–30
Precedence-free Phonology 244–9
Prevocalic Tenseness *see* tenseness
prominence 93–6, 185, 245
prosody (intonation) 186

RCVP 255–69
recursion 34, 38, 235, 255, 261–70
rhymes 3, 73, 140, 147–9, 180, 187, 195,
   255–61, 263–6
rimes *see* rhymes
rUmp *see* elements, |U|

#sC sequences 3–4, 98–110
segholates 112–21
segment(s) 3–4, 13–16, 37–42, 52–3,
   73–4, 124, 156, 161–2, 219–20,
   238–9, 244, 257, 259–60
skeleton 4, 63–6, 73, 80, 130, 161
sonorants 50, 100, 121, 186, 190–5, 201,
   257–60, 264–5
spell-out *see* phonetic interpretation

Strict CV 4, 73–5, 77, 80, 83–4, 145, 147–8, 163–4, 199, 216, 255
svarabhakti 185–95
syllabic consonants 257
syllable *see* syllable structure
syllable structure 3–5, 73–5, 100, 103, 200, 206–7, 240–1, 255–70 *see also* constituents

tenseness 77–9, 85, 90–2
templatic morphology 112–21
tone 93–4
turbid government 167–8

|U| *see* elements, |U|
Ultimate Head Parameter 247
underspecification 15

voice retention 51–9
voicing 54, 56, 58, 75, 120, 201, 202, 204, 207n3, 252n8
vowel harmony 17, 30n1, 34, 61, 62, 66, 67, 132
vowel-zero alternation 1, 6, 139, 141, 142, 156, 158, 182

vowels 1, 2, 4–6, 13–14, 16–17, 20–30, 31n9,10,14, 50, 55, 60–2, 64–8, 68n2–3, 75, 77–86, 86n2–3, 89–96, 96n1–4, 100–5, 115–16, 119, 122n8–11, 124–7, 130–5, 135n5, 139–42, 147–50, 151n2–3, 155–9, 164, 174–81, 183n3–7, 185–195, 211, 217n2, 222–5, 227–9, 230n2,8, 236, 238–51, 252n4–5, 257, 260, 264–5, 270 *see also* nuclei

weak 53, 74, 75, 112, 116, 122n9, 130, 139, 165, 185, 244, 257, 269
weakening 40, 45, 175, 182

X-bar 262
x-slot 145

yers 162, 164, 168
yod 158, 210–16, 217n5

zero *see* emptiness; vowel-zero alternation

Language Index

Arabic 75, 82, 84, 114–15, 118
   Cairene 75, 82, 89–96
   Egyptian 96n4, 96n8
   Moroccan 156
   Palestinian 82

Bantu (languages) 197–207
Bavarian *see* German, Bavarian
Bemba 198, 203, 205
Berber
   Tashlhiyt 260
   Taqbaylit 20
Brazilian Portuguese *see* Portuguese, Brazilian

Cairene Arabic *see* Arabic, Cairene
Connemara Irish *see* Irish, Connemara
Cypriot Greek 98–110
   writing system 110n6

Dutch 260, 262–5, 267

English 20, 42–3, 77–88, 98–9, 103, 105, 112–22, 124–135, 147–50, 156, 219–29, 238, 244–5, 257, 260, 263–4
   British v. American 150, 223

Fijian 244
French 101, 126, 128, 131–5, 139, 155–8, 209–17, 239–43, 247, 249
   Continental 169–70
   Old 239–40
   Parisian 210–11, 217
   Quebec 167–71, 210, 217

Gaelic *see* Irish; Scottish Gaelic
German 16, 19
   Bavarian 19–32
   New High German (NHG) 65
   Old High German (OHG) 65
   Standard 19–21, 30, 65, 114, 122n4
   Upper Austrian 22, 24, 29
Georgian 260, 267
Greek *see* Cypriot Greek

Hausa 82
Hawaiian 238
Hungarian 82, 267

Icelandic 82
Irish 187–8, 191
   Connemara 185–96
Italian 82, 100–4, 148
   Finale Emilia 163

Japanese 75, 101, 132–4, 139–50, 156, 197, 244, 250–1

Kashmiri 84
Kaqchikel 252n9

Lamba 198
Luganda 198, 204

Malayalam 51
Mehri, Omani 20
Mongolian 157–8
Mòoré 60–1

Old French *see* French, Old

Persian 238
Polish 49–59, 103, 158, 260, 267
   Cracow-Poznań 54
   Warsaw 54
Portuguese 158, 174–84, 238
   Brazilian 177–82
   European 100–1, 176–7

Pulaar 82, 236
Punjabi 238

Scottish Gaelic 185, 187, 195
Spanish 82, 101, 132, 134–5

Tashlhiyt Berber *see* Berber,
 Tashlhiyt

Taqbaylit Berber *see* Berber,
 Taqbaylit
Turkish 62–4, 66–7, 82, 132

Yoruba 238

Zulu 247

Printed in the USA
CPSIA information can be obtained
at www.ICGtesting.com
JSHW062321140924
69617JS00038B/72

9 781800 085299